American Dream
American Nightmare

American Dream
American Nightmare

Fiction since 1960

KATHRYN HUME

University of Illinois Press
Urbana and Chicago

Library of Congress Cataloging-in-Publication Data
Hume, Kathryn, 1945–
American dream, American nightmare : fiction since 1960 /
Kathryn Hume.
  p.   cm.
Includes bibliographical references and index.
ISBN 0-252-02556-3 (alk. paper)
  1. American fiction—20th century—History and criticism.
2. Failure (Psychology) in literature. 3. Literature and society—
United States—History—20th century. 4. Psychological fiction,
American—History and criticism. 5. National characteristics,
American, in literature. 6. Loss (Psychology) in literature. 7. Dis-
appointment in literature. 8. Economics in literature. 9. Success
in literature. I. Title.
PS374.F24H86   2000
813'.5409—dc21   99-050421

C 5 4 3 2 1

For Philip Jenkins,
historian,
who helped supply a sense of chronology
for one who is chronology impaired

Contents

Acknowledgments

I received very valuable criticism from friends and colleagues. They told me that the first version of this work was much too long. Future readers will thank them for so insisting. Christopher Clausen challenged many of my attitudes and made me modify them or justify them by context. Jackson I. Cope was the only reader to mark passages and books with an eye to cutting; from studying his judgments, I learned to cut yet more. David Cowart, Philip Jenkins, and John Whalen-Bridge made me rethink some of my statements on politics and insisted that I include a few references to earlier American literature. Daniel Punday provided bibliographic assistance at the outset of the project. I am grateful to all of them, and if I have not gone as far in various directions as they advised, the fault is mine, not theirs. Finally, I owe more than I can say with mere thanks to Robert D. Hume. He has provided endless help and encouragement and has never been too busy to discuss ideas and how one might write about them.

American Dream
American Nightmare

Inthoduction

Around 1960, American fiction cast aside many canonical limits and became a carnival of bustling diversity. Did the excitement of these developments blind critics to a surprisingly bleak outlook in many of these novels? For all the flash and energy of the narrative voices, a disconcerting amount of the fiction expresses bitter disillusionment with America and the American Dream. This study considers roughly one hundred novels—some very briefly, to be sure. Many more could have been analyzed or mentioned. Obviously, disappointment with America is not found in all novels of the period, nor in all the books by these particular novelists. Writers more concerned with language than story, who locate "art's deepest morality at the heart of linguistic creativity of which fiction is capable,"[1] and those for whom aesthetics, theory, and philosophy are the burning issues may not feel attracted to political ruminations. An immigrant like Bharati Mukherjee may argue in *Jasmine* that America offers sufficient reward for anyone willing to face the challenge of adapting to the country. A Tom Clancy thriller must make America seem preferable to the Soviet alternative for his near-mythic agon to grip readers. Nonetheless, few serious writers of this period celebrate this country as Ray Bradbury did during the 1940s and 1950s, when he wrote the stories that became *Dandelion Wine.* My map of the novelistic landscape since 1960 is not meant to be exhaustive. It explores the surprising expanses of this Slough of Despond rather than focusing on the higher plateaus whose inhabitants pursue their own ends and feel no worry about the state of the country.

Many books on recent fiction have the strengths and limitations of extreme specialization. One type proffers analyses of six to ten novels, with the occasional nineteenth-century or modernist precursor used for contrast or genealogy. Stimulating books by James M. Mellard and Jerome Klinkowitz are early examples; the pattern continues in studies by Charles Caramello and Alan Wilde. Another type uses ethnicity or gender to group a similar number of works: *Race, Gender, and Desire: Narrative Strategies in the Fiction of Toni Cade Bambara, Toni Morrison, and Alice Walker* (Elliott Butler-Evans); *Place and Vision: The Function of Landscape in Native American Fiction* (Robert M. Nelson). Scientific and technological metaphors dictate the choice of texts in criticism by N. Katherine Hayles, David Porush, Robert Nadeau, Susan Strehle, and Tom LeClair. Political argument defines texts for John Whalen-Bridge. Particular kinds of experimentalism produce the groupings in Robert Siegle's *Suburban Ambush* and Young and Caveney's *Shopping in Space.* These books and others like them create powerful and exciting readings or theoretical analyses in their chapter-length studies of single novels or novelists. They are immensely helpful for understanding how American fiction is developing. They do, though, have the unavoidable effect of reinforcing our sense that American fiction consists of isolated interest groups. I admire such books and owe them much, but I am attempting to view the fiction from a greater distance—and by using a wider lens. I want to avoid reinforcing the marketing categories; and, in my effort to find common ground, I want to put texts together that are not usually found in each other's company.

Projects that explore a wide spectrum of novels start with Frederick R. Karl's *American Fiction, 1940–1980,* a descriptive survey that may remain unmatched in coverage of its territory. Tony Tanner's *City of Words: American Fiction, 1950–1970* gives us searching analyses of what seem to him the more demanding and rewarding artists of the period. Marc Chénetier's *Beyond Suspicion: New American Fiction since 1960* studies the way that mainstream forms prior to 1960 suddenly became inadequate and yielded to new developments. Chénetier stresses the aesthetic novelty and variety of what he finds and in doing so offers an alternative to my political, social, and deliberately nonaesthetic and nonjudgmental mapping. Books on postmodernist fiction by Linda Hutcheon and Brian McHale do not limit themselves to American work; however, in the galaxy of titles that conform to their definitions of the postmodern, we find many from the United States.

My own enterprise is decidedly different. For instance, one can read an Ishmael Reed novel for its fizzy prose and zany plot—an aesthetic analysis and appreciation. This is valuable but does not do justice to his total project if it ignores the anger over America's racism and cultural imperialism. One can deal with the racial message by talking about "re-visioning" the history of Western civilization in *Mumbo Jumbo* and seeing how Reed's plots reflect his understanding of power and control. This is a technical and theoretical approach, and it links him to Foucauldian theory and to other authors concerned with control: Burroughs, Acker, Pynchon, and Mailer. (I have written such an article on Reed.) What I am doing in this study, though, is contextualizing Reed specifically with very different writers who also criticize Western civilization and, more generally, with dozens of authors whom he might not usually be compared to but who exhibit a parallel sense of estrangement from their country. Each novelist analyzed is situated in one or more specific conversations and then placed more generally among his or her peers. That, too, seems worth doing, especially since few critics have done anything with such a cohort or generational context.

Why do these authors exhibit such spiritual recoil from America? How does this disillusionment shape their fiction? The focal problems that organize each chapter respectively are immigration (chapter 1), lost innocence (2), lost civilization (3), spiritual quest (4), democracy's fragility (5), America as evil (6), anarchy (7), and the need for community (8). Books talk to each other if given half a chance, and these topics emerged because of the heated and complex discussions they generated among the books. Having surveyed the rival constructions of America's failings, I will look in the ninth chapter at the narrative and formal manifestations of the social malaise. Within each chapter, texts are chosen for differing ideologies and responses to the initial focus—immigration, anarchy, and the like. A few novels even express satisfaction with America; they argue against the assumptions of the others and provide some balance. No grand solution to America's problems emerges at the conclusion: conservative writers respond to one set of faults, radicals to another, and their solutions do not harmonize. Chinese Americans differ in some of their hopes from Native Americans. Women and men often wish to foster different changes.

Since my title is *American Dream, American Nightmare: Fiction since 1960*, I should explain what I mean by the American Dream. Many longings and desires are expressed through that rubric. Prosperity for anyone willing to work hard is a crucial component of the Dream, a house of one's own being the icon. In the past, immigrants knew that they might have a hard life, but they trusted that their children would be better off. For a long time, indeed, successive generations did acquire more personal property than their parents did. Reinforcing this perception is the technology that makes each generation seem better off. Indisputably, cars got faster, houses became larger and acquired more appliances, and more miraculous medical interventions proved possible. For each generation to be more prosperous than the last, however, the economy must continue to expand. That may ultimately cease, what with shifts in power toward developing countries, the country's debt, and the decline in nonrenewable resources. In a zero-growth economy, it will no longer be possible to believe that a gain for you is not a loss for someone else, and a central component of the Dream will vanish for good.

People have also hoped to enjoy certain liberties in America: freedom of worship, justice in the courts, and a classless society (or at least one where the class barriers were permeable to those who educated themselves). That all men are held to be created equal in the Declaration of

Independence has encouraged those who have suffered from cultural and racial scorn to hope that they, too, could make good. To young immigrants hoping for jobs, America is also the land of the pop culture they adore, a land of leisure, jeans, athletic shoes, and rock music. America can seem the land of romantic quest or fairytale reward. Fairness, material comfort, and freedom: these are probably the core values, but each generation adds contemporary interpretations of what these might mean. Of course, such dreams are not necessarily reasonable or coherent and compatible; even today, though, they influence our idealist expectations.

As a catchword to signal discontents with America, my use of the term "American Dream" has its drawbacks. Although the notion of a dream applies, with variations, to the hopes of anyone coming here as a voluntary immigrant, it can only be used in quotation marks for Native Americans or for Africans brought here as slaves. Slaves could dream of freedom in the North. After Emancipation, they could hope that someday liberty and justice would prevail for all. Nevertheless, despite the disparity between the ideal of equality and lived reality, Martin Luther King Jr. could say, "I have a dream. It is a dream deeply rooted in the American Dream."[2] For Native Americans, the concept of an American Dream is even less resonant, but those who enter mainstream life and a money economy want equal treatment: who would not? Even the most traditional tribal groups desire fairness in court so that their legal rights can be protected against mining companies or plans to divert water. Nor are they the only groups to wish freedom from government interference while they maintain cultures and religions at odds with mainstream values. The Mormons and members of various militia movements all want the liberty to lead their chosen lives, and they looked with horror at the way the government denied those rights to David Koresh's Branch Davidians. When I refer to the American Dream, therefore, I am using it as shorthand for a wide variety of desires, some opposed and some not even close to the yearnings of early European immigrants. When I talk of responses to the Dream's failure, I mean the many dissatisfactions expressed with America that are not just personal and not just complaints about life in general. One must, of course, recognize that the disillusionment with the Dream is so deep precisely because its ideals encourage us to hope for so much.

That the reality of America falls short of the ideal America is nothing new. American literature has always been critical of this gap, and many disenchanted novelists are now classics—Hawthorne and Melville, for instance. The early part of this century produced literature that rebuked America on many of the same topics as those explored here. In Cahan's *Rise of David Levinsky*, the protagonist becomes a millionaire but feels that he loses his soul, as do current immigrants in Russell Banks's *Continental Drift* and Oscar Hijuelos's *Mambo Kings Play Songs of Love*. John

Dos Passos's U.S.A. trilogy looks at the derailment of the labor movement, as does Thomas Pynchon in *Vineland*. Corruption and fragility of democracy were as pitilessly dissected by Frank Norris in *The Octopus* as by Pynchon, E. L. Doctorow, Don DeLillo, Ishmael Reed, Andrew Macdonald, and Robert Heinlein. Revolution was advanced as the cure in Jack London's *Iron Heel*, and modern upholders of revolution include Macdonald, Ernest Callenbach, and Starhawk. Life in the fast lane is much the same in spirit if not particulars in F. Scott Fitzgerald as it is in Jay McInerney and Douglas Coupland. While the small town got worse press from Sinclair Lewis and Sherwood Anderson than it does from Ray Bradbury, lost innocence is cause for ratiocination in both halves of the century. True, it tends now to be deconstructed rather than lamented, as seen in works by Toni Morrison, Gloria Naylor, Lisa Alther, Kurt Vonnegut, and Richard Brautigan. However worn the theme, though, it was still capable of producing two grand novels in Ralph Ellison's *Invisible Man* and John Barth's *Sot-Weed Factor*. The modernist writers tended to analyze social problems in class terms, whereas contemporary writers put more emphasis on race, ethnicity, and gender; however, the construction of classist poverty is similar in John Steinbeck's *Grapes of Wrath* and Carolyn Chute's *Merry Men*.

Are current dissatisfactions just an extension of those early in the century? For fifteen or twenty years, from the late 1930s into the 1950s, criticism of the country was largely inaudible. The government harshly suppressed dissent during World War II, and the war economy brought enough prosperity to diminish many economic dissatisfactions. Thomas H. Schaub describes the subsequent Cold War as a period in which "American intellectuals after World War II no longer seemed at odds with American culture, as they had been throughout the twenties and thirties." The resulting consensus culture meant "that a collaboration of business, government, and labor established a dominant center which either saw no need for extreme and divisive positions or actively worked to suppress them."[3] Liberalism, with its belief in gradually improving the extant institutions of America, replaced communism and socialism as the opposition to conservatism. The interim was long enough and the social conditions had changed enough in the 1960s and after for me to feel that the current dissatisfactions represent a new cycle of assessing the country and are not just a continuation of the old.[4] Much of the criticism grows out of a liberal moral uncertainty, triggered by the doubts about governmental, racial, and personal morality in the 1950s and 1960s.[5]

Politics changed, and so did literary taste. Old fictional patterns ceased to work well. Love, success, and many displaced mythic oppositions between good America and evil others no longer grip readers and writers of serious fiction. As I shall argue in the final chapter, the traditional literary themes and structures have lost appeal in part because so many Americans have lost faith in America's future, in America's righteousness, and in the power, meaning, and integrity of the individual. This represents a considerable change since World War II. When the traditional structures fail, novelists must struggle to create interesting and satisfying fictional patterns that do not rely on obsolete value systems, including confidence in the country. In *The Naked and the Dead*, Norman Mailer may worry about the ineffectuality of the liberal response to reality, but he does not doubt that World War II should be fought or that America should win. No such convictions provide stability for Joseph Heller's characters in *Catch-22*—let alone Joe Haldeman's Vietnam novel *1968*. The central solidity and rightness of what had once been America is gone.

America has always had its share of wrongs and evils, including government corruption, crime, and oppression on the basis of race, ethnic group, or class; in the middle of the century, however, many Americans believed that much of what was wrong was correctable. Until the 1960s, middle-class white Americans—those who were part of the Cold War consensus—believed in their own basic goodness. Those who were not part of the consensus had trouble making their complaints heard, especially at the legislative level or in the courts. Many Americans had faith in the possibility of progress and social improvement. In the 1990s, the middle class is more ethnically and racially diverse, and its members know from experience, or learn from the media, the drawbacks of America for those neither white nor middle class. Despite the comfort of property, this middle-class group feels frightened by riots or the threat of being mugged, and it also fears unemployment. Social changes have thus assaulted benevolist liberal beliefs. Furthermore, the lack of obvious political solution increases the frustration of both the middle and lower classes. Congress has not come up with an effective program to rectify racism, to educate more teens at risk of dropping out, to reduce our jail population, or to make sure that everyone receives basic medical services.

When I first started planning this book, I tried and abandoned many organizing strategies. Ethnic groupings produced bad generalizations about how African-American and Native American writers differed on some issues. Such marketing categories inevitably implied that only literature by white authors whose ancestors came from certain northern European, Protestant countries could be called American without hyphens and modifiers. Political stance proved no more effective as focus: novels like Leslie Marmon Silko's *Ceremony* and William Gibson's *Neuromancer* are both conservative, though in totally different fashions, and they are also radical in some respects. The solution finally chosen still has drawbacks. I cheerfully mingle writers whose ancestors inhabited this continent, Africa, the Caribbean, Russia, Great Britain, Germany, China, and elsewhere. They may be Jewish, Christian, upholders of Native American religions,

Vodoun believers, Wiccans, and atheists. They may be gay or straight, conservative, liberal, or radical, feminist or masculinist. Some come from working-class and some from Ivy League backgrounds. Simply claiming everyone as American lays me open to charges of cultural imperialism. Yes, they are all American, but they do not share equally in the benefits of being American and do not have equal access to power.

Objections can be raised to every term I use: Native American, Amerindian, tribal person, or Indian? American or U.S. fiction? I cannot satisfy all possible objections; at best, I can explain why I make some choices. In *Playing in the Dark*, Toni Morrison argues that white writers use black figures to create complex white characters but never manage to deal with African Americans except as psychic tools for their own self-exploration. When I introduce Morrison's own fiction into a chapter on lost innocence, I might be accused of using her vision to shed light on a white obsession. To my mind, what she does to that theme is riveting and challenging, and in no way subordinate, and it is far closer to my own judgment on the human value of innocence than traditional Adamic hand-wringing. That I explore what is being written about innocence in contemporary America is dictated by the large number of writers who still hold forth on the subject, but the topic is greatly changed by what Morrison's fiction does, and by what Ralph Ellison and Ishmael Reed do with the concept. Awareness of innocence's color-coding will let readers hear the texts argue with each other. Discussing innocence does not just illuminate the novels by white writers; it criticizes them and offers other viable visions of how we can relate ourselves to harm in the world.

In keeping with such eclecticism and with my desire to listen sympathetically to many standpoints, even when I disagree with them, "high" art mingles with "low" in this study. Most of the mainstream novels were reviewed in the *New York Times Book Review,* but I also discuss or mention occasional examples of speculative fiction, religious fantasy, and the spy novel when these can shed light on the larger area of American literary concerns. Some readers have objected to mingling popular with serious fiction. I do so because fantasy and science fiction have both been called the shadow or unconscious of canonical literature and as such are acknowledged to shed light on issues repressed or downplayed in more academically respected fiction.[6] Moreover, utopian thinkers seem to be the only writers who are explicitly concerned with how we might create a better government. References to film sometimes round out my presentation of the popular side of the topics being discussed.

Although I doubtless fail at times, I have tried not to assume that "white" or "Anglo-Saxon Protestant" is the default setting, and I label authors Euro-American, white, Catholic, or Protestant if such a descriptor is apt. When I take up a topic such as the fragility and even failure of democracy, I bring together authors from both the left and the right. Overall, this book tries to pay attention to different possible reader perspectives, implied and resisting. When my analysis builds on middle-class or white assumptions, I try to label them as such and offer alternative views. I do, though, focus on the possible responses of nonprofessional readers who read primarily for pleasure and information, for escape or consolation, for answers to problems in their own lives, for a sense of learning about themselves or about those different from them. The theorist who reads by means of Lacanian psychology or postcolonial formation of multiple subjectivities is not a typical reader, and I am not trying to reproduce all those reading responses. I am trying to look at implicit value systems rather than imposing critical frameworks from without. Insofar as possible, I want the books themselves to articulate their values.

The point of this book is to set up vigorous intratextual dialogues and to identify a core concern shared by a generation of highly diverse writers. Within this core of angry or disappointed comment, I try to bring out the differences and not flatten cultural disagreements. For instance, when looking at the loss of civilization, I start with James Welch's *Fools Crow*, whose tribes of the western plains saw no signs of moral idealism or superiority in the exponents of Western civilization they faced. Next, Saul Bellow and Walker Percy present conservative laments at the loss of the classical Judeo-Christian medieval tradition. Their assumptions resemble those of E. D. Hirsch in *Cultural Literacy*, though both are readier than Hirsch to recognize the racial and economic flaws that have destroyed so much of this civilization's credibility. Donald Barthelme's *Snow White* admits the same failure from a liberal perspective, adding gender to the flaws in that tradition's world picture. Ishmael Reed exhorts us to stop moaning over a stinking corpse that was rotten at the heart from its beginnings and to focus on the present. We should attend concerts of contemporary music, welcome living artists, support a diverse American culture, and look receptively beyond its boundaries.

Many recent critics seem to feel that American literature has exploded into a jumbled mass of disjunctive fragments, and the solution to date has been to categorize novels in terms of racial, religious, ethnic, gender, and sexually oriented groups. One of the central goals of this study is to show that a large number of seemingly disparate and unconnected writers between 1960 and 1990 actually share important common ground. Radically different as they may be in all sorts of ways, their estrangement from America gives them issues, problems, values, and often techniques that connect them as fellow members of a literary generation. After World War I, America had its Lost Generation. Thanks to the civil rights movement and the Vietnam War, among other factors, dreamers awoke. Since the early 1960s, we have had the Generation of the Lost Dream.

chapter one

The Shocks *of Transplantation*

Hacking stumps out of stony ground, draining malarial swamps, tending bobbins in cloth mills, enduring the heat and clangor of steelwork, carving granite mountains with hand tools to bear railroad tracks, following harvests up and down the country, digging coal from its seams in the earth: immigrants have joked about streets paved with gold, but most of them have known before they came that life would be hard. Death might claim them through sudden infection, cold, or work-related accident—but that was true in various homelands, too. Most immigrants who made their way voluntarily to the land now known as the United States could inspire themselves with some variation on the American Dream.

The American Dream is so associated with immigrants' hopes that incomers' experiences are a good place to start sampling a widespread literary dissatisfaction with America. Frank Lentricchia describes the Dream as having come over on the *Mayflower,* "the object of the dream being the person those pilgrims would become, could the dream be fulfilled: a new self because a new world" (194). Immigrants hope to better their position, if only by escaping an intolerable one: starvation, lack of land, and religious or political persecution. They have wanted to farm their own land or to escape an oppressive class system. They have wanted equality before the law. Even a job as a servant or in a sweatshop seems better than no job at all to the person squeezed off a family farm by overcrowding or foreclosure. The peoples native to the continent and the slaves forcibly removed from Africa were proffered no such vision of enriched life, and most of their hopes, at least initially, differed from the core desires that make up the Dream. For those who chose to come, however, America offered at least a chance of improving their lot.

Novels about cultural transplantation are not compelled to be sanguine. Autobiographies and biographies of immigrants incline toward optimism; rare is the impoverished, drunken failure who writes a life history and gets it published. However, Ole Rölvaag's *Giants in the Earth* portrays a series of disasters, ending with the protagonist's dying in a prairie blizzard. Written in Norwegian for old-country readers who wanted to know the experiences of their kin, and read in translation as a school text for decades in America, *Giants in the Earth* was able to tell truths avoided by Laura Ingalls Wilder, who was bound by the marketing demands for optimism in children's literature. Wilder glosses over the family failures and problems, and her own story of surviving those prairie blizzards teaches her readers to admire pioneer bravery. Her novels and others in the heroic tradition manipulate sympathetic readers into feeling that Euro-American settlers won their right to own the soil through enduring such hardships.

Novels of the last thirty years have focused on the estranging aspects of immigration, on the slippage between America's promises—equality, justice, prosperity—and the actuality of encounters between newcomers and the culture they enter.[1] The price of belonging is toted up and found to be dangerously high. What are the spiritual costs to a Haitian, Japanese, or Mexican immigrant who wishes to be American? How many generations are needed for the descendants to feel truly at home? How many years before they are routinely accepted as American? How much assimilation and how much rejection of the original culture does this demand?[2]

Where to start? Perhaps with an early immigrant wave. I know of no recent fictionalizations of Jamestown or Plymouth, but T. Coraghessan Boyle's *World's End* concerns seventeenth-century Dutch immigrants to the Hudson Valley. This account is useful for my purposes because, in addition to being breathtakingly vivid, it is structured by leftist assumptions of the sort that demanded revisions in the 1950s history-book vision of America. Reimagining immigrant experience in current novels is partly fueled by the increased acceptance of New Left values, such as the insistence that exploitive relationships be acknowledged as such. This mode of thought may take feminist, racially conscious, or economic forms, but it highlights systems of control and power, creates a hearing for suppressed voices, and generally tries to force a reevaluation of American culture by demystifying its triumphalist claims. Boyle's focus on economics and class make some of the basic leftist objections to America memorably clear.

In this chapter, Boyle will be followed by Russell Banks, who also creates an immigration narrative as a literary structure rather than a fictionalized set of family anecdotes. Banks is Euro-American but writes in part about Haitians of African descent. From writers to whom immigration is a literary situation, we learn what current conventions are and what sort of criticisms of America middle-class readers can stomach.[3] The chapter will also look specifically at how gender and race are used to construct and intensify the transplantation trauma. Julia Alvarez, Amy Tan, Maxine

Hong Kingston, Oscar Hijuelos, and Octavia Butler articulate challenges to 1950s assumptions about the openness of American society and the desirability of melting down all cultural difference. The chapter's conclusion will deal with a novel that dismisses all the complaints registered in the other novels. Bharati Mukherjee's *Jasmine* is a defiant success story, similar in its affirmation to optimistic autobiographies—though it is not in fact autobiographical. By producing it in the present atmosphere of victim politics and resistance to assimilation, Mukherjee introduces an individualist vision and invites reconsideration of quasi-libertarian political values mostly upheld on the extreme margins of our society. She also scrutinizes left-liberal assumptions made by middle-class people who know very little about the far left or about true poverty. She represents the opposite end of the political spectrum from Boyle; for this reason, each needs, in some sense, to confront the other.

The Trauma of Transplantation as Literary Topos: Boyle and Banks

World's End (1987)

Property is the root of all trouble in Boyle's seventeenth-century, Dutch-American world. The patroon, Oloffe Stephanus Van Wart, owns half of what is now Westchester County, New York, while the indentured Van Brunts owe their future lives' work and that of their children as well in return for their passage from Holland to the New World. The patroon "provided them with an axe, a plow, half a dozen scabious fowl, a cachexic ox, and two milch cows, both within a dribble of running dry. . . . As a return on his investment, he would expect five hundred guilders in rent, two fathoms of firewood (split, delivered and reverently stacked in the cavernous woodshed at the upper manor house), two bushels of wheat, two pair of fowl, and twenty-five pounds of butter. Due and payable in six months' time" (19–20). While readers may suspect irony when told that the cost of transporting the Van Brunts is "the princely sum of two hundred and fifty guilders" (19), we only realize how cheaply the family has been forced to sell its freedom when we learn that the transportation amounts to less than half a year's rent. Because the land is rich, if stony, their dedication to exhausting labor seems to promise eventual agricultural success. Unfortunately, malign spirits of place drive Harmanus Van Brunt, the family's patriarch, mad with an eating disorder. Further misfortunes send him over a cliff, deprive his son Jeremias of a foot, kill the wife and other son when lightning burns the house, and send the daughter, Katrinchee, raving mad, into life as a holy fool among the Kitchawank Indians.

Intertwined with the 1660s are two other eras: the twenty years following the stock market crash, and a few years starting with 1968. The Depression era Rombout Van Wart and then his son, Depeyster, still reside in Van Wart Manor. Though their acres are much diminished, the Van Warts own the local factory. Their financial power becomes clear when Depeyster in the 1960s is told that he needs $62,500 immediately; he notes that he has ten percent of that in his pocket and that the County Trust "would write him a note for six times sixty thousand. Without even blinking" (451). The title of patroon may have disappeared, but the reality of the position and its access to money and power survive.

The Van Brunts also bear the imprint of the past. Indeed, Boyle sets up elaborate correspondences among the three eras. In terms of class relationships, the Van Warts remain at the top, while the Van Brunts are curiously unable to make any but superficial improvements in their relative position. In the 1940s, Truman Van Brunt was a war pilot, served in military intelligence, and eventually got a college education, but he remains lower socially. His son, Walter, who fancies himself an existentialist hero, reluctantly works on the line in Van Wart Manufacturing for lack of anything else to do with his life. Later, when given an executive position, he tries to marry the boss's daughter, Mardi Van Wart, but she rejects him as too respectable for her decadent tastes. He does not escape employee status.

Eating disorders, mutilation, and betrayal figure in each generation, and the betrayals are perpetrated by a member of the oppressed group against those of his fellows who are trying to rebel or stand up for themselves or take leftist political stances. The first of all these failures is Jeremias's inner betrayal of self when confronting the patroon. The law may be against him, but the law is unreasonable, and he defiantly feels his own innocence. Ragged and wounded, he finds himself in the modest colonial manor, and suddenly he is overwhelmed by its luxury: "For all his anger and resentment, Jeremias was awed by it, humbled; he felt weak and insignificant— he felt guilty" (145). Between exploiter and exploited burgeons the sort of collusion that one finds between abused child and abuser or between hijacker and those abducted. He accepts the view of him imposed by the power that he is helpless to resist. In this scene, at least symbolically, we see Jeremias's spirit broken by his own response to material wealth; subsequent confrontations will show him backing down, no matter what proud defiance he had mouthed beforehand. Walter, too, will come to love the Van Wart life and outlook that he was raised to hate, and Truman (we deduce) did much the same when agreeing to betray his communist friends.

What all these repetitions suggest is that Boyle sees America as poisoned from its earliest years. A number of authors have taken this line and attacked the uplifting grade-school stories of Thanksgiving shared with the American Indians, Paul Revere's ride, and Washington chopping down the cherry tree. In *Breakfast of Champions*, Kurt Vonnegut calls early whites on the continent heartless and greedy pirates; Thomas Pynchon's *Gravity's Rainbow* laments Puritan intolerance as a fatal flaw that sent America down the wrong path; Kathy Acker sees the early settlers as militaristic, greedy, and religiously vicious in her *Don Quixote.*

Boyle looks at the colonial social patterns in much greater depth than do any of these other demystifiers. He shows how patterns established prior to the American Revolution continue—even into our own time—with little alteration. We fool ourselves with surface differences. Truman and Walter have college educations, for instance, and are not indentured servants, so how can seventeenth-century Dutch patterns of landholding matter now? Walter may think of himself as a wage slave, but he does not huddle in rags during a New York winter, nor does Depeyster Van Wart legally own the right to punish him corporally. Nonetheless, Boyle clearly feels that the limitations of factory-worker life are as onerous (within the range of possible lives available today) as those of indenture were earlier. Nor does the plot's final irony offer any hope for the future. The Van Wart heir is not in fact the child of Depeyster; his wife has been made pregnant by Jeremy Mohonk, the last of his tribe and a direct descendent of the Kitchawank Mohonk and Katrinchee Van Brunt. The poor may thus inherit the Van Wart earth, but the boy will officially be a Van Wart and will hold the Van Wart sway over any remaining Van Brunts or Catses or Pompeys or Cranes, and over later Irish and Italian immigrants to the region. The boy will own a factory and be able to get bank loans as a personal right when others cannot. Whatever his actual blood may be, the social structure will remain unchanged.

Boyle never tells us directly what hopes about the New World persuaded Harmanus Van Brunt to abandon the "ruined fishing nets" in Holland, so we do not know what he dreamed that America might be like. The land proved to be responsive to his husbandry; in different circumstances, he might have prospered. Regrettably for the history of the country, in Boyle's eyes, the American Revolution did not run deep enough. It was not a true revolution. Old imbalances were not corrected, and those in power under Dutch and then British rule remained in power afterward. The Constitution was framed to protect property, not people, and so the people continue to be maimed and haunted by property and its history. They also continue to betray themselves when confronted with images of the wealthy life of ease. Their collusion with the rich stems from hopes of improving their own lot and joining the rich but ensures that no real redistribution will ever take place. For that reason, Boyle gives us little hope of improving matters. Readers imbibe his bitterness along with the razzle-dazzle vividness of his three-strand, interlaced narrative.

Continental Drift (1985)

This novel by Russell Banks concerns two people, a Haitian woman and a New Hampshire man, and the experiences of the second will be dealt with in chapter 2. As a fictional narrative of immigrant experience, however, Vanise Dorsinville's adventures belong here. She is female, dark-skinned, and illiterate; as such, she is a figure of contempt but also of fear to lower- and middle-class white Americans. In their terms, she represents the lowest status possible. But when people from the bottom stratum of society like Vanise take part in mass movements and occupy ghettos that overflow and spread, they gain a power that is denied to them as individuals. Vanise's tragedy, moreover, challenges the values of a country that make her destruction almost inevitable; she suffers because a trawler captain's desire to "make a killing" (28, 198) outweighs his basic morality.

Banks looks at migration by the poor not as a specifically American experience but as a global phenomenon. "It's as if the creatures residing on this planet in these years, the human creatures, millions of them traveling singly and in families, in clans and tribes, traveling sometimes as entire nations, were a subsystem inside the larger system of currents and tides, of winds and weather, of drifting continents and shifting, uplifting, grinding, cracking land masses" (39). Whether in Somalia or Afghanistan, the fugitives will be preyed on by bandits (who are often themselves poor and dispossessed). Had Vanise and her nephew, Claude, known that such things happen to Haitians too, they might have been slower to depart the known, bad though it was. Such things, Banks seems to warn, always happen.

The first ship captain, rather than carrying them to America, takes their passage money and dumps them on North Caicos Island, a small landing point for both Columbus and Ponce de Leon. On the next leg of the journey, their latter-day Middle Passage, Vanise and Claude are kept below-decks in the noisome heat and darkness, repeatedly raped, and finally landed near Elizabethtown in the Bahamas. Here, Claude tends marijuana fields and Vanise is imprisoned and rented out as a prostitute. By now, Vanise has lost much of her spirit, but she helps plan their escape. When Claude kills her master, she has the presence of mind to tell Claude to search the whore-monger's pockets for the wad of cash he has on him at the end of an evening of gambling and peddling her body.

With that blood money, they can pay their passage on a boat run by an American looking for easy dollars. When the U.S. Coast Guard closes in, the captain forces the Haitians overboard, and though Florida is only two hundred yards off, they are unable to swim; only Vanise survives. Since she calls all day long on the loa Ghede, she is taken to this divinity's place of worship in Miami, and in the Vodoun ceremony, Vanise's former loa, Agwé, takes over her brother Emile. Ghede, also present, asks why Agwé has taken her soul away and is told that her drowned son has taken her soul with him to the loas' island beneath the sea. Agwé offers Ghede the soulless body of Vanise, and Ghede accepts; after various rites, including animal sacrifices, Vanise rises up, possessed by Ghede.

One cannot exactly say that America has swallowed her soul, but it may be fair to say that current immigration stories recognize her loss of soul as a fitting ending to the dreams of success. America had called to these people, lured them, "insisting, like the loas, on service and strategy, promising luxury and power" (231). They had duly served this loa, hoping for "all the things that Americans own—houses, cars, motorcycles, TV sets, Polaroid cameras, stereos, blue jeans, electric stoves" (345). If Vanise is lucky, she may get occasional illegal employment as a cleaning woman. More likely, though, her brother will sell her body. His own employment is unreliable, and his earnings would not let him carry her as dead weight.

Her being female, dark-skinned, and illiterate are reasonably reliable predictors of her fate. She will be raped and used sexually, and her only defense is withdrawal into herself. During her previous stint as a prostitute, "her mind, an utterly silent, burned-out charnel house by now, was filled with images of *les Morts* from the dark side, Ghede and Baron Cimitière, whose evil presence no longer frightened her" (228). No matter how evil she feels the loas' presence to be, their being with her and possessing her are vastly to be preferred to a daily life of forced sex. Only religion keeps her alive, for whatever good that may be.

ϙ ϙ ϙ

A glance at another constructed—as opposed to familial—immigration story brings out the plot devices an audience expects of this form. Vonnegut's *Bluebeard* shows us blood money (here taken from a massacre victim), the immigrant couple betrayed by a middleman, and a life of lower-class labor for people who were educated and privileged in their own land, Armenia. Their son proves his allegiance to America through war service and mutilation, becomes an artist, and finds himself alienated from the gender patterns of Europe and America. Vonnegut remains a liberal, however, and reconciles the protagonist to life; in this sense, he holds out hope that one can still flourish in America. He does not challenge his readers with a serious critique of this country.

What critiques of America are readers of the *New York Times Book Review* willing to absorb? Boyle argues a more radical line than is usually popular and gets away with it because he leaves the modern middle class out of the picture. He describes an upper class and various wage earners who live working-class and lower-middle-class lives, but his critique leaves the powers of the middle class untouched. That being the case, most readers can enjoy Boyle's excoriating the grand exploiters without worrying about personal applications. Because readers' family property is likely to consist of no more than a suburban house or city flat, those readers can face with equanimity Boyle's insistence that property on the scale of Westchester County is the root of the portrayed evils. They can agree with his criticism of those in power who ignore all the personal needs and desires of the people who serve them as tenants, servants, and factory hands. Because the idea is not new, they can nod when he lambastes the wealthy for valuing money more than morality.

Continental Drift, insofar as the immigration story complains about America, does so to the effect that America represents the siren song of televisions and blue jeans that lures the innocent to shipwreck off the coast. That middlemen of all ethnic backgrounds prey on the immigrants is accepted as the way of the world, for Banks shows it in operation on the borders of Afghanistan as well as in the Caribbean. However, Banks insists that the boat captain (the protagonist of the other plot) is morally responsible for drowning his Haitian passengers, in part because he has chosen to try to make some fast money in an illegal fashion to satisfy his own cravings for the American Dream. Again, we are being shown what happens when American materialism causes money to be valued over morality. The results are disastrous, not just for Vanise and her fellow Haitians but also for the captain.

America's materialism and concomitant lack of serious morality are acceptable themes. The other important theme suggested by these novels— and other novels and films—is America as a threat to the immigrant's spirit or soul. Whatever made one fully human and a moral being in one's original country may not survive the transplantation. This issue arises directly in *El Norte,* a film about a sister and brother who are illegal Guatemalan immigrants. The sister is sick in the hospital when the brother needs to leave for a once-in-a-lifetime chance for a real job that would lead to legal status, and he almost abandons her. Her angry friend tells him that if he does so, his soul is dead. At the last possible moment, he changes his mind, attends what proves to be his sister's deathbed, and henceforth must be content with illegal manual labor. The film provides a feel-good relief that the brother has not lost his soul; if we strip his action of sentiment, however, we know that his returning for twenty minutes with his sister costs him any viable future in America. He sacrifices his future for the past and present; many immigrants choose to salvage the future and must live with the guilt. Others persuade themselves that the old patterns of loyalty are not appropriate in the new setting.

Everything in America seems strangely incompatible with old ways. The idioms, the sexual patterns, the rules governing politeness and generosity, the moral supports in times of trouble, and the definitions of success all differ from their equivalents in various old countries. Total assimilation means rejecting one's ethnic group, but resisting transformation creates contradictions that will plague the hybrid life of immigrants and their semiassimilated children and grandchildren. Somebody—whether immigrant, offspring, or both—has to pay in the coin of the soul for the transplantation, a fact not usually obvious to those trying to make their way across the borders.

Transplanting Gender and Race: Alvarez, Tan, Kingston, Hijuelos, and Butler

Gender and race heighten the pressures on those undergoing the transformation. Authors who are relatively close to their ethnic roots have been able to create compelling pictures of their families' original cultures that bring out contrasts and make readers from different backgrounds understand the shock of immigration. Although writers like Amy Tan or Maxine Hong Kingston are closer to these immigrant ancestors than Boyle is to the Dutch of colonial times, we must remember that their pictures of China are still fictions, imaginative edifices built from an imperfect understanding based on research, anecdotes, and brief visits. These fictions will reflect whatever biases the writers feel toward the Chinese and American cultures that have uplifted or plagued their own lives as Americans of Chinese ancestry. That plausible and fascinating cultural studies can be done on purely fictional foundations will become clear in this chapter's discussion of Octavia Butler's Xenogenesis trilogy, since her speculative trilogy involves future aliens yet uses the same crises and causes for lament found in realistic fiction. The books to be discussed next are Julia Alvarez's *How the García Girls Lost Their Accents* and Amy Tan's *Joy Luck Club*; both deal with women from patriarchal societies and the particular strains this imposes on top of immigration. Maxine Hong Kingston's *China Men* and Oscar Hijuelos's *Mambo Kings Play Songs of Love* look at the effects on patriarchal men. The Xenogenesis series transforms these same issues by looking at how contact with a three-sexed alien race affects both men and women as they become immigrants to an uninhabited, postholocaustal Earth.

How the García Girls Lost Their Accents (1991) and
The Joy Luck Club (1989)

One step ahead of Trujillo's police, the little García girls move with their parents from the Dominican Republic to America. On the island, they were among the first families and lived in splendor: luxury cars, private guards, and servants. In America, they live in very straitened circumstances until Dr. García can pass the test that will license him as a physician in the United States. The girls' initial reaction to America is understandably negative. As they become teenagers and as their parents grow more affluent, their distaste is not so much for America as for their halfling status. "Cooped up in those little suburban houses, the rules were as strict as for Island girls, but there was no island to make up the difference" (107). Once at boarding school, however, they "learned to forge Mami's signature and went just about everywhere, to dance weekends and football weekends and snow sculpture weekends. We could kiss and not get pregnant. We could smoke and no great aunt would smell us and croak. We began to develop a taste for the American teenage good life, and soon, Island was old hat, man. Island was the hair-and-nails crowd, chaperones, and icky boys with all their macho strutting and unbuttoned shirts and hairy chests with gold chains and teensy gold crucifixes. By the end of a couple of years away from home, we had *more* than adjusted" (108–9).

Adjustment is not permitted to become assimilation, however. Their parents want them to marry boys from the island, lest the grandchildren speak only English. Their father in particular will not let them develop American independence. When ninth-grader Yolanda must write a speech in praise of the teaching nuns for teachers' day, she writes a daring American speech that expansively imitates Walt Whitman and claims that the *"best student learns to destroy the teacher"* (145). Her mother approves, but her father is horrified by this immodest flouting of authority and furiously tears up the speech. "It was bad enough that his daughter was rebelling, but here was his own wife joining forces with her. Soon he would be surrounded by a houseful of independent American women" (145–46). Yolanda narrowly escapes physical violence.

Another of the four daughters, Sofía, suffers his sexual tyranny. "'I don't want loose women in my family,' he had cautioned all his daughters. . . . They grew up in the late sixties. Those were the days when wearing jeans and hoop earrings, smoking a little dope, and sleeping with their classmates were considered political acts against the military-industrial complex" (28). He rummages through Sofía's drawers and comes across letters. "After his initial shock, the father regained his own fury. 'Has he deflowered you? That's what I want to know. Have you gone behind the palm trees? Are you dragging my good name through the dirt, that is what I would like to know!' The father was screaming crazily at the youngest daughter's face, question after question, not giving the daughter a chance to answer" (30). Sofía eventually marries the correspondent (with whom she had indeed slept), but her father never really forgives her, even when she gives birth to a son, the only male offspring for two generations in the family. He coos adoringly above his grandson's cradle, ignoring his granddaughter and showing only minimal civility to Sofía.

The girls' happiness as adults is severely compromised by elements in their upbringing. They get divorced, and two of the four spend time in mental institutions. Sandi suffers from anorexia, and during her hospital-ization, she comes to believe that she is changing into a monkey. She des-perately reads works by Freud, Darwin, and Nietzsche, trying to keep her brain human. On a symbolic level, she is struggling with the contradic-tions in her upbringing. By island standards, American behavior is primi-tive or degenerate (that is, monkey-like), while Americans would say the same of life in the Dominican Republic. Whichever culture Sandi chooses, the other tells her she is devolving into an animal.

At the beginning of the book, which is chronologically the end, Yolan-da returns to the Dominican Republic as an adult, privately hoping that she will discover it to be her real home and claiming that she has never really felt at home in the United States. At the end of the book, chrono-logically the beginning, she presents herself as parallel to a kitten that she, as a child, took from its mother in a way frightening and damaging to the kitten. She was similarly taken from the island and feels a continued vio-lation at her center because of that. However, her adult ignorance of is-land mores suggests that she will not find it easy to return.

America does offer the girls freedom, and at times they welcome this as superior to island patterns. The mistakes they make through wrong choices, however, leave some of them dubious about the value of bound-less choice. The same problem—endless choices and no clear rules—is felt by immigrants from other quarters. Amy Tan shows daughters of Chinese immigrants going through some of the same trials as they fight to integrate two cultures in their own lives and particularly to make sense of the con-tradictory definitions of woman.

The Chinese culture, like that of the Dominican Republic, is also patri-archal, so much so that women form a world of their own, and what Amy Tan describes in *The Joy Luck Club* is mostly the tensions between four Chinese mothers and their American-born daughters. Many Euro-Ameri-can readers will tend to side with the daughters and feel with them the embarrassment they suffer at their mothers' Chinese ways. Lena St. Clair recalls that "a man at a grocery store yelled at [her mother] for opening up jars to smell the insides" (109). Waverly Jong, a child chess champion, is irritated beyond control by her mother's behavior. "My mother would proudly walk with me, visiting many shops, buying very little. 'This my daughter Wave-ly Jong,' she said to whoever looked her way" (101). "She used to discuss my games as if she had devised the strategies" (187). Wa-verly tells off her mother a couple of times in public and once stops play-ing chess for a few days in rebellion. When she takes it up again, her mother provides none of the previous support but instead says, "It is not so easy anymore" (189). Indeed, Waverly loses her touch, can no longer sense "the magic within the intersection of each square" (190), and soon has to quit playing.

The mothers have a corrosive effect on the daughters' later lives as well. Sons-in-law, in particular, draw mothers' cool assessments, and against their own wills, the daughters find their love diminished by the criticisms. Waverly suffers from her mother's outspoken comments: "But by the time my mother had had her say about him, I saw his brain had shrunk from laziness, so that now it was good only for thinking up excuses. He chased golf and tennis balls to run away from family responsibilities. His eye wandered up and down other girls' legs, so he didn't know how to drive straight home anymore. He liked to tell big jokes to make other people feel little. He made a loud show of leaving ten-dollar tips to strangers but was stingy with presents to family" (192).

Lena St. Clair suffers similarly from criticisms that are at once oblique and direct. Her mother cannot understand why Lena and her husband would squander so much money on a renovated barn on four acres of land. Lena recalls her husband Harold attempting to explain their decision to his mother-in-law: "'Well, you see, it's the details that cost so much. Like this wood floor. It's hand-bleached. And the walls here, this marbleized effect, it's hand-sponged. It's really worth it.' And my mother nods and agrees: 'Bleach and sponge cost so much'" (163).

As Amy Tan creates these relationships, readers sympathize with the daughters but cannot ignore the mothers, because the mothers prove to be right. They decide that bad fortune or a bad marriage will result from something apparently meaningless, like freckles on a face, and their prognoses prove correct. Their grounds for judgment may seem totally illogical by American rules, but readers have to admit the soundness of their assessments. Rose Hsu Jordan contrasts the Chinese and American vision of a daughter: "It was only later that I discovered there was a serious flaw with the American version. There were too many choices, so it was easy to get confused and pick the wrong thing" (214). Rose has a breakdown when her husband divorces her because every decision involves choices and different directions.

The messages implied by the mothers' descriptions of their lives in China are similar. Their lives were devoted to upholding family and to keeping promises no matter what the cost. They are proud of how they managed to do this. Some of them found the need for cunning and developed cleverness that they did not know they had. Two are very proud that they ultimately discovered that they could think or speak for themselves. They lived pressure-cooker lives at the invisible, subordinate level, but invisibility to the male power structures makes them no less real. That these women are still alive attests to their toughness and their unyielding will to survive. In the film based on this book, the episodes set in China are pallid and unimpressive compared to those in the novel. The power of Tan's Chinese women is far greater in the book, and viewers learn less than readers about Chinese culture. In the book, the women feel devastated that their Americanized daughters seem weaker in crucial spiritual respects than they themselves are, even though one daughter is an architect and another a tax attorney. In addition, all the mothers suffer from the fact that their daughters do not talk to them or confide in them. Readers from non-Chinese backgrounds who are used to a wide generation gap will understand the daughters' reluctance, but Tan makes us understand that much good might have come out of open conversation.

Lindo Jong explains it for the mothers:

> It's my fault she is this way. I wanted my children to have the best combination: American circumstances and Chinese character. How could I know these two things do not mix?
>
> I taught her how American circumstances work. If you are born poor here, it's no lasting shame. You are first in line for a scholarship. . . .
>
> She learned these things, but I couldn't teach her about Chinese character. How to obey parents and listen to your mother's mind. How not to show your own thoughts, to put your feelings behind your face so you can take advantage of hidden opportunities. Why easy things are not worth pursuing. How to know your own worth and polish it, never flashing it around like a cheap ring. Why Chinese thinking is best. (289)

The Chinese way offers simplicity. Obedience makes life straightforward. Furthermore, a daughter who truly respects her mother may feel more self-respect. American society is not easy on female self-confidence and is harder still on the pride of those who do not count as white. If the children of immigrants feel ashamed of being with their mothers in public, they will feel no respect for themselves on those occasions. That kind of respect, however, the mothers do not quite achieve from their daughters, and so they see their daughters as relatively weak and unhappy, fluttering and flapping like birds with broken wings.[4]

The advantages of the Dominican or Chinese patterns of life are their relative simplicity: female roles are circumscribed and well explained. Private contradictions, such as women's power behind the scenes, are also well understood among the women. Living up to an explicit pattern where the consequences of failure are so appalling that one might literally prefer death does clarify choices. One's goals are clear, and one's measures of success are obvious. When one has a clear code, life provides report cards, and one can enjoy that periodic affirmation of success. America offers the luxury of choices, careers, and personal success measured in the same terms as used by men. It does not insist on subordination to one's mother, husband, mother-in-law, or first wife. This might seem enticing and alluring; however, one does have to make choices, and all sorts of things can go wrong. Alvarez and Tan are not saying that America is necessarily bad but that it does not specify goals and supply the emotional models and comforts that help one attain them. Life does not issue ongoing report cards; one has to manufacture one's own ego-support structures, and the women depicted in Alvarez's and Tan's novels are ill-trained to do this. The third generation may have it easier, and the fourth may not see what the problem was, but the first and second generations suffer because a cultural definition of gender is being dismantled as part of the process of cultural transformation.

China Men (1980) and The Mambo Kings Play Songs of Love (1989)

Kingston's novel informs many white, middle-class Americans of their culture's practice of feminizing Asian men.[5] However, while Kingston decries such cultural castration, she also condemns Chinese men for imposing similar oppressions on their own women. The women described by Alvarez and Tan find in America an attractive, if disturbing, freedom; they find something that seems, at least on the surface, to augment their lives. The men in both Kingston's and Hijuelos's novels are faced instead with a diminution of self in their gender identities. America's demands and damages are thus rather different for women and men.

Kingston begins with the legend of Tang Ao, a man who sought "Gold Mountain," the popular Chinese name for America.[6] When he arrived there, he was captured by women and turned into a woman. His ears were pierced, his feet broken and bound, and he was fed foods supposed to improve his womb. He was forced to wash the stinking bandages used to bind his feet. When he was finally permitted to go forth on small feet, it was to serve a meal at the queen's court. Thus, she tells us, were men forced to become women in America.

Even the Chinese workers who did exhausting physical labor, such as hammering and chipping tunnels through granite or creating pineapple and sugar fields on Hawaiian mountainsides, were feminized by the legal limitations set upon them. They built with their muscle and sweat the great farming areas of California but could not own property. They could not plead cases in court, attend white schools, or become citizens. Only men were allowed to immigrate, so they could not readily father families, since any American (male or female) marrying a Chinese person forfeited American citizenship. Indeed, Chinese men were largely deprived of any sexual outlet. Once the railroads were finished, the jobs they were permitted to hold were those considered too low for white men: cleaning clothes, cooking, serving food, and other functions usually performed by women in both American and Chinese societies. For part of the latter half of the nineteenth century, American women were similarly denied voice and power. They could not own property, argue in the courts, attend universities, vote, or hold most jobs. As Euro-American women improved their lot, though, the laws saw to it that racial others continued to be denied any such improvement. Kingston documents the legislation that aimed at subordinating the Chinese and refusing them citizenship, despite their labor in opening the American West.

Kingston makes plain the sufferings undergone by these men in their desire to make money to support their families back in China. In their own eyes, they lowered themselves unspeakably by doing female things. The Confucian system in China made women essentially unclean and inferior; to work in a laundry and wash clothes contaminated by female effluvia was a pollution practically beyond imagination. Moreover, since women were not permitted to immigrate on the same terms as men until 1952, the all-male Chinese communities were forced to perform female as well as male functions within their own enclaves as well as in white society.

In Kingston's view, America has much to answer for in terms of institutionalized humiliation and oppression of these men. Add to that the lynch mobs and occasional massacres, and those Chinese pioneers who helped build the American West had cause to feel that America treated them badly. Nor have the sexual stereotypes changed much. David Henry Hwang's play *M. Butterfly* explores the Western desire to interpret the Asian male as lacking masculinity, and he relishes that male's revenge. As Frank Chin in *Donald Duk* sums up the occidental vision of the Far East, "Chinese are artsy, cutesy and chickendick" (3). Nothing of the Chinese heroic tradition is permitted to cross the language and cultural barrier. Kingston remarks on a poem written on the walls of the detention center of Angel Island that "the poets had come to a part of the world not made for honor, where 'a hero cannot use his bravery'" (55).

That Americans deny Chinese men full masculine identity is well established in this novel as well as in other examples of Chinese-American literature. Kingston attacks such prejudice. At the same time, she attacks the Chinese concept of masculinity for its insistence on degrading women to prove its own superiority. The men experience mistreatment amounting to women's daily lives but choose to reinforce such treatment of women rather than apply what they have learned as a lesson in humanity. Kingston tells of her father swearing: "Dog vomit. Your mother's cunt. Your mother's smelly cunt" (12). She laments: "What I want from you is for you to tell me that those curses are only common Chinese sayings. That you did not mean to make me sicken at being female" (14). The evidence, however, suggests that the Chinese idioms are all too meaningful. Cousin Sao receives imperative letters from his Chinese mother: "I order you to come back. . . . You don't need to save enough money to bring a litter of females. . . . Sell those girls, apprentice the boy, and use the money for your passage" (172). The constant verbal abuse (and even a beating) is located in America and, as Goellnicht argues, is the result of cultural castration (201). Both women and men thus suffer from the effect of America on family cultural patterns; in this book, readers are not shown any clear picture of what America offers in compensation.

A very different sort of gender clash is at work in Oscar Hijuelos's *Mambo Kings Play Songs of Love*. Like many Chinese immigrants, his Cuban musicians enter an ethnic network and essentially never leave it. Eugenio, the child of one musician, must thus make his own terms with America, for his parents do not make much of a bridge for him between transplanted Cuban life and polyglot, multiethnic New York. The novel consists of the life-saga of Cesar Castillo, narrated during the two or three days it takes him deliberately to drink his diseased kidneys to death while playing records of his music and remembering his past. The narrative consists of three components: the history of Cesar's life told as he dies; his last hours in the Hotel Splendour in 1980; and, surrounding that, the musings of Eugenio, the son of Cesar's dead brother, Nestor. While some children of immigrants produce their novels through the persona of a child of immigrants who has become a writer, Eugenio has no claims to be a writer, and he appears truly lost.

Hijuelos himself is the child of Cuban immigrants and is the age of Eugenio, both being born in 1951. While the novel may indeed be purely a work of fiction, he writes about experiences of the sort presumably happening to Cubans of his parents' generation, and he certainly builds a sense of authenticity with his details. Hijuelos shows no particular animosity toward America and its culture. Nonetheless, Eugenio's state at the end of the novel reminds us that any immigration extorts a high price.

The finest reward that America had to offer Cuban musicians (in their estimation) is established at the outset. The most successful Cuban with their background is Desi Arnaz, the husband of Lucille Ball and, in the character of Ricky Ricardo, a star in the *I Love Lucy* television series. Even to make a spot appearance on his show (as the Castillo brothers do six years after their arrival in America) is to have gained the first rung on the ladder of success and to see the higher rungs stretching invitingly above them. Had they been luckier and perhaps a bit broader in their range of talents, they too might have soared from Oriente province to Hollywood. In his old age, Arnaz lives in luxury near the Pacific. His garden is laid out to remind him of his favorite plaza in Santiago, the place he used to take girls when he was young. Arnaz will never go back to Cuba; that option was eliminated for most of the novel's characters by Castro's revolution. However, he is wealthy enough to replicate his favorite corner of Cuba in California and to be generous to countrymen.

Success in America for these characters is media oriented and media shaped. Nestor and Cesar's highest achievement is to play at being immigrants and walk through silly stage business until they can perform a song that Nestor wrote. For Eugenio, watching reruns of that episode of *I Love Lucy* "was like watching something momentous, say the Resurrection. . . . because my father was now newly alive and could take off his hat and sit down on the couch. . . . He could play the trumpet, move his head, blink his eyes. . . . For me, the room was suddenly bursting with a silvery radiance" (4). When Nestor has gone offstage, Eugenio remarks that "the miracle had passed, the resurrection of a man, Our Lord's promise which I then believed, with its release from pain, release from the troubles of this world" (8). Television can thus raise the dead and give release from pain. In the final chapter, when Eugenio no longer believes God's promise, he still clings to the hope that Desi Arnaz can fill the hole in his life and save him.

Cesar suffers very little from being transplanted for the simple reason that he lives largely within the confines of a Cuban network of relatives, friends, Spanish speakers, Cuban food, and Cuban music. Even though he learns enough English to serve as emcee for the Mambo Kings, he never suffers isolation or loss of roots. In a real sense, he never becomes American. Nestor strives more consciously to avail himself of America and studies *Forward America!*, a book whose blurb promises, "Whether you're rich or poor, Chinaman, Indian, or from the planet Mars, this book can *change your life!*" (119). Nestor, though, is too emotionally blocked by unrequited obsession over a Cuban woman; he cannot fully commit himself to his wife or America, and his melancholy robs his life of much savor, though it makes his music compelling.

Cuba is thus the land of true love for Nestor and the land of the only real love for Cesar, the love felt for his mother. His happiest memories concern childhood, when he was spoiled by his mother and servant women, and he tries to relive these moments during the one time he revisits Cuba. His father is a violent tyrant and, like Fidel Castro, makes it impossible for Cesar to live at home. Even his mother is critical of his drinking. Nevertheless, Cuba is redolent with the enfolding, obsequious, nurturing love of Latin women for an adored man-child. America, by contrast, is characterless and sexless, and Americanized women do not supply such slavish, enfolding support for the male ego. Hence, these Cubans stay ensconced in a Cuban enclave and fiercely resist any attempt by their womenfolk to take on American ways or values. Cesar, as a first generation immigrant, is not unhappy with his lot, even though it involves a long, slow decline, musically and physically. He lives for rum, countless sexual encounters, and music. His lack of introspection and reasonably amiable personality save him from acute misery, even when he is reduced to serving as the repairman for an apartment building.

The second generation, seen in Eugenio, shows more strain. He evinces little talent for music. He proves too American to fit Cuban cultural patterns but is not American enough or ambitious enough to create a coherent and rewarding life for himself. Like his father, he is prone to depression. His life seems curiously suspended; he only comes alive when viewing reruns of that *I Love Lucy* episode. In Desi's house, Eugenio hallucinates seeing the television rerun again, and in this hallucination, he embraces his father and feels solid flesh. "I started to feel myself falling through an endless space, my father's heart. Not the heart of flesh and blood that had stopped beating, but his other heart filled with light and music, and I felt myself being pulled back into a world of pure affection, before torment, before loss, before awareness" (404). Eugenio cannot find meaning in love, sex, or music. His life, in a country that does not evoke memories of moth-er-love, lacks the emotions and intensity he expected from observing the older generation. With nothing in his American life to make him feel the darling of the world, he feels himself to be soulless.

For contrast, we might note that the film version of the novel, *The Mambo Kings*, is a success story. Eugenio does not exist. Cesar is shown shortly after Nestor's death running the little club that Nestor had defined as his version of success—a more modest goal than Cesar's big-time dreams. The brothers are shown speaking quite passable English when they go to America, and all the Cuban characters speak English when together, thus nullifying any sense of the ethnic enclave being limiting as well as supportive to the brothers when they try to come to terms with New York. Cesar's physical magnetism is enough to give viewers radiation burns, but he never has to deal with his own aging into unattractiveness, as the fictional character does. With no long decline and sodden death for Cesar, and no damaged second generation, the portrayal of immigrant life is much rosier. The problems deriving from gender remain unprobed.

Boyle shows the Van Brunts betraying their own spirits or souls to the Van Warts when they see the wealth and become co-opted to the domi-nant view of their own inferiority. Tan shows mothers thinking their daughters to be severely deficient in spirit and warped by America. King-ston shows some of her Chinese men compensating violently for their perceived loss of masculinity. With Hijuelos, we find another version of this threat to spirit or soul. Someone from a macho culture faces consid-erable adjustments with regard to women when coming to America. Nestor's most moving creation is his song, "Beautiful María of My Soul." Maria is the woman back in Cuba who has been his dream-love. Neither this fantasized woman nor the mother of Nestor and Cesar can be trans-planted to America. Maria as the Virgin Mary (another Maria concerned with souls) is also someone whose influence wanes in America. What those women stand for in the sexual and psychic economy in Cuba is lacking in American culture. Eugenio has absorbed expectations that his masculini-ty will be nurtured by female forces; the words of his father's music tell him this, and so do the lives of the immigrant generation. These expectations will not be met in his own life. His lack of musical ability, coupled with his melancholy, compound the problem; from his cultural point of view, the country he lives in and he himself lack soul. Not even the fabulous Desi Arnaz can supply this want. His hallucination of falling into the endless space of his father's heart is an ecstatic vision of annihilation, male into male, deprived of feminine and homeland nurture.

Preserving the old gender patterns may put off the evil day, but no group can resist the cultural pressures of America forever. *The Godfather I* and *The Godfather II*, for instance, show Sicilian gender roles preserved; the first film makes that point overtly when Don Vito is asked to arrange vengeance for an immigrant father who raised his daughter like American girls and let her go out unchaperoned only to be sexually assaulted. The Corleone family remains strong—in this vision—by holding to old patterns. Its members also remain unassimilated in crucial ways, and crime sets them apart even when Italian descent ceases to be a barrier. Given the nature of their "business," the second generation is unable to assimilate, and at the end, Michael Corleone is pondering the limitations of his chosen life. His wife has left him, relatives and former friends have betrayed him, and he has lost all chance of fulfilling his original ambition to become a senator or governor. Whether culture or profession keeps one from assimilating, the resulting life seems ultimately somewhat damaged, and damaging to the soul, even to the soul of a murderous crime lord. The old ways and the old gender patterns can be made exotically interesting—and viewers may be impressed by the power and confidence of the mafia dons—but those old ways have prevented full Americanization. When Michael's child or grandchild tries to make the transition to legality and legitimacy, he or she will only be able to do it by rejecting the strong family and all its concerns. The payment in the coin of the soul is simply being deferred to a later generation.

The Xenogenesis Trilogy (1987, 1988, 1989)

Octavia Butler's speculative fiction often refers directly or indirectly to the African-American experience. I do not mean by this that her futuristic stories simply reconfigure American racial relationships through allegory. Rather, she explores what happens emotionally when two cultures, human and extraterrestrial rather than black and white, become entangled. In this trilogy, humanity of all colors finds itself in the situation of Africans because the aliens have a crushing technological power to enforce their will and vision, no matter what the humans may wish, just as Europeans and white Americans exercised such powers in Africa and the New World.

In classifying Butler's work as fiction about immigrant experience, I am stretching a point. Butler's future people are merely traveling to a changed Earth and to a Latin American region rather than to their homeland, North America. Although they dislike the conditions of their being preserved alive, their discomforts are minimal compared to those of the slaves shipped to America. The books are thus one or two removes from the usual immigration to America story. Nonetheless, they constitute variants on that theme, and they make especially vivid some of the fears, ambiguities, inescapable guilt, and permanent dissatisfactions that immigrants rarely realize will be their lot. Furthermore, what Butler does with racial difference is particularly sophisticated and subtle; the distancing provided by extraterrestrials perhaps frees her to get beyond the obvious problems that racially distinctive groups have faced when entering America. For all that Butler's surface concerns are not blatantly critical of America, the patterning of these experiences is American, and most of the characters, with their prejudices and strengths, are from the United States, so what she does with them lends itself to commenting on America.

The protagonist of *Dawn*, the first book in the Xenogenesis trilogy, is Lilith Iyapo, an African American.[7] The setting is the devastation following a nuclear holocaust. All higher life forms would have been wiped out had not some aliens intervened to the extent of rescuing the few remaining humans—a few thousand, perhaps. The humans are interrogated, tested, and put in and out of biotechnical storage. When the novel starts, roughly 250 years have passed since the war, and the three-sexed alien species, the Oankali, have managed to cleanse and improve the biodiversity in a few tropical locations on Earth. The Oankali want to start new settlements on Earth—but on very nonhuman terms. The first volume concerns Lilith's training to go down to Earth, and the second and third concern the immigrant conditions and the first generation born of mixed Oankali-human blood.

The first parallel established between Lilith and her African ancestors is her helplessness in the hands of the aliens. Their technology is superior to any that existed on Earth, let alone that which Lilith may personally have comprehended. Oankali mechanisms are all biological; their spaceship is an organism, as are all their equivalents to toilets, food synthesizers, electric runabouts, and elevators. They collect and manipulate genes as easily as humans digest meals, although they do this conscious of and controlling every change on the atomic level. In the face of such power, Lilith makes very little headway in getting what she wants. Although the Oankali value humans to a degree that Lilith can never fully understand, they value them for their bodies' ability to grow cancers but see the individuals as perilously riven by the conflicting imperatives of hierarchical drive and intelligence. Those two elements in human nature ensure the destruction that did indeed ensue. Thus, the Oankali value in Lilith the cancer that she loathes but distrust or condemn qualities that seem to her natural and even desirable. This causes her great frustration. They can greatly extend her life, give her perfect memory, cure all physical ailments, and increase her strength, but she feels like a pet, not an equal partner.

The second parallel concerns sexuality. The Oankali are driven to mingle genetically with any suitable species they find. The price they exact for saving humans is hybrid offspring. Even as white masters took African women and did what they could to cheapen and deny black male sexuality and black pairings, so here Lilith learns that there will never again be purely human children. People can choose Oankali-ensured sterility in human settlements. They can also bear hybrid children who will seem monstrous—children with sensory tentacles, extra limbs, and strange skin, children of three sexes who must go through a prolonged metamorphosis before they become sexually mature, children driven by imperatives that the human parents can never understand.

Not only must the races interbreed as the Oankali decree, the family patterns will alter. Neither human nor Oankali couples ever copulate without the third-sex ooloi to take part in the experience. While the ooloi produces sexual ecstasies by direct neural stimulation, the woman will never lie with the man again, and all joining of sperm and egg and subsequent genetic engineering take place within the ooloi, where Oankali and human characteristics are mixed to create the new race. Humans cannot circumvent the rules because those rules have been made biological. Smells and feelings of aversion and avoidance keep people from touching each other, and trying to go against the sensation makes one sick. In the next generation, we are told, males will largely become wanderers and gatherers of genetic information, returning at intervals rather than participating everyday in the family. Historically, the black family in America underwent pressures that also drastically reduced paternal presence.

In addition to such social changes, Lilith also undergoes a change from the daily occupations of America and the Oankali spaceship to an impoverished biosphere where she lives along a river and grows crops in little clearings hacked from the jungle. That change is even more drastic than those undergone by the Chinese described by Maxine Hong Kingston, who are sent from Chinese villages or small cities to clear terraced fields for growing pineapple or sugarcane in Hawaii. Instead of an African extended tribal family or the nuclear family upheld by American law, Lilith must participate in a family where any child is not just the offspring of herself and a human mate but is partly the "master's" as well; the child's mixed blood is always visible. The children, with their ability to interact consciously at the genetic level with all biota, are always strange to the parents. They do not even have a language for explaining to pure humans what they as hybrids feel and perceive when tasting plants at this genetic level. As in immigrant families where the younger generation prefers English to a parental language, these families suffer from large areas of noncommunication and from major differences of attitude.

Even hierarchy within the family is disturbed, for human patterns cannot prevail in the face of the actual power of the Oankali. Similarly, in Chinese and Hispanic cultures, the patriarchal patterns are undermined in America. One of the most compelling reasons for human resisters to refuse joint marriage with the Oankali is the distress that some of the human males feel at ooloi manipulating them, as if the ooloi were treating them sexually as females. Their understanding of the sexual relationship is inaccurate, but their feelings are violently strong, and their definitions of gender are even more shaken by the Oankali than are the definitions of the Chinese men described by Kingston.

As in other immigration stories, the second generation—here the first hybrid generation—has predictable problems with identity. The males and females make the transition relatively easily, though Lilith's son Akin, the male protagonist of *Adulthood Rites*, regrets that his metamorphosis makes him look much more like an Oankali and more readily provokes resisters to violence against him. When the first hybrid ooloi appear in *Imago*, however, the problem of identity becomes acute. What the Oankali most valued about humans was their ability to form cancers, to turn on growth that had been genetically turned off soon after birth. Under Oankali manipulation, the cursed disease becomes the basis for new abilities to regrow organs, regenerate any tissue, and change shape as needed. The hybrid ooloi have this shape-changing tendency to such an extent that until they manage to stabilize themselves with human mates, they find themselves changing shape into whatever they are near; they can resemble any life form, including slime molds. In the distant future, when the new Oankali-human species leaves Earth and goes seeking new races to mingle genes with, this ability to shift shape will make contact with the new races less traumatic, since the ooloi will be able to make themselves less monstrous-seeming to the new life forms. For the time being, however, such gifts create more barriers between children and parents, human and Oankali, and make it difficult for the hybrid children to establish an identity.

Butler is not simply arguing that people should welcome change or the mixing of cultures. Rather, when we are faced with situations in which mixing is inevitable (as it has become in this country) and rapid change is unavoidable (as it is in our technology-driven society), we need to know and recognize the effects. Butler does a brilliant job of analyzing Lilith's internal conflicts. Lilith does not want sterility and death, but she wants fully human children. She is forced into an Oankali family and, with some hate and anger, accepts the psychological and chemical bonding. Every so often, though, she goes off on her own to think of the past and curse her present. She feels guilty for betraying humanity and admires the determination of resisters to stay fully human, even though she believes that their way leads only to death. She loves her Oankali mates yet cannot help having feelings of hostility and guilt over that love and that hostility. She loves her hybrid children but has to control her reactions to tolerate their differences.

Butler's preference seems not for cultural hybridity as such but rather for allowing as many culturally different enclaves as possible.[8] The human-Oankali communities develop local patterns since human languages determine the groups, so Mandarin-speaking villages differ in their customs from those of English speakers. Through Akin in *Adulthood Rites*, Butler argues that a fertile human-only group should be permitted to exist, and the Oankali eventually permit a low-tech human group on Mars. The Oankali argue that permitting humans to continue to breed is sheer cruelty since their genetic contradiction will inevitably kill them off. Butler's claim that they should be allowed what they want, no matter what "higher" wisdom suggests, would permit arguments that Native American tribes should be allowed to live free of all contact with Euro-American culture, including school, if they wish. It would also permit some purely Chinese or Mexican enclaves, or polygamous Mormons or David Koresh's Branch Davidians, to exist without violent interference from authorities and without persecution for their sexual practices. If members of such groups want the benefits of the majority culture, they will have to deal with it on its terms, but they should not be forced. There are problems with this argument; for example, children might be prevented from making choices by parents. Butler, however, is not an author to promise a rose garden.

๑ ๑ ๑

Among the authors who stress race and gender as defining elements of the immigrant experience, we see much sense of loss over the discarded cultural values. Even Kingston, who has reason to wish Chinese patriarchy modified, is indignant at the ways in which Chinese people were forced against their grain by discriminatory laws. These authors are not arguing that the original ethnic cultures were better in all ways; rather, they maintain that depriving people of their culture does damage that is not confined to the immigrant generation. True, these immigrants chose to come to America, and some chose to Americanize, but color would prevent some from full assimilation even had they wished to discard their heritage. Moreover, these writers feel that the original cultures did offer something superior to American materialism; they would be happy to see America somehow revitalized by learning from other peoples. The writers see their ancestral cultures as promoting values other than money. Scholarship and learning stand out in Kingston's China. Sensuality and elegance adorn

Hijuelos's Cuba. Devotion to duty even unto death gives Tan's older women a burnished strength. Furthermore, in all these novels, we see a stronger, multigenerational family structure. These writers agree that they do not wish to lose their heritage or see it reduced to a meaningless holiday or two. As the children absorb American values, they lose these ancestral strengths and seem—both to their parents and, sometimes, to themselves—to have lost their souls or spirits. Occasionally, a writer can find power in being able to draw on both cultures; Kingston perhaps describes that stage in *The Woman Warrior,* and Butler articulates it in *Imago.* The 1980s and 1990s have seen the argument that those with mixed blood or dual cultures can consider themselves superior to the "pure" and monocultural. Biculturality is possible; one need not feel excluded by either. For most of the writers of the last thirty years, however, such a stage is more a promise than an actualized reality.

One of the strengths of these novels is their ability to portray the ancestral cultures in ways that make them comprehensible to readers of Euro-American backgrounds. The very comprehensibility rests on fictions that permit the experience to be so revealing. The novels present readers with a banquet of strange flavors, but they are flavors modified so as not to appear too hot, strong, or alien. Not surprisingly, food is important to some of these writers. Hijuelos fills his air with the smells of pork and fried plantains. Amy Tan describes many Chinese specialties, and Julia Alvarez raves over the flavor of ripe guavas. For readers, such descriptions of food actualize the argument that other cultures are worth learning to appreciate. We benefit and will gain enjoyment if we can learn to savor their differences. Food is an unthreatening way of arguing the case for difference with readers from different cultural backgrounds.

Immigrant Success: Mukherjee

Jasmine (1989)

America looks pretty good to a young Indian woman from Hasnapur, where people defecate in the fields and the decomposing corpse of a dog disturbs one's ablutions in the filthy river. Or so Mukherjee argues in *Jasmine.* Her protagonist starts as an unwanted fifth daughter in a family that is ill-provided to pay dowries. A bull gores her ineffectual father. Widowhood renders her mother an empty husk, and her own future depends on the good will of her ambitious but not very competent brothers. By the end of the novel, Jasmine is living with an American nuclear physicist and heading for California with him. Mukherjee takes a somewhat libertarian position that the individual is responsible for what she makes of her life, no matter what her starting point: no sympathy is due to an underdog. Jasmine is admirable in many respects. She does and survives what very few peo-

ple of any class, culture, or gender could, and she enjoys what she is making out of her life. Mukherjee rightly calls this a fable rather than a realistic novel, but she does what many novelists do not: she shows us the victims trampled in the dust as well as Jasmine's victories.[9] The self-centered,
individualistic side of this book challenges and denies the complaints about
immigrating to America that are seen in the books just discussed. Mukherjee believes in immigrants' ruthlessly cutting off the past and forgetting
it, in their living for the present and future, in their adapting to the new
culture. The American Dream works in this novel, but Mukherjee is clear-
sighted enough to present a tally of victims. In doing so, she makes plain
the unrealistic expectation embedded in the American Dream—namely,
that everybody can prosper.

The early successes of Jyoti (later Jasmine) include learning fluent English in her village school and marrying a supportive, modern Indian man.
After his murder, she is helped in America by a Quaker who teaches illegal alien women how to avoid the behaviors that will draw police attention. Through this woman's daughter, she becomes the valued caregiver
to a professional couple's daughter in New York and learns her way about
Manhattan. Jasmine earns lots of extra money translating for scholars and
businessmen. When she leaves New York, she meets another strong-mind-
ed woman who gets her a job in a bank in Iowa, and Jasmine ends up living with the banker, one of the most important men in town. When she
leaves him, it is to rejoin the male half of the professional couple, Taylor,
to go to California, where he will carry on his research in physics and, if
they marry, she will presumably become a legal immigrant. As she takes
off from Iowa, not stopping even to pack a bag, she feels exhilarated. "Adventure, risk, transformation: the frontier is pushing indoors through un-
caulked windows" (214). The frontier, with its promise of openness and
possibility, still beckons. At each successive stage, she wins a new name.
Jyoti was her name in Hasnapur; Jasmine with her husband; Jase when
exploring New York; and Jane in Iowa. To succeed, she must create new
selves fluidly and without nostalgia for any of her pasts. That Mukherjee
chose Jasmine for the title suggests that she thinks the new Indian woman capable of taking on the world.

The banker's ex-wife calls the protagonist a "tornado" (182) because she
sweeps into town and ruins lives. Without usually meaning to do any such
thing, Jasmine does exactly that. A Sikh terrorist kills her first husband;
the bomb was meant for Jasmine, because her modern behavior makes her
a whore in the eyes of the fanatic traditionalist. When the trawler-captain
who illegally gets her to Florida rapes her, she stabs him. Her success as a
caregiver in New York is one reason that the wife decides to leave Taylor
for another man; she thinks that their adopted child, Duff, will be adequately looked after, and she also believes that Taylor has fallen in love with

Jasmine. When Jasmine ends up in Iowa, she gets a good job in a bank and wins the heart of the banker, Bud Ripplemeyer, causing him to break up his marriage. She becomes the dream woman of a young local farmer, who wants her to run away with him. When Jasmine, farm matters, and financial hard times become too much for the admirer, he hangs himself. At the end, she leaves Bud, now confined to a wheelchair, to go west with Taylor and build with him an unconventional family, consisting of the two of them, Taylor's adopted child, Duff, and Jasmine's unborn child by Bud. Bud will be devastated by her desertion. The Indian husband, the boat captain, the professional couple, Bud's wife, Bud himself, and a neighboring farmer: these are people whose lives are destroyed or damaged by her, whether she meant any harm or not.

Jasmine is successful because she becomes different people to meet the shifts of circumstance. What she says about a Vietnamese boy adopted by Bud applies to her as well. "Du's doing well because he has always trained with live ammo, without a net, with no multiple choice. No guesswork: only certain knowledge or silence. Once upon a time, like me, he was someone else. We've been many selves. We've survived hideous times. I envy Bud the straight lines and smooth planes of his history" (190). Her triumph is finding a series of selves that can operate independently in a world totally different from her original village.

Mukherjee frequently reminds complacent American readers of what lies behind their comfortable and convenient lives. When Jyoti bathed in dirty water and her fingers hit a dog carcass, "the body broke in two, as though the water had been its glue. A stench leaked out of the broken body, and then both pieces quickly sank" (3). She continues: "That stench stays with me. I'm twenty-four now, I live in Baden, Elsa County, Iowa, but every time I lift a glass of water to my lips, fleetingly I smell it" (3). For her, that putrescent dog is what her past life was and what she will become if she fails. Another such mental association is formed when she uses a shower for the first time in her life. Clean hot and cold water: they represent pure luxury. However, she uses it after being raped and after stabbing the rapist. Whenever she uses a shower later, she cannot avoid remembering this grisly purification from the past. Nor can she discuss those acts with anyone; no one in Iowa would understand or sympathize with murder. Even though the rape took place on American soil, it belongs to her previous life. To someone with her or Du's experiences, America offers opportunities that seem unbelievably rich, even when she and Du are insulted or humiliated by American tactlessness or racism.

When evaluating Jasmine's successful adaptation to America, we have to assess her abandonment of Bud. Is this so cruel that we should withdraw our sympathies? Is it a critique of contemporary culture, and is she showing that she has learned its lessons only too well? She has indeed learned many things that make this decision thinkable. "In America, nothing lasts. I can say that now and it doesn't shock me, but I think it was the hardest lesson of all for me to learn. We arrive so eager to learn, to adjust, to participate, only to find the monuments are plastic, agreements are annulled. Nothing is forever, nothing is so terrible, or so wonderful, that it won't disintegrate" (160). Another insight into American life came to her when she ordered too many goods by mail, and Taylor taught her to write "RETURN TO SENDER" on the package. When Taylor comes for her in Iowa, she hesitates over leaving Bud, saying, "I want to do the right thing. I don't mean to be a terrible person" (213). Taylor's answer: "It's a free country." *"Just pull down an imaginary shade,* he whispers, *that's all you need to do."* She sees her position as being "caught between the promise of America and old-world dutifulness. A caregiver's life is a good life, a worthy life" (213–14). She chooses the promise that is America and heads for California without any baggage. She chooses a free and independent self over service.

For some readers, this is a brave development for the girl from a Punjabi village, marking a feminist discovery of self. For others, it represents a change for the worse felt throughout all of America, the change by which Bud's neighbor would sell his family farm and run a franchise and another neighbor would shoot Bud in the back, blaming him for banking conspiracies to defraud the honest farmer. Small farming-community innocence is disappearing in America, as it is in India. Jasmine's village teacher was shot by Sikh extremists; Bud is maimed by the farmer. Are her acceptance of rootlessness and her ability to shrug off obligation and compassion symptomatic of attitudes in America that lead to the growth of such violence? Mukherjee does not answer the question. All her words for Jasmine are neutral or positive, and the ending is filled with exuberance, seeming to be a paean to freedom, but the image of ditching a loving man confined to his wheelchair is so strong as to leave one disturbed. However, as Jasmine explains it, she is not running away from Bud; she is going toward something she wants or needs. Mukherjee thus challenges immigrant tales of discontent and the loss of soul; she points out that one can lose one's soul in many fashions, including chaining oneself to a half-paralyzed husband. Instead, she offers affirmation of the self and of the need to make life-enhancing decisions. As readers, we may still wonder if self-absorption will not bring serious problems in its wake, and we certainly see them in terms of Jasmine's tally of victims. Nonetheless, Mukherjee gives us this formula for how to take the New World by storm, for how to survive with your soul intact.

A film with an equivalent outlook is *American Pop*, in which a Russian Jewish boy is the first immigrant generation. He works in the entertainment world and marries off his only son, Ben, to the daughter of an Italian gangster to strengthen their professional relationship. Ben dies in World War II, but his son Tony runs away from his mother's second family and enters the music world. He becomes a composer and drug addict and fades away. However, he also had a son. That son, Pete, also enters the music world. He pays his way by peddling drugs but eventually gets his songs performed and performs them himself. Roots are totally lost: Pete knows nothing of his Italian or Russian Jewish background; like his mother, he is a blond from Kansas. Creativity and fame in the entertainment business are achieved. The film acknowledges without moral comment the gangsterism and drugs that constitute the underside of the entertainment industry. Perhaps performing the music at shattering volume before frenzied crowds produces ecstasy. If so, there is a public transcendence, but there is no private happiness. The overall tone at the end is much like that of Brat Pack and Generation X fiction: the fast lane offers success but little joy in *Less Than Zero* and *Bright Lights, Big City*. The emphases in *American Pop* are different from those in *Jasmine*, but the hardheaded acceptance of the present, the shedding of the past, the embracing of things American—these are similar.

It was suggested at the outset that *World's End* (as strongly leftist) and *Jasmine* (as strongly individualist and therefore quasi-libertarian) are inimical, politically speaking, so that confronting one with the other should be instructive. Thanks to the differing core values in each, however, they scrape along each other's side rather than collide head on. Property serves to focus *World's End*, while individual experience is what matters to Mukherjee. Jasmine rises as an independent person but not as a property owner. She eagerly expands her mind and experience, not her bank balance. She leaves Bud, taking nothing with her, and does not feel tempted by his wealth when deciding whether to stay or enter the world of risk again. She was once as helpless as the Van Brunts but has escaped—in part through help from others that Boyle's characters lacked; in part because she has adapted to the modern world and is prepared to leave her past behind her.

One could not live her life in colonial America, so Jeremias cannot be blamed for not living in her way. Walter Van Brunt could have tried in 1968, however, but he was not willing to leave his hometown or forget the past to create a new future. Obviously, Jasmine would not have done well had she stayed in Hasnapur. She escaped so that she might refuse the definitions imposed on her by her mother, her gender, and her religion. She consciously cultivates the ability to forget the past. Boyle insists that the past binds us; Mukherjee would agree but argues that individuals can cast off that binding. Therefore, what holds the Van Brunts down is not just the capitalist system but weakness and a choice on their part to stay in their ancestral home. Boyle sees his characters as victims; Mukherjee would consider them responsible for their own lack of success, especially in the later eras. A standard critique from the left and the standard answer from the right: Boyle leaves out individual responsibility and Mukherjee ignores the fate of the many Jasmines who failed to get the help she received along her way. Jasmine could so easily have become a Vanise Dorsinville.

Constructing the Immigrant Experience

The uprooted person has taken many metaphoric forms in literary history: the exile in Anglo-Saxon poetry; the pilgrim of the medieval world; the tourist of Pynchon's *V.*, and now the immigrant. Brautigan makes immigrant unhappiness his symbol for the nature of human life in *The Tokyo-Montana Express*. He starts his melancholy meditation with materials from the nineteenth-century diary of an immigrant Czech, much as Kingston begins *China Men* with the legend of Tang Ao. The modern-day characters echo the emblematic experiences of Tang Ao and Francl in that they too will never again feel at home or truly happy.

Summing up novels of immigrant experience is difficult, because doubleness and emotional contradictions are so fundamental to their nature. The doubleness takes many forms: ambivalence toward both America and the country of origin; contradictory values absorbed from each culture within the protagonist; clashes between older and younger generations in which both seem partly right. Moreover, much of this literature has more than one face. It says one thing to assimilated, middle-class Euro-Americans whose immigrant ancestors are a century or more in the past, but the message differs for those sharing the same ethnic background as the protagonist. A novel will carry yet another message for an African-American reader who knows how quickly the new ethnic group will leapfrog over ill-paid and ill-regarded African Americans. Furthermore, a tradition-oriented Native American reader may well feel impatience with complaints from any such invading group.

When Euro-American readers consider the attitudes expressed toward this country, they find a novel's impact intensified when the author produces a foreign view of America or when they are shown another culture in enough detail to feel the logic behind its strangeness. "Exotic" is a taboo term in postcolonial studies since it carries the baggage of orientalist projections, but such a shaping of the alien to make it acceptable is very much at work here. Part of exoticism is attraction; readers can enjoy learning about distanced or framed alien life patterns. America itself becomes new again through being rendered strange. Kingston's and Hijuelos's Americas show us a land of railroad construction and mambo nightclubs. In the Xenogenesis trilogy, the Oankali are equally exotic to all readers, no matter how long their ancestors have been on this continent. The calculated and constructed strangeness of immigrant cultures of origin must attract but also repel readers. Otherwise, the characters would have no reason not to buy a return ticket. In *The Mambo Kings Play Songs of Love*, Cuba offers a life deemed to have soul or meaning, but it also imposes paternal and dictatorial tyranny, whereas America offers freedom from such tyranny but no soul. The basic contrasts associate America with freedom, materialism, and individual pleasure; the original cultures are seen as offering extended, usually hierarchical, families with strong family support systems, codes of honor, and clear moral instructions. These instructions are enforced with such social pressure that there are few alternatives to correct conduct except death. Moreover, in any of the societies with strong hierarchies, life is hell for someone who does not fit the pattern. America's offer of freedom and pleasure is hard to turn down, but the responsibility to make all the decisions can be overwhelming, and the lack of codes reduces most people's sense of there being any meaning in life. Extended families and heroic adherence to a code of honor are exotically attractive, but forced obedience and the frequent chance of death are less enchanting. No matter how readers identify with either culture, they will find their emotional allegiance split and a sense of satisfaction denied.

Not only do the texts produce conflicting responses, they produce different responses in different readers. The impact of *China Men* would engage one set of sympathies from Chinese-American men (who might welcome the exposure of the peculiar sexual nature of the legal attack on their status in America). Feminists might feel anger that the "women's" lives forced on these men made them more determined to subject women to the worst of their own cultural gender practices. In essence, the texts with strong racial, gender, or ethnic orientations project little-heard voices within the culture. At the same time, they seduce members of the majority culture with something to shake their assumptions of monolithic culture and the melting pot because the vision offered is undeniably other yet attractive.

The impact of these texts is not one clear note; rather, it is a complex fugue of competing values. Readers are reminded very forcibly that life, maturely understood, involves compromises and inevitable losses as well as potential gains. Immigrant parents must learn that they will never understand their children or be close to them in significant areas of experience, and those parents must sacrifice a great deal of their own happiness in the hopes of benefiting those same alien offspring. Another way of discussing this impact is to liken it to a set of complex flavors. Readers from that particular cultural background may enjoy the validation of their family's experiences or may find matter to ponder in the differences from family accounts of the transplantation. The literature also makes difference and diversity enjoyable, like foreign foods. This message of diversity is partly structured to reach middle-class Euro-American readers, who represent a nationally influential bloc in terms of buying books and calling for legislation. All the pleasures that derive from vivid writing and intriguing exoticism work to make such readers more willing to accept the presence of cultural diversity. Sufficient exposure to something at first considered exotic can soon render it merely unusual and ultimately welcome as variety. Even very monocultural Euro-Americans would miss sweet-and-sour pork and pizza, adaptations of once-exotic viands. The authors not only try to influence readers' minds and emotions but, literally and figuratively, try to change mainstream tastes as well. Their sales and places in the current canon depend on succeeding in offering just the right amount of difference. As Trinh T. Minh-ha puts it, these writers must project "the possibility of a difference, yet a difference or an otherness that will not go so far as to question the foundation of their beings and makings."[10]

chapter two

Mythical *Innocence*

During the middle of this century, innocence flourishes as a liberal myth. It signifies harmlessness and thinking well of others. It enshrines belief in America's benevolence, whether exercised at home or abroad. It can still mean sexual ignorance. It encodes belief in ideals and betterment. Stories concerning falls from innocence are one way that white-oriented American literature explains uneasiness and discontent with America. Life is not all one imagines or wishes or thinks one's due, yet America offers such bounty that perhaps one's poverty or alienation is caused by something one has done. Out of the Protestant heritage of early settlers come images of the American Adam in the new-world paradise, and his fall creates a pseudohistory to account for a life of greatly diminished expectations and hopes. Among the many American Adams discussed by R. W. B. Lewis are Arthur Mervyn, Natty Bumppo, Donatello, Redburn, Pierre, Billy Budd, Daisy Miller, Isabel Archer, Huck Finn, Jay Gatsby, Ike McCaslin, the invisible man, Holden Caulfield, and Augie March.[1]

Innocence takes many shapes, individual and communal. It may be embodied in a character or rendered pastoral as rural community life. In the twentieth century, it is often projected onto the low-tech past to create a prealienated condition designed to explain our dejected state. It can, however, operate in a high-tech setting: the film *The Right Stuff* represents the early astronauts and test pilots as wisecracking and shallow but nonetheless heroic innocents, and behind that portrait is awareness of Watergate and Vietnam, where such military and governmental purity would lose its luster. Innocence can even exist in the world of crime: *Atlantic City* shows a small-time crook "innocently" delighted when he lives up to the film noir icon of trench-coated killer. He looks back to the old days of Atlantic City's crime-controlled gambling as simple and open compared to the drug world of the present-day crime business. Innocence claims the goodness of American motives when America acts abroad. It draws on idealized images from childhood. Frequently it reflects a middle-class desire to imagine its mode of life as harmless and not exploitive.

In addition to the national, middle-class, and childlike components of the innocence idea-complex, we also find white uneasiness over African slavery or over the displacement and slaughter of Native Americans. Leslie Fiedler shows how American Adams rely on their companions of color. In *Playing in the Dark*, Toni Morrison argues that the presence of that racial other coddles white uneasiness over racial cruelties by sanitizing the relationship between the races and helping the white Adam feel personally innocent of responsibility toward their condition.

In the nineteenth and early twentieth centuries, authors dealt with the loss of innocence. Since the 1960s and even the 1950s, writers have felt compelled to admit that our innocence, personal and cultural, was never real. Ecological doomsayers have done their part to destroy comfortable belief in a clean wilderness and the endlessly and naturally bountiful farm. Vietnam, Watergate, and the Iran-Contra affair have damaged the politician's ability to proclaim the good intentions of our government at home or abroad. Nevertheless, artists have not jettisoned the theme. Innocence is as popular a topic as ever, but novelists partially deconstruct it, prove that it never existed, problematize it from minority viewpoints, and even construct nonwhite alternative visions of innocence. Cut off one head of the hydra, and two appear in its place. That authors continue to wrestle with the issue proves the tenacity of this literary theme. Evidently, many American writers remain tightly linked to this imaginary state, which has its roots in European and Christian myth.

The fall from innocence can be seen in purely individual terms, but most of the novels tie that individual fall to the loss of childhood and the disappearance of a sense of home that is associated with the small American town or rural community. Since the 1960s, the small-town idyll has become implausible (as it was earlier for Sinclair Lewis in the 1920s), so we have to go back to the 1940s and 1950s to find a detailed rendition of such an Elysium. Ray Bradbury's *Dandelion Wine* felicitously exemplifies this Euro-American pastoral celebration of the small American town and guiltless boyhood. With this as a starting point for the discussion of innocence (and with a few contrasting references to villages in Mukherjee's Punjab and Tan's China as reality checks), the chapter will then look at two African-American constructions of innocence. Toni Morrison's *Bluest Eye* and Gloria Naylor's *Mama Day* show us innocence of the individual and pastoral sort, and we will see how different their assumptions are from Bradbury's. Following this, the chapter will explore how Russell Banks and Lisa Alther attack the destructive dreams generated by white, small-town concepts of innocence in *Continental Drift* and *Original Sins*. The next section analyzes two books with an identical theme: a young boy shoots someone by accident. Brautigan and Vonnegut both use this image to embody the loss of innocence, and both make connections between the spiritual state of their protagonists and America. They project through their stories a sense that the liberal ideal has failed, and they may be aestheticizing the national loss of innocence in Southeast Asia. The chapter will then look directly at how the Vietnam experience affects our national and personal myth of innocence in novels by O'Brien and Haldeman. Even prior to Vietnam, Ralph Ellison and John Barth argue that innocence prevents our understanding our true identities; the chapter will then limn this theme. From very different perspectives, Ellison and Barth undertake to attack what they see as a burden of false innocence in *Invisible Man* and *The Sot-Weed Factor.*

Innocence cannot be ignored in a book on the American Dream, however tired we may be of new-world Adams and men who head for the frontier rather than deal with political and social complexity. A central tenet in the white American Dream is the belief that an individual's prosperity can be gained without harm to others; in other words, the pie is always expanding and one's increased share does not come from someone else's portion. Innocence as not doing harm thus lies at the very heart of the Dream. The rich complexity of approaches to innocence in this chapter demonstrate the power that this often dangerous idea still exerts on American imaginations, no matter which race's cultural perspective an individual starts from.

Constructing the White American Pastoral: Bradbury

Dandelion Wine (1957)

Part of what makes *Dandelion Wine* so convincing a celebration of innocence is Ray Bradbury's persuasiveness in constructing an idealized child's point of view. Waukegan, Illinois (which Bradbury calls Green Town), could be called an ugly town, with its harbor, coal docks, and railroad yards, or so Bradbury admits as an adult. As a boy, though, he was "fascinated by their beauty. Trains and boxcars and the smell of coal and fire are not ugly to children. . . . Counting boxcars is a prime activity of boys" (ix). Coal, with its dark iridescence, makes "a ton of beauteous meteors" as it rattles down the chute into the cellar. Bradbury's choice of words establishes that he is constructing a magical world: the book begins and ends with Doug Spaulding in a third-story cupola bedroom, looking out over the town and orchestrating its getting up and going to bed. From his "sorcerer's tower," he exhales, and streetlights go out like candles; he exhales again, and the stars begin to vanish. He conducts an orchestra of birds in their orisons as the sun rises. He is a magician on the first and last days of the summer of 1928, and there is more than a touch of a god in Doug as well, since his gestures invoke both creation and apocalypse.

Bradbury intensifies all the best moments of this summer, and one of his techniques for doing this is to invest them with the numinous. Doug is stalked by an eerie, almost hysterical sense that something will reveal itself or happen to him, and when the mystic breakthrough in consciousness occurs, he discovers that he is alive. He looks up and sees his father "standing high above him there in the green-leaved sky, laughing, hands on hips. Their eyes met. Douglas quickened. Dad knows, he thought. It was all planned. He brought us here on purpose, so this could happen to me! He's in on it, he knows it all" (10–11). Doug's father picks up strange auras of woodland Pan or of "Bacchus and his pards." They had been gathering grapes, and Douglas, "eyes shut, saw spotted leopards pad in the dark" (10) and feels ecstasy. By transforming his father into a god showing only his benign aspect, he makes the American arcadia a nonoedipal world. Other manifestations of the divine occur. Doug's best friend, John Huff, is "the only god living in the whole of Green Town" (102), and Doug is devastated when John moves away. Similarly, Doug's grandmother is a goddess "with the look of the Indies in her eyes and the flesh of two firm warm hens in her bodice, Grandma of the thousand arms, shook, basted, whipped, beat, minced, diced, peeled, wrapped, salted, stirred" (223–24). Her food is a divine mystery, and the importunate visitor who keeps asking the names of dishes is accused of blasphemy. As people eat, their mouths are full of miracles. The innocent world is one where oral gratifications are the sacrament, where the divine and mundane are not separated by impermeable barriers.

This American arcadia has multigenerational families, like any traditional village in China or India. In two houses side by side are Great-Grandma, Grandma and Grandpa, Dad and Mom, and Doug and his younger brother Tom, as well as the boarders at Grandma's who are practically part of the family. However, we find none of the tensions seen in the Chinese village (such as the tyranny of a first wife over others). Wisdom from the old is freely offered and cheerfully accepted. When a boarder, Bill Forrester, buys ten flats of a grass that will spread and replace ordinary grass yet not need mowing and that will be able to choke out weeds, Grandpa pays him for the flats and tells him to put them in the dump. Doug's grandfather declares to Bill: "Dandelions and devil grass are better! Why? Because they bend you over and turn you away from all the people and the town for a little while and sweat you and get you down where you remember you got a nose again. . . . A man toting a sack of blood manure across his lawn is kin to Atlas letting the world spin easy on his shoulder. . . . Spin those mower blades, Bill, and walk in the spray of the Fountain of Youth" (50–51). Grandpa's numen is Atlas; he also defends the dandelions because of the dandelion wine made from the flowers, a wine that preserves the memory of summer when drunk in winter. "They picked the golden flowers. The flowers that flooded the world, dripped off lawns onto brick streets, tapped softly at crystal cellar windows and agitated themselves so that on all sides lay the dazzle and glitter of molten sun. 'Every year,' said Grandfather. 'They run amuck; I let them. Pride of lions in the yard.'"(12).

The multigenerational family lives in harmony. On summer nights, Doug's grandfather, father, various uncles, and cousins come out onto the porch "into the syrupy evening, blowing smoke, leaving the women's voices behind in the cooling-warm kitchen to set their universe aright" (30). Later, the women follow. "What they talked of all evening long, no one remembered next day. It wasn't important to anyone what the adults talked about; it was only important that the sounds came and went over the delicate ferns that bordered the porch on three sides" (30). This harmony among the generations extends to people not in the family. Doug and his friends listen to old Colonel Freeleigh talk of the distant past and privately call him a time-travel machine. Others get along with their elders in meaningful ways, too. Young Bill Forrester, a reporter, falls in love with Miss Helen Loomis, aged ninety-five, and spends the afternoons of three weeks savoring the exotic locations she saw in her travels during the latter half of the nineteenth century. Their love shows itself in talk and eating together, and they hope, if there is reincarnation, to recognize one another in a future life by their both ordering lime-vanilla ice cream. Here and elsewhere, oral gratifications make this world beautiful. When Doug's great-grandmother dies, even her death is put in terms of food: "I've tasted every victual and danced every dance; now there's one last tart I haven't bit on, one tune I haven't whistled. But I'm not afraid. I'm truly curious. Death won't get a crumb by my mouth I won't keep and savor" (184). She talks to Doug without talking down to him, and he responds in kind. There is no generation gap in white America's dream of its own innocence.

The pleasures of the pastoral world also stimulate other senses. One of Bradbury's lovely set pieces is Doug's acquiring a new set of sneakers. He moons over the "Cream-Sponge Para Litefoot Shoes" for days and then talks the shoe-store owner into letting him pay part of the price by running errands. Mr. Sanderson agrees to the trade, feeling for a moment the magic that Doug feels in those shoes, and asks Doug if he would like a job in a few years as salesman. "'Gosh, thanks, Mr. Sanderson, but I don't know what I'm going to be yet.' 'Anything you want to be, son,' said the old man, 'you'll be. No one will ever stop you'" (24). In the realm of innocence, there are no limitations on the future. Doug hares off, his winter shoes forgotten on the floor, while Mr. Sanderson slowly "headed back toward civilization" (25), the civilization of stiff shoes and dark suits. Doug does not yet have to light out for the territories to find an antidote to civilization; the two are still intertwined in this arcadia.

Only three things threaten this golden age: misunderstanding the nature of happiness, quarrels, and death. Leo Auffmann tries to build a happiness machine—a strange forerunner of virtual reality rigs—and succeeds in this fantastic enterprise. His wife, however, is far from enchanted with his obsession; from the outset, she opposes him. "Can that machine make seventy-year-old people twenty? Also, how does death look when you hide in there with all that happiness?" (56). When the machine catches fire, she makes sure it is burning fiercely before letting their son call the fire department. The devastated creator gradually comes to see what real happiness is: the nuclear family, ensconced in its house. He sees his six children about their tasks and games, supper being put on the table, fresh bread coming out of the oven. That view, with its promises of food and love, is the true happiness machine, but seeking pleasure for its own sake can destroy such true happiness.

The quarrel that threatens Bradbury's arcadian peace is a silly dispute between two ladies in one of the ladies' clubs, but it gets worked up into accusations of witchcraft and might have turned very nasty. Here Bradbury deliberately softens the tone of small-town life, for in such circumstances, quarrels are real, and their bitter histrionics can start a feud that will last for years. Such feuds occur in Amy Tan's Chinese villages. They also appear, sharpened by religious fanaticism, in Mukherjee's *Jasmine*, since both Jasmine's husband and teacher are killed in factional violence. The period Bradbury describes did see some white American towns lynch African Americans. While American religious divisions rarely if ever caused the sort of violence shown by Mukherjee, they did produce social friction. Doug sees nothing of the potential power of that ugliness. When he and his brother Tom discuss this witchcraft quarrel, Doug is half-disappointed that it came to nothing. Witches, he feels, would add something shivery and deliciously frightening to the everyday.

Death provides some of the necessary shivers and challenges to a world otherwise too safe. Miss Helen Loomis, Colonel Freeleigh, and Great-Grandma all die in the course of this summer. Doug himself catches an unidentifiable fever so virulent that he nearly dies. Even as Doug becomes conscious of being alive, so he gradually faces the truth that he will die: "SO IF TROLLEYS AND RUNABOUTS AND FRIENDS AND NEAR FRIENDS CAN GO AWAY FOR A WHILE OR GO AWAY FOREVER, OR RUST, OR FALL APART OR DIE, AND IF PEOPLE CAN BE MURDERED, AND IF SOMEONE LIKE GREAT-GRANDMA, WHO WAS GOING TO LIVE FOREVER, CAN DIE . . . IF ALL OF THIS IS TRUE . . . THEN . . . I, DOUGLAS SPAULDING, SOME DAY . . . MUST . . ." (186). He cannot bring himself to finish the sentence but later admits the ugly word.

Those deaths, though, belong even in arcadia, and the people who die do so full of years and go not unwillingly. Death also comes, however, to the unwilling through violence, and at the center of this lyrical novel is a long chapter devoted to the "Lonely One," who has killed three women of the town. He—or some stranger—is stabbed to death by Lavinia Nebbs, a maiden lady who seeks the thrill of fear by walking through the town's ravine after dark. Doug, Tom, and their friends are devastated that the Lonely One has been removed from their emotional landscape. After discussing what the Lonely One *must* look like—tall, pale, skeleton-thin, with bulging green eyes—they decide that the little, red-faced, fat man whom Lavinia killed cannot be the murderer. Their relief at this imaginative reprieve from boredom is immense; "August won't be a *total* loss" (179), nothing but "vanilla junket" (178).

Incompatible fantasies conjoin to make the world of *Dandelion Wine*. Wilderness and civilization do not exclude each other. Father-son relations are nonoedipal. No generation gap sours family life, and familial relationships are harmonious. The numinous appears frequently, even if it is not recognized as such. Oral gratifications are the highest to be explored and exalted; not surprisingly, then, one finds no overt sexuality. Obviously, this is a dream, not anything that could exist. It would be found unpersuasive by many kinds of readers: the person passionately devoted to cosmopolitan life, the African American whose relatives would have been relegated to the wrong side of the tracks in this town, the reader who prefers Trollopian novels of political sophistication. Someone aware of the political and moral crises that took place while this work was written (1946–57) might find its arcadian escape into a peaceful past irritating. By setting the story in 1928, Bradbury can ignore the Rosenbergs, the Korean War, the McCarthy hearings, and the start of the civil rights movement. Bradbury's magic world can only work for those susceptible to its fantasies, but many Americans do respond to current complexities by glorifying small-town civilities. They would like to think that there was a time and place where events like those historical events named above were absent or unimportant. For those readers, Bradbury invests this white vision of innocence with brilliant intensity. And for those with a sense of history, the 1928 setting is a tacit admission that this Shangri-la could not or did not last. The stock market crash of 1929 forced many white Americans to "grow up" and face the fact that life was not benign, that success was not assured, that they could not count on being anything they wanted.[2]

Constructing Black Innocence and Arcadia: Morrison and Naylor

The Bluest Eye (1970)

Slavery and Jim Crow laws do not foster Adamic fretting. The pain of unsuspecting young victims is commonplace, but worrying about loss of one's personal innocence is likely to strike an African-American novelist as a selfish and self-indulgent white luxury.[3] A somewhat different kind of innocence, however, does enter their worlds indirectly, as a contrast to the way things are. Toni Morrison, for instance, invokes an absent world in which natural black "funkiness" (to use Morrison's term) is the behavioral norm. This mythically powerful realm acquires a kind of innocence because black authenticity is not compromised by white influences. The sunniness of that original state is suggested by her invocation of the southern towns from which her people moved north:

> They come from Mobile. Aiken. From Newport News. From Marietta. From Meridian. And the sounds of these places in their mouths make you think of love. When you ask them where they are from, they tilt their heads and say "Mobile" and you think you've been kissed. They say "Aiken" and you see a white butterfly glance off a fence with a torn wing. They say "Nagadoches" and you want to say "Yes, I will." You don't know what these towns are like, but you love what happens to the air when they open their lips and let the names ease out. (67)[4]

But that is how they invoke their hometown when they have left for the North in hopes of bettering their economic condition. Morrison also makes another distinction. Some "do not have lovely black necks that stretch as though against an invisible collar" but are instead "sugar-brown" (67–68). In other words, their lighter color tempts them to try to be more white, to act in white-approved fashions. This is their fall:

> They go to land-grant colleges, normal schools, and learn how to do the white man's work with refinement: home economics to prepare his food; teacher education to instruct black children in obedience. . . . how to behave. The careful development of thrift, patience, high morals, and good manners. In short, how to get rid of the funkiness. The dreadful funkiness of passion, the funkiness of nature, the funkiness of the wide range of human emotions.
>
> Wherever it erupts, this Funk, they wipe it away; where it crusts, they dissolve it. . . . They fight this battle all the way to the grave. The laugh that is a little too loud; the enunciation a little too round; the gesture a little too generous. They hold their behind in for fear of a sway too free. (68)

One result of conforming to white demands is the destruction of real sexuality. "She hopes he will not sweat—the damp may get into her hair; and that she will remain dry between her legs—she hates the glucking sound they make when she is moist" (69). When Pauline Breedlove was still a girl in the South, she experienced orgasm in the following terms: "I begin to feel those little bits of color floating up into me—deep in me. That streak of green from the june-bug light, the purple from the berries trickling along my thighs, Mama's lemonade yellow runs sweet in me. Then I feel like I'm laughing between my legs, and the laughing gets all mixed up with the colors, and I'm afraid I'll come, and afraid I won't. But I know I will. And

I do. And it be rainbow all inside" (103–4). Once she moves north, the colors go out of her life, and she succumbs to the demands of whiteness.

In addition to this hidden rainbow world of black authenticity, with its innocence that is defined as lack of white defilement, Morrison is aware of the Green Town ideal; she shows, though, how her characters are barred from enjoying such a life. The world of Dick and Jane that starts chapters in *The Bluest Eye* is also the world of *Dandelion Wine* in a slightly modified form. Dick and Jane's family is nuclear rather than extended, but they are white, conventional, and happy, living in small town or suburban comfort. By contrast, the ironically misnamed Breedlove family never owns a house, suffers poverty, and struggles under the weight of community disapprobation. Cholly is unreliable as a breadwinner. Pauline dreams of looking like Rita Hayworth and loves her white employers' child more than her own. Pecola is at the bottom of every childrens' pecking order. When she sees dandelions, the pride of Doug Spaulding's grandfather, Pecola senses something in them and feels a "dart of affection" but then accepts what she has been taught rather than what she sees and feels: "They *are* ugly. They *are* weeds" (43). She and her friends Frieda and Claudia MacTeer live in a world where they usually cannot afford any of the ice cream that consoles Doug on a hot day. Doug's grandmother's boarders are all practically members of the family; in contrast, the MacTeers' boarder starts pawing Frieda as she reaches puberty. Doug's fever is assuaged by the bottled smells of air from fine, clean places; Claudia's fever involves her swallowing Vicks salve, vomiting on the covers, hearing her mother curse her, and suffering a humiliating sense that falling sick is her own fault.

This is not a world in which Bradbury's sexlessness has any place. Pecola knows three prostitutes. "Nor were they protective and solicitous of youthful innocence. They looked back on their own youth as a period of ignorance, and regretted that they had not made more of it" (48). Experience without guilt is possible. Morrison describes such people:

> Then they were old. Their bodies honed, their odor sour. Squatting in a cane field, stooping in a cotton field, kneeling by a river bank, they had carried a world on their heads. They had given over the lives of their own children and tendered their grandchildren. With relief they wrapped their heads in rags, and their breasts in flannel; eased their feet into felt. They were through with lust and lactation, beyond tears and terror. They alone could walk the roads of Mississippi, the lanes of Georgia, the fields of Alabama unmolested. They were old enough to be irritable when and where they chose, tired enough to look forward to death, disinterested enough to accept the idea of pain while ignoring the presence of pain. They were, in fact and at last, free. And the lives of these old black women were

synthesized in their eyes—a purée of tragedy and humor, wickedness and serenity, truth and fantasy. (110)

The acceptance of it all—wickedness but also humor and truth—is impossible within a world obsessed with innocence. To wish to stay cocooned in the innocent, tidy world is to reject "the dreadful funkiness of passion, the funkiness of nature" and, thus, authentic black feelings. Morrison's towns are not arcadian. People and their problems are too vivid to be contained by the limits of Bradbury's white pastoral. Poverty denies the validity of that vision, as does racial mistreatment. Innocence in the white sense is only that time when a child is too young to understand what the world is like; it is not a state to be preserved as a moral virtue, since it will only leave that child open to getting hurt.

For further angles on innocence, we might consider a few aspects of Morrison's much more complicated novel, *Beloved*. Bradbury reduces all sensuality to oral gratification and extracts all sexuality from the world. Morrison's very different sense of innocence lets her merge oral and sexual sensations when Sethe and Paul D. remember her union with Halle:

> she remembered that some of the corn stalks broke, folded down over Halle's back, and among the things her fingers clutched were husk and cornsilk hair.
>
> How loose the silk. How jailed down the juice. . . . What he [Paul D.] did remember was parting the hair to get to the tip, the edge of his fingernail just under, so as not to graze a single kernel.
>
> The pulling down of the tight sheath, the ripping sound always convinced her it hurt.
>
> As soon as one strip of husk was down, the rest obeyed and the ear yielded up to him its shy rows, exposed at last. How loose the silk. How quick the jailed-up flavor ran free.
>
> No matter what all your teeth and wet fingers anticipated, there was no accounting for the way that simple joy could shake you.
>
> How loose the silk. How fine and loose and free. (27)

In Sethe and Paul D.'s joint memories of that long ago time, the sex is no more moralized than food. Bradbury cannot imagine sexuality in innocent terms, so he makes oral gratifications supreme, thereby eliminating sex. Morrison makes black sexuality in its authentic state different from white; it is a thing quite apart from sin or fall. She can infuse sexuality with food images and food with sexuality, thus sensualizing and glorifying the world of all the senses.[5]

Beloved grows out of murder, as do the novels by Vonnegut and Brautigan to be discussed later. Where white liberal writers choose to lament over an "innocent" crime stemming from youth and lack of judgment, Morrison's protagonist tries to murder her own children rather than permit slavers to recapture them and her.[6] She succeeds in killing only the baby, and her life is emptied of human relations as a result. As her older children grow up, they run away. The community rejects her. She allows her life to be swallowed by the ghost of the dead child and nearly succumbs to it.[7] Certainly, the narrator of Brautigan's *So the Wind Won't Blow It All Away* would understand that development. But Morrison does not end the story with futile regrets and obsessive mental flagellation. Instead, she shows how the community can help, how Sethe can be reached by a friend, and how even with such a crime in her past, she has to realize that "you your best thing, Sethe. You are" (273). No matter what the crime, life and one's self still need to be nurtured. Life properly shared with the community makes individual actions much less important and individual emotions much less all-encompassing. To cling to them is self-indulgent.[8]

Insofar as innocence by any definition seems valuable to Morrison, it would be a state of freedom from white expectations, standards of beauty, and rules of behavior. She values intense, funky relationships undefiled by white rules. She appears to endorse something like an essentialist vision of blackness or, at any rate, a sense that rural black culture had a coherent, humane, supportive code fundamentally lacking in white society, a code understood by all blacks who have not allowed themselves to be whitened by majoritarian values. Black authenticity is evidently capable of embracing nearly all experience and not just one's attempts to be good, generous, and nurturing. One falls to the degree that one's image of one's self is contaminated by whiteness and extracultural codes. Morrison never shows a community totally unmarked by whiteness, though Pilate's house in *Song of Solomon* may come close.[9] That uncontaminated ideal flutters at the edge of her literary horizons, though. It is an emotional utopia, if not a political reality.

Mama Day (1988)

Gloria Naylor constructs an isolated community in which a large measure of freedom from whiteness is possible; for women, that includes independence from and equality with men. Naylor's arcadia is the island of Willow Springs, located just off the coasts of Georgia and South Carolina but not claimed by either state. Thus, this place is not entirely part of the United States. Instead, it belongs completely to its black inhabitants. From 1823, the island has been held by free black descendants of a white man and black woman. Rumor has it that their foremother, Sapphira Wade, killed her white master after securing the island for her family, so this originary blow, real or imagined, at white, male oppression may be a founding act for the island culture, an act that makes Naylor's black style of

innocence possible. Local custom and agreement keep anybody from selling any part of the island to developers. While many inhabitants work on
the mainland, or even go to distant cities to pursue careers, they can always come back, sure that their community will not have changed radically. The life led there is low-tech, and compared to the rat-race pressures
that one of the two main characters, Cocoa, experiences in New York, it
may seem paradisal. However, Naylor's arcadia is not soppily idealized.
When Cocoa's city-bred husband, George, suggests they play Adam and
Eve, Cocoa tartly remarks, "Just go on and roll around in those woods with
your clothes off, and the first red ant that bites your behind will tell you
all about paradise" (222).

The community is relatively well defended against the pressures of
whiteness. We see Mama Day watching television, but she often leaves the
sound off and simply evaluates faces, interpreting the tics and fears that
do not show in words. The culture shown by the television certainly offers her nothing she wants in life and provides much to condemn about
the outside world. For Mama Day's generation, Candle Walk Night—held
December 22, in place of Christmas—is a time to exchange food and items
made with one's hands; but the younger generation, those who work beyond the bridge, exchange items from catalogs, and some even drive rather than walk. This might look like the destruction of culture, but Mama
Day notes that she knows Candle Walk was different in her father's time,
and his was different from a previous generation. Like the medicine man
Betonie in Silko's *Ceremony*, Mama Day accepts that ceremonies have to
change if they are to remain alive, so readers are told not to assume that
this means the end of all that matters about that celebration. In other
words, this is a living community; with ceremonies as with television, it
absorbs and makes its own what it wants of the outside, but it is not overwhelmed by white patterns. As a slightly unusual twist, Naylor sets part
of the story in 1999, so readers can see that the community retains its
independence even beyond the 1980s setting.

Naylor does not uphold the notion that nearly ideal circumstances will
produce nearly ideal people; in this, she differs from many utopian and
arcadian traditions. Accusations of witchcraft happen here, and the dangerous magic can claim lives in a fashion not true in Green Town. In Rudolfo Anaya's *Bless Me, Ultima*, readers also find real witchcraft in a Chicano town. The solidity of magic in these ethnic communities reminds us
that Bradbury's Green Town witchery is phony, a remnant of a real tradition but in the twentieth century only a child's fantasy. In Willow Springs,
Cocoa nearly dies as the result of Ruby's witchcraft and poison, and the
redness in Ruby's name coupled with her erotic jealousy link her to the
loa Erzulie. Naylor does not show Vodoun as an openly practiced religion
with hounfors, houngan, vevers, processions, and animal sacrifices, but she

does expose to view small evidences of its presence, such as someone buying a mojo hand for luck in the evening's card game. Since much of the narrative consists of dialogue between Cocoa and the dead George nearly twenty years after the events, one can say that Naylor does a bit of Vodoun herself, making the dead speak so even readers can hear.[10]

Vicious magic is one way in which the nearly ideal community proves itself less than a paradise. Another way in which its people fall short of ideal is their inability to recognize real joy. As in the case of Bradbury's Leo Auffmann, one inhabitant of this arcadia mistakes the nature of happiness but is taught better. Under Mama Day's tutelage, Bernice learns how to make her life productive. Instead of valuing cars and material goods, she learns to value her own work. She learns to cook things from scratch rather than to buy ready-made food. She gardens, sews, and does things that take time and attention, and ultimately turns her life into a series of fruitful processes, the sort of life Leo Auffmann's wife led as she fixed supper for her family. We also see death in arcadia, and that death is not confined to the elderly. Bernice's idolized child dies in the tempest, and so does Cocoa's nearly perfect husband, George, whose weak heart bursts in his attempts to save her.[11] Those are major exceptions, but life does not protect one against major exceptions. This arcadia gives us shocking death as well as death in old age. The old here are wise beyond the ways of the young, so the generation gap is minimized. Cocoa may be feisty and impatient of advice, and she has survived in New York City, but she knows through experience that Mama Day's suggestions work out. She never really thinks that Mama Day is an old woman who must be humored but can be safely ignored because she is out of touch with the real world.

The "funkiness" seen in Morrison is not an ideal directly invoked, but Naylor's equivalent is her sense that people must be true to their inner selves. Mama Day knows that Cocoa is tempestuous and demanding, and Mama Day laughs fondly when remembering that as a five-pound baby, Cocoa was exactly the same as she struggled to live. Miranda considers certain modes of conduct loving and others not, but she recognizes Cocoa's right to develop as her inborn personality dictates, merely warning her of possible consequences. Being authentic to your inborn self characterizes the culture, something quite different from trying to restrain your personality and actions until they fit Christian and other social codes of conduct.

Someone who is work- and technology-oriented rather than people-oriented, and who wants a standard against which to measure achievement, would find life here lacking. Certainly, this will apply to many urban readers and to anyone who accepts culturally male patterns of behavior, like George. Someone who values social interplay and freedom from rat-race pressures might indeed find this the way to enjoy life while learning about

one's true self and one's neighbors. This lifestyle also empowers women—
Mama Day being a traditional herbal doctor, midwife, and witch—so readers seeking lifestyles that encourage strong and competent women will find
it attractive. The echoes of Shakespeare's *Tempest* notwithstanding, one
should not read this island as a magical never-never land.[12] This world is
closer to the harshness of reality than is Bradbury's Green Town.

Deconstructing the Dream of Small-Town Innocence: Banks and Alther

Dandelion Wine showed us the white dream of small-town innocence.
Russell Banks and Lisa Alther are white writers who have tried to come
to terms with the legacy of that dream in more recent times. Both show
characters who were raised to believe in the Green Town dream and whose
lives are warped or even destroyed by their belief in that fantasy or by their
disappointment in its failure. Banks seems angry that it should have proved
false; he would still like to believe that hard work and decency are enough
to win a comfortable life in a nice town. In the first part of this century, a
general handyman (carpenter, painter) could live in a comfortable house,
raise three children, and make occasional trips by train across the country to visit family (one of my own grandfathers lived such a life). The skills
of this sort of trade have not changed that much in the intervening years,
but today's painter-handyman often subsists in borderline poverty and
struggles with unpaid taxes and payments on the vital truck, and, as like
as not, he lacks medical insurance. Banks's characters feel this constric-
tion of expectations from what their parents and grandparents could gain
with such blue-collar skills. Alther's vision is even darker than Banks's
because her small town is southern, and race is an inescapable flaw in the
picture of innocence. Both are shocked by the effect that the American
Dream has on lives and ask what their characters could or should have done
to make a more equitable life for themselves and others. Neither finds
much of an answer.

Continental Drift (1985)

Can a small-town American make the money needed to live a comfortable life? Not many can, not unless it is done by illegal means and by destroying others. This seems to be the conclusion Banks comes to in *Continental Drift*. Bob Dubois starts in Catamount, New Hampshire, in 1979,
and is stabbed to death two years later in Miami. After his death, his family returns to Catamount, and we see them estranged, jailed, or bound to
a life in which they find no promise of a better future. One need not live

in Haiti to know the sort of hopelessness that provokes emigration. Small-town America, whether in New England or the Midwest, can prove a dead end and make a lie out of the American Dream.

Bob Dubois grows up swaddled in small-community assumptions. His mother had always believed that because God had made her poor, he would make her sons rich and famous. Anything Bob or his brother achieved would cause her to "smile and nod approvingly, as if to say, See, God's looking after you, just like I said He would" (273). Thus, like Doug Spaulding, they start with no known limitations. The boys' principal distinction is their high school hockey playing on a championship team. They thought themselves "destiny's darlings" and reveled in small-town fame, much as does John Updike's Rabbit, who was a high school basketball star. Such boys become accustomed to success, to self-esteem, and the respect of others. Bob's dream, shared with his best friend, Avery Boone, was to build a boat, take it somewhere distant and exotic like the South Pacific, and "make a killing" (28). That is Bob's set phrase for making the kind of money he wants, and those words will turn literal when he commits himself to making big money. To begin with, however, he believes that he can live the American Dream and that it will take no special dedication, training, or education on his part to achieve it.

His dreams do not materialize. For one thing, he is a tradesman rather than a professional. "Dubois thinks, A man reaches thirty, and he works at a trade for eight years for the same company, even goes to oil burner school nights for a year, and he stays honest, he doesn't sneak copper tubing or tools into his car at night, he doesn't put in for time he didn't work, he doesn't drink on the job—*a man does his work*, does it for eight long years, and for that he gets to take home to his wife and two kids a weekly paycheck for one hundred thirty-seven dollars and forty-four cents. Dirt money. Chump change" (4).

As he faces the commercial demands of Christmas, unable to afford the gifts his children want, he focuses on his situation: "everything he sees in store windows or on TV, everything he reads in magazines and newspapers, and everyone he knows—his boss, Fred Turner, his friends at the shop, his wife and children, even his brother Eddie—tells him that he has a future, that his life is not over. . . . all a guy like that has to do is reach up and grab it" (14–15). Similarly, Kurt Vonnegut analyzes this American condition in *Slaughterhouse-Five:*

Americans, like human beings everywhere, believe many things that are obviously untrue. . . . Their most destructive untruth is that it is very easy for any American to make money. They will not acknowledge how in fact hard money is to come by, and, therefore, those who have no money blame and blame and blame themselves. This inward blame has been a trea-

sure for the rich and powerful, who have had to do less for their poor,
publicly and privately, than any other ruling class since, say, Napoleon-
ic times. (112; italics in original)

Just before Bob explodes and smashes all the windows in his car, he finds
himself in Sears saying, "I want . . . I want . . . I want"—the lament of Saul
Bellow's Henderson. This craving for something beyond will never be
satisfied because there will be something yet more to want. Bob feels "the
hard, metallic bubble once again, still located low in his belly, but expanding toward his chest and groin now and rapidly growing heavier" (13). Doug
Spaulding felt something rising and swelling inside him like this, but his
sensation led him to the awareness that he was alive. Bob Dubois comes
to the conclusion that he is dead, his wife is dead, and his daughters are dead.
In search of a new life, Bob sells up and takes his family to Florida so he
can join his brother and make a new start in life. When shipping illegal
Haitian immigrants in, he escapes the Coast Guard by forcing his passengers overboard at gunpoint.

Bob thus loses his "soul" in his efforts to "make a killing." As he guilt-
ily wanders around with the money he collected from his passengers in
his pocket, he can only marvel at the difference between his own corrupt
state and the innocence that still exists for his infant son. He changes his
son's diapers, staring: "he has a penis. Just like me. An ordinary, circum-
cised penis. A doctored tube coming out of his digestive tract, that's all. It
was contracted and short, shrunken to little more than thimble-sized from
the cold and sudden exposure to the air. Below it swelled the testicles in
their tight pouch, like the breast of a tiny, pink bird. There was no mystery, no power, no sin, no guilt. Just biology. It was terrifying for that, and
for an instant, wonderful" (396–97). Bob's major sin is murder; his minor
transgression is adultery. However, he reverts to nakedness and the shame
that came with the Edenic Fall to express his own sense of despoliation.
His phallocentric power as captain—reinforced by the phallic pistol used
to herd the Haitians into the water—contributes to this identity of his sin
as genital, and so does his Catholic background. He tries to return the blood
money to the Haitian community but is stabbed when he literally crosses
the tracks.

In the novel's envoi, Banks lists the fate of Bob's family, and the lives of
his children duplicate their father's and those of his peers in Catamount.
His son, in particular, becomes a plumber, another tradesman like his father. The novel ends, echoing and radicalizing a classical and medieval
formula: *"Go, my book, and help destroy the world as it is"* (421, italics
in original).

Banks never really deconstructs the Dream. In essence, he sees that it
no longer works (but, by implication, thinks that it once did) and resents

this fact on behalf of his characters. His tone never quite reaches T. Coraghessan Boyle's level of gritty anger. Banks does not give us a politicized
or historical understanding of why Bob Dubois cannot make money. He
believes in the basic decency of Bob, in the possibility of people's being
decent, and, therefore, in their deserving something like the American
Dream. While Banks mostly shows crooks making money (and dying bank-
rupt), he does not question that there should be a good reward for the right
kind of legitimate work. He simply acknowledges that his characters do
not manage to achieve it and that they lose not just their souls but their
lives in the attempt.

Original Sins (1981)

What are America's original sins? Once we become aware of them, what
can we do about them? Lisa Alther asks these questions and uses a small
town as the locus for her study. Whereas Bradbury's Green Town, Illinois,
and Banks's Catamount, New Hampshire, both lack explicit history, Alther's Newland, Tennessee, loudly proclaims its past, and in that past lie
keys to the present. Newland was a Confederate town, and it currently
possesses a substantial black population and a cozy class system that keeps
problems from being apparent to residents of all classes. The book is structured around an Edenic image. In the first chapter, five children have
climbed up the Castle Tree, a great weeping beech, and we see their childhood through conversations from and memories of time spent in that tree.
At the end of the first chapter, the children are told that they are too old
for such goings on and are chased out of paradise by their southern history teacher, in whose yard the tree stands. At the end of the book, those still
alive return with five children of their own, and the children climb the tree
while their battered and weary parents wonder if life can be made any better
for the next generation.

The aptly surnamed Prince sisters, Sally and Emily, are daughters of a
mill owner. Jed and Raymond Tatro are sons of a mill worker, and both
families share a colonial ancestor who was half French and half Cherokee.
The fifth child, Donny Tatro, is the descendent of slaves who worked for
the Tatro family, and his mother still works for the Princes as a maid and
babysitter. As children, they play together with minimal race- and class-
consciousness. They all picture themselves as going to New York and becoming famous, and "they knew that whatever they decided on—baseball
star or ballet dancer or waitress—they'd have no difficulty doing it, since,
number one, they were special. And number two, they lived in the Land
of the Free" (3). Doug Spaulding and Bob Dubois likewise believed that they
could be anything they wanted.

They play at being American Indians, Confederates, and Americans de-
feating commies. That Cherokees once owned the land produces no guilt:
they know Injun Al French and his daughter, Betty, and they themselves
have Cherokee blood. Since all of them are comfortable, there is nothing
to worry about in the destruction of the original inhabitants. They are similarly ignorant about the Confederacy. To them, "Confederate" means brave
and gallant, and "Yankee" is an all-purpose term of condemnation that is
still useful because northern mills put economic pressure on their own.

Then doubt sets in. Studious Emily does not win the spelling bee that
they had agreed would be the first step toward playing "The Sixty Four
Thousand Dollar Question" (a television show soon to become infamous
for being rigged). They learn the facts of sex and become self-conscious.
Donny learns enough race history to cease saluting the Confederate memorial when they walk past it, and when they all attend a downtown movie
theater together, he is forced to sit in the "colored" gallery. They are already
drifting apart when their southern history teacher tells them they are too
old to play in his tree. The sins that drive them from this Garden of Eden
are the lack of academic application (spelling), the awareness of sex, increasingly specialized gender roles, color, age, and southern history.

Those who remain in Newland and try to live the small-town life fail
to achieve the satisfactions their parents did. Jed's belligerent temper leads
to relative failure at work and less than good communication with his wife.
He dies, along with his best friend's wife, in a drunken auto accident. Sally becomes far more independent and ambitious than any of her models
from the previous generation, but her attempts to create a new pattern get
her beaten by her husband, Jed, and result in her widowhood. She may be
better off eventually, but she has certainly not found what small-town life
once seemed to promise her.

Donny, caught between his wife's desire for a house and his own inability as a working-class black to earn a middle-class salary, heads for New York
and joins the Black Panthers. Though still poor, he feels better about himself, having traded his subservience for belligerence and pride. Raymond and
Emily head to New York for employment and college. After working for
various liberal causes, Emily focuses on sexual exploitation and patriarchal
power and becomes a feminist and, ultimately, a lesbian. Her years in college gave her no practical training for life in the business world, and her
reluctance to play submissive secretary gets her fired. Raymond becomes a
well-read Marxist and interprets the world he knows in terms of the hidden economic flows of power, the money bleeding from the southern mills
into the pockets of northern owners. He tries to retreat from the capitalist
world by living in a log cabin, but this dream of self-sufficiency is ruined
by a new strip mine, whose runoff floods his gardens. He has proved total-

ly unable to communicate his vision or win anyone to his insights, and this frustration drives him to start constructing a bomb. He does not know whom to use it on but wants to damage some capitalist institution.

In short, Donny wishes to fight but has few fighting skills and no financial power. Raymond wants to change the capitalist system but is so totally lacking in interpersonal skills that he cannot communicate. Emily wants to deal with men on equal terms but has done nothing to gain the necessary training to achieve any sort of professional status. That none of Alther's characters fully understands reality is suggested by the fact that they all see different realities: all are true but incomplete.[13] Donny sees white injustice to blacks, but not the male injustice to females that he perpetrates on his wife. Emily sees the gender biases that victimize her without making much sense of the economic and educational factors behind them (which are Raymond's specialties).

Alther projects both sympathy and sardonic disenchantment with 1960s "enlightenment." She clearly agrees that the stratified, racist, and patriarchal society of such a southern town is immoral. All her characters become what they are in part because of hurt and anger at the way that their small-town assumptions have betrayed them. However, Alther also insists that the South's emphasis on a personal approach to everything has real virtues. She likes the politeness of that culture, even when she has one character admit that it can also be called "a scum of civility over a swamp of injustice, exploitation, misery, and hypocrisy" (244). Alther cares about racial, gendered, and economic flows of power but notes the lamentable failure by the ideologues of these visions to escape from *the* basic problem of subsuming people into categories instead of treating them as individuals. Both Raymond and Emily reach this insight: Raymond's voting-registration friends despise all southerners, which he sees as morally equivalent to despising all Negroes; Emily's lesbian friends condemn all men, and earlier friends had condemned all southerners yet despised southerners for supposedly condemning all blacks. In Alther's vision, this passion for overgeneralization, with its consequent exclusion of human individuality, is our society's fundamental sin, as slavery was our original sin.

This is a book that will not make many readers comfortable. Liberals from outside the South may enjoy the satiric look at Newland but will feel less easy with the satire on social crusaders in New York. Those from within the southern world may feel a reverse pattern of attraction and repulsion. To a young reader in the 1990s, the 1950s and 1960s look like a bizarre other world. Alther can keep diverse groups of readers happy because of her humor. Scene after scene provokes loud laughter at the human comedy. Laughter at the characters, their worlds, and our worlds is reason enough to read, but it is not a political answer. This is very dark comedy, because Alther has addressed seriously this problem of the American myth of the small town and its innocence but finds no solution.

From Innocent Food to Guilty Guns: Brautigan and Vonnegut

Loss of innocence leads to frustration and to a sense that life has lost any logic or coherence. The result is not just a sense of regret that the child's meaningful world has disappeared but a sense of guilt and a need to find some crime that would explain being flung from paradise. Liberal discomfort over the gap between the Declaration of Independence's rhetoric and current reality produces some of the free-floating guilt in the fiction of this era. Books frequently figure violent crimes or actions committed by major characters that somehow justify the loss of life's logic and happiness.

In *Dandelion Wine,* murder is exterior to the community, committed by a stranger and hence no cause for communal guilt. The Lonely One's actions are not interpreted as a comment on the town or on male sexuality in general; he is simply a mad dog who needs to be destroyed. However, in many novels from the 1960s and later, the actions are internal to the local society and are not easily explained away. In Joseph Heller's *Something Happened,* a man smothers his son while trying to help him. Updike's first two Rabbit books center on a baby drowned by a drunken mother and on a runaway waif's burning to death at the hands of neighborhood vigilantes. In the 1960s and 1970s, we find books like *One Flew over the Cuckoo's Nest, An American Dream, The Book of Daniel, Bless Me, Ultima, Sula, Woman on the Edge of Time,* and *The Public Burning.* All of these feature one or more murders, some the worse for being judicial and institutional rather than mistakes or crimes of passion. Brautigan's *So the Wind Won't Blow It All Away* and Vonnegut's *Deadeye Dick* stand out for their sad, lyrical tone used to explore the feelings that grow out of a shared central image: a boy shoots a gun and accidentally kills someone. Both books reek of the resultant guilt. Brautigan's narrative ties that guilt to an exposé of small-town America, while Vonnegut's novel refers more generally to acts of violence committed by America at large.

So the Wind Won't Blow It All Away (1982)

Brautigan's narrative takes place in 1947–48 in western Oregon and makes brief references to 1979, the time of its writing. February 1948 is when the protagonist, Whitey, shoots his friend in an abandoned orchard where they like to shoot apples (the gunslinger nation's treatment of the Edenic apple tree). At times, it almost seems as if Brautigan were answering Bradbury point by point, so often do Whitey's experiences appear to imitate darkly those of Doug Spaulding. These shadows cast on Bradburian innocence stem from poverty, and the atmospheric guilt is partly an expression of what America makes the poor feel.

Doug soars when he contemplates new sneakers. Brautigan's boy is just as emotionally involved in his footwear. Wet feet prompt him to comment, "They were at their half-life, which is the best time for tennis shoes. They felt as if they were truly a part of me like an extension of my soles. They were alive at the bottoms of my feet" (5). He goes on to remark that when they were totally worn out and his fatherless family did not have the money to buy another pair, he felt guilty: "I must be a better kid! This was how God was punishing me: by making me wear fucked-up old tennis shoes, so that I was embarrassed to look at my own feet" (6). He did not link the dead shoes with "the reality that we were on Welfare and Welfare was not designed to provide a child with any pride in its existence" (6). Doug's love affair with the shoes is ecstatic, and while his family may not be wealthy, it is not on welfare. We find another such shared evocation of childhood when Whitey notes the coal along the railroad tracks as being like "gigantic black diamonds" (14).

Whereas Doug is upset by the deaths around him, Whitey battens on the funerals that take place next to their temporary lodging and develops a piercing interest in the deaths of children. Doug feels the expanding physical pressure that leads him to conclude that he is alive. Whitey's friend feels a similar (though negative) pressure of something going to get him, and in his case, it leads to his death. Doug's grandfather feels rejuvenated and empowered by mowing the lawn or dealing with dandelions; Brautigan's narrator hates mowing the lawn and weeding. Doug loves his grandmother's kitchen and her magic preparation of meals. Brautigan gives us instead the picture of three months in a welfare apartment that had a gas stove: "We were all terrified of gas, especially my mother. She had a mind like a gray library filled with gas-leak death stories" (49). Once Doug has restored fructifying disorder to the kitchen after the well-meaning tidying by Aunt Rose, he and the boarders and family experience a marvelous midnight meal. In contrast, Brautigan's narrator gives us this scene: "Every meal was a nightmare with my mother having to build up her courage to cook. We usually had dinner around six, but with that gas stove, dinner arrived on the table as late as midnight" (49). The mother finally breaks down, and they eat nothing but cornflakes and sandwiches. As Whitey puts it, they "just sat around in silence, waiting for the gas to get [them]" (50). The only happy overlap between Bradbury's and Brautigan's worlds concerns the elderly: both Whitey and Doug get along with older people and experience no generation gap.

One assumes that the people in Bradbury's world are sensible and unthreatening. However, readers do not feel so in Brautigan's setting. "If you saw a twelve-year-old kid with a rifle standing in front of a filling station today, you'd call out the National Guard and probably with good provocation. The kid would be standing in the middle of a pile of bodies" (102), Whitey avers, noting that the youth's reasons would be that he did not like gym and that McDonald's had not put enough sauce on his hamburgers. Brautigan's speaker concludes his fantasia by stating that "they'd let him out of prison when he was twenty-one, with a baby face and an asshole three inches wide" (103). This is Brautigan's picture of a mad killer and thus his analogue to Bradbury's Lonely One, but his language and the references to jail-rape could never exist within the horizons of Doug Spaulding's world. However much Brautigan's narrator wishes he could live a happy small-town life, Brautigan's use of such language denies the existence of such a clean, well-behaved world. Whether Brautigan actually had Bradbury in mind is not my point. Bradbury lovingly models American innocence; according to Brautigan, that innocence is not real because that pictured life demands a modest level of wealth and practically ignores the existence of evil. Readers enjoy the fantasy only at the expense of those who are excluded from it.

Whitey fruitlessly wishes to regress to oral gratifications, as seen in his obsession with hamburgers. When he buys bullets for his newly acquired gun, he has enough money to buy some bullets or a hamburger. Instead of feeding himself, he chooses to feed the gun: "When I got home I would show them to my gun. I would load and unload my gun a couple of times. That would make the gun happy because guns like bullets" (74–75). For months following the shooting, Whitey thinks of nothing but what might have been, which takes the form of hamburgers. He fantasizes Superman telling him to buy a hamburger; he interviews short-order cooks about hamburgers; he tries to read up about them in the library. He puts his obsession in cinematic terms: "I have replayed that day over and over again in my mind like the editing of a movie where I am the producer, the director, the editor, scriptwriter, actors, music, and everything. . . . I have been working on the same movie for 31 years. . . . I have, more or less, about 3,983,421 hours of film. . . . I call my picture *Hamburger Cemetery*" (74). Brautigan does not mention Vietnam, so one might be mistaken in equating bullets or hamburger with the "guns or butter" arguments of Lyndon Johnson's era. The year of the novel's publication, 1982, is late for such a topical reference, but the percentage of the Gross National Product spent on the military was still high. Brautigan's mindset is strange enough—and his points about poverty real enough—that he may not have needed Vietnam to trigger guilt. This regression to an oral obsession may just be a response to guilt that reflects the desire to be a child, or even an infant, since Whitey's childhood gave him few of the oral gratifications enjoyed by Doug Spaulding.

Deadeye Dick (1982)

Vonnegut questions innocence from several perspectives. He seems to think that making money innocently is difficult or impossible. He expresses an uneasy awareness of black servants and the racial injustices of the country. He draws on America's treatment of immigrants to demonstrate the nation's distance from its ideals. Most centrally in this book, however, he associates guilt with guns—personal guns and the big guns of the military.

Varied immigrant experiences provide background texture to this novel. The Waltz family is of German extraction, and Rudy Waltz's father actually knew Hitler in his prewar Viennese days. In America, the businesslike members of the Waltz family became well off from selling a patent medicine and running pharmacies with soda fountains. More recent immigrants in Midland City, Ohio, the Italian Maritimo brothers have become a major force in the construction business. Early in the narrative, however, we see their illegal entry into the land of promise: "Somewhere in the seamless darkness, which may have been West Virginia, Gino and Marco were joined by four American hoboes, who at knife-point took their suitcases, their coats, their hats, and their shoes. They were lucky they didn't have their throats slit for fun. Who would have cared?" (15).

Vonnegut clearly would like to share a picture of small-town innocence with Bradbury and others. The corner drugstore-soda fountain, a mecca for oral gratifications in Doug Spaulding's world, remains an important locus in Vonnegut's world. He waxes satiric on a Waltz Brothers drugstore's transformation into a simulacrum: "I gather that it is part of a cute, old-fashioned urban renewal scheme. . . . And there is an old-fashioned pool hall and an old-fashioned saloon and an old-fashioned firehouse and an old-fashioned drugstore with a soda fountain. Somebody found an old sign from a Waltz Brothers drugstore, and they hung it up again. It was so quaint" (37–38). When Rudy himself works the night shift at a pharmacy, he deals not with ice cream but with an amphetamine addict who tries to wreck the store. Like Doug, Rudy loves the kitchen of his boyhood. Indeed, he spends most of his childhood time in the cramped, warm kitchen with the black servants and loves that life compared to the undemonstrative and chilly world of his parents. However, Vonnegut makes clear that the tiny kitchen "was the only room in the house where any meaningful work was going on, and yet it was as cramped as a ship's galley. The people who did nothing, who were merely waited on, had all the space" (30–31).

Such criticisms remind us that Rudy's childhood innocence grows in a world of false values. Then he fires a rifle from the cupola to celebrate his being called a man and simply because "the rifle enjoyed [being loaded] so. It just ate up those cartridges" (61). Eight blocks away, a pregnant woman is killed while vacuuming her house, shot between the eyes. Thereafter, only guilt is possible for Rudy, a guilt that results in a repression of self and service to others that demands no personal feelings from him. Rudy becomes neuter in all ways, including sexual. His only remaining pleasures are oral, and Vonnegut inserts recipes into the text to map the desperate narrowing of Rudy's life.

Brautigan links the personal level with America only indirectly. Vonnegut makes it explicit; indeed, he suggests layers or planes of correspondence like those so entrancing to the Elizabethans. At the funeral of the amphetamine addict, who killed herself by consuming drain cleaner, Rudy notes the following parallels:

> The corpse was a mediocrity who had broken down after a while. The mourners were mediocrities who would break down after a while.
>
> The city itself was breaking down. Its center was already dead. Everybody shopped at the outlying malls. Heavy industry had gone bust. People were moving away.
>
> The planet itself was breaking down. It was going to blow itself up sooner or later anyway, if it didn't poison itself first. In a manner of speaking, it was already eating Drāno. (197)

He implies other such correspondences. Concerning the government's sale of radioactive concrete, he says, "In this case, the government was about as careless as a half-wit boy up in a cupola with a loaded Springfield rifle—on Mother's Day" (215). The neutron bomb that depopulates Midland City is readily admitted to be a mistake (or possibly an experiment by the government) rather than a foreign attack; it is a "friendly" bomb, both in the sense of coming from the government and in the sense that it kills people but leaves property unharmed. The government that uses such a device on its own city, whether deliberately or carelessly, is like the boy with the gun or worse. The radioactive concrete (which originated in Oak Ridge, Tennessee, the home of the atomic bomb) and the neutron bomb seem to be Vonnegut's images for what has changed the American world. The liberal hopes of gradual betterment (embodied in the text by Eleanor Roosevelt) seem doomed if such bombs exist. These are the bullets shot by irresponsible boys at a higher level. Innocence in a world that lets boys use guns or governments use such bombs is no longer possible.

The Slaughter of Innocence in Vietnam: O'Brien and Haldeman

The image of the shining knight on a white horse that America has assigned itself in its foreign interventions lost its credibility during the Vietnam War. Not surprisingly, Vietnam novels show the loss of innocence on both the personal and national levels. What I wish to concentrate on here, however, is an interesting and desperate strategy for recuperating some measure of personal innocence, for turning the experience of being a soldier into something other than the bloodguilt brought about by the country's repudiation of the war. Soldiers who returned home had to face obloquy of all sorts—being spat upon, socially humiliated, jeered at by antiwar activists. When fighting, they knew that friends, even girlfriends, were demonstrating against the war and their actions. An issue, then, for anyone who did not simply assume that America was right to fight and that the Vietnamese were better off dead would be to justify his own role in the killing.[14] Or, given that a soldier simply tries to stay alive and rarely worries about morality, this matter of guilt is one for writers to worry about. All the themes associated with innocence and its loss are reworked in the two novels discussed here, and they take on new shadows from contact with Southeast Asia.

The Things They Carried (1990)

Like *Dandelion Wine* or Erdrich's *Love Medicine*, this novel coalesces from stories; they are unified by their focus on a small group of men and by recounting the deaths that froze or polarized these men's emotional lives. Tim O'Brien makes much of the fact that the subjects are eighteen or nineteen; they have no sexual experience, and they moon over hometown girlfriends whom they hardly know, wondering if they are virgins.[15] They rely on magic—one wears a girlfriend's pantyhose around his neck like a scarf as protection against grenades and bullets—and they carry odd mementos that remind them of their hometown lives. O'Brien's great set piece on the loss of innocence concerns one soldier's seventeen-year-old girlfriend, Mary Anne; she comes for an illegal visit and gradually becomes addicted to danger. She learns to shoot and goes out on ambushes with Green Berets, joining them in their jungle cult of death (emblematized by piled-up human bones instead of Conrad's ivory tusks). Eventually, she disappears into the jungle, a spirit haunting the shadows. Her disappearance into Vietnam's Heart of Darkness is so striking because she starts as a bubbly, flirtatious, innocent cheerleader type in peddle pushers and a pink sweater; she is last seen wearing a necklace of dried human tongues.[16] O'Brien frequently calls a story true and then asserts its pure fictionality, so readers have no grounds for labeling this, though its Conradian echoes and general implausibility make it seem the most obviously fictional of his tales. Clearly, however, O'Brien feels that Mary Anne's experience is one way that American innocence could respond to the adrenaline rush of this life, and he tells the story in terms designed to make it most shocking to American stereotypes of innocence.

The Native American whose literary role is to be foil to these white

American Adams in Blunderland is Kiowa, who is nicknamed for his tribe. He is more mature than the rest: he controls his own desire to babble when it gets on someone else's nerves and encourages others to babble when they need to, giving helpful advice when they feel paralyzed by guilt. He is a religious man who can enjoy a quiet moment in a Buddhist shrine. He will encourage one of these boys mooning over a girlfriend's picture by admiring her beauty. For several of the company, his death in a flooded shit field is the point at which they feel they have lost their own selves, the time when they died even though their bodies continue meaningless lives in America. Had he merely died of his wounds, the event would not have obsessed them so, but his drowning in sewage expresses their sense of their own fate. One of the company chose the shit field as the spot to camp; another turned on his flashlight briefly to show Kiowa the picture of his girlfriend; another grabbed Kiowa's foot but could not hold on as the mud sucked him down. Each feels guilty over Kiowa's death; but as is often the case in this novel, the verdict is rendered ambiguous: "'Nobody's fault,' [Norman] said. 'Everybody's'" (197).

O'Brien also writes about "The Man I Killed." From the O'Brien persona's emphasis on his feelings, one can read it as at least quasi-autobiography, particularly because he imagines for the corpse much the same motives for going to war that O'Brien himself often admits to in interviews—fear of disgracing himself by refusing. Then he undoes the truth claim by denying that he killed anybody to his daughter. Then he tells the episode again as if his daughter were old enough to hear the truth, and he admits to having tossed the fatal grenade. Then, sixty pages later, he says, "I did not kill him. But I was present, you see, and my presence was enough. . . . and I remember feeling the burden of responsibility and grief. I blamed myself. . . . But listen. Even *that* story is made up" (203). Then he claims that in "story-truth," he killed the man. Then, in answer to his daughter's question of whether he killed anyone, he replies, "I can say, honestly, 'Of course not.' Or I can say, honestly, 'Yes'" (204). O'Brien refuses any straightforward admission of personal responsibility, taking all and none. Guilt and innocence alternate and run together.

O'Brien sees himself keeping Kiowa, Ted Lavender, Curt Lemon, and others alive by writing about them; more than that, he is trying to save his own life with his tales. Like Scheherazade, he holds off death with story. In that, he differs from the soldiers in the film *The Deer Hunter* (1978), who do not feel they can talk to anyone about their experiences.[17] One should note, though, that the dead whom O'Brien saves this way (with one partial exception) are the American dead. He and his friends become relatively innocent—or at least justifiable—in their own eyes and arguably in the reader's because they all suffered. That they killed Vietnamese, turning a Vietnamese baby and nurse, via napalm, into a "crunchie munchie" and "crispy critter" does not much upset the emotional balance of these stories, because the narrative focus directs our sympathies toward the Americans. We can of course deliberately read against the grain, but we are invited to sympathize with the American boys who are so young that they have not lost their virginity and who may die any moment. That makes them innocent after a fashion in a common white American scheme of moral existence; and with the army giving them orders, the blame becomes diffused, dispersed on America and thus, perhaps, on no one—or on the reader as much as the soldiers. Guilt and innocence, fiction and truth flicker until they run together into something that can claim none of those clear, precise names. The flickering state keeps us, as readers, from passing judgment and makes us question our own stands.

1968: A Novel (1994)

Tim O'Brien's first novel about Vietnam, *Going after Cacciato*, ends on a strongly fantastic note; *The Things They Carried* limits itself to the more or less realistic. Joe Haldeman's two Vietnam novels follow the same pattern. His first, *The Forever War*, casts the experience in science-fiction terms, while his newer effort, *1968: A Novel*, is much more confined to everyday plausibility. Both of Haldeman's novels try to recoup a kind of innocence, but this analysis will focus on the more recent novel because of its similarities in technique to *The Things They Carried*.

Spider Speidel's initial innocence is established by his still being a virgin and is maintained at the end by his feeling fairly sure that he never killed anyone: his gun was defective, basically unusable during his three weeks of active duty before the ambush that ends his service career. Furthermore, one might argue that Haldeman makes an insanity plea of sorts. Spider starts seeing horrible things that he can occasionally prove not to be real. He sees the black sergeant fuck a corpse's head and the radio/telephone operator eat an ear off another head; the latter, however, proves not to be true, because he subsequently sees the head with both its ears still attached. What of the former action? He cannot be certain. The army's word for this is schizophrenia, and that is what he is treated for, with drugs and electroshock. He narrowly escapes a lobotomy. Post-Traumatic Stress Disorder would not be recognized for a few more years.

The ambush during the Tet Offensive that destroys his already feeble equilibrium kills virtually all his companions. Both Batman and Moses, the code names for an African American and a Jew, die horribly before his eyes, as does the sergeant and the RTO. A North Vietnamese boy comes to shoot Spider but runs out of ammunition, so Spider lives, having survived the moment when the trigger was pulled but no bullet exploded his head.[18] Both Batman and Moses seem more mature and courageous than

Spider, so when they die (at least in Spider's later accounts of the massacre), he seems by comparison the weak one left to deal with the horrors all alone. As in the case of O'Brien's Kiowa, the death of Moses (and, to a lesser extent, that of Batman) is the point at which Spider loses his own life, even though his body continues to exist and function. The racial and religious others died; without them to make him feel like part of the gang and an adult, he is lost.

Haldeman complicates his picture of innocence lost by granting Spider a lyrically described sexual encounter. Too ignorant to know the meaning of her terms, Spider pays the maximum for the whole works from Li, a Vietnamese prostitute. His very first time with a woman, he tries all orifices and exposes all his own intimate surfaces to digital, oral, and genital contact, except for wearing a condom when penetrating her vagina. He is delighted by the physical ecstasies. Owing to Li's having syphilis and to his incomplete protection, he gets chancres on his mouth and anus but not on his penis; so while an army incompetent is dealing with his "schizophrenia," Spider is diagnosed as homosexual and given aversion therapy. His parents are informed that he is queer. This results in his father's leaving the house while he is there and in his parents' moving without leaving an address for him. Furthermore, the electroshock destroys his memories of that one sexual experience, so he does not even know how he got syphilis, and that inability is chalked up by the army to his repressing awareness of his homosexuality. To his father, as to the army, Spider would be much more acceptable had he massacred a village full of women and children than he is as a supposed gay.

When being shot at, of course, one does not worry much about the morality of taking part in a war; one just tries to stay alive. After the war, many soldiers had to find terms that would justify their military experience, claiming military innocence or at least helplessness to act other than they did against the enemy. Spider instead must uphold sexual innocence yet does not even have memories to help him. War guilt gets translated into sexual terms, with an updated meaning for sexual innocence as nonhomosexuality.

In addition to these troubles, he suffers terrible oil burns when learning to make doughnuts, thus undergoing something similar to an exposure to napalm. As in O'Brien's novel, suffering the enemy's hurts works emotionally on the reader to free the American soldier from personal guilt over the morality of that particular war. Anyone still inclined to place blame (including Spider himself) is deflected by the way that military guilt is transformed into a false sexual allegation. Spider's innocence is recouped, albeit at a price so steep that we do not know whether he can pull his life together.

In both O'Brien's and Haldeman's books, the American Adam's experiences are made more poignant by the death of African-American, Native

American, or Jewish characters, and regret over their deaths replaces any felt uneasiness over their peoples' historical treatment in the United States. In both books, most of the tension over killing the Vietnamese is transmuted into other tensions from which the author and characters can emerge more or less exonerated. They escape the moral issue of killing in an unjust war by virtue of their own suffering and our focusing on that rather than on the suffering of their victims.

They also escape by insisting on ambiguity of interpretation. Did Tim O'Brien, the character, kill a man or not? What happens to Spider? He tells six versions of the story, some of them while he is in the mental ward heavily drugged. In his mind, the stories become science fiction and feature space suits, jump jets, and laser fingers. They could easily have been episodes in Haldeman's earlier novel, *The Forever War*. Both O'Brien's and Haldeman's characters try to escape a sense of guilt by spreading blame so that all and none are responsible for American and Vietnamese deaths— or, America is responsible, but the individual is not. Because the soldiers all worry far more about American deaths than Vietnamese fatalities, naturally enough, the public issue of the morality of that war gets replaced with different guilts and answers. No one reading the books would say that the characters recapture a sense of true innocence or blamelessness, but some of them manage to distance themselves from the public issue.

In *Shattered Dream: America's Search for Its Soul*, Walter T. Davis sees the war in Vietnam as having destroyed the stories that America had told to itself. One national narrative was the story of freedom, democracy, opportunity, plenty, and justice. The other was the dream of American exceptionalism or Americanism, basically the positive picture of American imperialism, which includes "innocence, purity, uniqueness, superiority, invincibility, a conflict between good and evil (civilization vs. wilderness, cowboy versus Indian, and so on), limitless possibilities, a 'can-do' optimism, and regeneration through violence" (113). Davis interviewed many veterans and studied the religious or secular narratives that they were trying to piece together to help them in their state of storyless chaos. He does not mention a sexual narrative, but that seems to be what we have here, particularly in Haldeman's book. As in Banks's *Continental Drift*, where Bob Dubois reflects on his own guilt through the symbolism of his infant son's anatomy, these two authors are putting together a symbolic story that can be told in sexual terms borrowed from Eden. Innocent boys, without sexual experience, must deal with the pain of their treatment by girlfriends at home, must deal with prostitutes, with seeing soldiers wounded in ways that destroy their genitals; they must go home to women who will never understand what they have experienced. By allowing sexual tensions to replace anxieties over the morality of killing, among other techniques, these authors substitute the fig leaf for the olive branch as a subject for contemplation. America's long literary fascination with the Edenic Fall makes that substitution viable and invisible for a large portion of an American audience. How much sense would that strategy make to someone from a nonbiblical culture or someone not so conditioned to define innocence in sexual terms? Some, no doubt, but the moral sleight of hand might be harder to overlook.

False Innocence: Ellison and Barth

To find innocence celebrated unself-consciously, this study had to go back to the 1950s and Bradbury's novel. Doing justice to the array of approaches to innocence demands a further dip into that earlier period, the Truman and Eisenhower years, when America was perhaps most sure of its own righteousness. Hitler and Pearl Harbor had made most Americans feel justified in their country's wartime actions, even if the atomic bombs raised anguished doubts in the minds of some. Those same years, however, also produced two great novels that show innocence in adult figures and use that abnormal state to attack the very concept as it applies to America: Ralph Ellison's *Invisible Man* in 1952 and John Barth's *Sot-Weed Factor* in 1960. While Bradbury was singing the song America wanted to hear, they were challenging it. The invisible man, Ebenezer Cooke, and their shared predecessor, Candide, are all products of a Christian education; for Ebenezer and Candide, the education is classical as well. All three suffer while learning the difference between real life and moral ideals. For Ellison and Barth, of course, real life is America. Whereas Barth and Voltaire play to easy laughter through fairly gross exaggerations and burlesque, Ellison's protagonist is serious and fairly realistic. The laughter at his innocence is there but is less raucous and much darker. Indeed, one might call it a color-coded laughter that is legitimate from a black reader but sometimes morally troubling from a white.[19]

Invisible Man (1952)

The issues in *Invisible Man* are usually articulated in terms of W. E. B. Du Bois's double consciousness, the relationships between the novel and its precursor texts (black and white), its politics, and the shocking nature of certain episodes, such as the Battle Royal and Trueblood's incest.[20] To contextualize the book in terms of a larger (mostly white) American concern with innocence shifts our sense of the book's issues slightly, even though white patterns of education and religion must still be contrasted to black authenticity, which is beautifully expressed in the yam-eating scene.[21] In Du Bois's sense of race, as in Toni Morrison's, black authenticity is in the blood and evidently available to anyone black who wants it.

However, in Ellison's handling of the issues, as in Gloria Naylor's, authenticity seems to consist of the individual's truth to self and not just to blackness. Such authenticity is not a great well that anyone black can draw from but rather something by now deeply obscured, at least for the educated, and it can only be achieved painfully and in compromised form. Ellison does not seem to support the essentialist black position that blackness consists of certain known, inherent qualities. The protagonist seeks the blackness of blackness and wonders how it fits himself, and he seeks his own core being. In identifying the true quest as a search for an individual core rather than blackness, Ellison resembles Naylor's Mama Day more than Morrison's Guitar Bains in *Song of Solomon* or her girls from Nagadoches and Mobile in *The Bluest Eye*. Identity for Ellison is constructed by all one's cultural influences, even if some of those are white.

Much of the novel shows the protagonist's willed blindness or innocence. Even when Dr. Bledsoe reveals his own realpolitik and says he will keep his power if it means hanging every Negro in the county, the invisible man still thinks Bledsoe means him well and is acting in his best interests. Similarly, the invisible man misses all the signs that the Brotherhood is using him and has no interest in helping his people. By now, the invisible man has identified enough of what is authentic in himself to be unwilling to prostitute himself to yet another white political structure. However, he sees no black structure that draws him either: the numbers and preaching empire of Rinehard and the agitation of Ras the Destroyer are not for him. Part of his problem is his determination to be a leader and his inability therefore to join a community as an equal. Toni Morrison would deny that authentic blackness or self can be found in isolation, believing instead that it must come with active membership in a community. The invisible man has never managed to fit himself in with others. He goes into hibernation, consolidating his spiritual insights until he can understand the blackness of blackness, the ambivalence of love and hate, and then chart his own course.

The narrator's innocence throughout is a burden. It keeps him from seeing things as they are. As the institutionalized black doctor and war veteran says of the narrator to the white millionaire, "he believes in that great false wisdom taught slaves and pragmatists alike, that white is right. I can tell you *his* destiny. He'll do your bidding, and for that his blindness is his chief asset" (95). His innocence is his belief in the twisted doctrines he has learned: humility but not equality, turning the other cheek.

Whereas Toni Morrison identifies black innocence with a state outside of or beyond the influence of white society, Ellison does not define any kind of true innocence, only this false, imposed kind. He rejects that false innocence for keeping the invisible man invisible even to himself. What one really is does not consist of an external and idealized Christian moral

scheme, but neither does it consist of something essentially and purely
black. It consists of finding the self, whatever that self may be. By an external, idealized standard, Jim Trueblood, who slept with his daughter,
should be an object of revulsion. Everyone tells him how wicked he is, and
he cannot pray, cannot think what to do. Finally, he sings some blues, "and
while I'm singin' them blues I makes up my mind that I ain't nobody but
myself and ain't nothin' I can do but let whatever is gonna happen, happen. I made up my mind that I was goin' back home and face Kate; yeah,
and face Matty Lou too" (66). He is what he is and finds that more real than
the preacher's words about wickedness. His wife talks of sin, but he mostly
views his situation in terms of dealing practically with consequences.[22]
Whatever his problems may be and whatever damage he has done, Jim
Trueblood has found himself. He is authentic, a desirable and difficult state
to reach in a white-dominated world.

The Sot-Weed Factor (1960)

What is innocence anyway? And why should we value it? Whereas the soda
fountain and the small American town of the first part of the twentieth
century comprise the *locus amoenus* for many white meditators on this
theme, Barth dives further back into the abysm of time. He asks about the
innocence of America's foundations in terms of the sexual innocence of
his protagonist. He exposes the great American theme to coarse laughter
by casting it in terms of male virginity. A man can protect his chastity for
religious or spiritual reasons; in our secular society, though, any other reason tends to strike us as ridiculous and possibly discreditable. Ebenezer
Cooke's idiotic lack of practicality, his social uselessness, and his flowery,
elaborately erudite justifications for his stance throw his education and his
culture's official values into disrepute, for his valuing celibacy outside of
marriage is indeed the official Christian value. From his words and deeds,
that restraint comes to seem preposterous. Eben's virginity may prevent
him from seducing the unwary, but that does not keep him from doing great
damage to the women in his life. His refusal to treat Joan Toast as a prostitute is indirectly responsible for her being raped and poxed by pirates, her
becoming addicted to opium, and her dying a few years later from her diseases and childbirth. His sister's life, though not as blighted, is also rendered difficult by his obsession with chastity (and, therefore, with sex).

On another plane, Barth explores the supposedly innocent, Edenic character of the New World and explodes myths of our foundations right and
left. He does not take on the Pilgrims (and Puritans), peoples assumed at
the mythic level today to be righteous if not necessarily attractive. Leave
that to Kathy Acker: "these New Worlders had left England not because
they had been forbidden there to worship as they wanted to but because

there they and, more important, their neighbors weren't forced to live as rigidly in religious terms as they wanted" (*Don Quixote*, 117–18). Barth looks instead at Maryland, his natal territory.[23] Eben enters this New World after walking a pirate ship's plank, managing to swim ashore only to find on the barren strand a black slave tied up and left to die slowly. Eben gains help from a sick American Indian chief and next approaches the English colonists, whose sole concern is profit from tobacco, and who offer him no help. Thus, in short order, Eben experiences piracy and rapacious commercialism, which are built by a system that drives Native Americans from their ancestral lands and exploits mistreated black slaves.[24] As he ventures further, he sees the exploitation of women as whores and of both sexes as indentured servants. He experiences the helplessness of the many who are too poor to buy justice in the courts. The local political conspiracies, perhaps evocative of the McCarthy era, leave him totally bewildered. American myths of a hallowed new beginning in a regained paradise do not stand scrutiny. The land does not seem paradisal, what with mud, floods, prostitution, drugs, casual violence, rape, abortion, and other dangers. Nor can it be parsed as the howling wilderness compared to the paradise of the orderly garden that Christians will impose, for the white Christian society seems a vicious, lawless, Hobbesian world where life is nasty, brutish, short, and also elaborately conspiratorial.[25]

Eben is led to confront his innocence, which does make him focus most of his attention on himself, and he sees that it causes as much harm as might have resulted from any concupiscence on his part. By giving up his virginity and by accepting disease as a necessary corollary to experience, he marries Joan Toast and wins back his estate. With that, he can enter the economic sphere at a level that will permit him and his sister to live very modestly but in a fashion that he deems suitable to their education and refinement. He puts his artistic skill, such as it is, at the service of a kind of truth, for he exposes the corruption and roughness of Maryland in hopes of offering those considering emigration a more accurate picture than the come-ons used to recruit people for the New World. Eben cannot discover experience that merely seems neutral; it remains diseased and attached to guilt. Eben accepts it, though, and does not mourn nostalgically for his prior existence.[26]

Barth develops what he calls the tragic view of innocence, "that it is, or can become, dangerous, even culpable; that where it is prolonged or artificially sustained, it becomes arrested development, potentially disastrous to the innocent himself and to bystanders innocent or otherwise; that what is to be valued, in nations as well as in individuals, is not innocence but wise experience" (vi). If innocence is possible, it exists only for the very young and inexperienced and amounts to ignorance. In other words, Eben's innocence is a false burden—and so is America's. Eben's sense of being special is analogous to American exceptionalism. Eben satirizes seventeenth-century Maryland, but Barth satirizes twentieth-century America, in particular the world of the 1950s, during which time *The Sot-Weed Factor* was written.

Eben's concept of innocence shows the limitations of that white notion. He is inescapably self-centered. He does not find a more authentic self but accepts external moral schema: he goes from the culturally accepted first stage of innocence to the culturally determined second stage, diseased experience. His concern with external schema shows in his need to live a gentlemanly life, which allows him to supplement his income with clerkly chores but not to dirty his inept hands with manual labor. Barth thus stays within a generally white concept of innocence, as do Bradbury, Alther, Banks, O'Brien, and Haldeman. African-American writers like Ellison, Morrison, and Naylor open up different possibilities and, therefore, different paradigms of action. They do not fit a single black pattern, though all value authenticity by some definition and reject an externally imposed moral scheme.

๑ ๑ ๑

If one turns to Native American literature, one certainly finds innocent victims in unwary tribal people who are exploited by white society. The protagonists of N. Scott Momaday's *House Made of Dawn* and Leslie Marmon Silko's *Ceremony* are both innocent in that sense. However, I do not sense, in the novels I know, that personal unfallenness is a relevant concept to these writers. Ignorance and inexperience are not sanctified and valued for their own sakes. Furthermore, authors like James Welch in *Fools Crow* and Silko in *Ceremony* would greet the idea of white innocence with grim scorn and dark laughter. American Adams somehow fail to show to advantage when massacring Indian camps, slaughtering buffalo, stealing cattle, and shooting rare mountain lions.

To end this chapter, let me demystify Bradbury one more time by contrasting his vision with that of James Baldwin. Bradbury describes summer evenings when adults sit on the porch talking and Doug Spaulding listens, willing it to go on forever. Those, however, are whites in small-town darkness. Baldwin describes a similar situation in his story "Sonny's Blues," but his African Americans in urban darkness bring a different awareness to the human currents. The narrator is remembering his mother:

> The way I always see her is the way she used to be on a Sunday afternoon, say, when the old folks were talking after the big Sunday dinner. . . . And the living room would be full of church folks and relatives. . . . For a moment nobody's talking, but every face looks darkening, like the sky outside. And my mother rocks a little from the waist, and my father's eyes

are closed. Everyone is looking at something a child can't see. For a minute they've forgotten the children. Maybe a kid is lying on the rug, half asleep. Maybe somebody's got a kid in his lap and is absent-mindedly stroking the kid's head. Maybe there's a kid, quiet and big-eyed, curled up in a big chair in the corner. The silence, the darkness coming, and the darkness in the faces frightens the child obscurely. He hopes that the hand which strokes his forehead will never stop—will never die. He hopes that there will never come a time when the old folks won't be sitting around the living room, talking about where they've come from, and what they've seen, and what's happened to them and their kinfolk.

But something deep and watchful in the child knows that this is bound to end, is already ending. In a moment someone will get up and turn on the light. Then the old folks will remember the children and they won't talk any more that day. And when light fills the room, the child is filled with darkness. He knows that every time this happens he's moved just a little closer to that darkness outside. The darkness outside is what the old folks have been talking about. It's what they've come from. It's what they endure. The child knows that they won't talk any more because if he knows too much about what's happened to *them*, he'll know too much too soon, about what's going to happen to *him*. (114–15)

In this play of lightness and darkness, of innocence and knowledge, the contrasts to Bradbury's idyll say it all, and the existence of Baldwin's version challenges the grounds on which Bradbury's is built.

chapter three

Yearning *for Lost Civilization*

The decline of Western civilization: automatically, one thinks of the Judeo-Christian, Greco-Roman, Medieval-Renaissance-Enlightenment tradition. Those extensively educated in this tradition are trained to scorn people whose frame of reference is popular culture, and they mourn the loss of gentility, stability, and public respect for social order and cultural monuments that are currently associated with that tradition.[1] This attitude is often perceived as Eurocentric, and fewer Americans now feel bound to its values. Much of this chapter is devoted to authors who do look to that European and biblical past for solutions to America's present. For the sake of raising submerged issues, however, we might choose a different starting point. By the standards of *another* Western civilization, the life led by Native Americans living in the western half of the North American continent, one might argue that Euro-American culture was vicious and riven with hopeless moral contradictions. Its high ideals were not much in evidence to those driven off their ancestral lands, massacred, and corralled on reservations whose acreage was frequently reduced by unilateral abrogations of treaties. Which group was really civilized, and by what standards of civilization? In *Fools Crow*, James Welch makes the case for the American Indians, the people dismissed as primitive in histories written by the victors. Obviously, my two senses of "West" are a geographic wordplay, but the contrasts between what is meant by civilized life are offered for serious consideration in this chapter.

After experiencing a Native American view of Euro-American culture, one can then look at novels upholding traditional Western civilization with new eyes. Authors who claim this heritage are frequently conservative in their values. Saul Bellow and Walker Percy write out of Jewish and Catholic traditions respectively, but both lament the decay of civility and morality in America, and both track the change in manners to World War I and a failure in education. Bellow explores that failure in gendered and racial terms in *Mr. Sammler's Planet* and *The Dean's December;* Percy does so more in terms of science in *Love in the Ruins* and its sequel. To both writers, we have lost a tradition of civilization and have become new barbarians. Donald Barthelme recognizes the loss of Euro-American civilization in *Snow White;* but as a liberal, he seems interested to see what might emerge as a new framework of values. He acknowledges that the old order provided meaning, manners, and an entry into the corridors of power for some; he is also aware that it served others very ill, so he shows only detached regret for some of what is being lost.

Yet another approach to culture—one might call it Americentric—is taken by Ishmael Reed. He flagellates mainstream culture for nostalgically desiring a corrupt past rather than engaging in the present and working to ameliorate its faults. The moral corruption at the heart of Western civilization is depicted in his *Flight to Canada,* and he lambastes the backwards orientation in *The Free-Lance Pallbearers.* Reed asks, Why should we morbidly worship the paintings and music of dead artists rather than enjoy and encourage living creators? Using his own version of the Arthurian tradition, Reed argues that just because a cultural artifact comes from the past does not make it automatically worthy. Such dead culture was once topical and enjoyed by its contemporaries. Our culture will some day be similarly looked on as classical. Why not give it due attention now, even as past stages of culture were relished in their own time?

Which Western Civilization? Welch

What makes Euro-Americans or heirs of Western civilization accept a social system other than their own as civilized? Texts and literacy come to mind: the developed ability to store knowledge in libraries and communicate over distance and time are recognized. A political and personal morality with low levels of violence is another element in this conception of civilization. So are monuments made from shaped and enduring stone: these are seen to guarantee a degree of civilization, although respect for the truly monumental in the ancient world ignores the fact that the larger constructions have historically been the product of some form of slave labor. Technology must be developed in certain valued areas of endeavor: metalwork, whether in iron or gold; glass crafting for ornamental vases, windows, or lenses; ceramic skill that produces regular-looking vessels whose glazes depend on tightly controlled chemistries. Cities, because they demand elaborate government, are also deemed civilized. They become more civilized if human waste does not offend the senses. Industrial production spells a modern civilization. The ultimate proof of cultural prowess lies in weapons technology. If one country can conquer a land whose civilization is markedly different, then that winning country treats the loser as less civilized or as decadent and therefore less worthy of respect. In other words, representatives of Western culture look for the elements in which they themselves excel and reject as barbarian those cultures without these indicators of civilization, even if the vanquished country has virtues that their own signally lacks. Euro-Americans can recognize and admire artistic work in gold, whether the crowns of Macedonia, the belt clasp of Sutton Hoo, or a Fabergé egg. Those trained in what remains of the Western tradition can rarely recognize the differences between an artistically shaped and a utilitarian arrowhead because that artistry comes from a different intellectual matrix. Those not present at the sacred act or enlightened as to its traditions will see no special civilized virtues in Navaho sand paintings or any other performative art. Those eating supermarket potatoes or corn are likely to think them superior to the smaller strains cultivated by the pre-Columbian Indians, though many tribes deserve the credit for elaborate, long-range plant breeding of types suited to each local pocket of soil and each microclimate.[2]

Euro-Americans are not the only writers to feel that a lost civilization spells the loss of something vitally needed by our current culture. The tribes of the American West also have lost the full range of functions from their ancestral culture. Those on reservations retain some practices and remember enough traditions from those earlier groups to feel that the tribal life of the past was probably more coherent in its values than that of the present *and* that it offered more civilized patterns of behavior than the Euro-American tradition. In *Fools Crow,* James Welch tries to reconstruct what one such Western culture might have been like. The Blackfeet in the Montana region that he describes doubtless differed in many ways from the neighboring Assiniboine, Cheyenne, Sioux, Mandan, and Crow tribes, but those differences dim when tribal lives are contrasted with the lives of the sodbusting settlers, let alone with lives possible in the age of interstates and the Internet. Readers with other tribal affiliations or preferences for nonnomadic existence might prefer the native cultures of the Southwest or Northwest, but Welch makes general arguments applicable to many if not all native cultures; in doing so, he offers us an interesting challenge and contrast to the Euro-American concept of civilization.

If technology, literacy, and humane attitudes are what define civilization, then these tribes have no claims in two out of three categories. The Plains Indians have left us no stone monuments or ruins: they lived in lodges and tipis built from buffalo hides and wooden poles. They did not work metal and so have left no gold artifacts to titillate our greed. They painted some sacred pictures on animal hides but left no form of casual writing. Their low-tech life rendered them vulnerable to the weapons and troops of the whites expanding westward. What they do have—in this novel, at least—is a culture that treats its own members in a humane fashion. Welch thus implicitly challenges Western assumptions and redefines what makes a culture civilized. Welch himself is descended from two neighboring tribes, the Blackfeet and Gros Ventre, as well as from whites, and he attended schools on Montana reservations. He is also a graduate of the University of Montana, and he is distant enough in time that a good deal of what he portrays comes from reading as well as from his grandfather's stories.[3] As we saw with immigration literature, however, constructs of alternative cultures can be partly or entirely fictional to the writer and yet still function as comments on American culture today. To the whites of 1870, the Blackfeet had no civilization, but Welch argues otherwise with considerable eloquence. Whereas the films *Soldier Blue* and *Little Big Man* make the argument for Native American civilization as part of a larger agenda of discrediting white American imperialism in Vietnam as well as in the American West, Welch needs no such excuse. His Marias River massacre is not My Lai; it happened in its own right.

Fools Crow (1986)

In Welch's historical novel, we find no centralized political authority and hence no government as the West is wont to judge it, and yet Western countries are plagued by dictators, jails, and bureaucracy. The Kainahs, Siksikas, and Pikunis are all Blackfeet, and each group is further subdivided into traveling units consisting of a few families, of which we follow the Pikuni "Lone Eaters." All the Blackfeet share a sacred place on top of Chief Mountain, where ancestral chiefs had gone for visions. The groups have no coercive power over each other, however. Any action taken in concert is agreed on by consensus, and the subgroups feel free to take different stands on such issues as how to treat the Napikwans (whites). Similarly, within the Lone Eaters, there is little hierarchy by white standards. One man is chief, but he arrives at decisions through discussion with representatives of all the tribal societies, and in matters of war, another man is war chief. Nor do we find a religious hierarchy. Two men have significant medicine bundles, and both carry out different sorts of healing: Mik-api (proprietor of the Thunderpipe bundle) seems to do more with herbs and compounds than Boss Ribs (bearer of the Beaver bundle), but we are shown no sign of rivalry or disagreement between them. The group is lucky to have two such repositories of medicine and power within it, but such medicine bundles can be sold to other groups. Hoarding such a good is not part of the cultural outlook. Mik-api's bundle comes from the Nez Percé tribe, and he gave all his belongings for it in hopes of saving his wife's life. The Lone Eaters acquire another kind of medicine when Heavy Shield Woman asks the help of all the tribe in acquiring the Medicine Woman bundle, whose sacred objects are associated with Feather Woman. The group values such bundles but does not cling to them; when a fitting apprentice or the right kind of situation for passing the bundle on comes about, it will be yielded up.

The lack of central organization and power of compulsion is reflected in the fact that the individual lacks a controlling center, as manifested by the changing of names throughout life. The protagonist starts life named Sinopa, becomes White Man's Dog in childhood and adolescence, and is awarded the name Fools Crow after an exploit in which he kills a Crow chieftain. Furthermore, the individual is not impermeable; evil spirits can enter one, and while they may be driven out by means of appropriate ceremonies, they may transfer to some other unlucky person. Totem animal spirits also have a proprietary relationship that penetrates one's unitary self. One's spirit can travel to more than one level of reality. All these characteristics create a human being quite different from the Christian soul, the Romantic individual, or the scientist.

One characteristic of Indian life as described here and in other novels is the oneness with nature valued by the tribe. This unity is a cliché in discussions of Native American literature, but the near universality of this element cannot be dismissed simply because everyone notes it. The attitudes toward nature are one of the most obvious differences between Euro-Americans and Native Americans.[4] The biblical Book of Genesis gives man dominion over animals and plants; the result is a belief that if some plant or animal native to a location is not useful, it can be killed or removed so that something else more useful may take its place. Leslie Marmon Silko makes the point that from her tribal perspective, the landscape given by nature, parched or rugged or harsh though it may be, is perfect; a person's task is to learn to fit in, to survive with a minimum of change to that landscape ("Landscape" 84–85). Humanity may learn to value the green and gentle portions all the more but should not just try to rip out the prickly native vegetation to plant and irrigate unnatural crops. Similarly, in *Fools Crow*, the Lone Eaters see their high plains as the "ground-of-many-gifts" and the buffalo herds as the supreme gift.[5]

Another characteristic of Native American life is the immanent nature of divinity. People act out their lives within a living mythology and may themselves speak with divine figures such as Raven, who comes to both Mik-api and Fools Crow; during these visits, Raven gives them specific information permitting action and not just general wisdom that a skeptic might say rose from their unconscious. Toward the end, Fools Crow has a dream telling him to go on a journey, and as he follows the instructions, he finds himself no longer in the depths of winter blizzards but in a land that is always in summer, and while there he talks to Feather Woman herself. She tells him about the future of their people and that this future is their defeat and diminution under pressure from the whites. The buffalo and other animals will be exterminated, and so will most of those who depended on the buffalo for their lives. Obviously, this particular vision quest is fictional, but anthropologists around the world have recorded accounts of such experiences. Though Western culture has heavily discouraged more than one mode of consciousness, others are well known to other peoples. Welch describes what it might be like to live within a culture where walking and talking with gods and culture heroes is still possible, even as it was for the patriarchs in the Hebrew Scriptures and the heroes in Homer.[6]

Another feature of this Native American culture is the way that dreams unite the individual with the divine and with nature. Dreams may tell where game is or give warning about a horse-stealing expedition. Calling up significant dreams is a recognized and cultivated power. The young bring their dreams to elders or to the group for help with interpretation. The dreamer can redream the troublesome material the next night, hoping to work out the problems the second time around. In *Fools Crow*, the child One Spot has nightmares about wolves after being bitten by one, but he is helped to think of the wolf as a power animal that may be his helper in later life, so his later dreams still feature the animal, but it no longer threatens him so terrifyingly. In other words, Welch's American Indians interact with their dreams, seek them, return to them, question them, and generally rely on them for a different perspective on their waking actions. The unconscious (or spirit world) is thus more accessible and provides a very different dimension to life than a "dream" of material success.

As Paula Gunn Allen has pointed out (*Sacred Hoop* 78–82), Western fiction is based on conflict; Native American fiction, like Native American religions, is based on ceremonies designed to bring about transformation or to integrate individuals with their tribe or world. *Fools Crow* is a bildungsroman, but it starts at a nondramatic point in adolescence and ends with Fools Crow as a respected member of his tribe but not at the resolution of some great crisis. What we read about are the various points in his life when Fools Crow makes meaningful transitions from younger and more naive stages to wiser and more richly endowed states of mind. We see a few ceremonies that he participates in, and the story ends with the whole tribe dancing to welcome the first rains of spring. He knows what the end of his people will be and sees his role as helping them live correctly so that they can face annihilation or diminution within the white world, but he has no particular strategy in mind. He can only shape his life and help them shape theirs to meet the demands placed on them. If they achieve the right balance, they can face with dignity whatever happens.

The life of this culture is not based on money or material wealth; it is noncapitalist. Little is taken from the environs, and that which is taken— mostly buffalo—is fully utilized. Migration, hunting, and gathering roots and berries all work with nature, not against it. Minor warfare among these tribes is common, but genocide, the novel implies, is not, and neither is violence within the tribal group. Socialized behavior is brought about by peer pressure: teasing and mock-insults keep youngsters in line. Banishment, usually temporary, is used only in extreme circumstances. The point of life in this culture is not to leave a visible monument but to live one's life as part of a community, to see one's life cycle unfold, to earn the respect of one's group, and to face whatever comes with as much dignity as one can muster. Welch claims that such a life was comfortable and offered much to enjoy.

A cartoon I once saw shows two subcontinental Indians in Nehru jackets walking and talking: one asks, "What do you think of Western civilization?" and the other answers, "I would be in favor of it." Clearly, from the perspective of Welch's Western civilization, Euro-American culture does seem in need of being civilized. Whatever Christianity may say about loving neighbors or compassion or keeping promises clearly did not carry over into dealings with the Native American other. Whatever classical philosophy may have said about stoicism, about not attaching oneself to material goods, did not carry over into the land rush. Instead, the imperial impulse took the fore—the part that favored chosen people above gentiles, that divided the world into Greeks and barbarians, and that saw barbarians as more convenient when dead. Whatever it is that would outrage white men were a white woman raped or a white child killed does not carry over to their treatment of American Indian women or children. Naturally, one could question Welch's own picture and suggest that there are more regrettable elements than he admits. His Pikunis are already trading with whites for guns, whiskey, pots and pans, flour, sugar, and cloth. They are no longer purely dependent on their own efforts and materials. He says little about the damage done by frequent intertribal raiding parties (admittedly less damaging than nuclear war). Moreover, he portrays women as content to work far harder than men, while the men have leisure for sitting, smoking, and telling stories. His Pikunis do not indulge in much physical cruelty except in rituals voluntarily undertaken, but some tribes carried out systematic torture on enemies. In *Fools Crow*, readers see slave women who marry and gain nonslave status but learn little about those who remain slaves or the conditions of their servitude. In other words, this is hardly a complete or critical picture of Pikuni life, and Pikunis cannot stand for all Native Americans. Rather, Welch constructs a life that contrasts sharply to materialistic, consumerist, and imperialist culture. Welch may only have seen himself as writing a historical novel about his ancestors and about the Marias River massacre, which his great-grandmother survived. He may see this only as a challenge to Hollywood stereotypes of impassive Indians—though Hollywood itself has been destroying its own stereotypes, and the Lakota in *Dances with Wolves* show humor, expressiveness, variation in attitude and outlook, and civilized codes for handling quarrels and differences of opinion. Welch's portrait also functions as a reproof to Euro-American culture of the 1870s and just as much to the culture of modern America.[7] The Euro-Americans were the force that wiped out the buffalo without remorse, that plowed up the plains, that did their best at times to wipe out the natives. They could not see civilization in people who lived in tipis, yet Welch maintains that these natives had noncoercive governments—something America has never managed even when colonies lived in small-scale arrangements. The Indians enjoyed relatively nonmaterialistic lives and took only renewable resources. Although their lives were low-tech, they lived with what he claims to be a decent degree of comfort and felt themselves to have many causes for celebrating the goodness of their lives. As Welch describes this life, his American Indians could feel positive about their government and their family values; this stands in stark contrast to most of the other authors discussed in this book, who feel discomfort or despair on exactly those points.

The whole impact of the book (and of films like *Little Big Man* and *Dances with Wolves*) depends on the claim for the humane qualities of this culture. Fools Crow, as he grows up, is obviously becoming a sensible, reliable, and responsible man who does much for others and leads his own life according to the customs and values of the group. He is forward looking but not hasty to act, and he enjoys his life. He loves his wife; he has a son; he is respected by his people. Bellow's Mr. Sammler, as this chapter will show, is so cantankerous and alienated throughout most of the book that he has few human contacts, and fewer of them actually respect him. Dean Corde has friends, but what readers mostly see is his frustration and humiliation as his friends and school turn against him for his articles on Chicago. Walker Percy's Thomas More drinks, slashes his wrists, and gets divorced. Donald Barthelme's Snow White, while not a naturalistic character, is emblematic of middle-class, white, female discontent and offers readers few reasons to respect her. No spiritual center dwells within her or within her culture. What can such characters tell Fools Crow about leading a civilized life?

Must primitive mean savage, marginal, harsh, and inflexible? Must low-tech mean barbarous? Must illiterate mean an impoverished mental life? Welch says no. He stresses that life is best lived in a close-knit community and that one's sense of accomplishment should come from benefiting that community. In this novel, life consists of relations with other people and is experienced as the unfolding of a known pattern; it does not consist of the acquisition of bulky material goods that must be guarded from theft and that keep their owner chained to them. Nor is it a life that separates mind from body. As ultimate argument, Welch could point to the fact that whatever the drawbacks of such low-tech and small-scale life—

and drawbacks there are—these cultures did not threaten the existence of all life on earth. They were renewable, as the petroleum-based, high-tech pattern is proving not to be.

The Obligations of Civilization: Bellow

America can be lauded as the land of revolution and everything new, the democratic society in which one can rise despite lack of birth or breeding. For many immigrants, these very qualities define the American Dream; but for others, their implications spell out America's failure to produce or embody a true civilization, with its classical education and social stability. From such a viewpoint, the United States boils with an infernal urge to destroy all tradition and hence all that gives conservative life true meaning. Civility has broken down in the face of robbery and rape, literally in the streets and figuratively in economic dealings. Children show neither respect nor love. The Beatles or Boyz II Men have replaced Beethoven, while replacements for Plato, Spinoza, or Kant neither exist nor (worse yet) are felt to be lacking in the current cultural frames of reference. Knowledge of the great ideas and names of the past has dwindled beside knowledge of show-business celebrities and is seen as useful principally for playing "Trivial Pursuit" and "Jeopardy!" These days, few people pretend to have the background needed to appreciate all forms of classical culture—literature, philosophy, architecture, sculpture, art, music, history—and fewer still try to acquire it. Among these writers, however, is a clear sense that one answer to America's problems lies in this past, in its morals and values, in the cultural works themselves—if only Americans could bring themselves to put in the effort needed to understand and assimilate them. The answer, in other words, is not found in the liberal hope of gradual improvement, nor in a radical vision of a utopian future, but in a return of some sort to past values. Because any widespread cultural return is clearly not going to happen, these writers are as much concerned with the factors that prevent it as with the sense of loss. They must consider what they believe to be the true nature of humanity, the proper relationship between humans and technology, and the implications of history, ancient or recent. They must also ponder the potential of an American future in which that past is forgotten.

Mr. Sammler's Planet (1970) and *The Dean's December* (1982)

Bellow portrays life's possibilities in these two novels as spread along a spectrum. At one end is murder. When Mr. Sammler was a starving and freezing fugitive during World War II, this quiet, cultured, reclusive, sophisticated man killed a German and *loved* doing so:

Was it only pleasure? It was more. It was joy. You would call it a dark action? On the contrary, it was also a bright one. It was mainly bright. When he fired his gun, Sammler, himself nearly a corpse, burst into life. Freezing in Zamosht Forest, he had often dreamed of being near a fire. Well, this was more sumptuous than fire. His heart felt lined with brilliant, rapturous satin. To kill the man and to kill him without pity, for he was dispensed from pity. There was a flash, a blot of fiery white. When he shot again it was less to make sure of the man than to try again for that bliss. To drink more flames. (140–41)

Even the mild scholar is a willing murderer in extremis, and if he is, then so potentially are all men. At the other end of the spectrum, Bellow's well-educated journalist turned academic dean, Albert Corde, looks out from his porch and undergoes a mystic experience as he feels himself being carried over the water into color. He passes through blues of an Italian landscape sort, "very close to the borders of sense," experiencing them as freedom and joy: "It was like being poured out to the horizon, like a great expansion. What if death should be like this, the soul finding an exit" (286). Part of experiencing this fusion with the visible world consists of the physical facts of his standpoint, for "he had to look through the rods of his sixteenth-story porch" (285). Corde asks himself: "Did the bars remind you of jail? They also kept you from falling to your death" (286). He finds mystic ecstasy reachable because of patterns of restraint. Those may limit some forms of freedom, but they protect him as well. One is tempted to see those bars as symbolizing social structures, the restraints whose truest and best forms Bellow would like to discover. What limits to liberty will give us our truest freedom?

For most liberals and radicals, man is born tabula rasa and will become whatever nurture encourages. To a conservative, man's basic nature offers fewer grounds for optimism. Ultimately, man is a killer, and any theory of culture must deal with this fact. Given opportunity and freedom from punishment, killing is what humans will do. Sammler meditates on this truth:

> No wonder princes had so long reserved the right to murder with impunity. At the very bottom of society there was also a kind of impunity, because no one cared what happened. Under that dark brutal mass blood crimes were often disregarded. And at the very top, the ancient immunity of kings and nobles. Sammler thought that this was what revolutions were really about. In a revolution you took away the privileges of an aristocracy and redistributed them. . . . How those middle-class Sorels and Maurrases adored it—the hand that gripped the knife with authority. . . . For them an elite must prove itself in this ability to murder. . . . The superman testing himself with an ax, crushing the skulls of old women. The

Knight of Faith, capable of cutting the throat of his Isaac upon God's al-
tar. . . . The middle class had formed no independent standards of honor.
Thus it had no resistance to the glamour of killers. (144–45)

However, man is not *just* a killer. Man also has a moral nature in Bellow's
world, and the tension between the drive to kill and the moral nature is
normally resolved only by what Sammler calls kinds of madness (197).
These crazy behaviors are our various means of organizing life, from the
rituals of dressing oneself each morning to the ideologies one is willing to
die for.[8] Sammler studies such insanities, from French sultanism to Polish
anti-Semitism. He observes the current "acceptance of excrement as a standard" (43), the obsessions of Elya's son and daughter, the baglady-like magpie
instinct of his own daughter. Wherever he looks, he sees madness.

On one end of the spectrum, then, are the ecstasies of killing and of
debasing oneself in shit or rage; on the other are mystic perceptions, made
accessible in part through inner order. In Bellow's world, Western civilization is the bridge, the way to escape the first and reach the second. He
asks about the loss of this bridging culture in a pair of matched novels, *Mr.
Sammler's Planet* and *The Dean's December*. The first centers on a dying
patriarch who represents the basic values of the old culture. The second
weighs American barbarities against those of communist regimes and centers on a dying matriarch who represents the nurturing values and impulses
that any culture ought to have.

When Mr. Sammler regrets the unrecoverable past, he sees our losses in
terms of aristocracy, education, models for civilized behavior, and religion.
His obsession with aristocracy emerges in his horrified fascination with a
black pickpocket. When threatening Sammler through the wordless ritual display of his penis, the thief was "oddly, serenely masterful. The thing
was shown with mystifying certitude. Lordliness" (50). Thinking back on
the episode later, Sammler ponders his reaction: "The black man was a
megalomaniac. But there was a certain—a certain princeliness. The clothing, the shades, the sumptuous colors, the barbarous-majestical manner.
He was probably a mad spirit. But mad with an idea of *noblesse*" (293–94).
Aristocracy, for Sammler, combines "lordliness," duty (ideally), power (to
kill or use sexually), a nonmaterialist set of values, and "sumptuous" elegance in clothing. The pickpocket overwhelms other revulsion with his
exquisite sartorial sense. Aristocratic values also surface when Bellow
strives to express the height of ecstasy or mystical exaltation. The words
used are satin and silk, luxury fabrics long associated with aristocratic
privilege. Bellow does not explicitly advocate a return to an aristocratic
mode of society, but the many functions of that image in Sammler's mind
remind us that hierarchy has endured as a social pattern far longer than
democracy.

Sammler muses on how American education has failed to transmit his notion of culture to the younger generation. Elya Gruner's daughter, Angela, is described as having "a bad education. In literature, mostly French. At Sarah Lawrence College" (11). Her brother, Wallace, is called a high IQ moron whose degree from MIT has done nothing to make him a competent or responsible person. The student activists that Sammler hires to read aloud to him do very badly because they do not know and cannot pronounce the words used by his cerebral authors. Sammler himself automatically relates current experiences to a French mathematician viewing Racine or to Balzac, Dostoyevsky, or Wells. When trying to express to himself his sense of Angela's sexual appeal, he falls back on the vocabulary and anatomical terms learned from Zola. He may not play "the old European culture game" (55), but it plays him. He never lacks a mental framework for explaining or assimilating events around him, even the mildly outré sexual escapades of Angela. Because of that education, he can always relate himself to what he learns about other people. As a child, he read English and became a Polish Jewish Anglophile. His fluency in French, German, some of the Slavic languages, and Latin are attested to in the novel. He has read major works of literature in all of these and the main thinkers of philosophical or political import. While he has had seventy years in which to acquire this and Angela is young, the reader knows that she never will try, because she sees no point to such reading.

The loss of such an education means, crucially, the loss of models for civilized behavior in all kinds of circumstances. Human behavior depends on learning by imitation, but that imitation must be culturally guided and proven by generations of testing. Sammler looks at students dressed as barbarian, buffalo hunter, squaw, poet, sexual fantasist, princess, troubadour, and guerrilla: "They sought originality. They were obviously derivative. And of what—of Paiutes, of Fidel Castro? No, of Hollywood extras. Acting mythic. Casting themselves into chaos, hoping to adhere to higher consciousness, to be washed up on the shores of truth. Better, thought Sammler, to accept the inevitability of imitation and then to imitate good things. The ancients had this right. Greatness without models? Inconceivable" (149). Furthermore, one must imitate the models even when one does not feel wholeheartedly the proper sentiments. Correct behavior, even if not entirely sincere, is better than self-indulgent honesty. Sammler tries to persuade Angela to ask her father for forgiveness even if she does not feel that she needs forgiving for anything. Preserving the forms and continuity is more important in his eyes than the hypocrisy. Similarly, when talking to the Gruner's chauffeur, he asks him of his children, "Do they love you?" and is told that "they act like it," to which he responds, "That's already a great deal" (269). Neither Angela nor Wallace nor Sammler's own daughter act in fashions that can be happily interpreted by their fathers as showing love, whatever the children may think.

Religion is the other major value lost with the disappearance of traditional society. Sammler muses on the fact that Angela's grandparents were Orthodox Jews: "This gave a queer edge to his acquaintance with her paganism. Somewhere he doubted the fitness of these Jews for this erotic Roman voodoo primitivism" (72). Religion, though, supplies the inward order so necessary for civilized behavior. When Sammler visits the body of Elya Gruner, he murmurs to himself, "Remember, God, the soul of Elya Gruner, who, as willingly as possible and as well as he was able, and even to an intolerable point . . . was eager, even childishly perhaps (may I be forgiven for this), even with a certain servility, to do what was required of him. . . . he did meet the terms of his contract. The terms which, in his inmost heart, each man knows. As I know mine. As all know. For that is the truth of it—that we all know, God, that we know, that we know, we know, we know" (313). If we do not have an ancestral religion to supply the terms of our contract, where can we turn for that inner order? Sammler looks at the American scene and finds no satisfactory answer.

He looks at the liberal answer and demystifies it: Liberty, Fraternity, Equality, Adultery. Sammler knows that one cannot look to the government for answers or help. He "vaguely recalls hearing that a President of the United States was supposed to have shown himself in a similar way [to that of the black pickpocket] to the representatives of the press (asking the ladies to leave), and demanding to know whether a man so well hung could not be trusted to lead his country" (66). Obviously, Lyndon B. Johnson was not a president to encourage a classical sensibility! Furthermore, Sammler accepts that the hierarchical society with aristocrats had problems and that the idea of individuality is probably true and good. We cannot just turn back the clock.

What he seems to find as answers—such as they may be—are first to ask forgiveness, whether of parents or of the tradition itself. Second, we must accept our own unoriginality and free ourselves from that Romantic bugbear, recognizing the need for appropriate models of behavior tested by generations. Next, we should behave in the fashions established by such models, even if we do not always feel the appropriate feelings; the forms help create the feelings, or can over time, and our individual feelings are not so sacred that we must indulge them senselessly. As Sammler tells Wallace Gruner, whose scatty behavior seems to Wallace himself a message to the world from his unconscious self, "Why send such messages? Censor them. Put your unconscious mind behind bars on bread and water" (243). His most positive recommendation is that "the best is to have some order within oneself. Better than what many call love. Perhaps it *is* love" (228).

Of course, this answer passes over a very large segment of the population. It offers few interesting options to women. They are to go about their Shavian business of trapping a suitable man and furnish their husband with some of those duties that keep him enmeshed in some of the lesser forms of orderly madness. Having no intellectual strength of note, their power comes from the mystery of their sex, and they lose that through promiscuity. Elya says of his profligate daughter that she has "fucked-out eyes" and is nothing but a "dirty cunt" (177–78); and yet, as Sammler realizes, "What she intended to be was gay, pleasure-giving, exuberant, free, beautiful, healthy" (69), a Pepsi-generation liberal ideal. However, women are offered a place, if subordinate, within the system. Sammler's vision, though, offers nothing to the underclass (represented by the pickpocket). A few bright children may acquire the requisite traditional education, in which case they—but not the rest—can be assimilated. Not even the future, represented by the discussion of life in a Moon colony, offers much hope either to the classical conservative or to members of the underclass. Only those highly trained in scientific and technological fields will be allowed into such a confined habitat. The dying man at the center of the text—doctor, father, charitable supporter of relatives, a man eager for bits of the old world tradition, and one who does his duty as he conceives it—expires, and no comparable representative of a supportive new order hovers in the wings.

The Dean's December forms the second panel of a diptych, for it recounts the death of a mother. Having looked at culture as a masculine construct, Bellow now investigates its feminine modalities. He reverses not only this polarity but also that of generational perspective. Mr. Sammler's Planet sees culture from the father's perspective as he looks at disappointing and disgusting children; The Dean's December is the story of adult children facing the failures—personal and cultural—of their parents.[9]

Valeria (named, appropriately, after a healing herb) is a Rumanian matriarch, a former party member and minister of health. We experience the last week of her life through the anguish and frustration of her Americanized daughter, Minna, and through the experiences of Minna's husband, a cultured American journalist and university dean. A major concern in this book is the contrast between the barbarities of a communist state and those of America; the novel also explores the cultural answers to such barbarities. Valeria and her female relatives constitute a coherent confrontation with tyranny. Their female network of emotional support is made vividly real for Dean Corde by its crazy-seeming inconsistencies. Valeria can love and be loved by the concierge, whose state function is to spy on and report on Valeria, a fact known and accepted as part of life. Valeria also supplies motherly emotional cushioning for several men, including a member of the hated secret police. Valeria's love for her daughter took the form of conditioning her to attach herself to science and then getting her to the West. Thus, Minna can rise above mundane struggles by studying the physics of star formation. Valeria's concern for her daughter also shows itself in her distrust of Corde, for she believes that a capitalist could not show the necessary emotional commitment to her daughter.

Death of the emotions is a major correlative to the death of the symbolic mother and the mothering functions of society. People do not form strong networks: "As matters are, people feel free to plug in and plug out. . . . They can pull out the plug when they've had enough of it, or of him, or of her. . . . It's the position of autonomy and detachment, a kind of sovereignty we're all schooled in. The sovereignty of atoms—that is, of human beings who see themselves as atoms of intelligent separateness" (259). Minna rebels against this, her American husband's picture of sovereign human atoms, "and how capitalism is the best because it fits this emptiness best, and is politically the safest, for horrible reasons" (260). As Corde realizes later, "She had her doubts about Corde's good intentions. About her mother there were no doubts; she came from her womb and they were bound by true bonds. . . . For a complex monster like her husband, goodness might be just a mood, and love simply an investment that looked good for the moment. Today you bought Xerox. Next month, if it didn't work out, you sold it" (284–85).[10] The capitalist American world, in these terms, lacks the reliable, nurturing, nonmaterialistic forces of mother love.

Corde focuses on society's lack of such nurturing functions in his article on Chicago. One of Corde's interviewees, Toby Winthrop, describes the time he suffered a drug overdose but was brought back to life and then how he helped someone in the extremes of delirium tremens, holding him down, sitting by his bed, and helping with the treatment: "I held his dick for him to pee in the flask. He had a bad ulcer in his leg. I treated that, too. That was his cure, and it was my cure, at the same time. I was his mother, I was his daddy. And we stayed together since" (190). The two recovering addicts have collaborated to found a drug-treatment center. Corde acknowledges, though, that few can find the center and respond to the treatment. Many hundreds of thousands more never do: "they're marked out to be destroyed. Those people are meant to die" (191). For the many, envisioned by Winthrop as submerged in shit, there are not enough mothers (and fathers), not enough mothering social structures, to help them and save them. Society has instead decided that they can die. Lenin and Stalin made such decisions explicit. American politicians would deny making such a decision; functionally, however, the result is the same. The surplus millions of the underclass are motherless children.[11]

Part of the death of the emotions is the modern split in conscious personality, the inability to feel one's emotions authentically, and the culturally imposed taboos on expressing serious emotions honestly. Corde comes up against this barrier several times when he tries to talk earnestly. He partly succumbs when interviewing the public defender, Sam Varennes. In the long talk with Dewey Spangler that turns out to have been an interview, Corde wonders, "Shall I talk? . . . I'll talk" (240). For him, earnest talk means moral talk, talk that assumes the reality of evil, morality, souls, and eternity. The terms apocalypse, Antichrist, and salvation (even if only as poetic images rather than doctrinal realities) are taboo in the secular world. They get dismissed as mysticism or poetry when he uses them in his articles, and every person to whom he talks starts to tune him out or turn against him when he introduces the terms into discussion.[12] Corde notes ruefully that "if you were going to be a communicator, you had to know the passwords, the code words, you had to signify your acceptance of the prevailing standards" (296). Perhaps because he refuses to limit his discussions to subjects encompassed by the prevailing codes, Corde finds himself departing from the rhetoric of his beloved objectivity and engaging with his subjects emotionally, in a whirling state of mind.

"Whirling" (160, 192, 203, 204) derives in part from Edgar Allan Poe's maelstrom, as Varennes suggests; perhaps also from Dante's second circle of Hell, where people whirl in storms of desire, whirling with no fixed point of reference, with no foundation on which to stand. Whirling is also the giddiness of fever, and those living in the world of the unemployed and unwanted live in "fever-land" (151). Spofford Mitchell, a black rapist and murderer, is explained by the white Corde as being "filled with a staggering passion to *break through,* in the only way he can conceive of breaking through—a sexual crash into release. . . . from all the whirling" (203). Whirling lives are those led by the condemned underclass; whirling states of mind are entered by Dean Corde when trying to come to terms with those lives and with the disintegration of moral order in his world. Whirling brings a heightened clarity of vision to Corde; possibly the whirling sensation attunes him to the God who speaks out of a whirlwind, even though God remains mute. Our giving up moral values on scientific, rationalistic, and pragmatic grounds has opened culture to "the great emptiness," and "from the emptiness come whirlwinds of insanity" (298).

Loss of the mother, loss of authentically felt emotions, and loss of the mothering side of culture have many of the same results as the loss of the father in *Mr. Sammler's Planet.* Gentle and unworldly Minna responds to her mother's death by saying, "I feel vicious" (255). For someone with a less well furnished mind, the result is literally vicious. Corde wrote in his article that "the advanced modern consciousness was a reduced consciousness inasmuch as it contained only the minimum of furniture that civilization was able to install (practical judgments, bare outlines of morality, sketches, cartoons instead of human beings); and this consciousness, because its equipment was humanly so meager, so abstract, was basically murderous" (192). Corde opines that "America no more knew what to do with this black underclass than it knew what to do with its children. It was impossible for it to educate either, or to bind either to life" (199). Bellow's terms are parental rather than strictly maternal, but the accompanying images, particularly the whirling and its threat of engulfment, in Jungian terms, belong to a vocabulary of the feminine.[13]

Bellow's politics in this novel are not confined to the gendered aspects of culture. As in *Mr. Sammler's Planet*, he explores the failure of liberalism: "We are used to peace and plenty, we are for everything nice and against cruelty, wickedness, craftiness, monstrousness. Worshipers of progress, its dependents, we are unwilling to reckon with villainy and misanthropy, we reject the *horrible*—the same as saying we are anti-philosophical. Our outlook requires the assumption that each of us is at heart trustworthy, each of us is naturally decent and wills the good" (197–98). Such blind liberalism, when motivating developers and boosters of Chicago, causes them to push for outdoor cafés, boutique developments, casinos, riverbank landscaping. No one faces the drugs and guns that are driving anyone with money to flee from the heart of the city. This terror, smoldering in the inner city, is the heart of darkness, because the inner city, as Bellow reiterates, is also an inner city of the mind or soul, a manifestation of our inner structuring and proof of our cultural failure to mindscape ourselves.[14]

Bellow does not give us a happy choice. Bucharest, Rumania, offers a high level of pain for everyone; even the elite is not exempt, since shifts in the party line often result in the barbarous elimination of former party bosses. Bucharest works on the "archaic standard, Oriental and despotic, affliction accepted as the ground of existence" (272).[15] Americans, by contrast, assume that pleasure, not pain, should be the standard by which to measure life, the ground of existence; pain is merely an aberration to be avoided at all costs. However, marginalization makes the underclass bear far more than its share of pain, and underclass lives seem much worse than the drab and painfully constricting lives of Bucharest. Bellow pulls the stops out to describe outrages revolting to protected, middle-class readers, yet these outrages are presented as commonplace in slums.

We find fugitive reference to a third possibility: Valeria's friends signify by their funeral clothes an attachment to "the old European life which at its most disgraceful was infinitely better than this present one" (212). Most of them, however, were from the boyar class and spent time, fashionably dressed, in Vienna, Paris, and London. The hierarchical and aristocratic model is also invoked for African-American gang leaders and outlaw chieftains, "black princes in their beautiful and elegant furs, boots, foreign cars" (149). Though drawn by their aristocratic features, Sammler decides they lack true nobility, even as the "big men" in Chicago who pay hitmen to eliminate opponents have the power but not the noblesse of true aristocracy. As Corde puts it, "I don't think you can be managerial and noble at the same time" (273). Again, aristocracy evokes fugitive nostalgia but is put aside as unable to solve America's problems.[16]

Although apocalypse is often invoked in this novel, we find a more coherent nexus of images that invoke Dante's *Inferno*. Those poor souls living in perpetual whirling are perhaps the inhabitants of Hell's second circle. The drug addicts sinking in shit, their hands held up for help, would have appealed to Dante. Those who can afford it literally live in the high towers above the sewer. Corde had described a Chicago sewage project boasting a capacity of "forty billion gallons, as wide as three locomotives side by side, running for more than a hundred miles deep under the city, maybe weakening the foundations of the skyscrapers. And all those tons of excrement, stunning to the imagination. It won't be the face of Helen that topples those great towers, it'll be you-know-what, and that's the difference between Chicago and Ilium" (235). This is *ecclesia super cloacam*, indeed, with the underclasses having to live their lives figuratively in the sewer.

In Bucharest, the crematorium inferno is a realm of fire and heat, reminiscent to Corde of German ovens for Jews, since he "tried by shallow breathing to keep out the corpse smoke, protect his lungs" (211). Yet the fire seems clean compared to the government, which Corde links to Goya's Saturn (68), the head gnawing insanely on a human form. Goya's image in turn echoes Dante's Satan devouring with his three heads the worst sinners in *Inferno*. Saturn alchemically is identified with lead, and one scientist in the novel makes extended arguments that the entire world is suffering from lead poisoning: "He was only investigating lead levels and this led him into horror chambers. Then he saw vast and terrible things all the way into the depths of hell" (225). Wherever we turn in the novel, we find inferno, an eternal city of dreadful night, an eternal dark night of the soul.

As in *Mr. Sammler's Planet*, Bellow offers moments of mystical ecstasy, nonrational arguments that eternity does exist and that "ordinary" consciousness is blind to a greater reality, as it also is to the destructions and resurrections we go through every minute of our lives (263). Corde looks out from his porch and feels himself somehow transcending into the color blue. His other apprehension of such mystery comes when facing the beauty of abstraction. The astronomer's sky, "tense with stars," draws him to its icy depths, to its orderly balances: "everything overhead was in equilibrium, kept in place by mutual tensions. What was it that *his* tensions kept in place?" (306). Like Boethius, Bellow wishes that the human emotional life were as orderly as the great dance of planets and stars, all held together by the fair chains of "love" (Boethius's term, which one would render more familiar as bonds of gravitational "attraction"). Corde finds the stars and their sky cold but finds almost more painful the "coming down," the return to the mundane, whirling, often infernal world.

Various metaphors emerge for the threat posed by the chaos of a non-moral universe—whirling, the Darwinian law of the jungle, random violence, and submersion in shit. Bars that can keep you from falling from your balcony while your mind expands and opens to the eternal are equivalent to models of behavior and the civic limitations on action necessary to create and preserve useful social order. One's immediate goal is to identify one's personal duty in life if one is to keep the insanity at bay. Once, when people were not individuals but peasants, craftspeople, and aristocrats, the bars and the duties were supplied as external patterns of hierarchy and subordination. Though characters show a furtive nostalgia toward the aristocratic splendor of the old order, Bellow does not really offer it as a viable possibility now. We have instead to find some way of building an internal sense of order. Sammler can still claim that in our hearts, we really do know, deep down, what we ought to do—an expression of conservative belief in an absolute moral order. By the time Dean Corde finishes educating us on the Chicago slums, however, readers may feel that members of the underclass are offered no such cultural inner voice, and if it is not inherent, then how can they or we ever find it again? Bellow upholds love, which he redefines as inner order, as a starting point. Love is a minimal unit achievable by just about anybody—witness the hit man who overdosed or the alienated Sammler—but Bellow does not show us how society at large might create that inner order, at least not in these two novels. The classics and religion can offer us the models, but how can that theory be turned into practice for either the decadent moneyed class or the deprived underclass? On that, Bellow is all but silent. Ridpath and Winthrop are the closest to models of behavior that he offers; both figure in Corde's articles on Chicago. The one tried to run a jail honestly; the other gave up his ambitions and personal life as a hit man to help others at a drug center. Society, far from welcoming them, has given them the cold shoulder. Attempting to rise above one's murderous impulses and achieve a philosophical or mystical relationship with life thus would seem to demand abnegation and self-sacrifice. Who in America will take up that challenge but a small handful at best? If America has failed—and ultimately it or its people have done so in these two novels—Bellow can offer no answer but individual self-discipline practiced in a decaying social environment that destroys more and more of the artifacts of civilization.

Why Science Cannot Be the New Civilization: Percy

Love in the Ruins (1971)

Walker Percy agrees with Saul Bellow that our current society is unlikely to improve itself. We cannot look to the government for a new vision. Not even the Roman Catholic Church offers an imaginatively compelling vision.[17] Nor is the future promising: Percy published *Love in the Ruins* in 1971 but sets it in 1983, providing such futuristic goodies as cars with only one moving part and the Catholic Church splintered into several schismatic sects. Lacking any other source of inspiration, his chief character turns to science. Our society treats science as the font of all provable truths and therefore the only system worthy of our trust. Could we use science to improve human mentality by stimulating the correct brain centers or by ingesting the right chemicals, for instance? These are questions that Percy asks in his paired novels, *Love in the Ruins* and *The Thanatos Syndrome*. Lewis A. Lawson suggests that the former should have been called *The Eros Syndrome* because that would better indicate the interrelated nature of these two futuristic speculations into social and personal morality. The first deals with America's failure in terms of liberal and conservative politics, race relations, religion, and sexuality; the major metaphor for our various mistakes is promiscuity. Both center on scientific experiments that alter mental patterns by means of chemicals. Needless to say, Percy proves hostile to these material solutions, but he analyzes the American problems from unusual and thought-provoking perspectives before coming to conclusions.

Whereas Bellow identifies one of America's major problems as an underclass that happens to be largely African-American (in his vision), Percy constructs the problem as racial and moral but derives it from the original act of enslavement rather than simply from intractable economic divisions in society:

> Even now, late as it is, nobody can really believe that it didn't work after all. The U.S.A. didn't work! Is it even possible that from the beginning it never did work. . . . that all this time we were not really different from Ecuador and Bosnia-Herzegovina, just richer. . . . Was it the nigger business from the beginning? What a bad joke: God saying. . . . so I gave it all to you, gave you Israel and Greece and science and art and the lordship of the earth, and finally even gave you the new world that I blessed for you. And all you had to do was pass one little test. . . . here's a helpless man in Africa, all you have to do is not violate him. That's all. (48–49)

This rambling indictment of "Visigoth-Western-Gentile-Christian-Americans" (49) comes from Thomas More, the protagonist, who believes he has come up with a discovery that might yet save America.[18] More is a bad Catholic, a boozy doctor, and a not very effective psychiatrist. His interests in the psyche and his scientific training, however, have allowed him to create a device that permits localized encephalographic studies of brain activity. At layers I and II of any animal, the readings are identical; in man, however, the social self of layer I and the inner self of layer II may be far apart. The outer for many people is active, while the authentic core is nearly dead: "Only in man does the self miss itself, *fall* from itself (hence *lap*someter!) Suppose—! Suppose I could hit on the right dosage and wed the broken self whole! What if man could reenter paradise, so to speak, and live there both as man and spirit" (31). A right order exists, we are thus told, and what we experience as our normal state is a violation of that order. Percy focuses on the fallen state of a specifically American spirituality, indicated by the main action's taking place on the Fourth of July.

This cleavage in self explains our social problems. What Percy calls angelism mostly haunts liberals. They become abstracted from themselves. One of his patients, Ted, talks in impersonal terms about his impotence, as if it were someone else's problem, and shows interest in the diagnosis only when it is scientifically unusual. More himself feels that "it took religion to save me from the spirit world, from orbiting the earth like Lucifer and the angels" (217). In his current inability to believe or feel sorry for his sins, he suffers from the concomitant physical complaints he tries to treat in liberal patients of morning terror and occasional impotence. In conservatives, the disparity usually manifests itself in "unseasonable rages, delusions of conspiracies, high blood pressure, and large-bowel complaints" (17). Conservatives are also likely to develop not abstraction from body and self but too close an identification with it, resulting in satyriasis. The protagonist himself is dogged by complaints of angelism and bestialism. He is thus liberal and conservative, a Janus figure reflecting the splits in America itself.

More's liberal tendencies show up in his rejection of southern white attitudes toward African Americans. He winces at phony traditional Christmas rituals based on black fawning before white masters. He is upset by his business partner, Leroy Ledbetter, because Ledbetter is both viciously racist and "a decent, sweet-natured man who would help you if you needed help, go out of his way and bind up a stranger's wounds" (129). A traditional southern conservative would have less trouble understanding that combination. His liberalism also shows in his hoping for salvation from science and in his tendency to prefer abstractions to real people.[19] Percy's satire on the American Catholic Church (a schismatic sect) may seem superficially leftist, for he derides its sanctification of private property.

More's conservativism comes out, however, in his satire on the beliefs of the left (16), in particular those that happen also to be against the teachings of the Catholic Church. The test case in this book is euthanasia, and More is allowed triumphantly to prove that in a specific case it would have been a tyrannical and misguided act. Percy's conservatism, shown at More's expense, manifests itself in the satire on More's belief that a gadget can cure the ills of the world. Liberals are more likely to seek material causes and solutions to the problem of evil than are conservatives, particularly religious conservatives. In the scene in which More signs his "pact with the devil," More is suffering from a euphoria induced by his own device; and in that state, he rapturously affirms liberal stances regarding the superiority of feeling good rather than bad, of being happy rather than unhappy. In his right mind, which for him is Catholic, there are many circumstances in which it is better to be unhappy, one being after committing some sin, when only one's unhappiness can help one to try to amend one's ways. The "devil," Art Immelmann, prompts him to agree that the purpose of life in a democratic society is "for each man to develop his potential to the fullest" (182). More would never have reached that conclusion had Immelmann not attached a treatment device to the lapsometer, which stimulates and depresses centers in the brain to create this liberal outlook.

Percy also follows a conservative line of argument in having More uphold the rightness of different traditions for different people. More is twice married, but neither wife becomes Catholic; they remain Episcopalian and Presbyterian respectively, until seduced by more trendy, charismatic faiths, and their changing is held to discredit them both. More gets along well with an agnostic Jewish doctor and is not interested in arguing over differences with the three kinds of Catholics. At the end, Protestants, Catholics, and Jews are sharing the same building for purposes of worship but are not practicing any ecumenical blending. A person is born in a tradition and should keep faith with it. More frequently compares himself to his collateral ancestral relative, Sir Thomas More; he invokes this sainted forebear in his moment of direst need and receives miraculous succor.[20] Such belief in the vitality of tradition and the power of ancestors over personal life is basically a conservative belief.

What More learns from his attempts to make sense of life, however, will not let him save America through argumentation. After he slashes his wrists in a fit of depression, he spends time in the acute wing of his own hospital. Both he and a fellow inmate, Father Smith, reach major insights but couch them in religious terms. Father Smith decides that principalities and powers have won and that humans have lost, and this is decoded by the agnostic Jewish doctor, Max Gottlieb, as meaning that the powers of evil triumph. For Max, Smith's belief remains the babbling voice of insanity. Likewise, when More tries to talk in terms of angelism—or of the soul, of sin and guilt, and of the soul of Western humanity—his listeners immediately remind him that technically he has not yet been discharged from the acute wing. To them, such talk is insane. It robs his arguments of all power for them; it makes his pleas for a hearing of his theories utterly unproductive. His moral terminology, like that of Dean Corde, is unacceptable to the world of today. His insights might save that world, but he will never be able to put them across. More can thus find no communicable solution in his liberal or conservative modes; he finds none in his religious mode either.

If we ask when Percy's world took the wrong turn, we find that, like Bellow, he traces the evils of the modern world to changes that were brought about by the two world wars, particularly World War I. Corde got his personal "catastrophe exposure" in the 1940s in Germany but found that secondary to his boyhood exposure to his father's books on World War I—frozen corpses used as walkways, the rats eating their way through the corpses and emerging through the mouths, and other such horrors. Tom More is reading Stedmann's account of Verdun and wonders: "Father Smith speaks of life. Life is better than death. Frenchmen and Germans now choose life. Frenchmen and Germans at Verdun in 1916 chose death, 500,000 of them. The question is, who has life, the Frenchman now who chooses life and will die for nothing or the Frenchman then who chose to die, for what?" (161). He cannot quite picture what they did die for, but life without that something seems unendurably trivial. While reading of Verdun, he hears a sportscaster analyzing the prospects of football teams. "Number one on his list were the Nittany Lions of Penn State. I do not care to hear about the Nittany Lions. But what would it be like to live in Pennsylvania and every day of your life hear sportscasters speak of the prospects of the Nittany Lions?" (161). (As someone teaching at Penn State, I know what he means.) Life filled with such trivia is what frightened More to the wrist slashing in the first place. Something changed during World War I, something about our attitudes toward death, our willingness to die for a purpose because it seemed deserving to us. We can no longer find such causes, perhaps because our expectations about pain and pleasure changed, and those changes are related to our putting our hopes in science and material causes. Certainly they changed for Europeans and thus brought Europeans and Americans closer together spiritually, to the loss of all concerned, according to these authors.

Percy's plot is ultimately inconclusive. More finally manages a confession of sorts and so heals some of his religious wounds. Right up to the end, however, More still thinks that this machine could somehow save humanity, and readers are given no clue that he realizes the error of this attitude, though we are clearly meant to see the futility of such scientific materialism. Immelmann misuses the device, so the resulting violence is not the instrument's fault but rather a useful warning that if a machine can be misused for political ends, it inevitably will be. More does not discuss the fact that the effects he achieves from the ionizing treatment are only temporary. His treatments would not effect permanent cures. Nor does he really consider the implications. If our emotions are so clearly affected by, or even caused by chemical reactions, what does this do to religious interpretation of those same emotions? More seems content with solving the lesser problem of his own sexual attraction toward three women.[21] This seriously narrows the book's ending. Somewhat like the authors who deal with Vietnam in chapter 2, Percy finds sexual problems more fascinating than major national and moral issues.

Another peculiarly inconclusive element in the plot is the takeover of the town of Paradise by the Bantus, who have been living for years in the swamp. Paradise, where a racial clash sparked off Christmas riots ten years before the epilogue, has become ninety-nine percent black not by the revolution described in the story, which failed, but through capitalist exercise of property rights. Squatting in the swamp for twenty years gave these Bantus ownership of the land, and oil discovered in that swamp brings them the wealth to buy out the white haven. More is now a poor doctor because the black hospitals will not allow him to use their facilities. He must be careful where he sits to eat, since he is technically not permitted to eat with blacks in many buildings. The Bantus, meanwhile, play golf in British plus fours and have adopted old British golfing terminology. Colley Wilkes, the black encephalographer who used to watch birds because it was the thing to do with his white colleagues, has become zealous in his hunt to see the ivory-billed woodpecker. Colley has worked to integrate the local Audubon society but does not want to rock the boat regarding the hospital and urges More that these things take time. The plot at this point may be satiric, but it is not serious. If showering wealth on the dispossessed were all that was needed, presumably the American Indians of Oklahoma in the 1920s would have made a different and better life for themselves than their oil money secured. If money were a sufficient solution to complex historical problems, who needs morality? Percy's point seems to be that people of any color, when they gain control, tend to be exclusive and misuse their power, a reminder that humans are a fallen species and need religious structures to improve their natural moral standards.

In his analysis of what is wrong with America, Percy seems to say that promiscuity in a broad sense is at the bottom of our problems. We chase after false gods and idols (cult religions, science, and ivory-billed woodpeckers). We rush into false foreign wars (the ongoing war in Ecuador, equivalent to Vietnam) rather than fixing up our own country's ills. We engage in casual sexual activities rather than focusing our efforts in sanctioned matrimony. We want to mix, mingle, and weaken traditions rather than uphold those appropriate to ourselves because handed down by our ancestors. This cultural promiscuity is symbolized throughout by the vines that More frequently mentions. Vines grow up over abandoned cars; they break through asphalt; they crumble suburban walls and clog drains. When More mentions vines aloud, others look peculiarly at him to the point that readers wonder if the vines are a symptom of his mental unbalance rather than being objectively real.[22] Certainly Max treats his reference to vines as a delusion. The vines that More "sees" go all the places they should not, violating boundaries and destroying the artifacts of culture. They are uncultivated nature breaking barriers of culture, the wild weakening the tame. Only in the final paragraph do the vines become positive: "To bed we go for a long winter's nap, twined about each other as the ivy twineth" (343). The energy thus harnessed in a culturally sanctioned manner becomes part of culture rather than its destroyer.

✿ ✿ ✿

Both Percy and Bellow agree that American culture is in a state of breakdown, and they see us embodying this fragmentation. They also agree that the past offered problems that were different but less crucial because they did not threaten the coherence of life. Both analyze the alienation caused by our cultural breakdown as a split in the self, Percy showing it with the lapsometer, Bellow with the death of authentic emotions and the cultural ban on moral vocabulary. They also both see some mystic value to terror, a link between terror and the Eternal. Both see man as fundamentally bad in his most basic form—man as murderer, whether killing Germans or giving euthanasia to the elderly. Both writers seem to feel that the quest for liberties has gone too far, and they try to identify cultural controls that are necessary and desirable, even if those curb liberties. In addition, Percy is very worried by possible liberal legislation that would force conformity. In both *Love in the Ruins* and *The Thanatos Syndrome*, he focuses on liberties he wishes to defend against scientific arguments. Both writers would like to see a return to more traditional family values and to at least some religious beliefs. Both rather halfheartedly uphold love in a deromanticized and domesticated form, and both see the impulse to help others (in the drug center, in the hospice for the dying) as a more admirable investment of psychic energy than romantic love. Both value a sense of place— Louisiana, Chicago, or New York—and lament the fact that place has ceased to be an important and desired element in modern life.

"In the United States of the 1980s. . . . no great poet or novelist was willing to identify himself as a conservative, although Walker Percy, the Catholic novelist, did admit to voting for Reagan."[23] Whatever the label they may prefer, these two writers in these books offer a mostly conservative analysis of what happened to the American Dream of liberty, the pursuit of happiness, and justice and prosperity for all. They do not like what they see and certainly do not seem to think that the government can take any steps to improve matters. They are both moral enough to refuse the easy out of claiming that the poor are always with us. Insofar as they see any answer, it operates on the level of the individual. The individual may establish internal order or rediscover faith. The more people who manage to take such control of their lives, the better for society, but no effective mechanism exists for encouraging such self-improvement. The sheer size of the American population seems to render traditional conservative beliefs ineffectual. After all, the Athens of Plato only numbered a few thousand citizens, a small community in contemporary terms and one with considerable cultural uniformity. Percy and Bellow prefer moral development to industrial power and efficiency, but the latter seem better adapted to the sheer size of the population. Given the Darwinian effectiveness of capitalism at taking over third-world countries and surviving in competition with rival political systems, the conservative desire for old ways betokens an unwillingness to face the moral problems of the underclass produced by such industrialism. Bellow admits that the rotting inner cities are the rotting heart of America or even the cancer in its brain that produces madness; but neither he nor Percy can find methods from the past that would apply to the current situation. America is losing its continuity with the Judeo-Christian, classical, European tradition, but it is not, as far as they can see, gaining some other culture that will bring orderly functions back to society. Their books are vivid, and Bellow's works in particular are fine examples of that older tradition, capable of giving the reader trained in that tradition much pleasure: their arguments about America, however, lead one through a burning building to a locked door with NO EXIT written above.

Life among the Cultural Ruins: Barthelme

Snow White (1967)

Most critics of Snow White worry over whether Barthelme is surrendering to contemporary culture or criticizing it. Trash theory and Christopher Lasch's culture of narcissism have been invoked to deal with the linguistic confetti that swirls in the thin air of this strange text.[24] My approach—seeing this novel as a deconstruction of the liberal worldview and the Euro-American tradition—is only one of several possible readings. I choose it here because it brings this book into the conversation about lost civilization. I stress the conventional elements rather than the strange qualities because the conventional facets add to our sense of what liberal cultural stances can say about this supposed breakdown in civilization. Barthelme shares many of the basic outlooks of Euro-American culture and sees no way through or over the walls he comes up against.

Liberal tags dot the text. One of the dwarves grouses that their leader, Bill, should be out "realizing his potential" (20). The dwarves tend to believe "the idea that man is perfectible" (8). Snow White enjoys the benefits of the well-off, middle-class woman in that she consults a psychiatrist and rails that he is unforgivable because he finds her uninteresting and her problems commonplace and boring. She reads Teilhard de Chardin and insists that her "suffering is authentic enough but it has a kind of low-grade concrete-block quality" (41). Toward the end, one of the dwarves agonizes over the final actions: "What gave us the idea that there was something better? How does the concept, 'something better,' arise? What does it look like, this *something better?* Don't tell me that it is an infant's idea because I refuse to believe that. I know some sentient infants but they are not that sentient. And then the great horde of persons sub-sentient who nevertheless can conceive of *something better*" (179). Perfectibility, the possibility of improving the basic nature of one's life or of life in general, the concern with individual potential and suffering: these are all part of the liberal world picture.

Snow White herself has received a liberal education, a thing of shreds and patches, at Beaver College. This evocative name suggests that she (and her education) lack the drive and focus of the animal that builds dams, so she must be a beaver in the sexual sense. Her education is too spotty and her engagement in it too shallow to give her claim to anything but sex-object status. She studies *Modern Woman, Her Privileges and Responsibilities, Classical Guitar I, English Romantic Poets II,* a psychology course, a painting course, "personal resources," and the contemporary Italian novel. Thus, she acquires a smattering of art and music, fragments of two literary traditions without grounding in their history or development, and courses aimed at making her feel important as an individual. She takes nothing that would impart a moral framework or a philosophical grasp of life. We are given the hint in one of the large-print, boldface pages that the second generation of Romantics has something to do with her dissatisfaction. Shelley, Byron, and Keats were indeed dissatisfied with life as they saw it. We are told that "they found an answer not in society but in various forms of independence from society: heroism, art, spiritual transcendence" (24). This is the liberal aim as it has evolved in America: development of the self as individual, not devotion of the self to society and realization of the self within the social framework. With this training, Snow White is now trying to deal with the world. Unfortunately, it does not prepare her for a job; as two men heading for a hiring hall note, being an A.B. (an able-bodied seaman) is better than having a B.A. when it comes to getting employment (89).

Partly from her reading of Romantic literature and partly from the popular culture around her, Snow White has absorbed unreasonable expectations about life. Like Emma Bovary, she expects love to be a transcendent experience, and she finds her attempts to lead a fairy-tale life frustrating. Philosophy or religious morality would have given her other contexts by which to measure and judge her desires, but she lacks such checks on her imagination. Like Rapunzel, she lets down her long hair from the apartment window and is disappointed that no prince responds to this signal; no one even tries to climb, although gawkers assemble and stare up at her distress flag. Her stream-of-consciousness fragments suggest that she wants "one plain hero of incredible size and soft, flexible manners" or, in other words, "film bliss" (31). She repeats "Someday my prince will come" (70) and lists the names of all the princes she knows of, fictional or real. She grumbles that the seven dwarves she lives with "only add up to the equivalent of about two *real men*, as we know them from the films and from our childhood, when there were giants on the earth. It is possible of course that there are no more *real men* here" (41–42). Eventually, she concludes that Paul, the "prince figure" of this story, is "*pure frog*" (169). She anathematizes the world "for not being able to at least be civilized enough to supply the correct ending to the story" (132). Or, as one of the dwarves admits, "What is troubling me is the quality of life in our great country, America. . . . I am worried by the fact that no one responded to Snow White's hair initiative. . . . it suggests that Americans will not or cannot see themselves as princely" (140–41).[25] Like Bellow, Barthelme is aware of the connection between European cultural roots and aristocracy, but he treats it with irony.

Snow White's dissatisfactions with her present mode of life are not difficult to fathom. She does retain fleeting memories of the Huntsman, the knife, and the forest, but those events evidently took place long ago. She has been the housekeeper and sexual companion for seven men who make their livings by washing windows on high-rise buildings and making Chinese baby food. They are distressed by her dissatisfaction and try to meet her demands; for instance, they use words in combinations supposedly not heard before. They mean well, but they are incapable of fathoming her emotions and resent the diminution in their creature comforts caused by her withdrawals, sulks, and lack of enthusiasm for them. She adopts unrevealing bulky Chinese outfits instead of the "tight tremendous, how-the-West-was-won trousers" (16) that they had admired immoderately. She finally stops doing all housework—not just the elaborate and demanding treatment of old books, but basic cooking and cleaning as well.

She calls herself a horsewife, although the rather tepid couplings in the shower do not justify the force implicit in her image of woman as a hard-ridden horse. Barthelme is at his funniest when commenting on horse-wives. Some of his headlines include: "FIRST MOP, 4000 BC," "VIEWS OF ST. AUGUSTINE," "EMERSON ON THE AMERICAN HORSEWIFE," "OXFORD COMPANION TO THE AMERICAN HORSEWIFE," "INTRODUCTION OF BON AMI, 1892," "ACCEPT ROLE, PSYCHOLOGIST URGES," and "THE GARLIC PRESS" (61). Thus, he sums up what the historical tradition—from the early Christian fathers to Julia Child—has stated as the female's role in society. When Snow White weighs up her current activities and those of other horsewives, she likens them (using language from the Song of Songs) to an immense reservoir of natural gas being burned off from an oil well because it is not economically feasible to ship the gas somewhere. Snow White's discontents are the sort that fuelled the middle-class feminist movement, but she shows no awareness of that movement, despite the ferment that led to the founding of the National Organization for Women in 1966. Insofar as the personal resources part of her education belongs to the education of women, it derives from the previous generation and training for the genteel housewife.

Most of Snow White's attempts to change her life consist of negations. She refuses to do housework or continue her sexual relations with the dwarves. She has no positive vision of what should come next, of what she should strive for. She does write what the dwarves call "a dirty great poem four pages long" (10). As the dwarves grumble to themselves, "The poem remained between us like an immense, wrecked railroad car" (59). Though she will not let them read it, she permits them to guess that the theme is loss. Confronted with this, they ask the real question: "why do you remain with us? here? in this house?" To this, she answers, "It must be laid, I suppose, to a failure of the imagination. I have not been able to imagine anything better. . . . But my imagination is stirring" (59). Barthelme's handling of Snow White suggests both sympathy and impatience; and in this, he rather resembles Lisa Alther on Emily Prince in *Original Sins*. Like Emily, Snow White has justifications for her discontents, but her expectations are unrealistic. This fault may be attributed to her society and education, but she has done nothing to correct it. The steps she takes to change matters do not demand much of herself. Crucially, Barthelme sums it up when, in a stream-of-consciousness passage, we find juxtaposed "want to know . . . effortlessly" (165)—her problem in a nutshell. Real knowledge and real change do not just happen, except in daydreams, fairy tales, and films. They demand sustained effort, and she is making no such commitment. Her education has not given her the discipline to make it, and neither her imagination nor her education provides a goal to aim for.

The impotence of traditional Euro-American culture is reflected in the status of the men in this novel. Barthelme's *The Dead Father* represents the patriarchy and the dead hand of tradition as a monstrous god-man. In *Snow White*, the dwarfish nature of most of the male figures suggests weakness and inadequacy. Paul, the prince figure, is the son of "Paul XVII, a most kingly man and personage. Even though his sole accomplishment during his long lack of reign was the de-deification of his own person" (27). The dwarves' father is supposed to have told them, "Try to be a man about whom nothing is known" (18). The leader of the dwarves, Bill, "wanted to be great, once" but failed when trying to "make a powerful statement" (51). Snow White, of course, complains that there are no real men anymore, no one like the giants of old. As readers, we cannot readily tell the various dwarves apart. The shriveled and ineffectual nature of the men seems to be equated with the state of the traditional culture. Whatever its virtues may once have been, it can no longer hold respect or capture the imagination of people trying to live their lives in America. The dwarves' hanging of Bill and accepting of the brutal Hogo as a member reflects the growth of violence and the loss of any ideals. They and their country appear to be sliding into barbarity.

Despite his sense that the old civilization is now lost, Barthelme himself is clearly comfortable with that past system, well able to play what Bellow calls the old European culture game. Barthelme can allude to Apollinaire, Henry James, Henry Adams, Malcolm Lowry, Stendhal, and various English Romantic poets; moreover, he can still find some readers able to follow his lead. Mostly, however, he admits that what characterizes our culture now is a lack of communication. Also characteristic is an alienation from authentic emotions and a general lack of direction. Unlike Bellow, he does not especially lament the lost civilization, but neither he nor Snow White sees what could replace it. When we have no cultural controls, then Hogo's thuggish behavior will become the norm. Quite possibly, women will assume the roles of slave and sex object assigned them in the dwarves' sexual daydreams. When Snow White proves unable to find what she wants, she is revirginated and assumed into heaven, thus ceasing to be a player at the game of life. Her apotheosis enshrines discontent, not vision or action. The dwarves, meanwhile, set off in search of a new principle, which for them means a new mistress. Given Hogo's influence, the next group doxy is unlikely to devote the time Snow White once did to treating and preserving the leather bindings of old books containing that old culture. Those repositories of the old system will molder away.

❧ ❧ ❧

I have talked in greater detail than usual about Bellow, Percy, and Barthelme, in part because the very texture of their fiction demands such engagement. Barthelme's experimentalism leads him to invoke popular as well as traditional culture, but he plays the same culture games as Bellow and Percy. For them, the Western literary tradition is a dense network of allusions, and writers win respect the more of the tradition they invoke and assimilate. These novels and others like them have created and fed the presuppositions of literature departments and literary criticism. Their theme is Western tradition, and their authors' training in that tradition gives them much to say on various levels. That granted, one must admit that these three writers find no solution to the fact that knowledge of and allegiance to this tradition is dying. Their intellectual rigor lets them conceptualize the various problems clearly and keeps them from the dishonesty of easy traditional solutions, however tempting, such as More's achieving untroubled faith again or Snow White's being won by a prince. Within the assumptions allowed by the tradition, they find nothing to lead them toward a future. They admit that Western civilization has failed. Among the most important reasons for that failure is the contradiction that permitted people to engage in slavery and still feel civilized and moral. Western civilization also abolished slavery (a fact sometimes overlooked), but the racial problems stemming from that catastrophic failure in humanity continue to mock the tradition's claim to our respect. Nor have these writers any answer to America's acceptance of economic efficiency and materialism over all other values, yet those are producing an ever-growing class of "useless" people. The problems of culture are intimately tied to those of education. What should our educational system look like? To this, these writers offer no answer. One must step outside of their tradition to find thinkers concerned with finding a better educational theory—namely, the utopian thinkers discussed in later chapters.

As a way of looking yet again at traditional Western civilization, this time from its underside, from within the fissure caused by its contradictions, this chapter will now turn to Ishmael Reed. The Western tradition, particularly in its late, liberalized form, tries to deny or hide from all forms of darkness: evil, unpleasantness, pain. Both racially and morally, Reed reinserts that darkness.

Blackening the "Fair Name" of Western Culture: Reed

The Free-Lance Pallbearers (1967) and *Flight to Canada* (1976)

In his first novel, *The Free-Lance Pallbearers*, Ishmael Reed occasionally refers to a strange corner of his stranger world, the Emperor Franz Joseph Park. A triumphal arch, with the Four Horsemen of the Apocalypse on top, forms the gateway. The sculpture of the arch has broken, and "the ground surrounding the arch was littered with the heads of the famous dead" (74). Inside the park are piles of cannonballs and old men laden with memorabilia of the two world wars. "A procession. . . . was composed of some elderly gentlemen who pushed carts filled with artifacts and relics. The leader of this parade was a wizened-faced creature dressed in a ragged World War I uniform. His cart contained some parched manuscripts belonging to Wilfred Owen, stacks of broken violin scrolls, some twisted marble toilet bases and a big rock, the only remnant of Hadrian's wall" (75). Later on, Reed brings us back to the park. "A bunch of ol [sic] people singing 'Roger Young' off-key, forgetting the words and trying to unload Hadrian's rock on suckers. A collection of rusty trumpets and a wheelbarrow full of heroic couplets and fugues. Who in his right mind would want to buy a rock or a wheelbarrow full of dead verse? Why, just the other day I saw a man running out of a bar yelling: 'Just like Munich, just like Munich.' WHAT THE FUK [sic] DOES MUNICH HAVE TO DO WITH ANYTHING?" (113). Reed's protagonist is publicly executed on meat hooks in this same Emperor Franz Joseph Park, a black man butchered by the Western tradition.[26]

By invoking the name of Franz Joseph, Reed seems agree with Bellow and Percy in identifying World War I as the point at which Western civilization died for Euro-Americans—or at least lost its authentic claim to their allegiance. Its claim may linger on through World War II to some degree and even turn up in barroom conversation now, but what do any of its parts have to do with anything contemporary, really? Reed rejects the history, the poetry, the classical music, the remnants of the Roman and Greek era, and the collectibles from the wars themselves. Contemporary reality in America is not Euro-American, it is black and white or multiethnic, and issues of importance (to judge from his satires) include Vietnam, LBJ, city riots, the fate of black leaders like Malcolm X, feminism, and the bias of the American system against black men. The classics, he insists, have nothing to say to or for black Americans and, by implication, to or for Native Americans, Chicanos, Caribbean Americans, and Asian Americans. In this novel, Reed does not explore the reasons for that irrelevance, but in *Flight to Canada*, the inadequacies of the European tradition become his subject matter.

Flight to Canada was published in America's bicentennial year, but it gives readers little to celebrate. Reed focuses on one strand of the Western tradition, the perpetually popular Arthurian material, and casts his Civil War setting in Arthurian terms.[27] Arthurian stories have proved their durability. First told in Wales and worked up by Geoffrey of Monmouth and Chretien de Troyes in the twelfth century, they were popular throughout the Middle Ages in England, France, Germany, and Scandinavia. They were brought together by Malory in the fifteenth century and allegorized and given Protestant values by Spenser in the sixteenth. Milton considered them for his epic in the seventeenth century. Although less favored in the age of the Enlightenment, they were much retold in poetry and prose in the nineteenth century and filmed, retold, and parodied in the twentieth century. They supply romance in virtually all senses of that word. They feature personal heroics. They conceive of spiritual quests in physical terms and make few demands on readers' understanding of complex philosophies. They tell us that magic still breathes life into the material world. They thus represent the romantic and heroic side of the Western tradition without the music and art, without the philosophy needed to deal with quotidian boredom or endure tragedy, without the technology and commerce that fuel daily life and raise questions about materialism. The stories are Christian, more in their trappings than their serious concerns. One may quest for the Holy Grail and seek transcendence; otherwise, many knights live by violence, and even the good guys who defeat the bad must do so through fighting in hand-to-hand combat. Hence, while the Arthurian materials do not adequately represent all of the Western tradition, they do perhaps represent a portion of it deemed extremely attractive to a broad section of the culture's white inhabitants, past and present.[28] They are popular in a way that Plato and Thomas Aquinas and Heidegger are not. To judge from the fantasy market, Camelot is indeed what many readers like to daydream that life might be, and that is Reed's complaint.

Reed's Camelot is a postmodern zone of overlap between the Civil War South and the America of the Kennedy years. He superimposes the 1860s and 1960s so that both happen simultaneously. Lincoln is shot, and the assassination is seen on television. Raven Quickskill escapes from his Virginia master, Arthur Swille III, and considers fleeing to Canada on a jumbo jet. An escaped slave who does not have a trade and who cannot make a living on the abolitionist lecture circuit can team up with a Russian Jewish impresario and make biracial pornographic films. Swille's anthropologist son (like Nelson Rockefeller's) is killed by primitive tribal peoples. The Lerner and Loewe musical *Camelot* made the Kennedy era into Arthurian romance. Reed also depicts the Swille family mansion in Arthurian terms; it is

> said to be the very replica of King Arthur's in the Holy City of Camelot, the Wasp's Jerusalem, the great Fairy City of the old Feudal Order, of the ancient regime; of knights, ladies, of slaves; of jousting; of toasting; Camelot, a land of endless games. Seeing who could pull the Sword out of an anvil of iron. Listening to the convoluted prophecies of Merlin the Druid. Listening to Arthur and his knights, so refined and noble that they launched a war against the Arabs for the recovery of an *objet d'art*, yet treated their serfs like human plows, de-budding their women at will; torturing and witchifying the resistance with newfangled devices. Dracula, if you recall, was a count. (15)

Jumbled together here is an attack on nonproductive aristocratic life and hierarchy with extremes of power and powerlessness. Reed's animus is sharper because these European ideals have been brought to the potentially democratic New World. Jefferson Davis was indeed referred to as "Our Arthur" or "The South's Arthur." The Confederacy did consider various aristocratic models of government, including kingship or linkage with the French Empire.

Reed essentializes his picture of the South in one emblematic practice: the whipping of slaves. The whip generates his picture not just as a tool for corporal punishment but as a fetish instrument of sadists and masochists. Reed's South is a land of decadence, drugs, and kinky sexual practices (above all, of flagellation). Gladstone's unexpected support for the Confederacy is interpreted as motivated by a shared love of flagellation. "Raised by mammies, the South is dandyish, foppish, pimpish; its writers are Scott, Poe, Wilde, Tennyson" (141). And, Reed continues, "It wasn't the idea of winning that appealed to them. It was the idea of being ravished. Decadent and Victorian writing both use the romantic theme of fair youth slumbering. Fair youth daydreaming. Fair youth struck down. In the New Orleans Mardi Gras, that great Confederate pageant, the cult of Endymion has a whole evening" (142). Swille collects whips and uses them or has them used on himself at his exclusive gentlemen's club. He takes a drug he calls siesta, under the influence of which he dreams of becoming a baron. His breakfast indulgence is two gallons of mother's milk taken from slaves (to be labeled an unforgivable theft in Toni Morrison's *Beloved*). In an episode redolent of Edgar Allan Poe's stories, Swille swives the embalmed corpse of his beloved sister. All this is a far cry from conventional Arthuriana, but Reed stresses the South's worship of aristocracy and its sense that the aristocratic is the ideal way of life. To have aristocrats, Reed insists, you must have lowly servants, whether serfs, slaves, or villeins.[29] In the American Camelot, you find "darkies and Injuns to set places, pour and serve at the Round Table" (98).

Not only did the Civil War era have such Arthurian and aristocratic leanings; Reed argues that they appear (along with their associated versions of slavery) today. The escaped slave Raven says to his Native American princess friend: "They're going to get your Indian and my Slave on microfilm and in sociology books; then they're going to put them in a space ship and send them to the moon. And then they're going to put you on the nickel and put me on a stamp, and that'll be the end of it. They're as Feudalist and Arthurian as Davis, but whereas he sees it as a political movement, they see it as a poetry movement" (96). The academics collecting their accounts of ethnicity are preying off the descendants of slaves and American Indians. As a result of the information they take, intellectuals can enjoy positions of power within a hierarchy and make careers or money off those with low status in the hierarchy, just as Harriet Beecher Stowe is accused of stealing the story of Josiah Henson to create *Uncle Tom's Cabin*. In the novel, Abraham Lincoln also exploits the slaves in that he decides to push for emancipation not on moral grounds but because he sees he can make that the issue to sway European opinion of the war and thus keep several nations from declaring for the Confederacy. Modern scholars exploit non-Euro-American peoples in ways that keep them from the product of their own experience and labor; those academics salve their consciences by making such minority victims into art, thus robbing even that experience of its political meaning.

In painting the South as fixated on pain and mindless pleasures, Reed debunks the romantic illusions fostered by *Gone with the Wind*. In popular mythology, the South is gracious, cultured, nonmaterialistic, and aristocratic in its values. These characteristics somehow let it serve as a living reproach to the commercial, money-grubbing North. Or so the Agrarian literary movement would have us believe in its 1930 manifesto, *I'll Take My Stand*. By claiming that whipping the slaves was central to the aristocratic picture, Reed literally blackens this fair culture. He inserts the black into it and tries to prevent white readers from shrugging off slavery as a relatively benign institution or, at any rate, from viewing it as dead now and therefore insignificant compared to the heroics, grace, and culture of the upper classes. By insisting on the parallels between the 1860s and the period a century later, Reed tells us that mainstream white Americans are still fixated on daydreams of aristocracy, of being lords and ladies and letting the lower classes wait on them, even though those lower classes are now wage slaves. In Reed's view, the Western tradition (defined in Arthurian, aristocratic terms) is not just a faded flower but was and is actively immoral, exploitive, and vicious. To yearn for it, therefore, is not merely silly nostalgia but evidence of mental and moral disorder. After all, justifications are offered for slavery in the Bible and accepted in classical political philosophy. With that rot at the heart of the Western tradition, how could anything fair develop?

❧ ❧ ❧

Of Bellow, Percy, Barthelme, and Reed, only Reed has a clear alternative to past cultures in mind, and he only hints at what that might be. Why worship barrow-loads of violin scrolls and dead versifying when we have a living culture that is being written and performed today? As is evident from his other books, Reed would have Americans buy paintings from living artists, go to readings by living poets, and generally orient themselves to the contemporary. Support artists; do not condemn them to difficult and impoverished lives only to go wildly overboard and pay huge sums for their creations after they are dead and cannot benefit. Major opera singers and virtuoso classical piano players make large sums; meanwhile, emperors in the jazz world make modest sums and must perform nightly and live an exhausting peripatetic life if they are to make enough to live. Why not redress that balance? The other authors are at best ambivalent and at worst hostile to the contemporary. Bellow in particular seems to feel that the inner-city slums have no culture; he is unwilling to recognize performance as the basis of a culture (because it does not last), whether the performance is personal style, the verbal contests known as the dozens, or jazz. For him, only the textual and the works linked to his recognized tradition qualify as worthy of study. Reed may not make systematic arguments and is unlikely to convert anyone who has the training to enjoy Western cultural manifestations, but his reasons are clear enough. A culture that produced the slavery that his African ancestors suffered from and the culture that is unable to eradicate racial prejudice has no right to sacred status and can make no meaningful demand on anyone nonwhite. Its loss may clear the way for a culture more appropriate to multiethnic America. For Reed, this is good riddance to bad rubbish.

Race indeed is a major issue on which the Western civilization of Bellow and Percy fails badly, and they recognize that weakness by presenting America's apparently insoluble problems in terms of race. Barthelme adds that people are barred from full participation by gender as well as by color; Snow White's problems are particularly those of the educated but underemployed woman. Bellow, Percy, and Barthelme all admit that Western civilization has at this point proved unable to propagate itself through education, and we see this with painful clarity as we read about the courses taken by Snow White at Beaver College. The tradition is simply too long and too complex now to be passed on to any but a few enthusiasts of the next generation, and even they must specialize in particular cultural areas. The classical education of the eighteenth century meant only Greek and Latin classics. The liberal humanistic education means all of English, and American literature and culture as well, along with a smattering of European great works. With the demands of cultural literacy, the smattering has been extended to Native American myths and to African and Asian classics. Moreover, science and related matters unknown in earlier eras make demands for attention in the curriculum that reduce further any training that could be given to putting across the Western humanistic tradition. Conservative writers may not wish to jettison the past, but they find no way to inculcate their love for this past in the children of their main characters.

Another way of expressing the problem is the one that Dean Corde faces when he finds that he cannot talk about what matters to him in vocabulary acceptable to the essay-reading public. He needs terms of morality; morality, however, has become a nonissue or a minor, private issue for most people rather than the central focus for shaping one's life. The philosophical and religious components of the Western tradition concerned morality and its practical applications in daily life well into the nineteenth century. These, however, are now out of fashion. We retain Arthurian romance, the pleasure principle, and romantic individualism but overlook or repress awareness of pain, the concept of duty, our obligation to society, and the necessity of finding ways to deal with boredom other than running from it. Part of the tradition that we have laid aside dealt with such matters.

In going back to the alternative Western civilization, Welch produces none of the modernist web of references for obvious reasons. He is operating partly outside the Western tradition as usually defined, and the culture he describes is nonliterate and thus lacks Western-style intertextuality, though Fools Crow's visions certainly invoke such other texts as Black Elk's vision. However, Welch focuses on the here and now, on the rituals, on the gradual transformation of his main character, on the permeability of the barriers between humans and their culture heroes and divinities. These subjects represent some Native American tribal values and make a feeling claim for the attractive side of one such culture. Ceremonies are texts of another sort, and they are repeated or described in his text. We see how balance in the individual life is attained and how mental balance is striven for even when the culture is dwindling before unbeatable forces. Again, Euro-American readers are invited to feel a sense of loss, not for something they have half-known but for something they never knew. His Native American readers will feel more attunement with the tradition than his Euro-Americans, but if either kind of reader responds positively to his picture, that reader is rejecting the Euro-American Western tradition for its materialism and blind, greedy, destructive energy. What Native American traditions still have to offer is not clear from this novel, for it does not seem adaptable to any but a low-density population, and Welch is not offering it as a possible future. Whites are not being asked to join it so much as to lament a cusp at which a bad choice was made. One must turn to Leslie Marmon Silko's *Almanac of the Dead* for radical prophecies of an Indianized future.

That Reed's stand might put all races on an equal footing is suggested by the rhetoric of a white reformer in Hawthorne's *House of Seven Gables:*

> Shall we never, never get rid of this Past! . . . It lies upon the Present like a giant's dead body! In fact, the case is just as if a young giant were compelled to waste all his strength in carrying about the corpse of the old giant, his grandfather, who died a long while ago, and only needs to be decently buried. . . . We read in Dead Men's books! We laugh at Dead Men's jokes, and cry at Dead Men's pathos! . . . We worship the living Deity, according to Dead Men's forms and creeds! Whatever we seek to do, of our own free motion, a Dead Man's icy hand obstructs us! . . . And we must be dead ourselves, before we can begin to have our proper influence on our own world, which will then be no longer our world, but the world of another generation, with which we shall have no shadow of a right to interfere. (182–83)

Note that Barthelme literalizes Hawthorne's image of the giant in *The Dead Father* and advocates shedding the past, even if he has no great faith in the children who will succeed that father. Hawthorne himself is not exactly agreeing with this young firebrand, but the speaker certainly sees jettisoning the past as upholding hope for the future of America.

Ignoring the past may be dangerous in terms of repeating it, but does studying the past prevent repetitions? Or does the distant past offer real answers in the world of the Internet, ICBMs, and cloning? Reed seems to feel the past can be ignored, in part because he wants a shift in cultural modality. Our Western civilization has been the world of the set text, of the scripture. He prefers a performative model: improvised music rather than the written text provides his pattern. There will be losses in any shift of paradigm, but Reed argues that there are likewise gains that can only be realized if we give up fruitless nostalgia.

chapter four

5eeking *Spiritual Reality*

Robert C. Post defines the realistic novel as "the aesthetic result of the attempt to represent in fiction a world in which value has no distinct ontological status, and in which human meaning is perceived to reside in the unending and indissoluble tension between self and society" (390). The novelists discussed in this chapter do not belong to the realist tradition but exhibit impulses akin to those behind America's shadow-filled alternate tradition, the nineteenth-century romance of Nathaniel Hawthorne, Herman Melville, and Henry James.[1] The contemporary novelists start from the belief that mainstream American culture has no spiritual dimension, and all seek ways of reinscribing the realm of the spirit in the imagination of their readers. Their conceptions of the lost dimension vary: for N. Scott Momaday and John Updike, spiritual reality consists of a traditional religion that is all but lost to their characters and perceived through a glass darkly. For Rudolfo Anaya and William Kennedy, the old metaphysic is no longer viable in its totality; they salvage fragments and create space for them in a materialist culture, if only through giving them voice in fiction. Norman Mailer and Thomas Pynchon create new spiritual schemata—Mailer's is devoted to individual behavior, Pynchon's to the nature of metaphysical reality.

What does spiritual reality consist of? Characters sense or experience some form of reality beyond the strictly material, and the author treats this without irony or skepticism. In other words, the novel constructs reality in a fashion that differs from secular and scientific reality and invites readers to reconsider the validity and human efficacy of the strictly phenomenal explanation. Characters who are at home with the spiritual dimension are often made to stand out against the background American culture; they are presented as engaging with life more strongly, and their intensity makes their fictional world resonate with meaning either for themselves or others around them. A character in such a novel often undergoes a transcendent experience, whether mystic epiphany, cognitive breakthrough, or a victory, a creation, or even a perfect physical performance. Many writers link this transcendent moment to magic. Life that includes any version of such a spiritual realm is represented as meaningful; life without that intensification, transcendence, resonance, or magic may well seem empty or pointless.

The lament that America lacks a spiritual dimension is analogous to the estrangements illustrated in the first three chapters of this study. Immigrants who find American culture soulless and feel that it robs them of their souls experience one version of this loss. To lose one's soul is to lose something that transcends the physical world of everyday life. Similarly, alienation deriving from loss of innocence amounts to a feeling that once upon a time, a spiritually satisfying order suffused life but has now withdrawn or been forfeited. The loss of a past civilization, if that culture embodied a truly effective code, whether cultural or religious, similarly cuts us off from means of transcending reality and death. All deal with a shared feeling of estrangement, but each explains the diminution in different terms. What we see in this chapter is a specific kind of rebellion against mainstream values: a rejection of the materialist economic and scientific constructions of reality. This is the operative reality of our politics and news, our corporations and educational system. The demand in scientific fields for reproducible results has led to a feeling that the material world offers our only provable truth. These novels implicitly claim that the material construction of reality is flawed or at best partial and proffer arguments in favor of the immaterial. These arguments may be intended literally or psychologically, but readers are usually discouraged from making that distinction. The magic is presented as effective, however inexplicable it is in scientific terms.

The Magic of Traditional Religions: Momaday and Updike

Momaday's *House Made of Dawn* and Updike's Rabbit books differ considerably in their impact and appeal. Both, however, show protagonists who suffer from their sense that the American Dream does not work. Furthermore, those protagonists believe that their lives have lost meaning in part because they themselves no longer feel attuned to the religions of their respective peoples: the spiritual cosmos of the Walatowa and Navaho; the Protestantism of Pennsylvania. For both protagonists, belief is intertwined with forms of physical action and with kinds of magic. For Momaday, magic is a Euro-American term for the implications of a native metaphysic; for Updike, it constitutes a curious addition to Christianity, an index of his protagonist's inability to feel the belief he craves.

House Made of Dawn (1968)

When magic is presented as part of a native metaphysic, it represents a fashion of talking about other levels of reality breaking through into this one. Someone properly trained in shamanic lore may be able to work searches or hexes by means of access to other levels of reality, and so can a witch. Correspondences between levels can be used by those trained in the lore. Even in Louise Erdrich's *Love Medicine*, where members of the tribe are building a factory to make plastic American Indian items to sell to tourists, the correspondences are known. Lipsha wants to mend a damaged marriage by making the partners eat the hearts from a pair of monogamously bonded geese. The marketability of an "Indian novel" presenting no challenge to a scientific metaphysic might suffer for lack of that marker of "authenticity." Similarly, Vodoun has become commonplace in recent African-American novels. Such magic material does not go uncontested by readers. I have had African-American students who were disgusted by *Mama Day* and *Mumbo Jumbo* for what they consider primitivism, and they interpret Vodoun's presence as a white market's demand for blacks to be portrayed as mentally childish and unable to deal with scientific reality. Other students, however, feel empowered by such claims to other levels of reality, and some who are white find it easier to put aside disbelief if claims for a spiritual dimension originate in some culture not their own. Hence, more than one kind of pressure from readers encourages narrative forays into nonmaterial reality.

Writers like N. Scott Momaday face conflicting demands when they make Native American spiritual values their subject. If they write only for those who know or share their particular tribal metaphysics, they may run into trouble getting published at all or find themselves confined to small presses. They can write so as to attract the reader who skims the *New York Times Book Review*; to do so, though, they must present their different reality in palatable and semicomprehensible forms. Many choose to write for both audiences, and this sometimes results in giving outsiders one reading and insiders another, a Janus-faced mode of production. James Welch does this in *The Death of Jim Loney*, where Jim's death looks to middle-class Euro-Americans like a defeat and a waste; to tribal peoples, however, Loney's death can be experienced as a triumph. He reaffirms his American Indianness by choosing to accept tribal values and death rather than give his soul over to white ways. Welch does not explain this; academic specialists have opened that hidden dimension to Euro-American readers.[2] Likewise, Silko does much with witchery in *Ceremony* that she does not explain, but native or acquired knowledge of that cultural phenomenon makes Tayo more heroic than he looks when judged by commonplace Euro-

American standards. Momaday's *House Made of Dawn* does not explain for nontribal audiences the compelling American Indian reality of the albino witch, with the result that the story can be interpreted in several fashions, all hinging on the status of such magic.

Actually, Momaday problematizes the concept of the witch for most readers and forces on them a consciousness of their own assumptions. The absolute evil attributed to the albino is undercut by the example of another witch mentioned in the novel. Abel's grandfather, Francisco, once loved a woman who was *"the child of a witch. . . . whom everyone feared because she had long white hair about her mouth"* (184; italics in original). Does a minor hormonal imbalance, now handled with electrolysis, make a woman deserve social hostility? That, at least, is the scientific way of interpreting the hair. The masculine-seeming beard on a woman rouses uneasiness for its transgression of gender norms and, within the local tribal outlook, might seem to correlate to the possession of uncanny powers for good or ill. If the rational approach guides the reader's mind, how can such a reader extend any respect to this fear of a witch or agree to the desirability of murdering the albino witch, who is, by scientific assumptions, not responsible for his own genetic abnormality?

Momaday also shows Native Americans who do not believe in witches. John Tosamah, a Kiowa, Christian preacher, and priest of the sun, sarcastically condemns Abel for his act: "He turned out to be a real primitive sonuvabitch, and the first time he got hold of a knife he killed a man" (136). Tosamah is given many vivid, sensitive, lyrical passages on Kiowa history, drawn from Momaday's own family, and this inclines readers to take him seriously. Tosamah is also, however, a slick Willie in the pulpit, the sort of man who rouses the readerly uneasiness that stems from dealing with a charlatan. He undermines the American Indian position on witchery by reducing "witch" to "man" but is himself undermined.

Witchery, with its spiritual implications, is at the heart of this novel, and readers are given ambiguous and contradictory hints as to how to evaluate it. Abel starts his life as an outcast. His father is unknown and definitely not a member of the tribe; his mother is dead.[3] Boarding school isolates Abel from the tribe, as does soldiering in World War II. He returns home, unable to communicate with his grandfather or fit into the old ways. As soon as he tries to take part in a ceremonial contest, he is viciously humiliated by the winner. He subsequently kills this mysterious albino. At Abel's trial, the local priest tries to explain that "in his own mind it was not a man he killed. It was something else" (94). The American legal system does not recognize the possibility of someone being a witch, however.[4] Furthermore, Abel's direct personal violence is not the approved, communal way of dealing with witchery within the Native American community. As Silko argues in *Ceremony*, such personal violence can feed the witch-

ery and do its work. To face the witch properly, Abel would have needed
to involve the whole community.

Readers can rationalize the witchery, though they will read more sympathetically if they realize that witches are real to many of the American
Indians of the Southwest. Abel's life is damaged *as if* by witchery, and his
trouble over an alleged witch can function symbolically, through rational
factors such as his orphaned state, school, the war, jail, and alcohol. That
would be a "scientific" or Euro-American reading. The chief result of such
an approach would be to see Abel's action as misguided, thus diminishing
his moral stature; it would not prevent readers from seeing his return to
the village as positive for his individual psychology, though such readers
might see the process as ultimately regressive. If, however, one grants the
albino to be truly monstrous and accepts Abel's conviction that he would
kill again were he faced with the situation, then one has a much stronger
sense of the cultural gap that Abel is crossing by an act of will.

Abel's eventual solution is to return to the village of Walatowa for his
grandfather's death and to participate in a ceremony of communal running
against evil—a very different sort of running from that of Huck Finn, Rabbit, Rojack, Francis Phelan, and all the American heroes analyzed by Leslie Fiedler. Even as his grandfather once ran, so he now tries. That he is
slow, out of condition, and not part of the official race will not matter. The
physical action of running and the physical pain open him to native patterns, and readers are evidently meant to see some hope and comfort in
this decision to enter the symbolic life of his ancestors and join in the
necessarily ongoing struggle to keep evil properly balanced with good.[5] Abel
has had his problems with the village. His upbringing, like that of Tayo in
Ceremony, shows the cruelty of the village toward those different enough
to be perceived as a threat to cultural uniformity. However, the rest of the
American world offers him unbearable factory work, beatings, and drink.
His social worker may have believed in "Honor, Industry, the Second
Chance, the Brotherhood of Man, the American Dream, and him" (99), but
she never understands him or his world. The white world seems to him
cold and dead. He feels better in a world with a spiritual dimension, even
if that sometimes manifests itself as malign magic.

He also feels better in a world where one shapes one's relations to one's
surroundings through such means as the "House Made of Dawn" chant.
The scientific mode of mainstream culture "objectively" isolates the self
from the world. The tribal outlook cultivates subjective reality and influences internal feelings through harmonizing them with that external
world:

Happily I recover.
Happily my interior becomes cool.

Happily I go forth.
My interior feeling cool, may I walk.
No longer sore, may I walk. (134)

The chant ends, "May it be beautiful all around me. / In beauty it is finished" (135). A world lacking this religious dimension, especially the part that would be called magic in the scientific realm, is not worth inhabiting for Abel. From the point of view of someone low in the economic scale, the wonders of technology offer little of value.

Rabbit, Run (1960), *Rabbit Redux* (1971), *Rabbit Is Rich* (1981), and *Rabbit at Rest* (1990)

Had Updike written a historical novel set in colonial days, he would have found a strong tradition of folk magic in the mid-Atlantic colonies, including herbal lore, hexing, and scrying (seeing at a distance or over time by looking into crystal or liquid). However, most such practices fell prey to science in European-derived communities.[6] Updike's Rabbit Angstrom embodies the values of the Eisenhower years of his adolescence. He lives through the cold war, Vietnam, the moon shots, the assassinations, the oil shortage, the hostage crisis, and on into the presidency of George Bush. He identifies with imperialist America, believes in its promise of freedom and initially in a material form of the American Dream. Critics argue over Rabbit's typicality or lack thereof (he is white, after all); over his intellectual consciousness or lack thereof; over his morality or lack thereof. They also differ in the degree to which they distinguish or do not distinguish between Rabbit's views and Updike's.[7] Many of these critics comment on religion in the tetralogy. Although I agree that Rabbit's ongoing quest for meaning would be satisfied by his achieving a stronger belief in his childhood religion, Updike shows him responding to something more nebulous, something closer to magic.

Rabbit's lost magic is primarily that of the game and the perfect physical performance, a magic he experienced when he was a high school basketball star. Rabbit does believe in God, and, oddly, he associates the intensity and magic missing in his adult life with God. Rabbit cringes when the pastor, Eccles, challenges him about this missing something. Rabbit "really wants to be told about it, wants to be told that it is there, that [Eccles is] not lying to all those people every Sunday" (112). Rabbit finds his answer, his justification, a wordless assurance that perfection exists with the next swing of his golf club:

> The sound has a hollowness, a singleness he hasn't heard before. His arms force his head up and his ball is hung way out, lunarly pale against the beautiful black blue of storm clouds, his grandfather's color stretched dense

across the east. It recedes along a line straight as a ruler-edge. Stricken;
sphere, star, speck. It hesitates, and Rabbit thinks it will die, but he's
fooled, for the ball makes this hesitation the ground of a final leap: with a
kind of visible sob takes a last bite of space before vanishing in falling.
"That's *it!*" he cries. (*Rabbit, Run* 112–13)

Here is Rabbit's theology in a nutshell: meaning, even religious meaning, comes from perfect physical action. God can be in a golf ball or a basketball and seems more accessible there than as the God who lets Rabbit's
drunken wife accidentally drown their baby girl. In *Rabbit, Run*, the first
of the four books, Rabbit finds his work selling vegetable peelers pointless
and his marriage hopelessly second-rate. His version of the American
Dream of success—community glory, team fellowship with himself the
first among equals—has been taken away from him, and what America
offers to adults with nothing more than a high school education does not
seem to him worth living for.

In *Rabbit Redux,* Rabbit finds two people who help articulate for him a
sense of life's meaning. Jill, the white poor-little-rich-girl who has run away
from her family in a Porsche, talks to Rabbit and his son, Nelson, about
"God, beauty, meaning," declaring that "Man is a mechanism for turning
things into spirit and turning spirit into things" and insisting that "the
point is ecstasy. . . . Energy. Anything that is good is in ecstasy. The world
is what God made and it doesn't stink of money, it's never tired, too much
or too little, it's always exactly full" (142–43). Although capable of feeling
this indwelling spirit in the world, Jill cannot deal with the dross of everyday life and has sought ecstasy in drugs instead.

Skeeter, Rabbit's other oracle, is a black Vietnam veteran and a fugitive
from the law. As Matthew Wilson notes, Rabbit "is fascinated by Skeeter
because he still feels the attraction of disruptive energies, an electricity . . .
an eruption of the demonic" (12). In other words, Skeeter possesses a certain charismatic magic. Skeeter wants revolution and what lies beyond
that: God descending. "He's coming, Chuck, and Babychuck, and Lady-
chuck, let Him in. Pull down, shoot to kill, Chaos is His holy face. The
sun is burning through. The moon is turning red. The moon is a baby's head
bright red between his momma's legs" (230). Nelson screams at the notion of God's approach, but Rabbit accepts it, as he accepts just about everything. At least such a God would be there, would prove his reality.
Rabbit tries to find some comfort in the Vietnam War, feeling that "America is beyond power, it acts as in a dream, as a face of God. Wherever
America is, there is freedom, and wherever America is not, madness rules
with chains, darkness strangles millions. Beneath her patient bombers,
paradise is possible" (49). Vietnam, though, cannot give him much sense
of God's purpose. When he and his wife Janice put their marriage together

again for the second time, he snuggles down in bed with her, and "all sorts of winged presences exert themselves in the air above their covers" (350). Even if these are only insects—and Updike does not say that—the phrase "winged presences" reminds us of fairies or angels, otherworldly or magical beings, invisible but somehow felt to be there, impinging on Rabbit's senses at their outermost range of consciousness.

Rabbit Is Rich shows Rabbit still believing in God, though he is no closer to behaving in an approved Christian fashion. He is well off, thanks to the Toyota franchise that Janice has inherited from her father. Rabbit gets moments of well-being from running, driving, or occasionally from sex, but real contact with any indwelling spirit has disappeared; indeed, sex no longer offers him much but a sense that it puts him in touch with death.[8] As Updike writes: "When Harry [Rabbit] was little God used to spread in the dark above his bed like that and then when the bed became strange and the girl in the next aisle grew armpit hair He entered into the blood and muscle and nerve as an odd command and now He had withdrawn, giving Harry the respect due from one well-off gentleman to another, but for a calling card left in the pit of the stomach, a bit of lead true as a plumb bob pulling Harry down toward all those leaden dead in the hollow earth below" (231). God has "shrunk in Harry's middle years to the size of a raisin lost under the car seat" (390). The little bits of contact with a nonmaterial reality come mostly when Rabbit drifts off to sleep. He remembers reading in *Time* about a book—unidentified, but clearly Julian Jaynes's *Origin of Consciousness in the Breakdown of the Bicameral Mind*—in which the author claims that "in ancient times the gods spoke to people directly through the left or was it the right half of their brains" (462). Rabbit identifies this experience with his own: "just before drifting off he hears Mom's voice clear as a whisper from the corner of the room saying *Hassy*, a name as dead as the boy that was called that is dead. Maybe the dead are gods" (462). As in William Kennedy's or Gloria Naylor's world, the dead are not just memories. While "the boy" may be dead, his mother can still talk.

In *Rabbit, Run*, Rabbit is simply an unheroic protagonist. By *Rabbit Redux*, he begins to take on mythic proportions. He is in some sense white, lower-middle-class America, and his puzzled and sometimes dreamlike encounters with Jill and Skeeter show America trying unsuccessfully to come to terms with drugs and racial issues. By *Rabbit Is Rich*, he is outwardly the American Dream incarnate: from failed salesman, to laid-off blue-collar linotyper, to well-off car dealer, he has moved from poverty to affluence. He owns a house in a semiposh development and belongs to a country club.[9] Nevertheless, like America, he is running out of gas and running scared. He has gained all that he ever dreamed of by way of personal earthly goods but finds life hollow.

Rabbit at Rest develops further this image of Rabbit as America—or at

least as the white America of his generation—since his son, Nelson, in-
dulges in the vices of a younger America. Father and son argue over the
meaning of the American Dream. Nelson insists that the $40,000 he makes
from the Toyota franchise are not enough: "People don't make money an
hour at a time any more; you just get yourself in the right position and it
comes. I know guys, lawyers, guys in real estate, no older than me and not
as smart who pull in two, three hundred K on a single transaction. You
must know a lot of retired money down here. It's *easy* to be rich, that's
what this country is all about" (31). When Rabbit discusses the American
Dream with his retired golfing buddies, they see two routes to happiness:
the chemical shortcut or a long life of hard work, and they admit that
"when you've gone the distance," the happiness is "behind you" (47). Pre-
ferring the chemical route, Nelson has squandered much of the family
assets on his cocaine habit. He wants the product of science and technology to make him happy by changing his chemicals.

Rabbit still wants to believe in God, but his God is silent. He wants to
believe in himself as "a God-made one-of-a-kind with an immortal soul
breathed in. A vehicle of grace. A battlefield of good and evil. An apprentice angel" (196). However, his heart operation suggests all too clearly that
he is just a soft machine whose valves can be replaced with pig-valves if
necessary. Rabbit muses that back in the 1960s, when no one else believed
in God, he did; but now, "He is like a friend you've had so long you've
forgotten what you liked about Him" (373). Trying for that ecstasy of energy and bodily perfection, Rabbit plays basketball with some black teenagers and succumbs to a heart attack. No grand vision, no reassurance that
all will be well. He dies in the hospital while trying to tell Nelson that
dying is not all that bad.

Throughout the tetralogy, Updike seems concerned to paint America of
the relevant decade (the 1950s, 1960s, 1970s, 1980s). Updike lovingly pens
in bits of news, pop music blaring from car radios, and consumer items.
Rabbit is in tune with all these fragments of America. Rabbit is haunted
in the first half of his adult life by the failure of the American Dream to
work for him. In the second half, he suffers from the knowledge that it has
worked, but that material prosperity is not enough to constitute a valid
dream. Those flashes of divinity from his youth, the moments of intensity when playing basketball or driving a golf ball, do not stay with him and
cannot be brought back to comfort him when he needs assurance. Intensity through drugs is not his style. Nor is his conventional religious training enough to give him a sense of fulfillment. The Dream is there, tanta-
lizing, and so is God, but Rabbit cannot grasp them or hold them tight.
Updike's faith may remain unshaken, but Rabbit's seems too stunted to
supply him with meaning. The novels charting Rabbit's life circle round
and round this absence of intensity, magic, and spiritual value. He has lost

something that might have worked in the past or for others; it seems banished from the rationalized American world as it has turned out for an ordinary white American.

The Melodramatic Imagination: Anaya and Kennedy

Whereas Momaday and Updike accept a traditional religion and show their characters striving (with different success) to assimilate that spiritual system, Rudolfo Anaya and William Kennedy seem to doubt that the old institutions can or should be entirely recovered. The systems they scrutinize for usable value are already fragmented and made up of conflicting traditions. Anaya and Kennedy push beyond material reality in hopes of identifying elements of older spiritual worlds that might still be able to function in modern culture. Peter Brooks describes a goal very like theirs in his discussion of the melodramatic imagination: "The melodramatic imagination is . . . a way of perceiving and imagining the spiritual in a world where there is no longer any clear idea of the sacred, no generally accepted societal moral imperatives, where the body of the ethical has become a sort of *deus absconditus* which must be sought for, posited, brought into man's existence through exercise of the spiritualist imagination" (209). The realm of the moral occult, which this imagination strives to understand, is one where "there is no clear system of sacred myth, no unity of belief, no accepted metaphorical chain leading from the phenomenal to the spiritual, only a fragmented society and fragments of myths" (210).

Bless Me, Ultima (1972)

Rudolfo Anaya's *Bless Me, Ultima*, like Momaday's *House Made of Dawn*, centers on witchery: in this case, it is a duel between a *curandera* (herbal healer) named Ultima and a *brujo* (sorcerer) named Tenorio and his three *bruja* (witch) daughters. Within this story, the protagonist, Antonio, tries to make sense of the various worldviews he is getting from his Euro-American grade school, the Roman Catholic Church, his vaquero father, and his farm-raised mother. He also learns from a playmate who knows Native American traditions and worships a human-sized golden carp as a living god. Ultima herself, a wise woman who works within the American Indian metaphysical view, teaches him about a cyclical and balanced universe. He hopes that by absorbing her wisdom he can escape the conflicting demands that he follow his vaquero father's wandering ways or his mother's rootedness in the soil or, indeed, her desire that he become a priest. Evidently, parts of *Bless Me, Ultima* are autobiographical. Given Antonio's final dream, we conclude that becoming a novelist is the solution to all the claims on the boy, the modification of archaic fragments to something

contemporary by translating them into fiction. The book was also written at a time when Chicano culture was organizing itself politically. As
Anaya himself describes it in "Aztlán," "The naming of Aztlán was a spon-
taneous act which took place throughout the Southwest, and the feat was
given authenticity in a meeting that was held in Denver in 1969 to draft
El Plan Espiritual de Aztlán" (232). Even as the community tries to define
itself as a movement of the spirit, Anaya works to preserve a picture of
spiritual elements in the community that are being overwhelmed by the
surrounding gringo culture.

As a *curandera*, most of Ultima's life is given over to gathering and dis-
pensing herbs. However, she is not just an herbal doctor and Christian
midwife. She has a familiar spirit, an owl, and when Tenorio shoots it, she
dies a few minutes later. Her human body will receive Christian burial;
as Antonio realizes, though, her real burial will be when he buries the owl.
(When she had agreed to fight the hex laid on Antonio's uncle by Tenorio,
she knew that this might lead to her own death.[10]) Before the story is over,
Tenorio and two of his daughters, Ultima, and a friend of the family have
died, and Antonio himself twice narrowly escapes being shot. While life
is going peacefully in the village, Ultima is assumed to be respectable.
When the issue of her purported powers is raised, she passes a test to de-
tect witches and so is absolved of any such evildoing, though Antonio
thinks he sees something that invalidates that test. Certainly, Antonio later
learns that she does have some wax and clay figurines that have evidently
been used against Tenorio's daughters. In other words, she may be a white
witch most of the time and is certainly a benign healer, but she is neither
ignorant of, nor entirely innocent of, darker doings.

Antonio's contact with his culture's various value systems is intensified
by ten densely symbolic dreams, described with a grandeur that makes
them sound like out-of-body experiences or trips to a spiritual otherworld.
In the final dream, he sees all the sources of holy power and meaning in
his life desecrated and dead: the Catholic Church (in which he never truly felt God even at his first communion), the carp slaughtered, Ultima
murdered. As these powers depart in the dream, they cry out, *"We live
when you dream, Tony, we live only in your dreams"* (244; italics in original). His dreams, and later his fiction and poetry, will be his magic; through
them, the ethnic magic will live on. He enters the ongoing flow of magic
but translates it into a new idiom.[11]

In "The Dynamics of Myth," Enrique Lamadrid points out that the novel
is "full of conflict, yet non combative" (244). The solution to conflict lies
in Ultima's way of seeing resolution by placing opposites in a system of
balances or in a continuity. When the viewpoints of the Luna and Marez
families are symbolized in his dream as sweet- and saltwater, the dream-
Ultima tells him how to reconcile them: *"The sweet water of the moon*

which falls as rain is the same water that gathers into rivers and flows to fill the seas. Without the waters of the moon to replenish the oceans there would be no oceans. And the same salt waters of the oceans are drawn up by the sun to the heavens, and in turn become again the waters of the moon.... The waters are one, Antonio.... You have been seeing only parts, she finished, and not looking beyond into the great cycle that binds us all" (121; italics in original). This wisdom-oriented Native American attitude toward life encourages one to harmonize contradictions and conflicts. As will be discussed later in the chapter, an attitude valuing courage over wisdom (like Norman Mailer's) demands repeated, agonized confrontations, as if the only way to reach higher vision is to hurl oneself head-on against a wall until the wall is breached.

Magic in this novel is also partly the "magic" of lost childhood, not unlike that in Ray Bradbury's *Dandelion Wine,* but Bradbury's flirtation with witchcraft is only a game. Anaya's witches do kill people and can cause melon-sized rocks to fall from the sky. The world of the 1940s that Anaya describes was a time of change; ways of life were dying out. The culture was under pressure from public schools and government programs to become more Americanized. The Luna farm life, the Marez vaquero life (destroyed by barbed-wire enclosures), the Indian myths concerning the goldfish, and the knowledge of plants: these are all being lost to cultural attrition. More generally, the matriarchal powers of the peasant, earth-oriented world are missing in mainstream society. The villagers are losing a world in which magic and their own dramatic role in the clash between good and evil is an accepted and accessible dimension of existence. What science offers in return is the Trinity site testing of the atomic bomb. The wisdom and humanity of Ultima make the magic seem basically good in this novel, worth the accompanying shadow of evil witchery. Science does unimaginable things like split the atom and detonate atomic explosions, but these are abstract, distant, and not of any use locally. Antonio seeks to rescue from the past at least elements of its spiritual life and perpetuate them in his fiction. He testifies to a world that may have experienced conflicting spiritual dimensions but did not suffer from their deadening lack.

Legs (1975), *Billy Phelan's Greatest Game* (1978), and *Ironweed* (1983)

According to Euro-American categories, Momaday and Anaya represent non-European ethnic traditions and can be considered marginal in relation to Western culture. In fact, what they do is very much what we find in a writer like William Kennedy, and his spiritual project resembles theirs more than Updike's. Discontented attacks on the scientific, secular worldview should never be casually equated with low-tech ignorance or non-

European superstition. Quite apart from the fact that Momaday, Anaya, Naylor, and Silko are highly educated, the same literary strategies are being used by Euro-American writers.

William Kennedy has become the chronicler of Albany, New York, and has written several books on an interlocking set of Irish-American families. He starts in the mid-nineteenth century with *Quinn's Book*, and later volumes so far cover the period up to 1958. I shall focus on three set in the late 1920s and late 1930s, because each features a different kind of magic. Kennedy's Irish immigrants show little anguish over not achieving financial success in America. Many of his characters are poor, but they know their Irish ancestors were poorer. They escape immigrant disillusionment with America, however, by valuing something more than money. His main characters can still touch magic in various forms. Kennedy writes a form of magic realism in which the ethnic background for the magic is Irish.[12] Ireland is a land, after all, in which a few pre-Christian folk practices have lasted into present times: holy wells, the banshee or *bean sidhe* (queen of the mound), and the goddess Brigid (now under the name of a saint). Kennedy's method of constructing reality is very much like those of Momaday, Anaya, and Naylor: their characters are officially Christian, but all respond to extra-Christian traditions and magic and make those define reality.

The kind of magic illustrated in *Legs* is essentially charisma, here portrayed as an intensity of engagement that makes Jack "Legs" Diamond himself and all life in his vicinity glow with meaning.[13] Diamond, the bootlegger and gangster, has this quality, and it draws to him men like the narrator, a lawyer named Marcus Gorman. Gorman gives up his political ambitions to serve Diamond and considers it a small price to pay for being so close to such an incandescent source of energy. To Gorman, Diamond is "one of the truly new American Irishmen of his day; Horatio Alger out of Finn McCool and Jesse James, shaping the dream that you could grow up in America and shoot your way to glory and riches" (13). Legs is "a fusion of the individual life flux with the clear and violent light of American reality, with the fundamental Columbian brilliance that illuminates this bloody republic" (14). Gorman notes this power the first time they meet: "Jack responded by standing up and jiggling, a moving glob of electricity, a live wire snaking its way around the porch. I knew then that this man was alive in a way I was not. I saw the vital principle of his elbow, the cut of his smile, the twist of his pronged fingers. . . . He hit you, slapped you with his palm . . . ridding himself of electricity to avoid exploding. . . . You felt something had descended upon him, tongues of fire maybe or his phlogiston itself, burning its way into your own spirit" (36).

Gorman is Catholic enough to be uncomfortable dealing with a man whom he suspects of being a murderer, but he is wooed with great skill.

Diamond offers him the chance to try a machine gun, and the target is an image of Dutch Schultz. The fact that the target represents a bootlegging rival bothers Gorman. He fears he may find himself in a situation where he must shoot at such a rival: "Powerful Irish Catholic magic at work that prohibits shooting effigies on the side of a barn. Bless me Father for I have sinned. I shot at Mr. Schultz's picture. And did you hit it, son? No, Father, I missed. For your penance say two rosaries and try again for the son of a bitch. . . . Millenniums of psychology, civilization, experience, turpitude. Man also develops Milquetoasts by natural selection. Would I defend him if some shooters walked through the barn door? What difference from defending him in court?" (40). Gorman proves to be a sharpshooter. When he admits to one of Diamond's men that he wiped out the cardboard Schultz's mouth, he is told: "Just what he deserves. The prick killed a kid cousin of mine last week in Jersey" (41). This response gives Gorman a sense of moral justification for his ethical lapse. When trying to come to terms with the murder of Charlie Northrup, Gorman thinks of the celebrity status of gangsters and their "permission from the social order to kill, maim, and befoul the legal system, for wasn't he performing a social mission for the masses? The system would stay healthy by having life both ways: first, relishing Jack's achievement while it served a function, then slavering sensually when his head, no longer necessary, rolled. This insight softened my hard line [on] Northrup. Maybe it was all a bootlegger's feud, which somehow made the consequent death okay" (85).

Diamond's energy takes several forms. He actually seems to luminesce when standing in shade. Gorman mentions having learned later about Kirilian auras and wonders if those are the energies he was able to see, indicating his attempt to rationalize and render scientific his subjective experience. Being close to such energy augments Gorman's own sense of energy. As he is drawn in, becoming an accessory, he finds the results empowering and intoxicating. Here, as when firing the machine gun, the effect is also sexual. His masculine drive is enhanced. The energy is also spiritual and a matter of style: Jack Diamond resembles Jay Gatsby and drives a roadster like Gatsby's. Indeed, the fictionalized Diamond knows F. Scott Fitzgerald and has been working for Arnold Rothstein, the original of the gangster in Fitzgerald's novel. Jack's energy is also that of the demagogue. One of his advisers suggests that he could accrue millions legally if he became an evangelist; and as the adviser outlines the sequence of events, we as readers agree that it would work—America would lap it up. So strong is his electric power over the living that Gorman experiences contact with Diamond's postmortem consciousness. As Jack's spirit finally disappears "into the darkness where the white was still elusive," Jack says, "I really don't think I'm dead" (317). Some of Gorman's earliest words in the novel are that he does not really think, cannot really believe, that Jack Diamond is dead, despite seeing that the back of his head has been blown away. Diamond seems a spirit greater than merely human, maybe descended from a higher sphere—or raised from a lower. One critic, Anya Taylor, even sees him as demonic and the novel itself as a reprise of Dante's *Inferno* (116). Those around him worry very little about his morality, however, and cannot get enough of their sense that they are in touch with the extraordinary.

That energy and its magic are too powerful for death to seem plausible; in this respect, Diamond has the same effect as the similarly charismatic Irish-American John F. Kennedy, whom many Americans were sure had not really died in Dallas.[14] Of course, one function of magic, of a nonmaterial reality, is to persuade us that something beyond the death of the body is possible; science has never provided us with evidence of this. William Kennedy finds such a power operating not in the licit structures of America but on the outlaw edges.

Diamond was finally rubbed out in 1931. *Billy Phelan's Greatest Game* and *Ironweed* both concern the same few days in October and November 1938, and they make passing references to Diamond as a recent celebrity and Marcus Gorman as a prominent lawyer. *Billy Phelan's Greatest Game* shows magic in the form of pool and card playing, gambling, and second sight. Knowing the odds and figuring them scientifically is one thing, but Billy can often reach through to touch magic when the pressure is on, though it takes special circumstances to rouse him to his best. "Billy roamed through the grandness of all games, yeoman here, journeyman there, low-level maestro unlikely to transcend, either as gambler, card dealer, dice or pool shooter. He'd been a decent shortstop in the city-wide Twilight League. . . . He was a champion drinker . . . a double-twenty specialist at the dart board, a chancy small-time bookie, and so on and so on" (6). Billy leads this life for the adrenaline buzz it gives: "he was really feeling the sweet pressure, and had been, all through the hand: rising, rising. And he keeps winning on top of that. It was so great he was almost ready to cream" (122). Billy wins, but winning rather than the money won is what matters; the money disappears quickly to more games, drinking, and generous handouts to those in need.

Martin Daugherty, a would-be fiction writer and successful journalist, is another channel for a different kind of magic in this novel. "The source of [his gift] was wondered at suspiciously by his Irish-born wife, who had been taught in the rocky wastes of Connemara that druids roamed the land, even to this day" (26). He knows that he will get phone calls from someone long absent from his life on the day the call indeed comes. He makes many clairvoyant leaps that always prove correct. He can bet on horses chosen for their names and win on such hunches and coincidences. Martin has occasional dream visions. What most of us take to be coincidence, he finds to be meaningfully connected.

The novel concerns an Irish-American political boss's son being kidnapped, the victim having grown up on the same street as both Billy and Martin. Billy gets himself barred from all the pool halls and gaming places controlled by that boss (all of Billy's world) because he refuses to spy on Morrie Berman. Berman had saved Billy's life in a brawl, but he may have a connection to the kidnappers. However, Billy does pass along an inexplicable reaction to his mentioning Newark, New Jersey, to Berman, and this proves to be where the kidnappers are caught. Martin tries to get Billy readmitted to the night world of Albany by writing a column on his magic insight:

> Yet even this was not a betrayal of Berman, for Berman had told Billy the truth [as he knew it] about Newark: Maloy was not there, and had no plans to go there.
> "Though I doubt he believes it," Martin wrote, "Billy knew Maloy would go to Newark at some point. He knew this intuitively, his insight as much touched with magic, or spiritual penetration of the future, as was any utterance of the biblical prophets which time has proved true." (272)

The power Martin attributes to Billy seems much more Martin's own kind of magic, but the column does its work and Billy is readmitted to the gaming world. The claims in the column make sense to the men of this world. One way or another, they are familiar with powers that go beyond the merely logical. In various ways, those with the magic are men who enjoy the proverbial luck of the Irish.

Ironweed portrays a man dealing with magic in terms of ghosts. Whereas Naylor's dead are audible under the right circumstances, and Anaya's dead appear in grandiloquent dream visions, Francis Phelan sees his ghosts in the streets, on a bus, or even building a bleacher in his backyard. Francis, Billy Phelan's father, was once a baseball player and is now a hobo. He has returned to his hometown of Albany after years of absence. One layer in the novel is a reprise of the *Odyssey*, complete with the grown son Billy corresponding to Telemachus; faithful wife Annie paralleling Penelope; Calypso represented by Helen, Francis's hobo-world wife; a welcoming bath; and a battle fought after the return.[15] Odysseus's reasons for leaving home did not make him an outcast. Francis, however, left (twice) to escape the consequences of his acts; he returns as a man haunted at first by the people he personally has killed, then by others, family and friends, who are dead. His life ceased to follow the common pattern when he used his third baseman's throwing arm to kill a strikebreaker with a rock; in the ensuing melee, two more bystanders were killed as well. In addition to those souls, he is also responsible for the death of his newborn son, Gerald. The baby slid from his father's awkward grasp and died of a broken neck. As a bum, Francis once killed another hobo who tried to hack off his feet with an ax to steal his boots. At the end of the book, he chalks up another death, for the vigilante whose back he broke has died. In what may or may not be the last couple of days of his life, Francis tries to make sense of what he is, what he has become, why he became a bum, and whether an afterlife is possible.[16]

Phelan's visible ghosts are not the only ones readers encounter in the course of the narrative. As he digs graves, he passes through the part of the cemetery where his parents lie: "Francis's mother twitched nervously in her grave as the truck carried him nearer to her; and Francis's father lit his pipe, smiled at his wife's discomfort, and looked out from his own bit of sod to catch a glimpse of how much his son had changed since the train accident. Francis's father smoked roots of grass that had died in the periodic droughts afflicting the cemetery. . . . Francis's mother wove crosses from the dead dandelions and other deep-rooted weeds; careful to preserve their fullest length, she wove them while they were still in the green stage of death, then ate them with an insatiable revulsion" (1–2). Kennedy gives us this wryly grotesque vignette independent of Francis's visions, so we cannot shrug off the figures he sees as the result of delirium tremens or insanity. The dead infant son, because of his innocence, enjoys an unusual postmortem existence, and Kennedy describes this at some length. Gerald is given the gift of tongues and strange physical perfection: "Gerald rested in his infantile sublimity, exuding a high gloss induced by early death, his skin a radiant white-gold, his nails a silvery gray, his cluster of curls and large eyes perfectly matched in gleaming ebony" (17). Gerald silently imposes "the pressing obligation to perform his final acts of expiation for abandoning the family" (19). Francis does not seem aware of these particular lives below the surface of the graveyard as we see them, but he knows himself to move in a world where the dead are still living in some sense, still shaping the present.[17]

Writers who treat the past as still living in the present tend to be conservative; liberals link the present to the future. Liberals see man as capable of moral improvement, whereas conservatives start with a Hobbesian or Darwinian concept of human nature or with original sin. Kennedy, writing out of conservative values, turns to the same image that haunts many conservative writers: man's ultimate nature is that of the killer. Saul Bellow recognizes this in his Mr. Sammler, and Walker Percy worries over it in terms of our eagerness to legalize euthanasia. Norman Mailer will say the same about Stephen Rojack and several other characters in *An American Dream*. Francis Phelan recognizes that he "seemed now to have always been the family killer" (145). Like Bellow and Mailer, Kennedy realizes that such a capacity for violence can bring one close to revelation. Francis feels it darkly when striking back at the American Legion thugs who have come to maim and kill hoboes in their cardboard camp. Francis, who earlier the same evening had given his own food to a homeless family with a young baby, feels ecstasy when hitting the backbone of a vigilante. He feels ecstasy without the violence when given the chance to take a bath and put on clean clothes: "A great sunburst entered the darkening skies, a radiance so sudden that it seemed like a bolt of lightning; yet its brilliance remained, as if some angel of beatific lucidity were hovering outside the bathroom window" (172).

After Francis takes his dying pal, Rudy, to the hospital—the third of his fellow hoboes to die in these two days—the narrative enters a strange conditional mood. Kennedy writes: "He would walk. . . . he would reenter the cold. . . . By dawn he would be on a Delaware & Hudson freight heading south toward the lemonade springs" (224). Lemonade Springs is one of the features of Big Rock Candy Mountain, an American folk version of the Land of Cockaigne and possibly here a happy image for life after death. Francis feels the corpses and ghosts fading from him. He may simply be dying: "Francis, this twofold creature, now an old man in a mortal slouch, now again a fledgling bird of uncertain wing, would sing along softly with the women" (222). But then again, he may not. His strange spiritual state may just reflect the point at which he has done sufficient penance for his murders and for leaving his family, and now he is shuffling off their weight. We are told that angels are manifested in the primum mobile and that Francis might like a cot in Danny's room, as if both pieces of information were equal in weight. He dies, he flees south again in a boxcar with a ghost, he escapes his ghosts and rejoins his family—we never know which of these possible endings is to be realized. A later novel, *Very Old Bones*, will place his death in 1943, so Kennedy evidently decided that this was not to be death, but *Ironweed* itself leaves us unable to determine the outcome. What we are left with is this strange spiritual state, with its awareness of a world beyond ours, brought about by the ghosts making a crossroads between the other world and ours.[18]

Francis is Catholic, though not exactly practicing. He still believes in some form of hell and heaven, though hell is clearer to him, "a foul mist above a hole in the ground where the earth itself purges away the stench of life's rot" (223). He is capable of hearing something like the music of the spheres: "the bottle and the moon made music like a soulful banjo when they moved through the heavens, divine harmonies" (225). His life of wandering seems partly a spiritual statement. Running was "a condition that was as pleasurable to his being as it was natural: the running of bases after the crack of the bat, the running from accusation, the running from the calumny of men and women, the running from family, from bondage, from destitution of spirit through ritualistic straightenings, the running, finally, in a quest for pure flight as a fulfilling mannerism of the spir-

it" (75). In this, he is like Updike's Rabbit and many other American heroes, for whom running is a natural expression of their souls. For Francis,
such fugitive existence nevertheless has meaning. The air he breathes and
the sky above him are loaded with meaning, which is sometimes made visible to him. He knows that he does not understand why his life has worked
out as it has, but he takes responsibility for his actions and yet knows that
they are part of a plan, even if he is not privy to the larger picture.

When Kennedy tackles magic in this novel, he goes far beyond mere
second sight, gaming luck, and charisma. Anya Taylor calls Francis Phelan
a Celtic warrior (114), and Michael Yetman sees him as a Romantic hero
and an American male hero who flees his weaker feminine side (102–3);
he is also a strangely saintly man with his life of penance lived in weeds
by railroad tracks, a violent saint. Kennedy is writing about the 1930s and
presents that decade as a time when the doors between the next life and
this were still open.

In *Very Old Bones*, Kennedy frequently uses the term magic but applies
it to the nonsupernatural. The power of the dead is reduced to metaphor
and memory, and gaming magic becomes sleight-of-hand cheating at cards.
The late 1950s, when the novel is set, appears to be the time when magic
started to withdraw, no longer available even to those whose culture fostered belief in it. The earlier novels show Kennedy creating worlds in which
magic in various forms exists, functions, and yields for many a sense of
meaning in life. By bringing out these more traditional and spiritual facets now lost to many middle-class Americans, Kennedy implies something
about our loss without ever establishing a direct comparison; he never
actually says that America has lost its magic. Most readers at the end of
this century have to acknowledge that the America they know lacks this
dimension, this spiritual quality, and marvel at this detailed, unfolding
vision of Albany in such spiritual terms. Science does not admit of ghosts.
The secular world does not take heaven or hell seriously. Kennedy's is an
Irish form of magic realism, and all the various magics in the novel—
whether characteristic of the bard and artist, the warrior, the gamester, the
man with second sight, the saint—are arguably Irish. In this novel, they
create a spiritual layer to experience that differs notably from any spiritual level still accessible through life conducted in shopping malls and on
the Internet.

Creating New Realms of the Spirit: Mailer and Pynchon

The differences between Momaday and Updike, Anaya and Kennedy, and
Norman Mailer and Thomas Pynchon are differences in degree, with the
spiritual realm being most coherently religious in the first two and least

religious in the last pair. Mailer and Pynchon both exercise their melodramatic imaginations, but when they borrow something from a religious tradition, it is likely to be esoteric or occult and possibly non-Western.

An American Dream (1965)

This novel is infamous for doing something offensive so well. Mailer portrays a man murdering his wife and, thanks to his privatizing of morality, presents this as justified.[19] He makes his case in prose so electric that it demands attention for the book even from those who would rather it be forgotten. One can deprecate the effect by calling the novel overwritten, but it throbs with erotic and magic-oriented vitality, and it impresses readers for distinguishing among gradations of sense-data that most of us lump together and pass through, virtually unaware. The narrative consciousness of this book has some kind of hyperlife. Such pulsing awareness, Mailer argues, is one of life's major desiderata.

Given a man's murdering a woman whom he could divorce, no one should be surprised that critics differ on how to read this novel. The important distinctions for my purposes involve Mailer's sense of magic. Some interpreters like Wagenheim and Gordon insist that it is not a realistic story at all, but a dream to be read in Freudian terms, a spiritual quest-vision in which the devil, a witch, and other symbolic figures are not humans, and Rojack's killing of the witch is not murder, any more than Abel's killing the albino is in *House Made of Dawn*. In "The Modern Dream-Vision," Gordon argues that "magic *does* rule in this dream-world: either we accept that as proved, or else Rojack is entirely insane, which would invalidate the whole novel" (103). Dreaming is Gordon's comfortable explanation that avoids insanity or treating magic as real. Others prefer to take the murder as the killing of a human and also accept the magic; I am inclined to do so, while not ruling out a Freudian reading of oedipal struggle with parental figures as relevant to how this novel works on psychological levels. Nor does treating the magic as real undercut Mailer's struggle with the concept of the American Dream;[20] the magic, as I am arguing here, is in fact part of his critique of America.

Norman Mailer's world is predicated on conflict and Darwinian struggle for supremacy and survival. Some elements he takes from Kabbalistic metaphysics. Some are macho and influenced by Hemingway. His medical morality makes cancer a punishment for spiritual failures. To this brew, he adds the hope of reincarnation. Throughout the novel, he imagines the world to be saturated with magic, and he seems to mean this literally; or, at any rate, he would like to believe in it.[21] The outlook is found in many of his writings, nonfiction as well as fiction. His is not just the magic of momentary intensity found in Kerouac's *On the Road*, where Dean Moriarty finds time standing still as he listens to a jazzman or responds to visionary primitivism in Mexico. Nor is it the more sentimental magic invoked in Waller's *Bridges of Madison County*, the magic of a supposedly perfect love and of a jazz musician's ability to reach magic through playing. Mailer's magic permits his protagonist to do things considered scientifically impossible, and the magic derives in part from a metaphysical background of Kabbalistic theogony. Mailer's God may not win in his struggle with the devil.[22] If God is to triumph, it can only be with the help of humanity. Every time a human fails in an act of courage, God is diminished. Every act of courage and every "good" orgasm give one access to God and give power to God's cause. Mailer defines sex in bad faith as masturbation, homosexuality, using contraception, or coupling with someone who does not matter. Such bad-faith sex and other failures of the spirit diminish the person who thus transgresses and open the body to cancer. Someone who always avoids challenge, who develops a weaseling soul, will lose that soul and be extinguished by death. Only the brave have some chance of rebirth.[23]

Mailer's example of someone living the American Dream is more extravagant than most. Stephen Rojack becomes a full professor at a prestigious school in an amazingly short time after gaining a Ph.D.[24] He has become a successful author and the host of a popular television program. People in the street recognize his face. He knows John F. Kennedy well enough to call him Jack. He marries a fabulously beautiful woman whose unbelievably wealthy Irish-American father is a gray eminence who pulls the strings of America and Europe through wealth, the mafia, and aristocratic Catholics. Rojack might have parlayed this nexus of American fantasies into a political career but has found politics a violation of his true self. Indeed, he does not altogether know what to do with his life and is hampered by the hopelessly storm-tossed state of his marriage. His lioness of a wife, Deborah, he feels, is trying to break his spirit before discarding him, and his manhood resists being broken. Instead, he strangles her, throws her off the balcony, and manages to escape the clutches of the law. At the moment of strangling her, he finds himself at one of his spiritual checkpoints. In a vision, he sees a door opening; however, he states that when he nearly lets up on pressuring her neck, "the door I had been opening began to close. But I had had a view of what was on the other side of the door, and heaven was there, some quiver of jewelled cities shining in the glow of a tropical dusk, and I thrust against the door once more" (38). From the point of view of living one's true desires, of reaching true courage, murder is appropriate, according to Mailer, and it carries with it tinges of exotic and apocalyptic fantasy.

No life of the spirit is easy. Rojack is as tempted as Saint Anthony to give in, to accept mediocrity or compromise, to flee the tests of his courage, and he does fail some tests. However, this life of the spirit is also in one sense blindingly simple: he hears voices. Almost always, they are to be believed and obeyed. Once, when a voice tells him to turn a whiskey bottle into a weapon, he decides that to be a temptation to be resisted, and he is right; usually, though, he need not worry about ambiguities. He knows what he should do at every point, thanks to these voices or this dissociation within his own consciousness, and his code simply demands that he always do what he fears most. When standing over his wife's body, something tells him not to telephone the police. Another "solution was finding its way up through myself, a messenger from that magician who solved all riddles was on his way, ascending those endless stairs from the buried gaming rooms of the unconscious to the tower of the brain" (47). When making love with Cherry, the singer Rojack falls in love with the same night that he kills his wife, a voice whispers to him: "Do you really want her, do you want to know something about love at last?" (131). When Rojack must atone for his unfair fight with Cherry's former lover, Shango, his mind and then Shango's umbrella say to him: "If you love Cherry, go to Harlem" (211). He argues with that voice, pleading,

> "Let me love her some way not altogether deranged and doomed. It makes no sense to go to Harlem. Let me love her and be sensible as well."
> "The sensible are never free," said the voice.
> "Let me be free of you."
> "Free as you wish," said the voice, and something departed from me.
> (211)

And free he is; a higher level of the divine voice departs from him. Clearly, he resembles Julian Jaynes's man with a bicameral mind whose gods speak to him and with whom Updike's Rabbit had identified.

Magic and the supernatural operate in several fashions in the story. Rojack's father-in-law, Barney Oswald Kelly, consciously made a pact with the devil to gain a child, with whom he later commits incest. As a result of the pact, Kelly knows by ESP which stocks will go up. Rojack's murder similarly introduces him into the devil's realm, although whether as challenge or pact is arguable. As Jessica Gerson points out in "Norman Mailer: Sex, Creativity, and God," the anal sex with Ruta (Deborah's maid) is part of a Faustian Walpurgisnacht (9). Rojack's powers manifest themselves when he is listening to the nightclub singer who wins his heart, for he is able to affect other denizens of the club by shooting psychic pellets at them. Not only do all of them respond, they know what is happening and apparently have similar, if weaker, powers:

> I fired a battery of guns at him. His laughter stopped in the middle; he scowled as if four very bad eggs had been crushed on his head. His nos-

trils screwed down to the turn of disgust I expected would be in the smell. He looked about. He, in his turn, calculated, (he was no stranger to such attacks) located me as the probable source, and proceeded to kick an imaginary foot deep into my crotch. My shield went down to block it. Blocked! "Your foot hurts," said my mind to him, and he looked depressed. After a while he started to rub the toe of that shoe against his calf. (102)

This is not just magic as metaphor; Mailer makes major demands on us as readers, demands that many readers resist and others accept by seeing this as part of the vibrant intensification of reality that Mailer is attempting.

Rojack faces a series of psychic tests that grow out of his relationship with Cherry. It culminates in voices telling him to walk twice around a terrace parapet thirty stories in the air. Only thus can he redeem his failures. He makes it once around the parapet, drunk though he is, but balks at a second attempt, despite learning from the voices that the second time would have saved Cherry and the child he believes he has begotten on her. His thoughts assure him that if he jumped the thirty stories, his violent death "would give some better heart to that embryo just created, that indeed [he himself] might even be created again, free of [his] past" (226). After Cherry's death, Rojack takes off for Las Vegas and finds that Cherry has left him the magic gift she herself had enjoyed in Vegas: "I knew the luck in the hand of each man who came to the table. . . . I kept an eye for the losers and worked up the fortune there. In four weeks I made twenty-four, paid my debts, all sixteen plus the loan for the car, and got ready to go on" (270). Like many an American protagonist, he has had problems creating an adult relationship with a woman, has felt but repressed an attraction toward a black man, has to some extent fallen from grace, and is heading away from conventional civilization toward the primitive (in his case, the Guatemalan jungle). Huck Finn, Rabbit Angstrom, Tyrone Slothrop, Stephen Rojack: the list of Fiedlerian American heroes continues to grow.

As Susan Glickman has pointed out, there are many parallels between this novel and Bellow's *Mr. Sammler's Planet*, including the ecstasy felt in killing Germans, the knowledge in one's heart of one's contract with the Creator, and the image of humans being fundamentally killers. In Mailer's world, this last facet applies to women as well as men, since Deborah and Cherry as well as Rojack and Kelly are given that trait. Bellow, however, sees the best life as service to others and as a contribution to a shared culture. In this, Bellow reflects the society-oriented, classical form of conservatism. Sammler tells Wallace to repress the sorts of impulsive messages from his subconscious that Rojack cultivates as the highest part of life. Mailer's "left conservatism," which belongs to the individual-oriented version of conservatism, defines life's aim in a much more romantic and libertarian fashion. Society matters not at all; its role in one's life consists of accidentals. Nor does the scientific perception of the universe matter; forensic science, after all, gives the police clues to the reality of the murder, but they prove unable to daunt Rojack's honed, combative will and are powerless before the demonic influence of Kelly.

What matters is the individual soul, its determination never to give in to fear, and its doing anything demanded by this cult of courage. As long as one lives on the edge, one will enjoy the sense of meaning, the magic that life produces for the spiritual elite. Failure to do so will quickly sink one into the complacent and meaningless life of the spiritless mob, and most Americans live their lives without that magic. Readers' responses to this stance depend on their own politics and their conception of the individual's obligations to society. Reader response is also likely to be influenced by gender. For many feminists, Deborah is an attractively powerful woman, and her murder is a particularly contemptible piece of masculine cowardice, emblematic of what they see as a symbolic expression of the all-too-common masculine response to women exercising power. For them, Rojack's fears that Deborah may break his spirit seem ludicrous, and his murderous response is indefensible. A male fan of the book with whom I talked sees the murder as both forbidden and wrong and yet necessary.

Mailer's spiritual dimension consists of the theogony demanding courage from humans and of the magical powers available to those who will take risks. The magic powers can be dismissed by readers as wishful thinking without weakening the feasibility of giving meaning to life through a macho code of behavior. In that respect, Mailer offers us a way of reinscribing meaning in our high-tech lives. We may even, he argues, come to feel we have souls after all. Had Rojack not guided his choices by the dictates of this spiritual realm, the American Dream would have smothered him by killing his soul—as it has done to most white Americans, by Mailer's reckoning. Perhaps Mailer feels the need to prove through Rojack that some white souls possess ultimate bravery, for by his own theory, blacks have an advantage over whites in this matter of spiritual courage.

Gravity's Rainbow (1973)

Identifying magic or claims for the existence of other realities is a fraught enterprise when one deals with postmodern fiction. Impossible contradictions in plot do not necessarily mean superimposed alternate realities, and symbols made sentient are not necessarily magical or divine figures. Kathy Acker's Don Quixote shows characters changing gender fluidly, but no magic is involved because no ontological weight adheres to these characters as beings in a world representing ours. In another author's hands, Barthelme's gigantic Dead Father would be a magical or semidivine giant in a fantasy world, but he too clearly represents the dead weight of tradition, patriarchy, and Joyce as an oedipal strong-precursor to Barthelme. Neither Barthelme's *Snow White* nor Thomas Pynchon's *Crying of Lot 49* seems to incorporate magic, despite their heroines' Rapunzel-like dreams of being locked in a tower and waiting for a prince. Furthermore, Pynchon's version of America is governed by forces behind the scenes, but not much suggests that these forces have spiritual as opposed to conspiratorial existence. Snow White's apotheosis does not persuade us that we have seen a true transcendence; Barthelme does not treat it realistically enough to make us offer the conditional belief we offer nonrational fiction.

Pynchon's *Gravity's Rainbow*, among its many violations of reality, however, does provide ontological weight for nonmaterial planes of existence and inhabitants of those planes. Its angels belong to Christian, Jewish, occult, Muslim, and poetic metaphysics; whatever their derivation, they regularly cross between their own world and that of war-torn Europe. Their very frequency makes them an accepted part of reality. The dead also cross over to communicate with the living. I shall focus on these two evidences for the "Other Side," Pynchon's term for all forms of nonmaterial reality. They contrast usefully to magic or religious claims found in other books discussed. Furthermore, Pynchon's handling of them relies on what passes for deadpan literalism in a postmodern text, the literary technique necessary to making readers accept these phenomena as in some sense "real." We can also look at Geli Tripping, Pynchon's self-proclaimed witch. While superficially she might seem comparable to Mama Day or Ultima, her magic remains a literary construct, and she never achieves their credibility or solidity. What determines the believable for literary magic comes out in the comparison.

To me, what proved unexpected about this postmodern rebellion against the purely material is its lack of affective power. Contact with angels or the dead produces not much wonder or fear, only a bit of surprise quickly allayed. Pynchon's characters operate in a world impinged on by all manner of unusual realities, and they hardly acknowledge that the conventional worldview has been overthrown, so calmly do they accept the new, more complex vision of reality. Indeed, as I have argued in *Pynchon's Mythography*, part of Pynchon's concept of what a hero might be is the ability to accept such a change in the weltanschauung without resistance or reluctance (180).

The most solidly realized of the looming angels is the earliest, the towering being glimpsed over Lübeck, Germany, during a British bombing raid, and even this entity was only seen by two people. Yet, as Guildenstern notes in Stoppard's *Rosencrantz and Guildenstern Are Dead*, the second man agreeing that he too saw the unicorn makes the experience as strange as it can get (21). One seeing it may be deluded, and by the time the mob is finished commenting, it will be a horse with an arrow in its head. A second witness establishes its presence for us as readers. So too does Pynchon's vividly luminous description: "only Basher and his wingman saw it, droning across in front of the fiery leagues of face, the eyes, which went towering for miles, shifting to follow their flight, the irises red as embers fairing through yellow to white" (151). They wisely do not report this sighting in their debriefing, but word gets around, and its existence seems supported by what others learn in their spiritualist contacts with the Other Side. Were this the only angel in the novel, readers might protect their own worldview by telling themselves it had to be some kind of interplay of light and clouds, but Pynchon's cosmos is riddled with spirits.[25] Slothrop sees them in a sunset: "out at the horizon, out near the burnished edge of the world, who are these visitors standing . . . these robed figures—perhaps, at this distance, hundreds of miles tall—their faces, serene, unattached, like the Buddha's, bending over the sea, impassive, indeed, as the Angel that stood over Lübeck during the Palm Sunday raid" (214). Galina is described as dreaming of herself as an angel-like figure looming over a miniature city, but the narrative voice invokes "these star-blotting Moslem angels" (341) as if Galina's dream were merely reflecting a previously seen reality. Those same angels are linked to the angel in Rilke's tenth elegy; it strides with printless footstep across the marketplace. These supernatural beings—even when identified as Moslem or as the Recording Angel or the Bright Angel of Death, or when given names of Kabbalistic angels—simply enter the landscape. Though linked to major religions, they do not function demonstrably as emissaries of God. They may bear witness come Judgment Day, but we know nothing of their obligations. Nor do they interfere with humans directly. They suggest that some nonmaterial dimension of reality exists, but the people who see them are basically too wound up in the war to draw any conclusions or entertain speculation. They soldier on, simply enlarging their weltanschauung to include hitherto unknown forces.

In addition to angels, we find the dead as actors in the novel. With such presences, Pynchon is entering the same fictive realm as Naylor and Kennedy and, to a lesser extent, Mailer and Updike, whose characters can talk with the dead in the graveyard or through a broken telephone or even just sense their presence. Sometimes Pynchon uses formal structures such as spiritualist seances with mediums and spirit guides. A roomful of the German high command question the shade of Walter Rathenau. When Blobadjian is apparently killed, we are told by the narrative voice that the "first thing he learns is how to vary his index of refraction. He can choose anything between transparent and opaque. After the thrill of experimenting has worn off, he settles on a pale, banded onyx effect" (355). His undertaking a quest at the command of a mysterious power merely seems to launch him into a life as real as ours but on another plane of existence. This is the dead-pan realism applied to something normally adjudged unreal. With the specific dead being so well realized, we are set up to accept the nonpersonalized multitude of spirits as well. When Slothrop is playing Orpheus with his mouth harp, spending some days naked on the mountainside, he finds himself sometimes near the sort of crossroads "where you can sit and listen in to traffic from the Other Side, hearing about the future . . . no serial time over there: events are all there in the same eternal moment and so certain messages don't always 'make sense' back here" (624). We have already been told that Slothrop, "just suckin' on his harp, is closer to being a spiritual medium than he's been yet, and he doesn't even know it" (622). In the passage on crossroads and symbols that reflect them, Slothrop actually "became a crossroad" (626) and sees the "stout rainbow cock driven down out of pubic clouds into Earth, green wet valleyed Earth" (626). When Slothrop loses himself between this world and the Other Side, he sees the interconnections of Earth in different ways and is remade by a new perception of reality.

Such layers of nonmaterial reality lack the excitement and sense of elevation delivered by various ethnic metaphysics or the visceral theogony and magic of Mailer. Still very much present in the narrative is the scientific world that gives us the V-2 rocket. Pynchon's supernatural agents supplement material reality but add nothing to various characters' emotional attachment to life, whereas for Naylor, Anaya, Momaday, Silko, Vizenor, Reed, or Morrison, a spiritual presence enhances the intensity of life and makes it more precious. If anything, Pynchon's supernatural renders life less comprehensible and less supportive. His supernatural diminishes humanity rather than raising it, in part because it simply happens; it does not constitute a body of knowledge that the apprentice sorcerer must study and master. No one calls up the angels, and while the dead are called up, we also see them coming across to Slothrop without his having to acquire training as a medium. No real mastery, with its implications of power and control, is present. Power and control belong more to the realm of science and technology, and for Slothrop, the nonmaterial beings appear unpredictably. Many structures in postmodern literature peter out into meaninglessness. Pynchon shows us magic as the supernatural woven into everyday life and yet not redeeming it, not elevating it to something that transcends the material in ways that help humans do so too. Pynchon's world devolves into paranoia but not meaning.

At first glance, Pynchon's witch, Geli Tripping, might seem to violate the uncontrolled nature of his supernatural. She has studied lore from other witches, has been taken to witches' sabbaths on the Brocken since her first menstruation, and uses her own vaginal secretions plus chanted spells to coerce somebody who does not know he has been bespelled. She wants to bind Tchitcherine to her with this love-spell. One could say that he might feel bound anyway, but that is true of Mama Day's "magic" notepaper used to nudge George's memory. One might say that Geli seems too wholesome to be a serious witch (and so very young as well), but Mama Day is wholesome also. Geli works the magic for her own benefit, and that may be at odds with the protocols of many white magic traditions; such motivations, though, are hardly unprecedented. In *Linden Hills,* Naylor's Luther Nedeed uses magic to ensure that his son will resemble his father in all respects. What he practices is black magic, but Reed's Papa LaBas's "knockings" in *Mumbo Jumbo* tell him things he wants to know, and Vizenor's Proude Cedarfair in *Bearheart* saves his own life when he faces the evil gambler in a spiritual and magical contest. Still, something about Pynchon's image seems frivolous, whereas Naylor's achieves a seriousness that makes her violation of the canons of rationality quite fictively real. Geli's power perhaps is too simply a metaphor for her sexual attractiveness. Her concerns do not seem to reach farther than the next man to take to bed, and the triviality of such an aim perhaps undercuts her supposed access to great powers. She seems more a cheerful pinup girl than a wise woman. Unlike Mama Day and Ultima, she is not a midwife and is not associated therefore with the creation of life, no matter how many men she beds. In sum, she neither has a full range of female magic, nor has she studied a learned tradition for long enough to produce any but trivial results. Overall, Pynchon's magic and his supernatural do not succeed in helping us relate to the world with more intensity, nor do they give us any sense of a transcendent reality that makes our lives more worthwhile. We are just the ants running in the grooves between cobblestones while giants riot overhead. Or we are the tiny people in a miniature city who cower while giants crush whole blocks with their bootsoles, or we are bugs in the manger straw threatened by the glaring radiance of the Christ child's halo and the sonic blast of his cry. Pynchon's major image throughout the whole novel is of a small, threatened consciousness, trapped in a maze-like, city-like structure, with a looming destructive power hovering just overhead.[26] That the forces above are supernatural brings no comfort whatever, even though they suggest the possibility of some existence beyond the material world and even of life after death.

ⓔ ⓔ ⓔ

Writers find various names for the nonmaterial dimension of reality: the divine, the spiritual, the supernatural, magic, aura, and intensity. Any of these imbue material reality with a glow that usually makes life feel worthwhile. Such metaphysical challenges to the phenomenal world (except Pynchon's postmodern Other Side) point to a sense of meaning having existed in the past, in religious and nonscientific cultures, in theologies public and private, but not in the life of America's mainstream culture. Most of the authors regret that absence. Only Pynchon produces a spiritual domain that is perceptible to many yet provides none of these assurances of meaning. We have Pynchon's portrait of the Puritans to know that earlier generations did not find the supernatural quite such an incomprehensible blank.

When these authors invoke a spiritual realm, they may be rejecting science, but they may also be rejecting institutional religion, substituting an invented metaphysic or, in Native American or African-American texts, elements of rival religions. What they gain is well defined by Robert Post: "In the reality of the spirit *everything touches*, everything is connected to everything else, and the usual constraints of time and space no longer apply" (375). Humanity no longer feels alienated, and life derives the feeling of meaning, at least, from most such connections.

The absence of spiritual activity from contemporary fiction is not just an American phenomenon; the secularization of the cosmos is felt elsewhere, too. The authors analyzed in this chapter, however, are imagining their critique of America in terms of such spiritualizing and intensifying magic. Many other authors discussed in this book use magic and the supernatural incidentally in their critiques, so those under discussion here should not simply be dismissed as a small band of lunatics. Russell Banks uses Vodoun possession in *Continental Drift*. Toni Morrison's ghost in *Beloved* is a magic return of the repressed, a horror that nevertheless leads to more engagement with life for Sethe. William S. Burroughs uses time travel and the moving of a soul from one body to another in *Cities of the Red Night*. One Indian in Leslie Marmon Silko's *Almanac of the Dead* is a psychic. Nanapush in Louise Erdrich's *Tracks* is capable of seeking game through out-of-body travel. Ursula K. Le Guin's *Always Coming Home* gives us magic in the sense of native metaphysics and a new perspective that changes our relationship to reality. Starhawk's *Fifth Sacred Thing* gives us active witchcraft and healing through changing ch'i energies; she also describes more challenging magic when her witches exert mental control over electronic circuits. None of these authors is indulging in purely escapist fantasy, where magic is rife but not meant to be taken seriously. If such antirational challenges to science are madness, the madness is widespread.

Furthermore, at times America itself has radiated a religious intensity of meaning. The land has lost the mythic structures its white settlers once projected on it, and many Native Americans have also lost the mythic structures of the land through being pressured to conform to mainstream beliefs. Even white Americans who have most benefited from the country have lost their sense that America is a sacred and untarnished political entity. They no longer can rely for spiritual uplift on the American secular religion of worshiping America; Updike shows that portal swinging shut, less with a bang than the agonized squeal of a rusty hinge, in his description of Rabbit's declining belief in America. Science, its attendant skepticism, and various analytic tools of political philosophy have picked apart America's myths and magic and demystified them. The values born in the Enlightenment that made both science and America possible seem to have given more lasting support to science and secular rationalism. In addition to sadness at the loss of soul, the loss of innocence, and the lost sense of civilization discussed in prior chapters, we are being asked by the authors in this chapter if our culture rests on beliefs in science and rationalism that may be "true" but are, in spiritual and even practical terms, fatal to us. If so, what is the value of this truth?

chapter five

The Fragility *of Democracy*

The critiques of America we have seen focus on ways that life in America supposedly degrades the existence of its denizens: it takes away one's soul, innocence, civilization, and access to a spiritual dimension of reality. The land itself is not the culprit, but the culture is felt to lack some essential values. Soul, innocence, civilization, and spiritual reality or magic are not entirely equivalent, but they function very similarly in literary terms and are all being used to give name to some elusive quality in life that the writers find wanting. This sense of loss may stem from nostalgia, one more version of yearning for lost Eden, but each concept expresses a different version of the psychological longing. Authors find the failure of the American Dream a useful metaphor for this loss. The sense that democracy has lost its virtues is a slightly different critique. Democracy as we know it was created here and defines America for much of the world. It is not a dimension of human spirituality but an American artifact.

The authors in this chapter all feel that our democracy has been undermined to the point that one must think in terms of its failure. They do not necessarily believe that some other country has contrived a better government, and they would not agree on what we now lack in terms of freedom, justice, or protection. Only a few, like William S. Burroughs, felt that they differed so from majority norms that they chose exile, and even Burroughs returned to Kansas at the end of his life. All of these authors feel that our government has lost its ability to recognize its own proper limits, to choose long-term over short-term gains, and to attend to voters' needs rather than those of corporations. Although their disappointment in our democracy can be reached from many starting points, this chapter focuses on three that grow out of conditions specific to the period since 1960. Belief in conspiracies, burgeoning in the wake of President Kennedy's murder in 1963 and subsequent assassinations, undermines one kind of trust in democracy. The conspiracy outlook mutated to encompass Watergate and other subsequent clandestine behaviors at high levels of government. Thomas Pynchon's *Crying of Lot 49*, E. L. Doctorow's *Book of Daniel*, Don DeLillo's *Libra*, and Ishmael Reed's *Terrible Twos* and *Terrible Threes* all scrutinize the American system through a conspiratorial lens. Their characters discover that the true powers making things happen in the land are not democratic and manifest but secret and immune to voter pressure. For these writers, voting is only democratic window dressing; the real decision-making process does not lie with the people or their elected representatives.

For writers who reject the corrupted democracy envisioned by the conspiratorial view, revolution is one solution—and this is the position argued by four authors covered in this chapter. Ernest Callenbach's novels *Ecotopia* and *Ecotopia Emerging* and Andrew Macdonald's *Turner Diaries* give us blueprints for revolutions that grow out of dissatisfactions with the shortcomings of American democracy because of its corruption, alleged conspiracies, and inability to protect citizens' long-term interests. Burroughs's *Cities of the Red Night* and Robert A. Heinlein's *Moon Is a Harsh Mistress* make revolutionary arguments but identify the danger not so much as corruption as a weakness in our concepts of democracy; both agree that we had our chance to establish true democracy and failed.

Since hindsight of the 1980s and 1990s tells us that neither revolution nor other major breakthroughs occurred, a few later writers and filmmakers pause to wonder why. Pynchon's *Vineland* is the most prominent novel of this sort. From the perspective of 1984, it asks where the 1960s took the wrong turn. Conspiracy, revolution, and puzzlement over the failure of the left: these are this chapter's three subjects. Disgust spurred by the first produces the second, and disappointment over the second begets the third. Among them, these three represent a range of political stances. Conspiracy fears came mostly from the left and center in this era, but Macdonald's come from the far right. Similarly, revolutions are proposed from both the green-left and the libertarian-right. Pynchon's questioning of why the left failed leads him to argue that American fascism is growing. Since Reed also sees fascism taking over the country, those two could be said to blame fascist impulses and powers for the failure of democracy.

Conspiracyland: Pynchon, Doctorow, DeLillo, Reed

That secret powers rule America is a fear with a very long history. David H. Bennett's *Party of Fear: From Nativist Movements to the New Right in American History* outlines the paranoid politics characterizing what was mostly a majoritarian position from colonial times on.[1] Protestants distrusted Catholics, for instance, and felt threatened by imagined Catholic plots to overthrow the government and instate papal control. This sentiment predates democracy in America, but the belief that orders from the

Vatican could compromise democracy was a much-argued issue in the election of John F. Kennedy. Hostility to Freemasons as alleged secret manipulators of the government was so active in the 1830s that it spawned an anti-Masonic political party and presidential candidate. Movements hostile to Jews, to people of African descent, and to the Chinese have accused these groups of trying to undermine white, Christian culture through secret agendas and unfair practices. Fiction picturing military invasion by these and other groups has been very popular.[2]

These politics embody the paranoia of a white majority imagining itself threatened by racial, ethnic, or religious conspirators within the country or their external kin. In the nineteenth and early twentieth centuries, such a paranoid vision let a powerful, expansionist people play with feeling threatened, thus producing an emotional sense of justification for imperialist wars in the Philippines and the Caribbean. In modern political terms, this sort of majority paranoia tends to come from the conservative portion of the political spectrum and sometimes reflects a fear of, or guilt over, those being exploited, a return of the repressed.

Since the 1960s, however, the politics of paranoia have shifted, and several of the books discussed in this chapter display a paranoid vision that emerged from the left. Senator Joseph McCarthy temporarily undermined the respectability of anticommunist paranoia in the early 1950s, but leftist paranoia filled the vacuum in the 1960s. For years, the focal points for this impulse were the Warren Commission and the Vietnam War, but the dead were resurrected to supply this paranoia with a genealogy: Sacco and Vanzetti and the Rosenbergs were canonized by writers like Kurt Vonnegut, Robert Coover, and E. L. Doctorow. They argue that these figures were framed by official institutions and suffered unjust deaths as victims of government conspiracy.

African Americans see white racist conspiracies to eliminate their leaders or their entire population. The John F. Kennedy, Martin Luther King Jr., and Robert F. Kennedy assassinations launched left-leaning visions of the country or even the world as run by secret groups. The CIA has been the most popular target for such fears, but the Trilateral Commission, the Rockefellers, Howard Hughes, the Council on Foreign Relations, the military-industrial complex, drug cartels, terrorist groups, and other such sinister embodiments of the "Establishment" (or its criminal analogues) have all been envisioned as the hidden power brokers.[3] Pynchon's *Crying of Lot 49* and Reed's *Terrible Twos* and *Terrible Threes* all use conspiracy as their metaphor for America, and to avoid hostile cries of "paranoia," they avoid specific recent events. Doctorow's *Book of Daniel* and DeLillo's *Libra* deal with fictionalized forms of the Rosenbergs' execution and JFK's death, and they emphasize the complicity of the government and government-related institutions in the deaths and cover-ups that resulted from their historical events. I call this phenomenon Conspiracyland because many middle-class citizens, whatever their politics, at first found the conspiratorial outlook as strange as anything seen by Alice. They fiercely resisted falling down the rabbit hole into this world where all the sensible-seeming rules underlying middle-class political assumptions had changed into sinister contradictions of their former selves. By the time Oliver Stone's film *JFK* appeared in 1991, however, many viewers took his conspiracy-oriented interpretation for granted. What once was deemed lunatic had become mainstream or was at least accepted as deserving equal time.

The Crying of Lot 49 (1966)

If one looks at Thomas Pynchon's *Crying of Lot 49* with the conspiratorial vision in mind, it reflects its 1960s origins quite strikingly. This is not a roman à clef. The Tristero system does not stand for the CIA, the Freemasons, or the assassins of Kennedy, and wealthy Pierce Inverarity is not Nelson Rockefeller or H. L. Hunt.[4] Rather, Pynchon cobbles his fictional world together from elements that invoke the accidentals and fringe features of various conspiracies, not the specifics launched by the assassination of 1963.

Pynchon's W.A.S.T.E. network is one of secret communication mostly used by marginalized persons of all sorts. In 1960s terms, it serves conspiratorial purposes, but with 1990s hindsight, we can see many elements of the Internet, with its bulletin boards for everything from Ku Klux Klan concerns to incest survivors. In his Tristero organization, Pynchon captures some of the illegal, secret violence of the CIA: Tristero agents dressed in black assassinate legitimate postal carriers down through the centuries. Another source for this concept of a secret alternative to mainstream society is the Freemasons, not for anything that they have been or done historically, but just for their existence as an alternative social order, usually understood as an alternative to Christianity, however skewed that perception may be. Pynchon gives his secret society a history back into the late Middle Ages even as the Freemasons trace theirs to the Knights Templars of medieval France.

The users of Pynchon's network are society's misfits. One such outsider is a right-wing extremist, Mike Fallopian, who canonizes Peter Pinguid instead of John Birch; Pinguid was a U.S. Navy commodore in the first clash between the United States and Russia, which happened off the West Coast during the American Civil War; to Fallopian, the Birchers are too left-leaning. Jesús Arrabal, a Mexican anarchist revolutionary, is another Tristero user. Oedipa Maas realizes that homosexuals use the network; so do members of Inamorati Anonymous, those who wish to free themselves from their dependency on any sort of love. People involved in psychic experiments use it, whether their experimentation concerns LSD or talking to Maxwell's demon.

The cast of minor characters in this novel manifests the strange diversity found among the people whose names have turned up in investigations of JFK's death. We find actors; mobsters; lawyers; Mexicans (instead of Cubans); a major financial magnate who appears to own every enterprise in a California city; a rock group; homosexuals gathered at a nightclub; a former Nazi and a neo-Nazi dealing in Nazi memorabilia; a bookseller; a stamp dealer; a literature professor; a disk jockey; and many others. George DeMohrenschildt, Guy Bannister, David Ferrie, Clay Shaw, and Jack Ruby would be at home in this lineup. When one considers Oedipa's touching all of these lives during the few days of the narrative and thinks of these contacts as connections—a conspiracy-world term—she could seem a very sinister figure indeed, even though she is not consciously conspiring with them. If one sees them all as long-term connections of Inverarity (which they are), the reader is given this sense of a network of diverse interests to some degree controlled by this shadowy magnate associated with narcissism as canonized in this country (San Narciso). That they all may be in on a joke conspiracy set up by Inverarity to baffle Oedipa is one explanation—but that is rather unlikely. Another, somewhat more plausible possibility is that they represent the real America. She calls the legacy of Inverarity's will "America," a supposed democracy where the real governing forces are hidden, and most of the populace has no idea what is really happening.[5]

Also echoing Kennedy conspiracy theory is the series of mysterious deaths, disappearances, and druggings. Oedipa's lawyer Metzger runs off with a nymphet and disappears. Her husband, Mucho, enters a private world generated by LSD and ceases to have any meaningful connection to everyday reality. Hilarius, the ex-Nazi, is carted off in a straightjacket after he holes up in his office with guns to protect himself from phantom Israelis. Mike Fallopian disappears. Randy Driblette, the play director, mysteriously commits suicide. Oedipa clairvoyantly realizes that an old sailor will soon burn to death on his mattress. The entire novel starts with Oedipa learning that Pierce Inverarity has died. A statistically improbable number of people supposedly associated with the first Kennedy assassination also died over a relatively short time, many of them under suspicious circumstances or obviously murdered—or so conspiracy specialists claim. Since some of the Kennedy-associated deaths would have happened after the novel came out, readers must credit Pynchon with a deeply imaginative insight into the way the world looks to the conspiracy-minded.

Where Oedipa in Conspiracyland differs most clearly from various other conspiracy investigators is in her strong intuition that an alternate order does exist. Several times she senses something like divinity but never manages to break through to that level of reality. Assassination buffs merely seek American political reality; Oedipa seeks the nature of reality at a different level. She looks down on San Narciso as a printed circuit and senses an "intent to communicate"; she is "parked at the centre of an odd, religious instant. As if, on some other frequency, or out of the eye of some whirlwind rotating too slow for her heated skin even to feel the centrifugal coolness of, words were being spoken" (13). Job heard God as the voice in the whirlwind. Oedipa several times feels the flicker of incipient meaning, described as the sort of flash warning that an epileptic may experience, but she never finds revelation. Possibly her life in the world of narcissism makes a breakthrough to the other reality impossible. Also, most conspiracy hunters conclude at least that a conspiracy exists. Oedipa remains unsure: "Either Oedipa in the orbiting ecstasy of a true paranoia, or a real Tristero. For there either was some Tristero beyond the appearance of the legacy America, or there was just America and if there was just America then it seemed the only way she could continue, and manage to be at all relevant to it, was as an alien, unfurrowed, assumed full circle into some paranoia" (137). Either she must declare America to be riddled by conspiracy—and with whom could she register this complaint?—or she must consider herself insane, a prospect not made more attractive by seeing Hilarius carted off in a straitjacket.

Oedipa is in the position of many people faced with the Warren Commission and the flying rumors and contradictory "facts" associated with the shooting in Dallas. She can try to persuade herself that making all the connections is insane—and so refuse to do so—or she must face the notion that America is a vast plot, not at all what she believed in her Young Republican youth at Cornell. Pynchon leaves her poised at a personal cusp; by the end of the auction, she may have reason to choose one way or the other, or possibly the conspirators will eliminate her. After all, the "men inside the auction room wore black mohair and had pale, cruel faces" (137), like all the other black-clad Tristero assassins. As the lock snaps shut, she sees the auctioneer "spread his arms in a gesture that seemed to belong to the priesthood of some remote culture" (138). The ending teeters on a sword-edge. No resolution is offered.

The Book of Daniel (1971)

Doctorow avoids having to rehash well-known and unanswerable questions about Julius and Ethel Rosenberg by writing about the fictional Isaacsons.[6] While Russian archives have subsequently identified Julius Rosenberg as a spy, readers of this novel when it first appeared could not have assumed that their beliefs about the guilt or innocence of the Rosenbergs applied to the Isaacsons. The separation from history provided by fictionalization still holds. Readers are thus immediately thrust into a position similar to that of the narrator, Daniel Isaacson, who tries to find out the truth of his parents' supposed spying. He knows various political versions, both left- and right-wing, and all the legal angles. He inherits the family hatred of Selig Mindish as accuser. His desperation to know what really happened is expressed obliquely by the behavior of his sister Susan, who tries to commit suicide at the beginning of the book and who, seven months later, dies from pneumonia and from a lack of will to live in a world of conspiratorial lies and stories. That desperation also shows in his schizophrenic shifts between first- and third-person narration regarding himself and in his occasional sadistic enjoyment of hurting his wife and son. Between Memorial Day, when Susan tries to commit suicide, and Christmas, when she dies, Daniel tries to find the truth, in part because he hopes it might help her. The biblical book of Daniel denies to Daniel an understanding of its allegorical mysteries: "Go thy way, Daniel: for the words are closed up and sealed till the time of the end" (12:9).[7] He cannot put closure to his interpretive problem and neither can Daniel Isaacson.

Like most investigators into recent conspiracies, Daniel finds justice in this country to be a sham. The FBI captures and convicts in the same press release. No one prevents the news media from condemning before trial. Evidence helpful to the defense is barred on grounds of national security. Daniel's own memories of his parents in prison give him no help. They maintained their innocence; since they also denied that there was any danger of execution, he has little reason to believe whatever they told him.

Ten years after the execution, a *New York Times* reporter offers his professional assessment to Daniel: "Your folks were framed, but that doesn't mean they were innocent babes. . . . your parents and Mindish had to have been into some goddamn thing. They *acted* guilty. They were little neighborhood commies probably with some kind of third-rate operation that wasn't of use to anyone except maybe it made them feel important. Maybe what they were doing was worth five years" (260). Daniel's adopted father gives him another reading. He says that "at the level of *Time* magazine the joke was how they [the Russians] copied everything and claimed it for their own. Well, of course the corollary of that is that it's our bomb they have and that means we were betrayed. After the war our whole foreign policy depended on our having the bomb and the Soviets not having it. It was a terrible miscalculation. It militarized the world. And when they got it the only alternative to admitting our bankruptcy of leadership and national vision was to find conspiracies" (270). He suggests that the Isaacsons' legal defense should have tried a different tactic, should have argued that not only were the Isaacsons innocent but so too was Mindish, and that both were patsies left to take the heat for the real passers of information. Were the Isaacsons innocent? Were they trivial spies or major espionage operatives? Daniel never finds out.[8]

Nor does America seem worth dying for to him, whether the site of sacrifice is being killed in Vietnam or being executed in the electric chair.
When Daniel goes to California, he sees that "power lines were strung
through the sky. Sulfurous smoke rose over the flatland. Steel cities vibrat-
ed the earth. It was the country of strontium children. LOVE IT OR LEAVE
IT" (320). America is not ideal and not wonderful, but it is his country; and
he feels at home, even among features he hates, such as army trucks, helicopters and jets, electronics firms—the "highly visible military-industrial complex" (320). For him, too, America is the land of the ubiquitous
FBI seeing to it that one is guilty and cannot ever be innocent. He knows
he will never get a National Defense Education Act fellowship. He will
not be drafted or given a government job. He feels he cannot even usefully demonstrate against the government because any negative act will be
seen as "genetic criminality" (89) and not an act of himself as an individual. His citizenship is hollow.

Those power lines crisscrossing the landscape are not entirely innocent
themselves. Any conspiracy-oriented vision of the world assumes that
power is what matters to humans. The point of conspiracies is to gain
power or shift the balance of power. Power, in English, is also electricity,
and electricity powers the electric chair. At one point, Daniel offers a
meditative ode on power that starts "om om om . . . ohm" and goes on:

> what is it that moves through others, comes from the sky and is invisi-
> ble, can only be detected after it's gone—not God, not the Lon[e]
> Ranger.
> ohm ohm ohm ohm
> what makes you smell when you touch it, blacken when you feel it, die
> when you taste it.
> ohm
> what is it that lightens the life of man and comforts his winters and
> sings that he is the master of the universe; until he sits in it.
> ohm[.] (275)

He quotes information on electricity; "The leading electric-power producing countries are the United States . . . and the Union of the Soviet Socialist Republics" (359). He argues violently with the doctor who wishes to
try electroshock therapy on his sister. All these discussions of electricity
circle the method of his parents' death. "I suppose you think I can't do the
electrocution. I know there is a you. There has always been a you. YOU: I
will show you that I can do the electrocution" (359). He proceeds to describe the grisly physiological details of what happened when his father
and then his mother were electrocuted. His mother had to be shocked twice
because the first brain-searing surge did not stop her heart. The Isaacsons

were caught between the two great national and ideological powers and, touching both, were killed by the power that shoots through them.[9]

Pynchon and Doctorow both have done much to present America not as the land of freedom and justice but as the land of riddle, connection, coincidence, injustice, conspiracy, and violence, as shown in *The Crying of Lot 49* and *The Book of Daniel*. Doctorow's *Ragtime* also explores injustice, while Pynchon's *Gravity's Rainbow* and *Vineland* express a conspiratorial vision with great force and prophetic eloquence. As these authors' historical materials make plain, however, they see the conspiratorial nature of the country's reality as going back in time—to the 1930s, even to the beginning of the century. Barth's *Sot-Weed Factor* would trace it further back to colonial times. We cannot comfort ourselves that the McCarthy hysteria, the Kennedy assassination frenzy, or the Iran-Contra investigations are isolated blips on a placid political scene. Belief in dark powers ruling the world was strong enough to inspire the seventeenth-century Salem witch hunt. America has no golden age in the past that we might hope to return to politically to escape the conspiratorial outlook. This country has never been free of political paranoia.

Libra (1988)

Don DeLillo's *Libra* mixes fiction with fact, insofar as anything about the Kennedy assassination can be called fact. Lee Harvey Oswald, David Ferrie, George DeMohrenschildt, Jack Ruby, and a few others were real people; others, such as the fictional "real" killer, Raymo, are placemarkers for whomever the real conspirators may have been. DeLillo states in an interview and in the author's note at the end that he is writing a novel, not trying to make the best possible scenario out of the contradictory evidence.[10] His Oswald is a created character based on somewhat arbitrary decisions as to what kind of person he thinks Oswald may have been, and the novel took off once DeLillo found the right voice for Oswald. His novel focuses on how history works, and he finds, both on the individual level and that of larger groups, that chance seems more important than expressed purposes. DeLillo himself has stated that the assassination gave us a different way of seeing reality, and we have moved from a coherent world to one of "randomness and ambiguity."[11]

Chapters alternate; there is one for Oswald, then one for everyone else combined, including the author-surrogate, Nicholas Branch, a retired CIA agent writing a secret history of the assassination for the agency.[12] Oswald's own words are quoted, and so apparently are the words of others, though we do not know from within the text to what extent Oswald's mother is a fictional tour de force or simply a transcription. Branch calls the Warren

Commission and its compendium of attendant data the "great Joycean book of America" (182), "the megaton novel James Joyce would have written if he'd moved to Iowa City and lived to be a hundred" (181). That the novel ends with a long monologue by Oswald's mother suggests Joycean aspirations to capture America as it was during the months leading up to November 1963.[13]

The title, *Libra*, refers to Oswald's astrological sign but also to the qualities attributed to Libras: the sense of being balanced, whether in the positive sense of being poised and sure or in the negative of being easily pushed in either direction (315). These negative qualities apply to Oswald and also to the conspiracies in the novel. Developments could easily have gone in different directions. Had Jack Ruby been more successful in business and not so deeply in debt to loan sharks, he might not have agreed to kill Oswald in return for canceling his debt. Had agents and former agents been kept busier by the CIA, and had they been given other things to think about than their failure to kill Castro and betrayal in the Bay of Pigs, they might not have found the idea of killing Kennedy so attractive. Had Oswald's Russian wife Marina not refused three times to come with him to Dallas, he might have dropped his plans for shooting. Some of the conspirators dislike Kennedy, or even hate his photogenicity and appeal to women, but none show monomaniac dedication to eliminating him. That just happens when enough agents experienced in "black ops" start to cross paths, swap their grudges, and amuse themselves by practicing their skills.

DeLillo tries to make sense of the qualities that would bring a conspiracy-controlled America into existence and focuses on the personal excitement offered by the possession of secrets. Win Everett, who hatches the first version of the plot, notices the effect of secrets on his daughter:

> When my daughter tells me a secret . . . her hands get very busy. She takes my arm, grabs me by the shirt collar, pulls me close, pulls me into her life. She knows how intimate secrets are. She likes to tell me things before she goes to sleep. Secrets are an exalted state, almost a dream state. They're a way of arresting motion, stopping the world so we can see ourselves in it. . . . My little girl is generous with secrets. I wish she weren't, frankly. Don't secrets sustain her, keep her separate, make her self-aware? How can she know who she is if she gives away her secrets? (26)

Oswald, we learn, would do odd things when a boy and let you think he was a fool or the reverse, "as long as he knew the truth and you didn't" (33). When Oswald attends General Walker's lecture, he feels exaltedly wrapped in the secret that he, Oswald, had almost killed Walker. One of his fellow workers gloats over how much fun it is to exchange secrets (274).

Attaching to secrets are the actions that they generate. Banister, formerly of the FBI, speaks of agents who are retired by the bureau:

Everyday lawful pursuits don't meet our special requirements. . . . For twenty-some-odd years in the Bureau I lived in a special society that pretty much satisfied the most serious things in my nature. Secrets to trade and keep, certain dangers, an opportunity to function in tight spots, wave a gun in people's faces. That's a charmed society. If you've got criminal tendencies, and I'm not saying this is true of you or me, one of the places to make your mark is law enforcement. . . . Spy work, undercover work, we invent a society where it's always wartime. (63–64)

In DeLillo's construction of the story, readers see how various groups of disaffected agents contrived, almost by chance, to kill JFK; how Oswald was peripheral to the plot and was basically unnecessary except to confuse the scene and be captured. For most of the story, we do not know which of several experienced mercenaries may have done the shooting from the grassy knoll. The guarded reference at the end to Ramón (Raymo) Benítez implies that he drove a taxi for some years afterwards. If he or someone like him was the assassin, that individual has not benefited except insofar as he can define himself by clutching his secret to his heart.

Having mentioned *Libra*, I cannot pass on without a reference to Oliver Stone's *JFK*. The film is a throwback to romantic notions of the lone investigator battling a coherent, malignant, purposeful conspiracy. It reeks of nostalgia with all the idealizations inherent in the nostalgic vision. Kevin Costner's Jim Garrison is young, reasonably handsome, and well dressed in light colors that spell out both southern gentleman and tropical exotic. He is at home in nightclubs where gangsters and low-life types mix with businessmen, yet no mud clings to him. He single-mindedly pursues his quest, devoting his life to finding the truth. Neither family nor threats can keep him from his appointed mission. He succeeds to the degree that he persuades the jury and the audience that there was a conspiracy and that the Warren Commission is a tissue of lies concocted out of fear over what would happen were the truth known. Perhaps the nostalgia for the single investigator reflects nostalgia for the lost innocence of a previous age in which such conspiracies were publicly absent. Of course, the Eisenhower era had its own brand of paranoia, but communist fears worried a different segment of the population from those prepared to swallow Stone's argument.

In terms of the particular conspiracy outlined, the film is much more radical than *Libra*, for Oliver Stone (and the character Garrison) lay the blame squarely on the CIA, insisting that not only high-level CIA officials but also the military brass were complicit and even active in rubbing out Kennedy. This was a coup d'état, as the film insists several times. To make this argument, Stone resorts to a somewhat shabby gimmick. A CIA specialist in black ops talks freely to Garrison. "X" asserts that Kennedy planned to bring troops home from Vietnam and that the assassination changed that policy immediately with Lyndon B. Johnson's National Security Memo 273. He insists that only top security forces could have changed the initial route, ordered the glass bubble removed, and refused to take the normal, massive security precautions. The ambush was a standard, military-style ambush with crossfire. Furthermore, the fact that the telephone system in Washington, D.C., was down at the crucial time of the assassination was no accident. Why was he killed? Who benefited? Who could cover it all up? These are answered by the needs of the military-industrial complex, among whose components are the services needing to justify their level of support, industries that supply armaments and matériel, and a newly acknowledged group, the southern and western power brokers, who sought to test their strength against the eastern establishment. In practical terms, American fascists overthrew the elected government. Or, as Stone asserts, secret murder lies at the heart of the American Dream. That is his image for how we have betrayed the Dream and what it stands for.

JFK reached a much wider audience and had more effects than *Libra* did. It provoked more than forty articles in the *New York Times,* triggered books and articles by the surgeons who autopsied Kennedy on the number of bullets found, and moved Congress to reclassify documents to facilitate future investigations (Friedman and Squire 50–51). Its vivid use of what it says to be the unaltered Zapruder film is disturbingly convincing, as nothing fictional is likely to be. Nonetheless, the film's ability to reach an audience seems to me undercut by the concessions to popular taste demanded by the cinematic medium. The regression to the use of the figure of the spotless, heroic young investigator is intellectually disappointing, especially compared to the more complex meditations on the individual in *Libra* or even in a popular thriller like Donald Freed's *Spymaster.* Stone insists that the United States is not what we thought but is rather a conspiracy of a traitorous sort. However, what Stone takes away with one hand, he returns to us with the other, reassuring us that the truth will out and the Lone Ranger will come to the rescue. That rescue is far from complete, but we are pressured to accept it emotionally as snuggly and satisfying by watching Garrison and his partly estranged wife in bed while they are reconciled to each other and go on with life as it was in the land of magnolias.

The Terrible Twos (1982) and The Terrible Threes (1989)

Given the frantic juggling of Freemasons, Knights Templars, Teutonic Knights, the Wallflower Order, and other such secret societies in *Mumbo Jumbo,* readers might expect Ishmael Reed to throw himself into African-American conspiracy theory in these conspiracy-oriented satiric novels.

Patricia Turner has analyzed a number of common African-American conspiracy theories in her book *I Heard It through the Grapevine*. AIDS is a
medical experiment in reducing the black population in Africa and the
United States. Crack and heroin are deliberately funneled into the inner
city to keep the African-American population too drugged to work or rebel.
The Atlanta serial murders supposedly involved children snatched for
medical experiments or (in a rumor actually evolving from Norman Spin-
rad's science-fiction novel *Bug Jack Barron*) as a source for healthy organs
to be transplanted into rich white recipients. Jonathan Vankin mentions
some other African-American conspiracy theories in *Conspiracies, Cover-
Ups and Crimes*. Jonestown was an experiment in mind control for killing African Americans, a racial variant on *The Manchurian Candidate*'s
picture of cued destruction or self-destruction. Vankin also points out the
pattern that African-American leaders who reach a certain level of power
and credibility get assassinated or killed with chilling regularity in what
may seem like suspicious circumstances: Malcolm X, Martin Luther King
Jr., Medgar Evars, Fred Hampton, Mickey Leland, and Ron Brown. Ishmael Reed mentions one or two such race-based theories—the extant concentration camps to be used on African Americans (*Threes* 107, 148) and AIDS
as a weapon used against blacks—but beyond those, he invents his own
conspiracies and cover-ups. Many liberal and middle-class readers are
unwilling to accept conspiracy as a sane and serious answer to certain
known crises, so he presents us with unknown or satirically altered versions of such crises.

One is the ongoing nuclear tension and temptation. Both books deal with
a conspiracy known by the code name of Operation Two Birds. The back-
room interests—the true but secret government of the country—consist
of an admiral; a Colorado beer baron; a white evangelist named Clement
Jones; the man in charge of White House Communications (Krantz); and
the secretary of defense. The plan is to bomb Miami and New York (the
major centers for the homeless), blame the attack on Nigeria—an emerging African nation rumored to have acquired nuclear capability—and then
nuke Nigeria to retaliate for its dastardly attack on the United States.

Krantz realizes in *The Terrible Threes* that he himself is being set up as
a fall guy who will be killed and blamed for Operation Two Birds and that
the secretary of defense and admiral have been "suicided" to prevent second thoughts. Krantz is ultimately revealed to be an extraterrestrial who
has become too involved in earthly temptations and joys to remember his
original mission: starting a nuclear war to exterminate humans so that the
extraterrestrials fleeing their own racial war could take over Earth. He is
thus actually an extraterrestrial conspiratorial agent.

Former Nazis also appear. They are necessary to a good conspiratorial
mix because of their place in JFK assassination theory: General Reinhard

Gehlen and his Nazi intelligence operatives were incorporated into the American intelligence network after World War II, and some were working with exiled Cubans. Reed invokes their presence in the spirit of the SS member who haunts the Reverend Clement Jones. Furthermore, higher-ups in the administration wear "Barbie" suits, the bold pinstripe favored by Klaus Barbie during his war crimes trial. The aims of Operation Two Birds are Hitlerian enough that the president of the United States is persuaded to declare Hitler's birthday a national holiday and award him posthumous American citizenship (*Twos* 58, 66). Other conspiratorial elements include blaming an anticommercial Christmas speech on Jews (who would naturally wish to ruin Christmas) and African Americans (because Christmas in the song is white). Clement Jones once preached sermons in which both groups were declared children of Satan. When Krantz is chosen as the fall guy, his supposedly Jewish name is used to suggest that he launched Operation Two Birds as part of a Jewish conspiracy.

Amidst all this conspiracy flotsam is an original element. Reed draws on various pagan, Christian, heretical, and Vodoun traditions to give us supernatural characters in the form of St. Nicholas, Black Peter (both the real Black Peter and an imposter), St. Peter, and Satan. St. Nicholas sweeps through Washington, D.C., exposing major players in the political game to the anguish of predecessors who made the wrong decisions, thus hoping to make changes for the better at the national level. St. Nicholas points out cusps in American history and tries to nudge leaders in the right direction. Black Peter is more concerned with ordinary individuals and shows them when they get close to the point of no return that if they change now, they can redeem their wasted or twisted lives. Satan does what Satan always does—he makes pacts and awards success in life in return for souls. He not only signs up the Reverend Jones; he is also making headway with the pope and a cardinal. Readers will remember the conspiracies involving papal investments and banks and the Masonic lodge network known as Propaganda Due or P2.

The scenes that stand out from the humorous conspiracy farrago are those showing the Dickensian ghosts of America past.[14] In *The Terrible Twos*, President Dean Clift (formerly a male model) is taken by St. Nicholas to see Harry Truman, Dwight Eisenhower, and Nelson Rockefeller. Truman remembers his decision to use the atomic bomb; Eisenhower laments authorizing the assassination of Patrice Lumumba. Rockefeller's scene is the most complex. He has suffered from his desire to be a "bit" tough at Attica in hopes of proving to the Republican party that he was not soft on racial issues. He also frivolously preferred having sex with his girlfriend rather than answering the phone during the Attica crisis; while he disported himself, thirty prisoners were killed. In *The Terrible Threes*, Supreme Court justice Nola Payne is shown a past justice who could have made a decisive difference to the course of American law: Judge Taney of the Dred Scott decision. Prodded by him, Payne changes her mind and votes *against* Clement Jones's Conversion Bill (which requires everyone in the country to become Christian or be expelled). She also gives up drinking. Reed uses conspiracy as a metaphor for America but does not believe in a coherent purpose behind the conspiracies. They make connections between circles of corruption but do not control the country or the world to some single end. Reed is enough of an optimist to hold that there is a right way to go at certain moral crossroads, and he can still believe that sometimes individuals might make the right decision.

Reed reiterates that "The Terribles" began in Dallas, Texas, on November 22, 1963, and have continued unabated since. What he sees in America is a Heart of Whiteness that is frighteningly like the Great White Hope to be discussed next in *The Turner Diaries*.[15] *The Terrible Threes* ends with the Amerikander party, led by a skinhead, gaining in the polls and the satanically controlled Reverend Jones leading the nation in hypocritical prayer. Reed has promised to write *The Terrible Fours* in the future. Readers will then be able to see if the conspiracies have multiplied or if that outlook becomes passé as 1960s assumptions and forms of naïveté fade away.

Calls for a Second American Revolution: Macdonald, Callenbach, Burroughs, and Heinlein

The Turner Diaries (1978; 2d ed., 1980)

Ishmael Reed and Andrew Macdonald (the pseudonym of William L. Pierce) are each other's nightmare: the former is an energetic, intelligent African American; the latter is a white racist. Reed focuses on the conspiracies and corruption of the white power brokers and suspects that revolution would come to no good end. Macdonald feels his values have enough majority backing that he seriously preaches overthrowing the U.S. government and supplies a detailed plan for carrying out such a revolution. Macdonald represents right-wing conspiracy theory and offers a Hitlerian paean to the white race. His picture of what lies at the heart of that race—the values that he upholds—are also those values that nonwhites would say despairingly are ineradicably and viciously white. Their complementary visions put an unusual fix on America.

Macdonald's *Turner Diaries* is both the story of a revolution and a racist utopia, and it has already made its mark on American politics. It was the favorite reading of Timothy McVeigh, the convicted bomber of the federal building in Oklahoma City. The novel's protagonist, Earl Turner, helps bomb the FBI headquarters to revenge the death of a fellow member of the "Order," the inner circle of the Organization, an Aryan supremacy

movement. The book shows how to carry out such an operation. McVeigh
seems to have followed the directions quite closely. Apparently, he acted
in part to revenge the Arkansas execution of an Oklahoma man who had
been a member of the real-life equivalent to the Order; he was executed
for murdering a black state trooper and a Jewish pawnbroker in the Order
campaign of 1983–84. The date for the Oklahoma City bombing (April 19,
1995) alludes to Paul Revere's midnight ride and to the destruction of the
Branch Davidian compound in Waco, Texas (important demands for liberty celebrated by the far-right); it also falls on the day before Hitler's birthday, a day of importance in *The Turner Diaries*.[16]

Macdonald's protagonist, Earl Turner, shows us the America of the early 1990s, a world degraded by the international Jewish conspiracy and
mongrelized by nonwhite "degenerates" present within the population:

> If the freedom of the American people were the only thing at stake, the
> existence of the Organization would hardly be justified. Americans have
> lost their right to be free. Slavery is the just and proper state for a people
> who have grown as soft, self-indulgent, careless, credulous, and befuddled
> as we have.
>
> Indeed, we are already slaves. We have allowed a diabolically clever, alien
> minority to put chains on our souls and our minds. These spiritual chains
> are a truer mark of slavery than the iron chains which are yet to come.
> (33)

In Turner's view, the diabolical, alien Jews have enslaved Anglo-Saxon
Americans with materialism, liberalism, feminism, and antigun legislation. They attack all hostile actions toward nonwhites as racism rather
than taking into account whether the actions were warranted by such prov-
ocations as sexual assault.

From Turner's diary, readers learn his views on many aspects of American culture: "Liberalism is an essentially feminine, submissive world view.
Perhaps a better adjective than feminine is infantile" (42). In the liberal
worldview, the lion and lamb will lie down in a padded nursery and live
happily ever after. Turner is just as hostile to conservatives, however: "They
are the world's worst conspiracy-mongers—and also the world's greatest
cowards. In fact, their cowardice is exceeded only by their stupidity" (63).
Conservatives, of course, wish to maintain the extant system and merely
reform it. Once the revolution has started, a conservative general in Northern California has to be assassinated because of his obstructive views:

> And he has denounced our radical measures in the south as "commu-
> nism." He is appalled that we didn't hold some sort of public referendum
> before expelling the non-Whites and that we didn't give individual trials
> to the Jews and race-criminals we dealt with summarily.

Doesn't the old fool understand that the American people *voted them-selves* into the mess they're in now? Doesn't he understand that the Jews have taken over the country fair and square, according to the Constitution? . . . Doesn't Harding understand that the chaos in his area will continue to grow worse until he identifies the *categories* of people responsible for that chaos and deals with them *categorically* . . . ? (173)

When Turner needs other targets, he has hippie dropouts, whom he castigates for drugs, unorthodox religions, Satan worship ("reminiscent of ancient Semitic cults"), ritual torture, murder, cannibalism, and sex orgies (66). Every traditional vice used by one race to dehumanize another is present here.

Earl Turner, a man with mechanical, electric, and electronic training, plays invaluable roles in the revolution of the radical right. He helps with communications, terrorist activities, counterfeiting paper money, and—with his suicide run—the bombing of the Pentagon. He also helps with the first steps of setting up a pure white community in the Los Angeles region, organizing food, and witnessing the Day of the Rope (the summary hanging or shooting of those who defiled or betrayed their race). He is invited to join the Order, the equivalent to the Nazi SS. He reads "The Book," with its Hitlerian master plan for the white race. He undergoes a moving initiation rite and, before his suicide raid, enjoys a rite of union.

After this rite, and just prior to his Pentagon attack, he looks at the other inner circle members:

> These men are the best my race has produced in this generation—and they are as good as have been produced in any generation. In them are combined fiery passion and icy discipline, deep intelligence and instant readiness for action, a strong sense of self-worth and a total commitment to our common cause. On them hang the hopes of everything that will ever be. They are the vanguard of the coming New Era, the pioneers who will lead our race out of its present depths and toward the unexplored heights above. And I am *one* with them! (203–4)

Earl Turner is both extremely individualist and desperately eager to submit his individuality to mystic unity with others, desperate enough that he accepts their definition of himself as someone who has failed and gladly buys his reinstatement by taking on a suicide mission.

From Macdonald's point of view, the Jewish conspiracy runs America. Its aims are not clearly defined, although it is seen as causing the degradation of the white race and the effeminization and enervation of white culture. African Americans are viewed as the pawns of the Jews, being, in Macdonald's view, too stupid to conspire. Macdonald's blacks are all lazy, natural rapists, irresponsible users of drugs (even when on duty in the army), easily corrupted with bribes, and cultural degenerates. The narrator gloats that when everyone is faced with starvation when the government is overthrown, only blacks resort to cannibalism. In opposition to these forces, Macdonald offers the successful conspiracy represented by the Organization. He provides a fictional blueprint for such a rebellion, the problems one has to anticipate, and the solutions he considers expedient. Whether the issue is communications, financial backing, or ways of bringing the government to its knees, Macdonald gives the reader a good course in terrorist tactics. The Oklahoma City bombing attests to his competence at providing instructions. When one compares Macdonald's picture of revolution to the painless, green-left blueprint for revolution that is presented in Callenbach's *Ecotopia* and *Ecotopia Emerging*, one has to admit a certain realism in what Turner describes. The peaceful changes envisioned in Callenbach's novels are implausible. Turner's new order deports those with African blood (so they will weaken the other side), shoots Jews, and hangs liberal whites from lampposts and freeway overpasses. This seems more plausible by the standards of most past revolutions. In the epilogue to Turner's diary, the world is well on its way to the extermination of all but the white race, and this outcome is seen as God's plan.[17]

Ecotopia is frequently taught on campuses; *The Turner Diaries* is not. They represent roughly the same level of literary value (minimal), and their ideologies—Callenbach on the green-left, Macdonald on the far right—are equally forcefully argued. Trying to teach Macdonald's novel as an example of revolutionary-utopian fiction, or of conspiracy fiction, or as an illustration of neo-Nazi concerns in this country might well cause a furor on a college campus. Some students would be outraged by the ideology; others would embrace it fervently. When I call Andrew Macdonald and Ishmael Reed each other's nightmare, I have that latter reaction in mind. Reed is all too aware of the undiluted and unmodified racism to be found within this country. His epigraph to *Reckless Eyeballing* reads, "What's the American Dream? A million blacks swimming back to Africa with a Jew under each arm." He cites as his source a book called *Truly Tasteless Jokes*, but it is no joke to Macdonald. He would rather kill all of them by firing squad; failing that, the swimming solution would be satisfactory.

Ecotopia (1975) and *Ecotopia Emerging* (1981)

Ernest Callenbach offers us another utopia produced by revolution, but his comes from the opposite part of the political spectrum. Basically, he asks what might happen if the radical values of the 1960s were allowed to take root and make a new culture. In these novels, the 1960s did not peter out, their energies dissipated. Rather, their energies resolved into action. American democracy failed to vote for costly cleanups and expensive economic changes, but in the smaller-scale world of Ecotopia, people prove willing to restrict their material wealth in favor of the common good. *Ecotopia* is a fairly crude and simple utopia set in 1999 and describing the Pacific Northwest as a separate country that seceded from the United States in 1980. *Ecotopia Emerging* is a much more interesting and complex book that describes how secession might actually take place. It is set in 1986; it refers to the other book as a piece of fiction, and it is crammed with statistics on how the United States is committing ecological and economic suicide. Both books are written in and about the later part of this century, but their values—as their characters admit, whether admiringly or dismissively—are the values of the 1960s. Callenbach takes up 1960s concerns but extracts them from their campus setting. As will be seen in this chapter's analysis of *Vineland,* Pynchon's focusing on campuses catches the childish and contradiction-riddled side of 1960s thought. Callenbach is more interested in collective behaviors and back-to-the-land movements. He is concerned with how we can extrapolate from the 1960s and make that decade's values real, and he offers us a detailed, radical critique of America and the American Dream.[18]

In *Ecotopia Emerging,* a number of basic principles are worked out for what is considered a sane future. There is no use of nuclear power; no manufacture or use of carcinogens or mutagens; no private automobiles. This last prohibition is the most radical and far-reaching in its consequences. Cities can no longer sprawl but become densely built population centers limited to 10,000 inhabitants, all linked by frequent, high-speed rail transport. The old cities have public transport and free municipal bicycles. Callenbach piles up the charges against the automobile: *"The automobile consumed well over an eighth of all the productive capacity of the American economy, and many individuals spent a quarter of their income on their cars. . . . The total deaths from accidents since cars were invented now approached two and a half million, but the fact that the weekly death rate was only around a thousand (plus another couple of thousand maimed) was regarded as a sign of the competence of American drivers"* (*Emerging* 80; italics in original). Callenbach adds to his case: "In the first half of the eighties . . . the net outflow of dollars to pay OPEC nations for oil amounted to the value of half the stocks and bonds listed on the New York Stock Exchange. Translated into real-world terms, this meant that in only five years the country had given away in order to maintain its car habit half of all the productive machinery, laboratories, land, buildings, transportation facilities, and food production resources accumulated by its corporations over the previous 200 years" (*Emerging* 153). If you grant Callenbach his figures (he does not cite sources), then his structuring of the new country to do away with automobiles is a sensible starting point.

Similar damning figures emerge on American agriculture. Callenbach argues that *"for each bushel of corn grown in Iowa, six bushels of soil erod-ed away; in eastern Washington, 20 pounds of topsoil were lost for every pound of wheat produced. Even in well-tended farm country such as Wis-consin, about eight tons of topsoil were being lost from each acre each year, and only about four tons regenerated. The national average net loss was almost nine tons per acre"* (*Emerging* 163–64; italics in original). The an-swer to this and many other problems is to go back to smaller-scale enter-prises. Big farms force too much damage on the land through specialization in one crop and the use of large machines that work best in straight lines. Callenbach wants us to return to small farms, to rotate crops, and to use integrated pest control. The product may cost somewhat more; if all costs (such as the loss of topsoil) are factored in, Callenbach argues, the efficien-cy is not inferior to that of big agribusiness. Furthermore, it is sustainable. His image of what such farming might be like is similar to William S. Bur-roughs's picture of articled communes in *Cities of the Red Night.*

Large companies cannot make small adjustments in their designs; any change may take a year or two to implement. Small businesses, Callen-bach argues, can. He makes all companies worker owned and operated, with no absentee owners. Furthermore, he insists that corporations exist to save their decision makers from personal liability, arguing that if all decisions are to be sane, "people must be made to bear responsibility for what they do" (230)—an important lever in reversing contemporary pat-terns. Indeed, personal liability is one of his chief legal tools. He also edu-cates us in total-cost accounting and insists that it must become a funda-mental principle. A company cannot pass on costs to future generations; the cleanup of all environmental impacts must be now and must be com-plete. When all such costs are figured in, alternative, ecologically sound measures become efficient and therefore acceptable.

The secessionist impulse grows gradually, and Callenbach portrays the process in considerable detail. First, the Survivalist party develops its ten-point platform and works for years on statistics, new ideas, new ways of implementing decisions and reaching consensus, and the like. Vera All-wen, the leader, popularizes survivalist ideas through a television talk show. A nuclear meltdown in the Pacific Northwest region gives the par-ty an immediate political victory over the pronuclear governor of the state of Washington. When the spread of cheap, effective solar cells lets a small, ecologically minded community disconnect from the power grid, the U.S. government's determination to bulldoze any houses not connected sparks off a great deal of local sympathy for the community's secession from the county, state, and country. One radical survivalist plants nuclear bombs in major eastern cities so pressure can be brought to bear on Congress. A sudden war in Brazil that demands American troops distracts public atten-tion and removes troops from the borders of Ecotopia. Since the war makes a military takeover in the United States likely, the survivalists decide to make a serious move for secession. Planning, luck, and unexpected world events combine to make the revolution possible, but even the unexpected in this scenario is quite plausible, except for the lack of violence and the inability of the U.S. government to retaliate effectively.

   Ecotopia, like most formal utopias, devotes chapters to education, health care, law enforcement, work in factories, travel, the arts, and similar subjects. Much is made of people enjoying a stronger and pleasure-oriented relationship with their own bodies. They also lead very open and expressive emotional lives. In both books, marijuana is as commonplace as beer, partly for its ability to focus one's attention on the here and now and on sensual enjoyments. Everyone is a backpacker and enjoys the wilderness without such props as all-terrain vehicles. Much schooling is devoted to living off the land, to animals and insects and plants and knowing their ecological functions. The workweek has been reduced to twenty hours and the standard of living is cut in half, but people are encouraged and trained to enjoy that leisure time. Even necessary drudgery, such as cleaning up the dishes after supper, is turned into entertainment with discussion, back rubs, jokes, and other group interactions.

   Perhaps most striking is the dismissal of the "rugged individualist" ideal in favor of a much more socially interdependent life. Marriage is important not just to the individuals involved but to the circles of friends they live with, and most people live in groups, sharing a wide variety of tasks like cooking and growing vegetables. Children get emotional support not just from parents but from all the adults in the group; thus, if a marriage breaks up, the consequences are less drastic for all.

   The ideals of hippies, flower children, collectives, and back-to-nature communes are thus transformed into a national pattern in both novels. Specialization is possible, although the intense specialization necessary for society seeking ever-higher technology is not. This society seeks to provide a comfortable life for everyone, but it does not allow expensive, high-tech solutions for the few. The utopia's medical system, for instance, does not go to extremes to preserve life at all cost, but it does far more than late twentieth-century medicine to make a hospital stay a healing, comforting, and even pleasant experience. Steady state, renewable resources, sustainable yield: these are the ideals, not novelties that result in progress, ever more complex technologies, and ever growing consumption. Reasonable though these ideals may sound to some readers, this fictional Pacific Northwest does not find it easy to separate itself from America's headlong rush down the path to bankruptcy and "permissible deaths" (55) for industrial progress. Even the U.S. Supreme Court interferes with the regional rejection of cars and the electric grid. The president of the United States scolds the Pacific Northwest for trying to withdraw from the automotive way of life and the national power grid: "it was irresponsible for the Survivalists to try to secure favored status for the Northwest at the expense of other Americans. Where was their sense of patriotism, he asked, where their dedication to the great American Dream of a continent united from sea to shining sea?" (*Emerging* 268). From the Ecotopian viewpoint, America is a country that has become insane and suicidal (Pynchon, in *Gravity's Rainbow*, considers us suicidal energy addicts). Somehow, collectively, America's people want "to drive off a cliff in a Cadillac rather than hike along the edge and enjoy the view" (*Emerging* 155); they are incapable of voting for long-term benefits over short-term gains. Pulling out is a matter of sanity and self-preservation, no matter that it can be labeled treason and no matter what the American Dream is or once might have been. Most American voters are blind to the conspiracies linking industrial giants, the government, the courts, and the FBI. Callenbach writes as one willing to give up on America, and *Ecotopia Emerging* is unusual in laying out a plan for revolution—a relatively peaceful revolution but a revolution nonetheless.

Cities of the Red Night (1981) and The Moon Is a Harsh Mistress (1966)

Macdonald's *Turner Diaries* and Callenbach's *Ecotopia* and *Ecotopia Emerging* are novels partly fueled by their authors' different conspiratorial visions of America, and both consider American democracy a failure. Two other novels are less conspiracy generated but show the same radical critique of American democracy: the prologue to William S. Burroughs's *Cities of the Red Night* (otherwise a time-travel and disease fantasy) and Robert A. Heinlein's *Moon Is a Harsh Mistress.* Both works complain that American democracy has destroyed its right to exist by meddling far too much in the affairs of the individual, telling people what to do and with whom to do it. Both want to see liberal forms of positive government dismantled and governing structures reduced to the minimum necessary to protect individual rights.

Burroughs looks to the pirate communes of the seventeenth and early eighteenth centuries for his model society. Like Kathy Acker, he sees pirates as antibourgeois and freedom seeking in their mode of life. His primary example, Captain Mission, established a very simple and limited form of government with a set of articles: "The articles state, among other things: all decisions with regard to the colony to be submitted to vote by the colonists; the abolition of slavery for any reason including debt; the abolition of the death penalty; and freedom to follow any religious beliefs or practices without sanction or molestation" (xii).

Mission actually located his group on Madagascar, but Burroughs states that similar colonies were established in the West Indies and in Central and South America; however, his critique, indirect though it may be, is directed toward North America. Had these communes flourished, especially if they added to those rights the right to follow any sexual practices desired without sanction or molestation, "mankind might have stepped free from the deadly impasse of insoluble problems in which we now find ourselves" (xiv).

Because America took the wrong road at the fork, it has probably lost true freedom forever:

> The chance was there. The chance was missed. The principles of the French and American revolutions became windy lies in the mouths of politicians. The liberal revolutions of 1848 created the so-called republics of Central and South America, with a dreary history of dictatorship, oppression, graft, and bureaucracy, thus closing this vast, underpopulated continent to any possibility of communes along the lines set forth by Captain Mission. In any case South America will soon be crisscrossed by highways and motels. In England, Western Europe, and America, the overpopulation made possible by the Industrial Revolution leaves scant room for communes, which are commonly subject to state and federal law and frequently harassed by the local inhabitants. There is simply no room left for "freedom from the tyranny of government" since city dwellers depend on it for food, power, water, transportation, protection, and welfare. Your right to live where you want, with companions of your choosing, under laws to which you agree, died in the eighteenth century with Captain Mission. Only a miracle or a disaster could restore it. (xiv–xv)

North America never really tried the freedoms that Burroughs mentions. Too many settlements were founded expressly to limit living patterns with their control-oriented forms of Christianity rather than to open up possibilities for enjoyment. However, Burroughs clearly feels that had such communes flourished in the Southern Hemisphere, they would have attracted so many people from the north that the example might have spread before industrialized populations rose to prohibitive heights. For all that his talk of pirate communes does not say much about North America, Burroughs's anger over lost liberties is directed toward the Land of Liberty: one of his plotlines contrasts Protestant, rule-bound Boston with a commune in Central America, much to Boston's disadvantage. Not only do the communards enjoy imaginative, mystical sex, but they are technologically creative as well (Burroughs sees a link between the two). Burroughs might well agree with William Slothrop in *Gravity's Rainbow* that pigs enjoying a cross-country trip were all that Boston was not. Of course, most Bostonians would have thought Burroughs's commune dwellers, with their public sexual practices and homosexuality, to be worse than pigs.

Robert A. Heinlein's *Moon Is a Harsh Mistress* shows us what life in

America might have been like had America's founders made better decisions in 1776 and had they embraced truly libertarian principles. To do so,
he has to cut through the historical distortions accreted to American conservative and libertarian thought—the racism, for instance, which has no
necessary place in conservative theory.[19]

Heinlein invites his readers to look critically at America by means of
three perspectival alterations. First, he takes as his subject a future culture that has developed on the moon by 2076 and for which he stages a
replay of the American Revolution of 1776, complete with a Declaration
of Independence that repeats the original word for word. Second, he sends
his protagonist on a brief visit to Earth, thus allowing himself to comment
unfavorably on America as it has developed by 2076. Third, Heinlein portrays the moon's culture, as it develops after its revolution, so that it embodies what he most decries in contemporary American social thought—
above all, its liberal concept of positive government.

The moon is a prison colony; because the warden does not care what
prisoners do, they can do anything they like, as long as they sell sufficient
grain to the catapult head to send food to the overpopulated Earth. Heinlein stresses that in this the prisoners (or "Loonies") are deprived of "the
most basic human right" (24), the right to sell to a free market—and indeed, the prices given for the grain are grossly insufficient—but the society is astonishingly free in all other respects. It has no laws. If the moon's
inhabitants want an education, they can pay someone to teach them. If they
want insurance, they can place a bet with a bookie. Any kind of family
arrangement is possible, and the preponderance of male convicts inspires
these people to invent a wide variety of group marriages. Because offensive behavior can get one ejected into the vacuum of space by those offend-
ed, people have learned to be polite and to adhere to rational social rules
regarding the rights of others.

This near-utopia is direly threatened, however, by a lack of water. The
moisture contained in the shipped grain is desperately needed on the moon.
Its loss will desiccate the moon within as little as a decade, so a cabal consisting of the hero (a computer repairman named Mannie), two friends, and
a sentient computer named Mike work behind the scenes to create a revolution. Rather than starve in a decade, they have to destroy a society that
is both tyrannically unfree and yet almost perfectly free. They do not fully realize how much of their freedom they will lose until their revolution
succeeds.

When Heinlein considers human nature, he is unworried by the propen-
sity to kill because he considers that ultimately rational; unlike Bellow
or Mailer, he sees no ecstasy in the act, viewing it as something that individuals will control in their own best interests. Indeed, human propensi-
ty to kill contributes positively, in a Darwinian fashion, to the elimina-

tion of the stupid, the unself-controlled, the vicious, the lazy, and the tyrannical. Humanity's fatal flaw is not murderousness but many individuals' determination to prohibit others from doing what they want to, even
if the action does no harm to the objecting individuals or to others. When
the Loonies are faced with putting together their own government, the
enthusiasts for legislated behavior come out of the woodwork with a vengeance:

> One female (most were men, but women made up for it in silliness) had a
> long list she wanted made permanent laws—about private matters. No
> more plural marriage of any sort. No divorces. No "fornication"—had to
> look that one up. No drinks stronger than 4% beer. Church services only
> on Saturdays and all else to stop that day. (Air and temperature and pres-
> sure engineering, lady? Phones and capsules?) A long list of drugs to be
> prohibited and a shorter list dispensed only by licensed physicians. . . .
> Look, lady, *aren't* any medical schools in Luna! . . . always somebody
> agreed with her prohibitions. Must be a yearning deep in human heart to
> stop other people from doing as they please. Rules, laws—always for *oth-
> er* fellow. . . . *not one* of those people said: "Please pass this so that I won't
> be able to do something I know I should stop." Nyet, tovarishchee, was
> *always* something they hated to see neighbors doing. Stop them "for their
> own good"—not because speaker claimed to be harmed by it. (161)

Clearly, Heinlein resents current American practices, many of them orig-
inating in liberal impulses to protect the buyer, the child, the minority,
the poor. He feels that people should band together and protect themselves.

Even the most perfectly laissez-faire society must have some government, and that is where trouble begins for the designers of the revolution.
For most of the story, Heinlein finds his ideal dictator in his sentient master
computer, Mike.[20] Mike can draw on a whole library of information, work
ballistic or engineering problems, create the video appearances of "Adam
Selene" (himself as leader), control telephones and other support systems,
count votes and make them come out as he wishes, and—above all—cal-
culate the chances of the revolution succeeding at every turning point. His
odds make policy choices easy for the central committee; essentially, they
never have more than one choice and so suffer no anguish of indecision;
nor are they surprised by many unforeseen side effects. The computer
makes the revolution possible, yet Heinlein allows Mike's sentience to be
destroyed by the final bombardment. Possibly, Mike has proved humans
to be superfluous. Possibly, he would prove to be the perfect, unstoppable
dictator. Possibly, his removal is necessary to let humans stand on their
own and prove what they can do. Regrettably, what they do is to demonstrate their rampant inadequacy. One part of Heinlein wants his people to
be adults and make their own decisions; another part of him hates the stu-

pidity and shortsightedness of the decisions they make. A subsequent Heinlein novel, *The Cat Who Walks through Walls*, shows later lunar society riddled with red tape, corruption, prohibitions, regulations, secret police, surveillance, and dangers. Postrevolutionary freedom has not been a success from Heinlein's viewpoint, on the moon or in America; in the later novel, his lunar symbolic equivalent to America is thoroughly riddled with conspiracy and corruption.

Heinlein's alter ego, Professor Bernardo de la Paz, puts the libertarian case to the constitutional convention: "Let your document be studded with things the government is forever forbidden to do. No conscript armies . . . no interference however slight with freedom of press, or speech, or travel, or assembly, or of religion, or of instruction, or communication, or occupation . . . no involuntary taxation. . . . What I fear most are affirmative actions of sober and well-intentioned men, granting to government powers to *do* something that appears to need doing" (242). However, when it comes to positive suggestions, Heinlein can come up with nothing better than a pious wish for a philosopher-king. While he finds such a figure conceivable in an individual (Mike the computer or Professor de la Paz), he sees no way of producing a line of such paragons to continue the light reins of ideal governance.

The political grail for Heinlein, as for Walker Percy's character Tom More in *Love in the Ruins*, is to find some combination of man and machine that will provide salvation or ideal government. Such a combination might offer us better results than American democracy has achieved. With a logical machine to handle the mechanical matters of a minimal government, and with a computer offering analyses of crises, humans might wreak less havoc than otherwise. They might follow more logical courses of action. Heinlein signals this hope in his hero, Mannie, who represents such a combination in that he has a bionic arm; thus, he combines with human priorities unusual skills, such as micromanipulation, that are usually possible only for machines. At the individual level, the combination of human and machine appears successful. At the national, it eludes America, and computer developments since the 1960s make that ideal seem unattainable. In William Gibson's *Neuromancer*, illegal manipulation of computers by hackers is taken for granted. Gibson's worldview belongs to the conspiratorial and, as such, is pessimistic. Few readers of current science fiction would be likely to trust to the impartiality and incorruptibility of computers as a government tool.

Although revolution was sometimes the war cry of campus radicals, it has never appealed to large segments of the population. Burroughs and Heinlein do not so much call for revolution as lament that the original American Revolution was not thorough enough, a point also made by T. Coraghessan Boyle in *World's End*. Macdonald and Callenbach are more serious about overturning the current U.S. government. Utopias almost by definition need either extreme isolation to be "possible," or they need a cataclysm that changes local conditions for mainstream society. Revolution supplies the necessary catalyst for change.

The Light That Failed: Pynchon

Revolutions for racial purity, for ecological protectionism, or for greater freedom: in the United States, none has in fact taken place nor even acquired much political power as a movement. A few instances of chemical pollution, insecticide residues, and endangered species have achieved national visibility. However, characters in Callenbach's *Ecotopia Emerging* would insist that our measures have been much too little and much too late, a Band-Aid that lets us feel smug at restraining ourselves rather than any sort of step that will matter to the long-range patterns of destruction. Even if political revolution was never a genuinely plausible idea in the 1960s, the belief that things were changing was real enough. The birth-control pill brought major changes in sexual mores. The war in Vietnam eventually ended. The civil rights movement gained momentum, and various minorities began to make their views heard. In the Reagan and Bush years, however, as the country turned toward conservative patterns, those who had experienced and welcomed the 1960s woke up to wonder what had happened. Why were even those modest changes fading?

Vineland (1990)

Vineland has been seen as a Reagan era lament for the lost age of the 1960s, an analogue to the films *The Big Chill* and *Running on Empty*.[21] To see where Pynchon is coming from, however, it pays to look at *Vineland* in conjunction with *The Crying of Lot 49*. Both are curiously critical of the 1960s and dwell on America's failures of the period rather than on the ephemeral gains. The protagonist of the earlier book is Oedipa Maas, an oedipal figure who seeks the cause of a cultural malaise and finds it to be herself. Toward the end of her quest, she finds herself wondering why she did not physically assault a seller of swastikas and SS uniforms and recognizes her complicity by concluding that she is cowardly and that "this is America, you live in it, you let it happen" (112). Oedipa, once a Young Republican, was never part of America's radical movement; however, many characters in *Vineland* are. This novel is Pynchon's *1984*; indeed, it is rather ostentatiously set in that Orwellian year. It looks at Big Brother–like security and surveillance and at the countercultural resistance to "Them," whether the resistors are the Industrial Workers of the World (IWW) in the 1930s, communist sympathizers in the 1940s and 1950s, or the campus radicals high on drugs and rock 'n' roll in the 1960s. Pynchon identifies two interconnected flaws in the logic of the 1960s: first, an important discontinuity in the radical-left political tradition, such that 1960s campus protests did not have real goals or encompassable aims; second, an erotic response to power and authority. He sees these as contributing to the wasted potential of the 1960s and making possible the rise of fascism in the near future.

Frenesi, a 1960s radical, comes of a radical family. Her mother and grandmother were union agitators who had real goals: they worked to make a specific company capitulate and tried to change particular labor practices. Eula, the grandmother, had been "bounced as a baby upon the knees of family friends known to have shot at as well as personally dropped company finks, styled 'inspectors,' down mine shafts" (76). When she marries a Wobbly, she gets used "to an idea of 'together' that included at least one of them being in jail in any given year" (76). When their daughter Sasha goes to work, she hears tales of the General Strike of 1934 from stevedores who threw ball bearings under the hooves of the police mounts:

> By the time the war came along she'd worked in stores, offices, shipyards, and airplane plants, had soon learned of the effort to organize farm workers in the valleys of California, known as the Inland March, and gone out there for a while to help, living on ditch-banks with Mexican and Filipino immigrants and refugees from the dustbowl, standing midwatch guard against vigilante squads and hired goons from the Associated Farmers, getting herself shot at more than once, writing home about it. . . . Growing up, Frenesi heard stories of those prewar times, the strike at the Stockton cannery, strikes over Ventura sugar beets, Venice lettuce, San Joaquin cotton . . . of the anticonscription movement in Berkeley, where, as Sasha was careful to remind her, demonstrations had been going on before Mario Savio was born, not only in Sproul Plaza but against Sproul himself. (77)

Strikes aimed at specific companies provide clear goals. The kinds of action open to the radicals are obvious, and the penalties (not just the law but management-arranged maimings or illicit surveillance) are also known. The campus secession that dominates *Vineland* is an act of a very different sort. For the stodgy College of the Surf to declare itself the People's Republic of Rock and Roll is a purely symbolic act. No chance exists that the campus might become an independent country, yet the declaration produces as much euphoria as would have fizzed up had they actually achieved independence from the U.S. government. The secession of Bolinas in Callenbach's *Ecotopia Emerging* at least happens in a context where the whole geographical region is testing an impulse to withdraw, and fundamental separation from the rest of the United States has already taken place with the banning of automobiles. Bolinas is a serious test case, where-as the People's Republic of Rock and Roll is merely a carnival.

During this 1960s rebellion, the students treat symbolism as if it were substantial. This is one of Pynchon's main criticisms. Frenesi belongs to a film collective whose manifesto proclaims that "a camera is a gun. An image taken is a death performed. Images put together are the substruc-ture of an afterlife and a Judgment. We will be architects of a just Hell for the fascist pig. Death to everything that oinks!" (197). The later collective she belongs to lives off slogans such as "film equals sacrifice" or Che Guevara's "wherever death may surprise us" (202). Frenesi likes to see the electricity she steals for floodlights as "draining off . . . the lifeblood of the fascist monster, Central Power itself" (202). These are all symbolic stances, however, not very substantial as blows to the system. When up against real guns, she and her cohorts are horrified and feel abused. Her mother and grandmother were both experienced with flying bullets and would not have made the mistake of thinking a camera in any sense equal to or equiva-lent to a firearm. Treating symbols as substance is a political mistake, one akin to the students not having specific, realizable goals.[22]

Frenesi makes another mistake that her mother, Sasha, at least resist-ed. Since her first Rose Bowl parade, Sasha "felt in herself a fatality, a help-less turn toward images of authority, especially uniformed men, whether they were athletes live or on the Tube, actors in movies of war through the ages, or maître d's in restaurants, not to mention waiters and busboys" (83). Sasha refused to give in to this "dangerous swoon" and even knows that her rebellions against authority figures may just be acts of denial. Frenesi, however, does not resist; moreover, her daughter Prairie, after being saved from abduction by the quasi-Nazi Brock Vond, goes back to the clearing in the same woods and whispers to the stars: "It's OK, rilly. Come on, come in. I don't care. Take me anyplace you want" (384). Nor is this weakness for powerful men just a baffling genetic trait. Frenesi's friend D. L. Chastaine also exhibits it; in her case, the feeling is tied to her love/hate relationship with her father, who was a military policeman. She shows her attitude toward men of power in her reaction to a mafia don, and she agrees to carry out his scheme for killing Brock Vond that involves seduc-ing Vond first.

This erotic response toward men in authority, especially when uni-formed, is something Pynchon first sketched a version of in *The Crying of Lot 49*. The California city that proves to be the center of that novel's spiderweb, the source for all the clues to the mysterious Tristero system, is San Narciso, and Pynchon traces the narcissistic spirit back to St. Nar-cissus and the Italian Renaissance, when cultivation of the self did indeed become paramount. Oedipa Maas registers at the Echo Courts motel, and the thirty-foot high nymph representing Echo looks, Oedipa realizes, rather like herself. In other words, the trouble is being cast in terms of men like Narcissus who love themselves and put self-interest above all else or in the mold of the women like Echo who love those men. Pierce Inverarity, Oedipa's former lover and apparently the secret owner of every enterprise in San Narciso, was one such narcissist, and men in uniform are surely a different form of the same preening self-love.[23]

Frenesi comes to see her radical activities as somehow childish and reluctantly comes to believe that a more middle-class way of life is adult and inevitable. Her parents' activities, perhaps because tied directly to adult labor, suffered from no such air of childish irrelevance. Pynchon thus criticizes America in general for oppressive capitalism but also takes to task its 1960s radicals for their childish irresponsibility, for not coming concretely to terms with problems, or indeed for not defining approachable problems at all. He also criticizes the eroticized response to authority, which he deems primarily a female problem. He notes that Reagan's being elected president was made possible by his having played uniformed roles, such as baseball player or officer; through those roles, he won the sexual interest of women and became a totem figure for men as well.[24]

In *The Crying of Lot 49*, Pynchon shows the suddenly expanded horizons of the 1960s that made anything—including communing with Maxwell's Demon—seem possible, but he also shows Oedipa realizing that too many people have been excluded from the network of power that is America. Pierce Inverarity's legacy to Oedipa turns out to be San Narciso and, by extension, America. However, it is an America imbued with the narcissistic spirit and is hence a land where too many are disenfranchised and disinherited, ignored by the democratic process:

> That America coded in Inverarity's testament, whose was that? She thought of other, immobilized freight cars, where the kids sat on the floor planking and sang back, happy as fat, whatever came over the mother's pocket radio; of other squatters who stretched canvas for lean-tos behind smiling billboards along the highways, or slept in junkyards in the stripped shells of wrecked Plymouths, or even, daring, spent the night up some pole in a lineman's tent like caterpillars, swung among a web of telephone wires, living in the very copper rigging and secular miracle of communication, untroubled by the dumb voltages flickering their miles, the night long, in the thousands of unheard messages. She remembered drifters she had listened to . . . and walkers along the roads at night. (135)

Nor are these the only sort of dispossessed. There are also those whose erotic practices are not countenanced, those whose politics are extreme, those displaced by computers, those grown too old, those with delirium tremens, those with nonwhite skin. Such people enter her quest, and she discovers that they communicate by the alternate postal system because they are excluded from the exchanges of those considered normal. She decides that only by accepting a paranoid vision can she begin to understand a reality in which oppressive government power is all too real. Life as a radical, an outlaw on the run, is indeed what some of the characters in *Vineland* take up, so in many ways, that book is a logical extension of the revelations in *The Crying of Lot 49*. In both, the 1960s form a curiously ambiguous cusp: had the revolution of 1960s radicals become real, it would have represented the opening of America. Since the radicalism of the 1960s failed, however, since it did not focus on feasible targets, since it did not get beyond childishness, the cusp turned out to be of another sort, the knuckling under to Big Brother and a future that appears to be headed for fascism. Insofar as the 1960s represented a new light, by the 1980s, that light has decisively failed.

Among films, *The Big Chill* shows the 1960s as a time of innocence, morality, and integrity. The 1980s are a period in which most of these same student radicals feel they have sold out—to business, to a safe but boring marriage, to a higher-paying job, to meaningless acting in a television series, to gossip-column writing. One of their number has committed suicide; as the mourners gather after the funeral, they look back on their college days as the point at which they knew the right road to take, but they realize that they have basically taken the expedient and profitable road instead. The suicide reminds them that back then, they would have considered themselves better off dead than doing the things they do now, the "adult" things that superseded the youthful ideals. No possibility of change is offered, and none of them seems to feel a real urge to sacrifice comfort for a more authentic existence. They do not even see what causes they should espouse anymore. They feel caught, living relatively uneasy lives of self-betrayal.

๑ ๑ ๑

The ideas that added to the strident tone of the 1960s were not in fact very new. One has only to turn to the McCarthy hearings of the 1950s to see the previous wave of paranoia. McCarthy and many mainstream politicians saw conspiracies in high places and felt American democracy had been compromised by such corruption. Moreover, the revolutionary alternatives represented by various communist countries were known in the 1930s and 1940s. Why did the 1960s seem different?

The Vietnam War was one reason; as an unpopular war considered unjust by many, it gave emotional weight to charges that the government was corrupt. Liberals tended to share the same outlooks on several issues, so they would be hostile to the war, open to the arguments of ecology, supportive of the civil rights movement, and critical of the CIA, FBI, and other bodies involved in covert operations, spying, and secret control. Support for peace and racial equality lent their stances a feeling of moral superiority. Because of the confluence of these issues, however, the hostility came to be directed toward the government and other large institutions and not just at overzealous leaders. In the 1930s and 1940s, communists were active in labor matters but did not have the power over major media that industrialists did. Their voices got little airing before middle-class audiences. In the 1960s, the liberals who turned against the government included Ivy League professors and major journalists. They could get media exposure for their views and could not be accused of being foreigners or bad losers. Their critique of democracy has a tone all its own because as a group, they were the beneficiaries of the American Dream, people who had done moderately to very well economically and educationally. In the Eisenhower years, they had been very much a part of the system. For such liberals to accept a conspiracy outlook demands their rejecting belief in a basically sane and improving world. Their entering Conspiracyland, as many ultimately did, coincided with liberalism's entering a decline. Not that liberals are the only critics of America; critics on the right reject democracy precisely because of its susceptibility to liberal assumptions and intrusive legislation.

Belief in American democracy was once practically an element of American spirituality. Many of the writers of this era feel wounded by the loss of that foundation. If any common assumption is visible among these authors, it might be that the individual is still important and still capable of making a difference at least to himself or herself and, possibly, to the broader community as well. The next chapter's novelists, however, those sharing a demonic vision, indicate that individuals have been rendered meaningless by the coherence and malignity of the powers marshaled against them.

chapter six

Demonic *Visions*

In the conspiratorial vision of America, respected institutions prove to be false fronts for unsavory interests. This may seem a bleak representation of the country, but it still permits characters some power to act within that world. Protagonists like Daniel Isaacson or Oedipa Maas may fail to resolve the tangled evidence into coherence, but they have at least attempted to uncover truth. Jim Garrison in *JFK* and the protagonist of the film *The Parallax View* go further in attempting to oppose and expose wrongdoing. Even the most nation-devouring network of plotters and assassins leaves a corner of the individual's mind untampered with; Shaw emerges from his brainwashing in *The Manchurian Candidate*. The demonic visions of this present chapter leave no such loopholes. They proclaim America to be profoundly fouled by evil. The victims' wriggles only bear witness to the cruelty of the power that torments them. Readers long for an escape route and, if white and middle class, long for reassurance that freedom and justice (as they have mythologized them) will prevail. What readers find is that the fire exits have been nailed shut.

Northrop Frye makes many acute observations about this kind of literary vision, which falls in the purview of his ironic mode and mythos. When discussing that mode in *Anatomy of Criticism*, he analyzes stories with protagonists who are "below" us as readers: "we have the sense of looking down on a scene of bondage, frustration, or absurdity" (34). Frye's five modes descend from mythic to romantic, from high mimetic to low mimetic, and thence to ironic. He writes that "irony. . . . begins in realism and dispassionate observation. But as it does so, it moves steadily toward myth, and dim outlines of sacrificial rituals and dying gods begin to reappear in it. Our five modes evidently go around in a circle. This reappearance of myth in the ironic is particularly clear in Kafka and in Joyce" (42). Among his categories of symbolism, the demonic belongs to this ironic world. The demonic building corresponding to the temple in the divine world is the prison or

dungeon. Fire, instead of representing purification or the source of revelation (as in the burning bush, halo, or mystic light), takes the form of an auto-
da-fé. The erotic, too, is infernalized; Frye argues that "the demonic parody of marriage, or of the union of two souls in one flesh, may take the form
of hermaphroditism, incest (the most common form), or homosexuality.
The social relation is that of the mob, which is essentially human society
looking for a pharmakos [scapegoat]" (149). When discussing the ironic
mythos, Frye identifies features of its oppressive phase as "prisons, mad-
houses, lynching mobs, and places of execution" (238). The only ray of hope
he offers relates to the cyclical nature of literary forms: "Tragedy and tragic irony take us into a hell of narrowing circles and culminate in some such
vision of the source of all evil in a personal form. Tragedy can take us no
farther; but if we persevere with the *mythos* of irony and satire, we shall
pass a dead center, and finally see the gentlemanly Prince of Darkness bottom side up" (239). This chapter will look at two novels with demonic
impulses that show some mythicized glimmer of hope at the end; the other novels discussed, though, remain locked in the infernal world of bondage, frustration, and ironized myths of killing.

The books analyzed in this chapter all argue that America is past redemption. In the first group, the government plays the villain and turns citizens
into sacrificial victims. Irony shades into the mythic with a vengeance in
these rituals. Ishmael Reed's protagonist dies after hanging on a hook for
three days; Robert Coover's Rosenbergs make their way to their electrified
autos-da-fé after spending their time in a prison, and Uncle Sam's rape of
Nixon is grossly shocking as a realization of the demonic erotic. In the second section of the chapter, institutions other than the government play a
similarly oppressive role: mental hospitals in Ken Kesey and Marge Piercy;
patriarchy in Kathy Acker. Mental hospitals can make the horror more intimate by invading the very minds of patients and altering thoughts or feelings. Patriarchy is a cultural rather than physical institution, and the feminist vision of its oppressions can be general as well as American. However,
Acker (and, later in the chapter, Andrea Dworkin) locate much of their action in America and blame America for failing to live up to its ideals of
equality, liberty, and justice. In the third section of the chapter, the rituals
of violence are played out as personal interactions, and here we find the perspective sometimes that of victim, sometimes that of perpetrator. Bret
Easton Ellis's *American Psycho* lets us inhabit the mind of the perpetrator
as he carries out his deadly rituals of torture and murder, and Norman Mailer's *Why Are We in Vietnam?* shows a protagonist who is both victim and
perpetrator involved in a ritual hunt. Andrea Dworkin's *Mercy* focuses on
the victim and the array of abuses women can suffer, with each episode
presenting one variation on rape, some of them explicitly linked to religion.

No matter what the perspective—victim or tormenter—we find ritual shaping the violence so noticeably that I once thought of calling this chapter "America as Black Mass." The final section of the chapter will look at books that peer through the gloomy shadows of bondage toward the emergence of new mythic possibilities. Both Gerald Vizenor's *Bearheart: The Heirship Chronicles* and Leslie Marmon Silko's *Almanac of the Dead* seek the holy moment when the world order as we now know it implodes. Their visions are world destroying, but holiness is possible, and some gleam of transcendence beyond all the horror can be sought.

Not surprisingly, we find in this chapter several authors who belong to nonhegemonic groups. Native American, African-American, and female experiences can all produce visions of unremitting bleakness. That their literary expression should involve the construction of ritual does suggest that the demonic vision moves us into a kind of sacred territory. I suggest that while many Americans have ceased to believe in the hell of theology, for some, hell has just moved closer to home and everyday life. Hell has also become a rhetoric of lament and accusation.

Murder as Central Ritual of the State: Reed and Coover

In *The Fictions of Satire*, Ronald Paulson points out that satires tend to spiral down to a central symbol of violence, an image that remains an ultimate horror or grotesquerie. He lists the copulation of ass and woman (Apuleius's *Metamorphoses*), the drowning of Paris in a flood of urine (Rabelais's *Gargantua*), the sawing off a man's head (Waugh's *Decline and Fall*), and the threat of firing Lilliputian arrows into Gulliver's eyes (Swift's *Gulliver's Travels*). Paulson argues that "these scenes represent the characteristic fictions through which the satirist conveys his subject matter: the corruption of an ideal and the behavior of fools, knaves, dupes, and the like" (9). Both Reed and Coover chose a form of ritualized murder: legal execution carried out by the state. Although the crucifixion produces a few echoes in each, neither author claims messianic status for his protagonists. Reed's Bukka Doopeyduk is more like Candide, a stumblebum innocent who proves ineffectual as a savior. Coover's Rosenbergs are working for a better world, and do come to see themselves as having a role they must play to be true to their principles, but the role is that of the victim, not the leader or redeemer. Coover presents them as brave little people, not the heroes of a romance of mythic stature. With legal execution as its central symbolic scene, the state has become the sow that eats her own farrow. By one formulation, the American state exists to protect the individual's rights to life, liberty, and pursuit of happiness. To consume that individual instead is the most profound denial possible of that basic function.

The Free-Lance Pallbearers (1967)

Bukka Doopeyduk dies spiked on meat hooks in the Emperor Franz Joseph Park. Like Damiens, the regicide described in Michel Foucault's *Discipline and Punish*, Bukka suffers while the state inscribes its Kafkaesque discourse of power on his body. What is the message? He and other minority citizens are meat to be eaten by HARRY SAM, who is both the ruler of the country and the country itself. His presentation to the public as meat is symbolic, but Bukka had discovered HARRY SAM's cannibalism to be literal as well.[1]

Bukka's experience with the country—incarnated in HARRY SAM—is not propitious. Bukka has dropped out of college and cleans bedpans in a hospital. His treatment in divorce court is grotesque. The hospital fires him rather than do the paperwork for garnisheeing his pay for alimony. Mistakenly identified as a radical black leader, Bukka is summoned to the government seat to be blandished by the Big Man himself (who shares a few mannerisms with LBJ). Bukka is overwhelmed to be offered a Nazarene bishopric and promises to assure the poor that "IT'S GOING TO BE ALL RIGHT, BY AND BY IN THE SKY" (133).

When Bukka hears screams that night, however, he seeks the source and finds men sodomizing each other. SAM roars at this interruption of his "Goat-she-ate-shuns" (135)—a fine term combining the pungent sexuality of the goat, the female role taken by some of the men, the sexual "eating" of each other (plus, as we will soon learn, the cannibalistic eating of children), the shunned nature of the activity, and the notion that these negotiations are how SAM's government works. Sam sodomizes those who want power; they, in turn, love it—or, at any rate, they come crawling back for more. Mailer in *Why Are We in Vietnam?* and Coover in *The Public Burning* lash us with this same squalid image of repulsively rendered male-male rape as a metaphor for the actions of governing power on those governed, particularly those with ambitions of their own to rise within the system.[2]

If grotesque sodomy is the first punch to Bukka's solar plexus, cannibalism is the second. After a slapstick chase sequence, he opens a door and is bowled over by "hundreds of tiny skulls" (137). Bukka realizes where missing children from the housing projects have ended up. This Candide-like figure had worshipped SAM and had believed his country's promises that life would get better, that hard work and determination were enough, that justice would prevail. He finds nauseating evidence that contradicts all his cherished convictions.

One final ugliness darkens Reed's image of this country. SAM manages to escape by diving down a toilet and going through the sewer into the Black Bay, an area lethally polluted by government documents, most of

them broken promises, spewed forth from the four great heads of Ruther-
ford B. Hayes, the president who dismantled the efforts of Reconstruction
to right racial wrongs. The trip down the sewer and the world of the bay
confirm the demonic excrementality of Reed's vision.[3]

   Reed's major images in this novel involve cannibalistic consumption of
the poor, power politics as sodomy, and shit gumming up life. Academic
research consists of pushing a dung-ball around the world. That dung-ball,
grown enormous, hangs over the three-day death pangs of Bukka on the
hook. SAM suffers from intestinal problems that have forced him to live
on a toilet for thirty years, and he smells atrocious. Bukka cleans bedpans.
The Black Bay's pollution involves the excrement of governmental words
pouring ceaselessly from large heads (double meaning) into the water. This
stercoraceous vision of an ironic world suits both the cannibalistic concerns (feces being the result of eating anything) and the anal locus of the
sodomies. Submersion in shit is one of Dante's circles of hell, an image
also used by Bellow to describe the life of Chicago's underclass. Being
gnawed on by Satan is another image from the *Inferno*. The infernal erotic—here the sodomizing of those who wish to rise within the structure—
is likewise appropriate. The electrified statue of SAM triggers thoughts of
the electric chair, that demonic perversion of fire.

   Reed may have gotten his image of the meat hook from the practices of
Chicago gangsters, but it suits his vision of the poor as rich men's meat.
In turning the oppressed into comestible meat, he is also touching on other
visions of ultimate repulsion. In Joseph Conrad's *Heart of Darkness,* sav-
agery involves cannibalism and brings forth the famous reaction to devolution from European ideals: "The horror." Furthermore, both James
Joyce's Stephen Dedalus and Russell Hoban's Riddley Walker realize that
what terrifies them about life is the reducibility of human life to flesh and
bone, with the implications that spirit may die or may not exist, and (for
Riddley) the awareness that those wanting power over others can torture
their victims' flesh and bone to make them do anything. These conceptu-
alizations of man's fundamental nature are not the same as Reed's, but they
all belong to the demonic—a terminal and apparently unredeemable picture based on man's physical nature as mortal meat. The particular spin
that Ishmael Reed puts on it—consume and be consumed—is devastatingly
appropriate to a critique of a consumerist culture.

The Public Burning (1977)

Robert Coover's brilliant novel has been analyzed as metafiction, a political novel, an example of the carnivalesque, a circus, a ritual, and a deconstruction of history—to name but a few useful approaches.[4] My reading
stresses Northrop Frye's demonic, which makes it grimmer than one em-

phasizing the merely carnivalesque, because this sites Coover among similar visionaries. No single reading, though, can do justice to this labyrinthine tour de force.

Coover takes us out of ordinary reality by overlapping two regions to create a "Zone"—Brian McHale's word for the nonrealistic territories created through the juxtaposition or superimposition of one region on another (*Postmodernist Fiction* 45–49). In this instance, the execution chamber and an adjacent room at Sing Sing Prison overlap with New York City's Times Square. The scaffold is built in Times Square, and everyone gathering to watch the spectacle can be described; however, the execution also takes place in the prison, and Richard Nixon can stumble backwards into the execution chamber at the prison and find himself in Times Square. The public exposure of the rite makes visible its obscene nature and turns the eager American watchers into ghouls.[5] Coover also collapses separate times in the fashion of Christian religious ritual. The miracle of transubstantiation, for instance, makes the contemporary blessing the actual Last Supper; the original moment impresses itself on the present, and the priest literally becomes Christ. Similarly, Coover briefly collapses moments of nuclear explosion: a moviegoer—by definition the American Everyman—wanders onto the scaffold and sits on the electric chair, where he sees a mushroom cloud. The electrocution of the Rosenbergs, enemies of the state for allegedly selling atomic secrets, conflates the present with the past and future incineration of enemies.[6]

Both electric chair and nuclear fire demonically distort purifying fire, and Nixon's Burning Tree Golf Course makes him a degraded Moses hoping to lead this chosen people. The settings, in keeping with the ironic world, are the prison, the scaffold, and the barren sites of Nixon's personal and public life. Also important is Nixon's iconic status: immigrant parents; relative poverty in childhood; hard work; the vice presidency; and, he is assured, eventual presidency of the United States. He *is* one version of the American Dream, yet his sense of estrangement from everything keeps him from glorying in his success.[7]

Part of what makes this murder a ritual is Coover's elaborate invocation of the three days surrounding the Rosenbergs' executions in 1953. *Time* magazine is the poet laureate, and words straight from the magazine, arranged as free verse, spangle the text with their distilled banalities. Betty Crocker, the commercial goddess of American cooking, serves as mistress of ceremonies for this commie-roast. Every senator and representative is introduced formally; all the Supreme Court justices have walk-on parts in a comedy routine involving their sliding in the dung from the Republican elephant, an animal participant in what at one level is a three-ring circus. The Hollywood and Broadway media treatment necessary for Americans to feel they are truly experiencing something are made available on the scaffold, where the wait is filled by entertainers doing skits based on the Rosenbergs' letters. Fred Astaire and Ginger Rogers do a dance based on the correspondence. Abbott and Costello, Andy Devine and Marjorie Main, Red Skelton, Jack Benny, Laurel and Hardy, and Ozzie and Harriet all turn the Rosenberg anguish into various sorts of popular entertainment (425–26). Coover's most stylish creation is the skit put on by the Marx Brothers. Ethel Rosenberg's having to be shocked several times becomes "Duh-four-shocksa New Worlt Sinfunny" (456). One aspect of ritual in this country is commodification of experience as show business, and Coover shows that process with grisly gusto.

The narrative tensions vibrate between two symbols of violence: the electrocution of the Rosenbergs and the rape of Nixon. Both are rendered in gross physical terms so elaborate and riveting that one cannot escape the horror and obscenity of this demonic vision:

> Julius Rosenberg's body is straining suddenly against the straps as though trying to burst from the chair. Air hisses from his lungs. His neck thickens as though swallowing something whole. The leather straps creak and there is a staticky crackling whine in the Square reminiscent of the classic mad-doctor movies—only more close up. The loose clothes flutter and his limbs shake. Greasy yellow-gray smoke plumes from the top of his head like a cast-out devil. Then abruptly, the whine stops. The body falls back into the chair, limp as a rag. (509–10)

When Ethel is electrocuted multiple times, "her body, sizzling and popping like firecrackers, lights up with the force of the current, casting a flickering radiance on all those around her, and so she burns—and burns—and burns—as though held aloft by her own incandescent will and haloed about by all the gleaming great of the nation" (517). This is demonic fire indeed.

Coover's world is stalked by such supernatural or allegorical powers as The Shadow and Uncle Sam. The Shadow, however, never appears, and may not exist except as an American projection upon the communist other—the setting is 1953, but the novel was written during the struggle with North Vietnamese communists, during continuing hysteria over Cuba, and at the time of the CIA's overthrow of Salvador Allende in Chile. Uncle Sam exists, though, right on the same plane as historical figures. He is raunchy, raucous, self-willed, cunning, energetic, and conscienceless. His way of making democracy work is to sodomize his chosen candidates for president, and he proceeds to rape Nixon shortly after the execution. Nixon whines, "You're not the same as when I was a boy," to which Uncle Sam sniggers, "You're forty years old, son: time you was weaned!" (531). Sam grunts and huffs as he inches in, with Nixon screaming and crying that he does not want the presidency any more:

"No!" I shrieked, giving way. And in he came, filling me with a ripping all-rupturing force so fierce I thought I'd die! This . . . this is not happening to me alone, I thought desperately, or tried to think, as he pounded deeper and deeper, destroying everything, even my senses, my consciousness—but to the nation as well! . . . Jesus, he was killing me! I'd been right about it all along! It *was* my execution! I was utterly gorged by him, he was slamming away in my belly, my chest, my very skull! I couldn't even breathe! I thought my heart would burst, my eyeballs would pop out! I was screaming and howling horribly but nobody came to my rescue. (532–33)

Uncle Sam's orgasm is of truly mythic proportions. Nixon, grateful to have survived, thinks of "Hoover's glazed stare, Roosevelt's anguished tics, Ike's silly smile" (533) and realizes that he should have guessed that they had paid some such price. As Uncle Sam reiterates that Nixon will become president, Nixon realizes, "Whatever else he was, he was beautiful (how had I ever thought him ugly?), the most beautiful thing in all the world. I was ready at last to do what I had never done before. '*I . . . I love you, Uncle Sam!*' I confessed" (534). The parallel to George Orwell's Winston Smith realizing that he loves Big Brother is unmistakable.

Coover achieves extraordinary intensity for this symbolic action by combining mythic dimensions with excruciating physical detail. Ishmael Reed's HARRY SAM also enjoys mythic dimensions, but his impoverished vocabulary (drawn from the blander phrases of LBJ) is no match for the explosively potent word-magic of Coover's Uncle Sam, whose verbal fireworks combine concentrated strangeness with wild creativity. As for gross physicality, I simply note that the quotations I used constitute a very short portion of much longer descriptions. For a male writer to describe unwelcome anal attentions does rouse anxieties, but Coover evidently got beyond those with a thoroughness not managed by Mailer (in *Why Are We in Vietnam?*) or Reed (in *The Free-Lance Pallbearers*). The result is devastating political satire, resulting in a depth of revulsion and rejection unusual even among demonic visions.

Coover's Nixon belongs wholly to the realm of Frye's irony. He is like us in that he has unfulfilled desires, wants to be liked but does not quite succeed, is dissatisfied with himself, mulls over mistakes, daydreams, exhorts himself, and carries on a complex inner life that is funny, painful, very human, and impressive as a literary creation even while it mostly disgusts as a political portrait. Nixon is like us but "below" in that we can see why he is not likable, and we feel the impulse to judge him. He is also a figure of bondage and frustration, yoked to Uncle Sam by his desires but always cringing, fearful of giving the wrong answers, never seeing what Sam has in mind, always groveling. He longs for better but lacks the intelligence, luck, or showmanship to make Sam like him. The book was published in 1977, long after Watergate—and after many delays—but it was written some time prior to that scandal, and the Nixon portrait Coover has created does much to explain the president's behavior in that fiasco.

In conceiving this portrait, Coover does one unexpected thing: he links the early experiences of Nixon to those of Ethel Rosenberg. Neither came from a wealthy family, and the recollections of primitive plumbing or dressing by a stove in the winter, of the love of acting, of the desire to stand out as a reformer—these shared experiences draw Nixon and Ethel together in strange ways. Had history gone somewhat differently, Nixon might have ended up rather like the Rosenbergs. In "real" history, Vice President Nixon apparently had little or nothing to do with the Rosenberg case, but Coover twins him with Ethel in part to show the strange nature of America. One can rise to be president if one does not fix one's attention too firmly on the injustices to the lower classes and the things that are wrong with the country. Small differences determine whether one will achieve rags or riches, the Oval Office or the electric chair. The fact that what determines your fate is insignificant contributes to the demonic nature of the vision. In the demonic, one has little or no control over one's fate. Nixon could so easily have ended up a buffoon, a man who stumbled over his own feet too often (politically speaking) and so lost his place in Washington, D.C. He gets what he thinks he wants but must "grow up" and learn that there is no innocence for those who seek power in America. The fate of innocence in this demonic vision of America is the electric chair. Rather than tolerate the uncorrupted mind, America destroys it.

When the Institution Steals Your Spirit: Kesey, Piercy, and Acker

One Flew over the Cuckoo's Nest (1962)

Ken Kesey's objections to America as a rigid and closed society are couched in terms that were old when Mark Twain wrote *The Adventures of Huckleberry Finn*. White, natural man is uncomfortable in civilization and needs the open, free life of the frontier. Where Huck could light out for parts west or Robert A. Heinlein's Mannie could head for the asteroids in *The Moon Is a Harsh Mistress,* Kesey's Randle Patrick McMurphy suffers because the mythic American frontier no longer exists. Put him among men, give him some adventure and danger, let him gamble, drink, engage in casual sex, and brawl, and he will be happy. McMurphy won a Distinguished Service Cross for leading a prison escape in Korea but was dishonorably discharged for insubordination. He has mostly functioned as a logger but does farm-work and other jobs open to transient laborers. His last brush with the law got him sent to a work farm, and he has taken a transfer to the mental hospital to escape the boredom of weeding. This interlude is merely an adventure to him, a chance to satisfy his curiosity and find new ways of indulging in mischief. However, it brings him up against an institution. In the venom expressed against that institution, readers get true 1960s values, emerging surprisingly early and foreshadowing the hatred of institutions that characterized the political left half-a-dozen years later.[8]

Kesey conceptualizes the tensions behind this novel in two fashions. One is gendered. McMurphy emerges as mythic white American maleness personified, while the hospital lives and breathes through the equally mythic American "momism" of Nurse Ratched. McMurphy soon shows the other inmates that the nurse's policies are designed to rob them of what little "manhood" they may have. McMurphy calls the nurse a "ball-cutter" (57) and plots to upset her, make her lose her cool, and ruin her system of control.[9]

Throughout, Nurse Ratched is the schoolmistress figure in the frontier myth who insists on men wiping their boots, speaking grammatically, avoiding bad language, and taking tea politely with the ladies. European men seem not to have suffered this sense that society and its functions are a female plot to castrate men; Jane Austen's men, or Trollope's, have not the slightest doubt that they have the real power. To behave with gentlemanly restraint makes them feel superior, not unmanned. Some American men are willing to give up their cowboy freedom and settle down— for instance, Owen Wister's Virginian or Curly, in the musical *Oklahoma*. However, America's literature is full of men who flee the responsibilities of a wife and children, or, if they contract such attachments, they come to see them as emasculating and soul destroying. Men with obligations to wives and children cannot risk being killed in a barroom brawl—or, rather, their wives cannot risk it—and so they ban male-bonded behaviors such as boozing and fighting. The word "commitment" is key to the final struggle in this book. McMurphy learns that, unlike a jail sentence, being committed to the mental hospital has no fixed termination. Commitment is thus potentially endless servitude, whether to the institution or to the obligations of society and family.

The central symbol of violence in this vision is lobotomy. A lesser punishment (masquerading as therapy) is electroshock therapy, a scaled down version of the electric chair and the demonized fire seen in Reed and Coover. Throughout, McMurphy treats the attacks on his brain as institutional substitutes for castrating him, which indeed they are. Castration makes male animals more biddable and compliant. McMurphy may be imperfectly socialized by a very narrow ethnic and class-bound concept of acceptable behavior, but he is sane. His behavior would seem entirely normal in a lower-class Irish pub during a Saturday night brawl. Because McMurphy does not fit middle-class WASP norms, Kesey argues, our institutions lobotomize him. Those men who are well adjusted simply do not know that they have been lobotomized. They have been castrated by a society whose values are feminine and hostile to the true natural man. Kesey recasts this basic opposition between nature and civilization in a second form to reinforce his message. The Native American, represented by Chief Bromden, is another version of natural man; and "the Combine" replaces female tyranny with the more generalized tyranny of white government and capitalism. Chief Bromden is a half-breed whose nightmarish visions establish him as insane by normal standards. Symbolically, though, the machinery he sees underneath the skin of doctors matches their lack of human feeling. Opposed to the mechanisms are his memories of the natural world: salmon leaping and slapping the water at the weirs, or a dog sniffing prairie-dog holes and then leaping in sheer delight at the vivid smells. From McMurphy's perspective, institutions castrate and feminize the individual; from Chief Bromden's view, they dehumanize and reduce the individual to a machine. Bromden escapes; like the dog, he may be heading directly for a collision and death, but, as with the dog, his fate is never divulged to the reader. One can hope that they both escape the juggernaut.

This fable has been frequently and often convincingly explicated. Placing the book within the context of Frye's ironic mode, however, gives readers additional explanations for features of the narrative. The mental hospital proves that one can tighten the screw and think of something even worse than a prison. Vision—which may take the form of Plato's Good or the impress of deity enjoyed on the Hill of Holiness in Edmund Spenser's *Faerie Queene*—becomes infernalized as Bromden's schizophrenic hallucination. The descent into ironic mythos accounts for McMurphy's electroshock crucifixion, where sparks play about his head like thorns. The terms of the basic conflict are peculiarly American—frontier man and Native American facing engulfment by evil, "civilized" forces. The hospital, readers are told in various ways, is a microcosm for the U.S. government, with its inmates representing citizens in their apathetic and controlled state. Everything has become centralized; there remains no room for Jeffersonian democratic rebellions.[10] Kesey could not foresee the rebellions of the later 1960s, but perhaps he fueled a taste for them with this highly readable tale.

Woman on the Edge of Time (1976)

Like Kesey's McMurphy, Marge Piercy's Connie Ramos has been committed to a mental hospital for violence. She has been there before. Her earlier stint grew out of a period of grief and despair during which she made the mistake of hitting her child hard enough to break the girl's arm. As a child abuser, she lost custody of the girl, was sterilized, and then institutionalized. Her second stint comes from trying to defend her niece from that niece's violent pimp; her smashing the pimp's nose seems little enough compared to the violence already done to the niece, but it is enough to get Connie committed again. Like McMurphy, Connie does not seem presented as truly insane. Piercy, however, shows us how words on documents and the assumptions of doctors and judges can make the individual "insane" and thus rob one of self-determination. Rather than let them carry out the amygdalotomy, a more up-to-date form of lobotomy, she poisons several doctors by putting insecticide in their coffee machine.

Piercy's is part of a small cluster of utopian novels to come out within a brief period: Ursula K. Le Guin's *Dispossessed* (1974) and Ernest Callenbach's *Ecotopia* (1975) precede hers, while Andrew Macdonald's *Turner Diaries* (1978) and Callenbach's *Ecotopia Emerging* (1981) come after. Her publication of *Woman on the Edge of Time* in 1976 points to a Bicentennial concern with where America is going, and she gives us a utopian possibility in her village of Mattapoisett; however, Piercy also provides two demonic societies. One is our American present, represented as a mental hospital. The other is a brief glimpse of an alternate future derived from the treatment of mental patients that we witness. In this future, a shadowy wealthy class living on space stations can replace organs and undergo treatments to keep themselves young and beautiful for two hundred years. All lesser folk are shaped to carry out their form of service and can expect to live only forty years or so. Such alterations of humanity to fit servitude resembles the futures envisioned by H. G. Wells and Aldous Huxley. A kept mistress suffers from a reduced intelligence and can hardly walk, so exaggerated are her anatomical curves. She knows she will be reduced to her component organs and chemicals when she gets too old or when she transgresses the rules. A security guard is a surgically enhanced killing machine; he no longer has sexual organs or needs, and all his skills are honed toward killing and toward loyalty to his multinational conglomerate.

Connie asks herself what a lone woman—one with relatively little education, a Chicana in an Anglo world, a woman branded insane—can do to change the system; the answer is "not much." She can achieve nothing democratically through the legal system or through written media. She chooses a terrorist role and strikes violently at the system, targeting the doctors and medical personnel responsible for the experiments. She knows the rest of her life will be hateful. Nonetheless, she dedicates her existence to the utopian future revealed to her, though she cannot know if she will succeed—indeed, she cannot be one hundred percent sure that she has really traveled in time. She, like the novel's readers, will always wonder whether the futures were just the hallucinations of a mind that well-educated doctors have declared schizophrenic. Piercy tips the scales against that interpretation, but it cannot be forgotten.

Throughout her life, Connie must deal with the hatred of self that she has internalized from her status as a Chicana and a woman. Kesey's early 1960s orientation is reflected in his claim that the masculine life force is being destroyed by an effeminized society; after a couple of decades of feminist criticism, the claim that society favors women over men seems strange. Such opposite accusations should remind us that calling society either patriarchal or effeminizing blinkers an awareness of the real complexities. When Connie poisons the doctors, she helps her best friend to escape the hospital in the confusion, declaring, "Hate them more than you hate yourself, and you'll stay free!" (366). That she recognizes this hatred as induced rather than natural is a victory, but that self-hatred is an abyss of bleakness that darkens Piercy's vision beyond the one that Kesey projects. All of society has worked together, if not conspired, to treat Connie in consistently degrading ways. The institution merely aggravates and symbolizes in stark form the harassments and oppressions of everyday life, and readers learn what Connie might have been in the figure of Luciente, the woman from Mattapoisett. Whereas the American government executes the victims of *The Public Burning* and *The Free-Lance Pallbearers*, the hospital merely destroys a few cubic millimeters of brain tissue. That betrayal is worse than mere execution. That the lesser institution is free to do so devastating a harm to powerless victims is truly demonic.

Blood and Guts in High School (1978)

Kathy Acker uses prison instead of the mental institution as her major image for a destructive organization. However, some of her prisons are symbolic and not actual institutions like Coover's Sing Sing, with its walls and bars and guards. As is the case with the hospitals of Kesey and Piercy, Acker's prisons reflect or represent society, particularly society as characterized by its patriarchally repressive elements. This society is not necessarily consciously organized and run as a conspiracy against women; rather, each semi-independent part of society turns out to function in parallel. Janey Smith, the novel's narrative focus, illustrates the ways in which women are victimized.

The novel divides into three parts. In the first, "Inside high school," comes the least obvious prison: Janey slavishly depends on, adores, and lives incestuously with her father while he is becoming involved with another woman and is pushing Janey out of his life. In the second part, "Outside high school," she is literally captured and held incommunicado by someone training her to be a prostitute; while there, she reads and comments on Nathaniel Hawthorne's *Scarlet Letter,* focusing on the scene in which Hester Prynne comes out of prison. The third section, "A journey to the end of the night," shows Janey in Tangier with Jean Genet, the notorious prisoner-outlaw-writer-homosexual; while in Egypt, she spends time in a real prison before dying. Alternating with the prison settings are outbursts of "wild" living: "*Wild* in the Puritan New England society Hawthorne writes about means *evil anti-society criminal.* Wild. Wild. Wild. Going wherever you want to go and doing whatever you want to do and not even thinking about it" (93). "Freaky" is another of Acker's terms for such nonstandardized behavior, and she values such behavior highly.[11] Also varying the displays of prison and wildness are the attacks on middle-class norms and ideals, the most memorable being a grotesque fantasia on President Jimmy Carter's asshole.

Incest, one form of the demonic erotic, is Acker's first image for the imprisonment of the young and female. While one's initial reaction on reading this section may be to take the incest literally, the nonrealistic variance between Janey's supposed age of ten and her relatively adult consciousness suggest that it has a symbolic dimension. Because she craves affection and acceptance, Janey enslaves herself to the paternal powers and their culture. This is the first training ground in female masochism.[12]

Once away from her father, in school, Janey joins the Scorpion gang. This is her wildness, and she and the gang vandalize and destroy to "cut away dullness, lobotomy, buzzing, belief in human beings, stagnancy, images, and accumulation" (37). The lobotomized nature of normal society is presented in her ritualized dramas that a salesperson must play out every day. Janey works in a cookie store and must deal with impossibly picky and inconsiderate customers (37–38). She is imprisoned by the conventions of politeness, by her need to satisfy customers, by her need to satisfy the management, and by her need to smother her own overwhelming anger. To accept the service role and grow to fit it would indeed be a lobotomy.

In the second section, Janey is locked up by Mr. Linker, a Persian lobotomist who is also a white slaver, and he trains her to become a prostitute— in feminist terms, this is a demonic enslavement. While incarcerated, she reads *The Scarlet Letter* and starts her book report: "We all live in prison. Most of us don't know we live in prison. A throng of bearded men, in sad-coloured garments, were assembled in front of a gaol. They were waiting for a woman named Hester Prynne to walk out of the gaol" (65). After pondering Hawthorne's attitude toward what he writes, she goes on: "It's possible to hate and despise and detest yourself 'cause you've been in prison so long" (66). This is a point that Connie Ramos understands only too well. In Janey's eyes, Hester is wild and free, driven by endless desire. She goes back to the scene of Hester's exit from prison, and considers the presence of Hester's husband: "Hester's husband's a scholar. A scholar is a top cop 'cause he defines the roads by which people live so they won't get in trouble and so society will survive. A scholar is a teacher. Teachers replace living dangerous creatings with dead ideas and teach these ideas as the history and meaning of the world. Teachers torture kids. Teachers teach you intricate ways of saying one thing and doing something else" (68). School is also a prison; this point is driven home when Janey sums up the move to take Hester's child from her, saying that "they want to keep the child so they can train the child to suck their cocks. That's what's known as education" (94). The incestuous relationship between Janey and her father, the practices of a prostitute, and the helplessness of the child or prisoner being trained to serve the dominant male establishment merge in this assessment of education. Also present is the desire for "living dangerous creatings" rather than dead culture, much as Ishmael Reed shows exasperation over the concern with heroic couplets, column capitals, and violin scrolls being sold in Emperor Franz Joseph Park when people could attend concerts of contemporary jazz by living giants and buy paintings by living artists. Acker's "plagiarisms" are a means of ripping and tearing those dead artists until they can be made to serve the needs of the present.[13]

Before and after going to prison in North Africa, Janey takes part in various dialogues. One, which starts immediately after her going to jail, is with President Carter. Like some of the satires on Nixon in Coover, Reed, and elsewhere in Acker, this portrait of a president plunges him into a heaving cauldron of scatological invective—into the world of the demonic. After being told that Carter is a pillar of American society, we learn that "President Carter's centre is an enormous HOLE. This HOLE'S DIAMETER, COLOUR, and ODOUR resemble a NEW YORK CITY SUBWAY TOILET that hasn't been CLEANED for THREE weeks. . . . [he] leaves a THREE-INCH WALL of SHIT around his ASSHOLE" (119). More in the same vein follows. Although Acker's mode is more personally abusive, her idea seems not unlike Reed's picture of LBJ, HARRY SAM, and the *ecclesia super cloacam* combination of respectability undercut by the presence of shit just below. The applications to Carter as a person are presumably minimal; but to bourgeois society at large—the world of repression described as a jail—this excremental portrait at least suggests Acker's feelings toward lobotomized society and some of its problems.

Janey dies for no reason except her inability to go on in a world of such total evil. After a section of drawings representing a book of the dead, we find the statement that "soon many other Janeys were born and these Janeys covered the earth" (165). Are they slaves and prisoners like the first Janey, or do their numbers suggest that they will be able to burst the repressive bonds of society? The final lines of this enigmatic novel may seem innocent in their uncomplicated lust, but in Acker's world, longing for the taste of a boy's lips leads to female bondage.

One Flew over the Cuckoo's Nest and *Woman on the Edge of Time* show a subgovernmental institution destroying an individual's mind to make that individual a dire example to others wishing to be different or simply born different in terms of skin and culture. Institutions steal one's spirit, leaving the husk of the body behind. Janey never reaches that point; the bleakness of Acker's vision consists of the foulness of all social structures, the sense that one can never escape them, the feeling that there is no alternative where things might be better. Through the violence of her desires, Janey keeps her spirit alive, although the invariance of her plaints also loses her some readers' sympathy. The surgical rituals of lobotomy and amygdalotomy are replaced in Acker's text by those of abortion, copulation, and the less obvious rituals of playing salesgirl and functionally lobotomizing oneself by adapting to the role. Whether in school, the hospital, or jail, whether in the courtroom or bed, the men in *Blood and Guts in High School* share the need to control their surroundings, and they impose that need on "wild" women. Janey's plight is insoluble because her wildness, consisting of so much sexual desire, ties her to those men and enslaves her because she wants to bed them. Truly, hers is a world of frustration and bondage, and the prisons she passes out of only free her into the grave.

Private Rituals of Violence: Ellis, Mailer, and Dworkin

We have just seen institutional—and therefore public—violence wreaked upon the individual. The rituals were all, to a degree, communal. The writers dealt with here concentrate on private violence. While a ritual element often characterizes the actions, private ritual lacks the mythic effect found in books like *The Public Burning*. If the previously discussed books verge on religious visions of the world, the current group embodies something akin to a magical belief structure.

American Psycho (1991)

Misogynists, sadists, masochists, and horror freaks can enjoy reading Bret Easton Ellis's *American Psycho* for its torture descriptions. However, book reviewers, students of contemporary fiction, and those who will not condemn a book without first reading it would be less disturbed were a clear moral norm present. Traditional satires let us know where the author stands and invite us to look down from the same elevated position on the antics of villains and fools. This novel deprives us of that comfortable defense; the author's voice deliberately absents itself, leaving readers with only the voice of Patrick Bateman, a psychotic killer indulging in his brand of the demonic erotic.[14] The first words are those inscribed over the entrance to Dante's hell. The last are "THIS IS NOT AN EXIT" (399).

The world consists of surfaces: brand names are mentioned for all the clothes, but only simulacra of humans exist inside those clothes. If there can be said to be depths, they are depths inhabited by monstrosities of violence not visible on the nominally human surface.[15] In Frye's terms, the frustrations are those of social climbing and snobbery; the bondage is that of Sisyphean repetition of meaningless acts, such as dining at expensive restaurants but never noticing or enjoying the taste of the food. The murders themselves are another repetition. Bateman presumably kills to endow himself magically with the vitality of the slain, or to eliminate people who may somehow enjoy life when he can feel so little, or even just to impose order on his world by controlling one person for a brief period. However, his disintegrating sense of reality demands more frequent murders to keep that illusion of control. These murders are leeched of any sacredness by the private and psychotic nature of the perpetrator. The only mythic elements are the slight invocations of *Inferno.*

Patrick Bateman is a white, twenty-seven-year-old graduate of Harvard Business School who is reasonably successful in mergers and acquisitions— and, as he points out, in murders and executions. His short professional life has seen the Ivan Boesky and Michael Millken scandals as well as the savings and loan crisis, not a very glorious era in American finance. Not until page 76 do we get any hint of his murderous activities; even then, the unwarned reader might brush off the reference as hyperbole. When Bateman starts letting such references drop in public, his friends all ignore them as weird or funny, never taking them literally. In public, Bateman is politically correct, deprecating anti-Semitic jokes, yet his murder victims are women, "bums" (many of whom are black), male homosexuals, and Jews, all the usual others felt to threaten the white, Anglo-Saxon male ego. Late in the novel, we realize that his activities extend back at least into his undergraduate days and that he may be responsible for hundreds of deaths. In this, he exceeds any real-life serial murderer;[16] however Bateman, as we know from the title, is not just an individual serial murderer. By calling this *American Psycho,* Ellis is making a statement about America and American society, and Bateman in some sense represents white corporate America. Since not all Americans are serial killers, we have to look at the component claims of this metaphor.

One element in American society blamed for this metaphoric psychosis is capitalism. The novel is set exclusively in Manhattan, chiefly in the financial district, where "making a killing" is everybody's business. So tightly focused is Ellis's geography that the New Jersey Meadowlands are experienced as disturbingly alien territory, and Arizona is as unreal as Novaya Zemlya. Just about all the characters handle accounts, use platinum American Express cards, and dress for success. That mergers and acquisitions are interchangeable with murders and executions is an obvious signpost; what leveraged buyouts do to the workforce, pension plans, and bondholders might be loosely compared to murder and execution. Certainly, workers are ruined or put out of work by such financial arrangements.

Rampant consumerism is another element in this diagnosis of America. Bateman enumerates what everyone is wearing, detailing the fabric, style, brand name, and price. This habit defines both his society and his own mind-set. His lunch buddies think in these terms also. They run through the rules for tasseled loafers in perfect seriousness, cite authorities, and rarely find themselves disagreeing. Those who dress for their kind of success would agree with their rules; by these tokens, they recognize their own kind and have no use for any other subculture. Bateman's depth of obsession shows in his understanding of female and children's codes as well as men's, but his extremism is quantitatively, not qualitatively, different from theirs.

Even as the dress code lets Bateman's circle recognize their own kind, it depersonalizes individuals. To each other, the men are semi-interchangeable. Paul Owen is always mistaking Patrick Bateman for Marcus Halberstam, and when Bateman kills Owen, Owen is nonetheless "spotted" in London by several people. Other characters repeatedly make similar mistakes. Even though everyone in this circle knows the other members, nobody knows anyone well, and nobody has true friends. This lack of authentic contact between individuals corresponds, at least symbolically, to the splitting in Bateman's personality that shows toward the end of the novel. First he addresses himself the way some people mutter vocative imprecations to themselves for being stupid. Soon, however, the disembodied voice describes what Bateman is doing as if Bateman were entirely separate from the speaker. In a sense, Bateman no longer recognizes himself.

Another element in this portrait of American psychosis is popular culture: television shows, rental videos, and rock music. The often-mentioned *Patty Winters Show* frequently features ugly materials: the murder of small children (138), victims of shark attacks (143), Nazis (156), mastectomies (161), women who have been tortured (236), and Ted Bundy (364). He rents videotapes that give him sadistic ideas and builds his own library of private entertainment by videotaping some of his own tortured victims in their throes. Bateman provides three entire chapters full of his own in-depth analysis of popular music. Ellis may be sarcastic in some word choices: a "killer bass" (135), for instance, or titles like "Who Dunnit?" (134), "Where Do Broken Hearts Go" (254), and "Is It Me?" (354). I find Bateman's flush of enthusiasm for one cultural experience disturbing, however, because of its apparent seriousness; in a different world, cultured Nazis loved Goethe and Beethoven, tastes bothersome to humanists who wanted to believe that those steeped in the classics would be humane. If Ellis is not saying that this music fosters a killer outlook—and if Bateman is not just spouting nonsense so Ellis can make fun of him—then Bateman's love for music creates an eerie but plausible cognitive dissonance.

An obsession with youthful appearance and fitness terrorizes the main characters and adds to the indictment of American capitalist society. The easiest way to upset somebody is to comment with seeming concern on a receding hairline or a softening chin. Bateman's morning routine involves Plax mouthwash, Rembrandt toothpaste, Listerine mouthwash, an ice-pack masque, a deep-pore cleanser, an herb-mint facial masque, two different brands of tooth polisher, Cepacol mouthwash, and a spearmint face scrub. Then he showers, using first a gel cleanser and then a honey-almond body scrub, and, on the face, an exfoliating gel scrub. Shampoo and conditioner differ depending on whether this is a weekday or weekend. He applies mousse, moisturizer, shaving cream, an alcohol-free antibacterial toner, an emollient lotion, and then gel appaisant. If necessary, he applies a clarifying lotion, an antiaging eye balm, a protective lotion, and a scalp-programming lotion. His workouts are similarly obsessive. At first he stresses the number of crunches; later, we learn of the guns and the three severed and grotesquely ornamented vaginas he keeps in his locker. Evidently, destroying other bodies magically helps him keep his own perfect and preserved.

The manipulation of the reader is one of the novel's most interesting features. By giving us an aristocratic protagonist—private money, Harvard, perfect body, handsome face, expensive clothes, competence in the money world—Ellis is going against real-life norms and glamorizing his character. Historically, serial murderers do not fit this profile, and glamour is rarely something they can claim. Unless the reader is mentally protected by Marxist or working-class hatred of capitalists and moneyed habits, however, that glamorization makes most readers wish to identify with Bateman. Structurally, the narrative builds toward Bateman's disintegration. As readers, most of us are eager for him to be caught, which would relieve our anxieties and assure us that good, or at least the social covenant, will reassert its protection. Working against this desire, however, is the narrative-generated impulse to identify with any first-person narrator (especially when glamorous) and, hence, involuntarily, to wish him to get away, lest our mental link with him subject us to the embarrassments and pain of being caught. Ellis refuses to reassure us. Though Bateman is very jittery and evidently much less in control than at the beginning of the story, he is still functional in public. He answers the question "Why?" with the statement that this is "how life presents itself in a bar or in a club in New York, maybe *anywhere*, at the end of the century and how people, you know, *me* behave" (399). Ellis then directs readers' attention to the sign over a nearby door that says, "THIS IS NOT AN EXIT." We as readers are offered no escape. We are left to suppose that Bateman's personal apocalypse—his world whirling into fragments of consciousness—will drive him to impose temporary order by killing more victims. By exercising absolute control over them, he can hope to control his shattering world, a motive for violence also probed by Saul Bellow in *The Dean's December*. Since no one believes Bateman, not even the friend who receives a long confession on his telephone answering machine, he can literally get away with murder in the Reaganite America of the 1980s. He simply does not stand out enough to draw speculative attention. Patrick Bateman is, Ellis insists, a distinctly American kind of psychotic, and he is right at home.

Why Are We in Vietnam? (1967)

Ellis argues that the values of at least a segment of society are best embodied by a handsome, well-dressed, psychotic, white killer. Norman Mailer sees America as turning out killers wholesale, and he too focuses on the white corporate executive world. Mailer's novel bursts with zest, high energy, and fizzy spirits, but the protagonist shows equally explosive anal obsessions and terrors, oedipal hatreds, and self-loathing.[17] The narrator is D.J., an eighteen-year-old boy remembering the hunting trip he took when he was sixteen (unless he is a black in Harlem fictionalizing himself as a white boy in Dallas, a possibility Mailer teases us with). The ritual is the fabled frontier rite of passage (adapted by whites from American Indian practice), the hunt. As Richard Pearce observes, however, "Mailer gives full recognition to the facts that frontier values not only derived from a past that never was, not only were unattainable, not only masked the real values of capitalism and imperialism—but have their own inherent potential for psychological and social destructiveness" (410). This potential destructiveness is something that Ken Kesey, say, overlooks when drawing on these same frontier myths for his concept of redemptive masculinity. Mailer's lyrical passages leave us no doubt that he loves America and its potential, but his murderous vision in this book shows that white America has failed the test of spiritual authenticity and is basically insane.[18]

On this hunt, D.J. reaches a cusp; he chooses one path—to become a licit killer, literally in war and symbolically in business, rather than an illicit killer like Ellis's Bateman. Readers are left to wonder if this is the best that one can hope for from the WASP male bred by America, since Mailer puts the problem in terms of maleness, whiteness, and Protestant American capitalist society and offers no model of experience except that of some kind of killer.

Some moments and peripheral experiences on this expensive Alaskan safari are reasonably authentic, and D.J. senses their power despite his disillusioned view of everything that is held up for his approval, particularly anything his father, Rusty, has arranged and paid for. When D.J.'s friend Tex kills a wolf, D.J. considers it rightly done by his lights, and their drinking the blood and their American Indian guide's asking the wolf not to warn the bears feels moderately authentic to him.[19] Shooting a ram with a gun meant for elephants does not feel right to D.J. Nor does using a helicopter to put people down near the wounded animal (thus avoiding a day's tracking in rough territory). Such a shortcut robs the ritual of any meaning and makes the animals just the victims of technology and overwhelming firepower. They, like the Vietnamese, are being most unfairly assaulted in ways that rob war of any enlarging spiritual dimension for the attackers. In Mailer's terms, danger undertaken in the right spirit can be beneficial to the soul, a romantic view perhaps, but necessary to his condemnation of the Vietnam War.

When D.J. and his father go after bear on their own, they wound one and trail it. After suitable stalking and exertion, after tasting their own fear in slippery hands and stinking sweat, they find the bear, posed on a ten-foot circle of its own blood. D.J. drops his gun and walks up to stare into its eyes:

> . . . when D.J. smiled, the eyes reacted, they shifted, they looked like they were about to slide off the last face of this presence, they looked to be drawing in the peace of the forest preserved for all animals as they die, the unspoken cool on tap in the veins of every tree, yes, griz was drawing in some music of the unheard burial march, and Rusty—wetting his pants, doubtless, from the excessive tension—chose that moment to shoot, and griz went up to death in one last paroxysm, legs thrashing, brain exploding from new galvanizings and overloadings of massive damage report, and one last final heuuuuuu, all forgiveness gone. (147)

Whatever authentic experience might have been gained is thus aborted, and D.J.'s bile bubbles over when Rusty claims the kill as his. His shot did indeed murder it, but that shot was unnecessary, and he had not faced it eye to eye. Here, Mailer writes, is the "final end of love of one son for one father" (147).

Balked of the primal wisdom magically available at a moment of death, D.J. strikes out into the wilderness with Tex, unarmed. They scare off a wolf by projecting their thoughts at it. The electromagnetic currents of the northern lights, whose influence on human minds Mailer treats as physically tangible, waken the boys in the night. Each feels an impulse to rape the other, to steal the other's power and magically add it to his own: "Tex was ready to fight him to death, yeah, now it was there, murder between them under all friendship, for God was a beast, not a man, and God said, 'Go out and kill—fulfill my will, go and kill,' and they hung there each of them on the knife of the divide in all conflict of lust to own the other yet in fear of being killed by the other" (203–4). Through this moment of demonic eroticism, they become blood brothers, and the book ends with D.J.

stating that "tomorrow Tex and me, we're off to see the wizard in Vietnam," concluding, "Hot damn" (208). But in Vietnam, they will hunt their prey with helicopters.

As if they were bars of iron being magnetized by the polar forces, their instincts are channeled into a certain kind of killing. Given Mailer's usual attitude toward fear, what emerges from this experience is not what should result from an initiation properly undergone. Mailer sees fear as the diminisher of the soul, and every time we give in to our cowardice, we reduce our own spirit and subtract from God's power as well.[20] After many such fearful denials, we lose our spirit, we encourage cancer (our body's response to such repressed fear), and we forego any chance of afterlife. Given the fear the boys feel, and the various fears that Rusty shows, even though he is "the highest grade of asshole made in America" (37), we deduce that America's unfaced fears are shaping killers. In his essay "The White Negro," Mailer praises people able to get beyond fear and violence to creativity, people who live on the edge as a spiritual discipline. Rusty shows no such hipness, and D.J.'s élan seems unlikely to last into adulthood. Rusty's fears involve corporate one-upmanship, prestige, success, and managing to behave and look like the really powerful men. In this, he shares a core of fears with Patrick Bateman. Bateman criticizes a restaurant's pizza but is grovelingly humiliated by proof that Donald Trump considers it the best in New York. Rusty cannot endure the possibility that "Medium Asshole Pete and Medium Asshole Bill" (50), his two corporate companions, should come back with better trophies than himself. Since one of them gets a bear, Rusty would rather die than face the laughter of his "friends" within the company.

Whereas Bateman is entirely the perpetrator of violence, D.J. is both the victim of his father's ego-driven pressures and also the perpetrator of more violence. He has not actually killed anyone, nor, we are assured, has he tried necrophilia (unlike Bateman), but he and Tex have fooled around with corpses, carrying out private autopsies in Tex's father's funeral parlor. Both boys look forward to Vietnam, another safari (at least to them) where the game is the wiliest of all. We assume that rather than learning a different wisdom from the hunt, D.J. will handle life by becoming like his father. Rusty talks of getting the better of other men in corporation terms as sodomizing them, and evidently D.J. will, too. What they fear is symbolically expressed as rape or disembowelment by some stronger male. Tex and D.J. may be killer buddies, but probably neither is capable of aiding the other without needling him for wanting help. Their friendship will thus be limited to superficially friendly rivalry. Their relationship enjoys more energy and zest than Bateman brings to any of his, but then, they are not clinically psychotic. They are just Texas men shaped by certain American assumptions of masculinity and ambition. That so little differentiates them from Bateman is what makes this vision demonic.

Mercy (1990)

Andrea Dworkin's protagonist, Andrea, is an articulate victim of male violence who would agree with Mailer's and Ellis's portrayals of American men. Most readers rightly see in *Mercy* an attack on men and patriarchy, not America itself, but I wish to focus on the specifically American elements in the novel. Dworkin's outrage at being cheated comes from her being denied that land's promised equality, freedom, and justice. She grew up a few doors from where Walt Whitman was born and starts every chapter by referring to him and his vision of America. His great faith in the country, his willingness to sing women as well as men—all being equal and all deserving—and his celebration of the body all seem to her the approach to life that should be enjoyed and welcomed by all Americans. She would love to greet all life as openly and unresistingly as he does in his effusions. The vileness that she sees in "Amerika," she feels sure, would have smothered Whitman as thoroughly as it is choking her. Instead of being able to celebrate people in this land, she can only lament the ways that men abuse women. Instead of the oceanic erotic, she cannot escape the demonic. This is a victim's "Song of Myself," each chapter with its central symbol of violence illustrating a different species of abuse described by the sufferer. Andrea seems less a continuous personality (whatever the autobiographical elements) than a generalized woman who has been abused. Hostile readers may think the tone hysterical, but it derives more than a little from the prophets of the Jewish scriptures. They too feel that a chosen people has failed to live up to its covenants, and they similarly lament and inveigh splenetically. Dworkin, in addition, feels personally betrayed by God, and she blames him.

The landscape, mostly the New York–Camden, New Jersey, region, and the mind-set are those of bondage and frustration, and they offer no escape. The name of the narrative persona, Andrea, is also one of painful irony. She says of her mother, "She named me Andrea for 'manhood' or 'courage.' It's a boy's name; the root, *andros,* means 'man' in Greek. It's 'man' in the universal sense, too. Man" (166). She plays variations on this theme: "my mother named me Andrea. It means manhood or courage. It means not-cunt. She specifically said: not-cunt" (225). Even if she won a Nobel Prize she would not be protected from drunken men on the street calling her "cunt"; but then, the New York neighborhoods that she inhabits are not populated by people who would recognize Nobel prizewinners. A male laureate would be mugged as readily as the next man, a fact she ignores.

When reading Dworkin, one has to decide what one means by "reason-able." She makes middle-class readers realize that their practical definitions are very self-limiting and rest on class and money. Andrea is raped several times because she had no money to sleep in places where she would be less vulnerable. However, her sense of what is reasonable acknowledges no prac-tical or prudential limits whatever. For her, freedoms must be absolute and total, without regard for culture, history, or local circumstances.

Is she "unreasonable" in thinking she should be able to live unmolest-ed? If she is not harming others, why should they assume that it is per-fectly acceptable to harm her? She criticizes the world for its prejudices and viciousness, but she does not blame herself for violating mores. As an American staying in Crete, she goes out at night, though local women do not. She asserts her values: "I've never been afraid of anything and I do what I want; I'm a free human being, why would I apologize? I argue with my-self about my rights because who else would listen. The few foreign women who come here to live are all considered whores because they go out and because they take men as lovers, one, some, more. This means nothing to me. I've always lived on my own, in freedom, not bound by people's nar-row minds or prejudices" (76–77). She despises what local custom allows men to do to women who are considered prostitutes but takes no steps to protect herself; when she gets the treatment, she feels abused. One can say that she is stupid to invite that trouble. Still, she is correct that the cus-toms are unfair to women, and she will only have freedom if she claims it. Otherwise, she voluntarily enslaves herself to culturally enshrined and brutally protected male selfishness.

This novel categorizes abuses. Infant girls, whose sucking reflex is abused by men, suffer in later life from breathing and eating disorders and frequent-ly attempt suicide when they grow up. As a young girl, Andrea proudly attends a film on her own and is molested by a man's fingers. Her attempts to be grown up and well behaved—not making noise, behaving politely— are held to discredit her by the very adults who have been drilling such submissive behavior into her. Hebrew school teaches her that her desire to attend the synagogue to receive God's comfort when her bleeding makes her feel ill is irreligious, given God's ban on bleeding women. She is raped several times under varying circumstances, each illustrating nuances and variations on the concept of rape. She describes brutal throat rape (with damage to the larynx) and blames the pornographic film *Deep Throat.* She chronicles the Nazis' treatment of women in the Birkenau concentration camp. She describes a love affair with a Cretan that ends in violence and a marriage to a revolutionary that ends with her being beaten into passive suffering. She shows the sexism of the peace movement for which she worked: men are gotten out of jail immediately, lest they be raped; wom-en, though, are left in for days despite the reputation of the jail for sexual and physical assault. She describes pornography as another form of assault. She pulls no punches with regard to patriarchal religion. The sanctified suicide of Israelites at Masada, she suggests, is somehow parallel to the suicides of women who as infants were abused by adult males: "God kept killing us, of course, to make us hard enough; genocide and slavery and rape were paternal kindnesses designed to build character, to rip pity out of you, to destroy sentimentality. . . . ignorant children shut up in Daddy's house, we yearn for Him and adore Him and wait for Him, awake, afraid, shivering; we submit to Him, part fear, part infatuation, helpless against Him, and we thank Him for the punishment and the pain and say how it shows He loves us" (274).

Even halfway through this anatomy of rape, Andrea still believes in the possibility of something better, something lyrically Whitmanesque:

And fuck meant all kinds of making love—it was a new word. It was fucking if you got inside each other, or so near you couldn't be pulled apart. It was joy and risk and fun and orgasm; not faking it; I never have. It didn't have to do with who put what where. It was all kinds of wet and all kinds of urgent and all kinds of here and now, with him or her. It was you tangled up with someone, raw. It wasn't this one genital act, in out in out, that someone could package and sell or that there was an etiquette for. . . . personal love ain't the only feeling—there's feelings of adventure and newness and excitement and Goddamn pure happiness—there's need and sorrow and loneliness and certain kinds of grief that turn easy into touching someone, wild, agitated, everywhere. (171–72)

Referring back to Whitman, she remarks, "I don't think a three-minute fuck was his meaning. I don't. It's an oceanic feeling inside and you push it outward and once you start loving humanity there is no reason to make distinctions of beauty or kind" (173).

What ground for activity does that encompassing desire have in a country in which these are the social and legal reactions to rape, she asks:

. . . are you cruel? He can't be killed; for what he did to you? It's absurd; it's silly; unjustified; uncivilized; crazed; another madwoman, where's the attic? He didn't mean it; or he didn't do it, not really, or not fully, or not knowing, or not intending; he didn't understand; or he couldn't help it; or he won't again; certainly he will try not to; unless; well; he just can't help it; be patient; he needs help; sympathy. . . . he needs time, education, help, support; yeah, she's dead meat; but you can't expect someone to change right away, overnight, besides she wasn't perfect, was she, he needs time, help, support, education. (329)

Dworkin makes a powerful distinction when she says that "the notion that *bad things happen* is both propagandistic and inadequate" (334). She devotes herself to arguing that *bad things are bad.* Her solution is literally terroristic: "It is very important for women to kill men" (331). Amnesty International, the United Nations, and the World Court will not help women; nor do men stop themselves. Only frightening men into change will get women anywhere. She signs off her prophetic judgment of the male world with "I declared war. My *nom de guerre* is Andrea One; I am reliably told there are many more; girls named courage who are ready to kill" (333). By this point in the narrative, she is addressing the whole world, not just America, but her animus is strongest against the United States. Cretan women, for instance, never have been promised the freedoms that America promised Andrea as a citizen. They are not being robbed of something officially theirs. She is.

The rituals in this novel are seen from the victim's viewpoint. The rapist partakes in a rite that may make him feel stronger or in control, but the victim is maimed and gains no benefit. Dworkin sees no ironic descent into the power of myth, no transcendence of the victim's spirit, no invocation of the goddess, who would have the power to wreak vengeance. Her women are simply ripped up and damaged. The multiplication of Andreas at the end resembles the multiplication of Janeys at the end of Acker's *Blood and Guts in High School.* Whether the number of women realistically promises enough violence to win male fear and respect (let alone whether this new basis for society would be an improvement) is unclear. Possibly, the women named Andrea and Janey will just be an army of new victims, their lives made impossible from the outset by fathers, religion, society, and the inequality between men's and women's average physical strengths that makes rape and battery possible.

◌ ◌ ◌

Kathy Acker's *Don Quixote* is another phantasmagoric exploration of abuses, bondage, and the demonic erotic. Within those private rituals are specific criticisms of America, and I would like to round out this section by paying attention to this rejection of America and its identification as a demonic landscape. One criticism is Acker's attack on Nixon (similar to that on Carter in *Blood and Guts in High School*), in which diarrhea, feces, vomit, and rape are scrambled together with the statement that American liberty is available to those with a wad of greenbacks in their pocket. Another is her picture of suburban life, in which her father straps her to a chair and forces her to watch electrocutions on television and then "electrocutes" her (demonic fire). Her third indictment of America consists of her attack on America's pious, foundational myths. Religious freedom was not what brought our ancestors to these shores: "these New Worlders had left England not because they had been forbidden there to worship as they wanted to but because there they and, more important, their neighbors weren't forced to live as rigidly in religious terms as they wanted" (117–18). She points out that in 1658, "the Massachusetts Bay House Deputies passed the Death Penalty against Quakers" (118). The protagonist learns about various clashes between money and principle, noting that when John Robinson, the speaker of the Virginia House of Burgesses died, his executor discovered that he had taken over £100,000 from state funds (this is in 1766!) that he had parceled out to well-to-do friends. In sum, the protagonist laments that "the United States is exactly as it was started: religiously intolerant, militaristic, greedy, and dependent on slavery as all democracies have been" (124).

All four of these writers—Ellis, Mailer, Dworkin, and Acker—cast the problem with America in terms of intimate relationships, especially those of a sexual nature. Ellis ties sex and violence to capitalism, materialism, and popular culture. Mailer turns the need to prove masculinity into American warmongering. Dworkin sees the social dynamics of rape as discrediting America's ideals. Acker finds love impossible in the world that derives from our colonial roots. In these ironic visions, any mythic elements (the hero against the beast in Mailer; Don Quixote as cultural "myth") are deformed and promise no transcendence or new start on the cycle of literary modes. The landscapes are infernal, and these writers seem generally to think Dante's advice good: "Abandon hope, all ye who enter here."

Seeking the Holy Moment When World Order Collapses: Vizenor and Silko

Northrop Frye promised that descent far enough into the demonic realm could bring about a reversal in orientation, a move from the ironic to the mythic mode. So far, we have only seen the twisted distortions of the mythic at the edge of the demonic vision. In novels by Gerald Vizenor and Leslie Marmon Silko, we pass that still center and find ourselves back in a mythic realm. Vizenor writes splendidly alien, grotesque, humorous, and sexually unusual stories—or so they may seem to a non–Native American. In *Ceremony*, Silko wrote a superb example of what was (to the post-1960s publishing world) *the* recognized Native American novel: an American Indian war veteran with psychological problems finds his way back to the old ways and old beliefs, a pattern probably given its attractiveness by N. Scott Momaday's winning a Pulitzer Prize for *House Made of Dawn*. In *Almanac of the Dead*, however, Silko turns to the gritty and grotesque, and to radical estrangement on a grand scale. Both Vizenor's *Bearheart: The Heirship Chronicles* and Silko's *Almanac of the Dead* are visionary, Vizenor in an apocalyptic vein, Silko in a prophetic. Vizenor shows the abrupt, surreal end of the white world; Silko shows it beginning to crumble. Both go beyond the horrors of cultural meltdown, partly because the white culture being destroyed seems no loss to them, and partly because tribal myths offer answers to what might be found beyond that destruction.[21]

Bearheart: The Heirship Chronicles (1978)

Previous readings of *Bearheart* have stressed Vizenor's zeal in attacking the constructed nature of what it means to be Native American. They have also stressed the narrative and formal originality of this novel.[22] This chapter is concerned with the novel's critique of America, which involves emphasizing the recognizable rather than the strange—regrettably, since that strangeness is what makes teaching this novel so disturbing but challenging. The high-tech American world crumbles almost at a snap of Vizenor's fingers: gas runs out, and the world we know ceases to be viable. Evidently during and after the patriotic hoopla surrounding the Bicentennial, Vizenor ruminated over the notion of America's future. He does not care in realistic terms what will bring white American civilization to a halt; he just wants to relish the morning after, to watch sardonically as officialdom disappears. One of the villainous characters notes regretfully that killing has become too commonplace: "What reason was there not to kill when money no longer worked?" (126–27). What indeed remains if transportation—as well as government, communication, and currency—has ceased?

Proude Cedarfair, a mixed-blood tribal shaman and trickster, is driven from his sacred cedar stand by the government's determination to steal the wood for fuel. The Bureau of Indian Affairs and its tribal henchmen actually try to burn him alive in his shack to get rid of him. His wife and randomly acquired mixed-blood companions follow him from the headwaters of the Mississippi to Pueblo Bonito in Chaco Canyon, New Mexico, a pilgrimage, a quest, a dance of death, and a journey through the *Inferno* all in one. They number thirteen, among whom are a strange clown, Benito Saint Plumero; a "small whitewoman" (78) and her seven-foot-tall companion; and a giant, sex-changed man-woman, to list only the more startling of them. The unusual nature of the episodes is suggested by their first few stops. At a refuge for "weirds and sensitives" (35), they are offered stuffed kitten for supper, and when they stay with the gay minikin friars, they discover that these homosexual brothers are starving to death and eating the corpse of each successive brother to die. Proude finds out too late that he has unknowingly eaten human flesh. Subsequently, he will pass up meals rather than eat dubious meat, but white Americans prove not so picky; they murder and quickly carve up the victim. In this, Vizenor seems to be paying anthropologists back for their rather prurient desire to attach cannibalism to whatever tribe they are studying.

The infernal attributes of the devastated country show in the mass movements of people and the people themselves:

> Late in the afternoon near Dumfries, the circus pilgrims [Proude's band] encountered hundreds of cripples, whole communal families of people with similar disabilities. The blind, the deaf, disfigured giants, the finger-less, earless, noseless, breastless and legless people stumbling, shuffling and hobbling in families down the road. Walking with the cripples were those suffering from various cancers.
>
> First the fish died, the oceans turned sour, and then birds dropped in flight over cities, but it was not until thousands of children were born in the distorted shapes of evil animals that the government cautioned the chemical manufacturers. (145–46)

Some in their march to nowhere have taken on new identities. People with deformed faces have plastic masks; those with twisted spines (scoliosis) have put on moth costumes and swoop about as the scolioma moths. Lit-tle Big Mouse, the tiny woman, is so entranced by the hordes of the de-formed that she dances ecstatically for them until she is torn to pieces by a group of slavering cripples. Evidently, she earns this sparagmos by roman-ticizing the idea of such deformity. One could argue that trying to evade death in this world is a questionable enterprise, given that starvation will soon strike down most of the population.

Proude is the most traditionally Native American of all those traveling. He has lived close to the earth, taking little from it for sustenance. More than once, he travels out of his body, back to the headwaters of the Mis-sissippi, where the skeletons of his father, grandfather, and great-grandfa-ther lie in the lake. He can hold his spirit in perfect balance such that he defeats the mythic figure of the Gambler, who gambles for lives.[23] Proude's spirit can leave his body and travel immaterially or in the form of a bear. He calls himself a trickster, though he seems less obviously so than Beni-to Saint Plumero, with the latter's much displayed sexuality, his strange humor, his grotesque physical form, and his passionate love for a bronze statue. Proude's trickery is subtle and often hidden from others. He hands over a medicine bundle in return for places on a special train, and all his companions excoriate him for this sacrilege, not knowing that the bundle he hands over comes from a museum and is thus desacralized and mean-ingless. He never explains his actions to them and ignores his loss of face in their eyes. He is more at one with the spirit world and the cosmos than with his fellow humans.[24]

Vizenor's protagonist is a trickster and traditionalist, but he is also so perfectly attuned to the world around him that he can avoid Vizenor's obsession, terminal creeds. Terminal creeds are statements of belief de-signed to hold the world still, to render it controllable; any statement that tries to pin down and define what American Indians are qualifies as such a creed. As Louis Owens points out in his afterword to the novel, *Bearheart* upsets Native American students because it shows "transsexual Indians. Indians in the novel were capable of cowardice as well as courage, of greed and lust as well as generosity and stoicism. And, according to the students weaned on film versions of Hollywooden Indians, Native American people could never be like that" (247–48). Somehow, Proude is the most Native American and yet the most flexible and undefined character, the most willing for people to be what they are and for the Earth to be and become what it is or must become. Because he never falls prey to terminal creeds, he is able to escape the world of frustration and bondage—literally of slavery and persecution as a sorcerer—and enter the mythic fourth world as a bear.[25] One other pilgrim also makes that transition; the rest of the pilgrims have fallen victim to their particular terminal creeds or betrayed values in some way that bars them from entry to the fourth world.

When government and commerce collapse, Vizenor suggests, proper human spirit still remains—at least in those whose spirit has not been deadened by materialistic living. That spirit can make its own arrangements if it knows how. To most Euro-Americans, the ending is mythologically enigmatic and unsatisfying. Is Proude dead? What does transition to the fourth world mean? Is this an answer that could work for others or only for trained shamans? Those whose terminal creeds include statements like "There is no world other than this one" and "No man can become a bear" will undoubtedly limit their experience to the world they define. They will never know what Vizenor's answer means. Those not able to see the world as Proude does but who are willing to experience Vizenor's fiction at least know that they have entered a world within America that is as alien as any they will meet in science fiction set on another planet. They can enjoy the disturbing originality that makes reading this book such a strange experience.

Almanac of the Dead (1991)

Vizenor focuses on peoples of mixed blood, in part because essentialist belief in pure blood is another terminal creed. Silko accepts the mixture of bloods as a given and focuses instead on the concept of tribal cultures. Part of being tribal is a low-tech mode of living that demands little petroleum-derived fuel, electricity, water, and fertilizer. Tribal identity demands belonging to a local, distinguishable group that is often set apart by a native language. Being tribal today also means being deprived of one's original resources by the colonizing intruders from Europe. Although tribal people were the original inhabitants of the Americas and Africa, they have been robbed of their lands and ways of life.[26]

Three issues combine to create the crisis Silko charts in this book, which is set in Tucson, Arizona. One is the theft of land from tribal peoples. In the United States, tribal people are a minority; in various Latin American countries, however, they are a majority, and that will make Silko's revolution thinkable. Another issue is the Euro-American civilization's overreliance on nonrenewable resources, particularly aquifers, fossil fuel, and the electricity generated from that fuel. Because she sets her story in the parched American Southwest, Silko focuses on water. One land speculator, for instance, plans a Venice-like town, serviced by canals and planted with nonnative trees and water plants, despite the way it will ruin all the wells supplying the surrounding area. Prophecy is the third issue that gives shape to the crisis. According to Silko, the ancient sacred traditions of the Native Americans predicted the coming of the whites. Those same traditions predict the whites' destruction and disappearance. Help to make this happen will come from spirits, including the ghosts of ancestors, who are angered at the abuse of their land. As native forces begin to gather, groups are inspired by such prophecies and devote their lives to hastening the day when the alien civilization will be driven from the entire continent.

Silko makes a place in her movement for anyone who will embrace tribal principles; those few whites devoted to ecology, for instance, may find themselves joining the movement and will not be repulsed. So may American blacks, and Silko speaks of African tribal peoples as included in this vision of the future world freed from white misappropriation. They, too, are still in touch with their native spirits. When slaves came to this country, some of their loas survived transplantation and have flourished, whereas true Christianity, according to Silko, has not. Being tribal is not a matter of race but a way of life, and the point of the movement is not to eliminate whites per se but to dismantle their civilization. Silko's visionaries are free enough of Euro-American cultural patterns to think in farsighted terms. They do not expect to win their war in a few years or even a few generations. They embark on a process of moving north that may take generations and cost countless lives. They feel, however, that they are part of a relentless force, like continental drift, that must slowly change the face of the Americas, Africa, and even, ultimately, Europe.

Silko's vision of Tucson is demonic not primarily for the destruction of white culture—a consummation to be wished, given her assumptions—but for the squalidness of its ways. People are murdered for their organs, and the local police look the other way because organ transplants are one of the few profitable businesses in this Tucson of the near future. Videos of abortion, of the scraper encountering the struggling fetus, are slavered over as a kind of snuff film. She shows bribery in the courtroom and the unlovely workings of the law enforcement agents in both Mexico and Tucson, including their ties to organized crime, drug smuggling, and insurance frauds. She describes in considerable detail Judge Arne and his sex life with his basset hounds.[27] Silko likens this union of animal and man to some of Zeus's activities, but the judge becomes no more godlike for taking his basset bitches or being taken by the basset stud. Or, if there is any mythic dimension, it seems ironic, the degradation of myth into perversion, the demonic erotic attaching to this degenerate scion of white southwestern culture. The true myths in this novel concern the rising of the people and the predictions they will make true regarding the end of the white race and its culture.

Like Vizenor, Silko savors the disintegration of the white civilization. Water is running out, and many buildings are abandoned and empty. Whites, foreseeing the rush of Mexicans, are trying to barricade themselves and gather weapons. They are not prepared for the masses of humanity heading in their direction. The government has moved troops in and is preparing to mow down unarmed mobs; we are told, though, that even they will sicken of endless slaughter, and the numbers still to come will be greater than their capacity to murder. The thrust of this book is toward massive destruction and certainly toward the disappearance of life as urban and suburban readers know it. Death on an inconceivable scale will add to the demonic nature of this vision, but the prophecies suggest that eventually the narrative treatments of this world will cycle from the ironic to the mythic. Silko's own narrative shows some pure mythic vision and not just the degraded, ironized mythic images found in other works discussed earlier in this chapter.

◑ ◑ ◑

In their attack on America, these novels naturally point at America's famous virtues. Liberty is infringed upon by the government, hospitals, and prisons. Justice is made a mockery of in the courtroom. Ruling figures—Johnson, Nixon, and Carter—return as grotesques to haunt us. Classics like *The Scarlet Letter* are interpreted as telling us why America is what it is and how it became so from its historical roots. A fabled rite such as a bear hunt shows us how unheroic the mainstream culture has become. Instead of the heroic male in these novels, we get the rapist, the torturer, the murderer, the cannibal, and the judge whose sexual pleasures are consummated with his dog. Instead of the heroic woman, we get "ball-cutting" Nurse Ratched; the lying, scheming, lazy wife in *The Free-Lance Pallbearers*; and a woman whose lovers are her dogs in *Bearheart*. Marge Piercy does produce a heroic if lone terrorist in Connie. Ken Kesey and Gerald Vizenor produce trickster protagonists, and Robert Coover gives us the earnest Rosenbergs. The trickster and the woman desperate to the point of murder and madness: these are the closest to heroes offered in the demonic

world. The fate of Proude Cedarfair is enigmatic, but the others are executed or sacrificed, the fate of true humanity in the demonic world.

Rather than concluding this chapter by restating the accusations leveled
at America in the novels studies here, let me instead offer two more examples of America as an ironic realm. In *Geek Love*, Katherine Dunn
shows the American nuclear family as a traveling carnival in which the
mother and father deliberately and lovingly damage their fetuses so that
freaks will be born to keep the family business healthy. After all, what
better gift could parents give a child than guaranteed employment just for
being itself? Conjoined twins, a flipper-limbed aqua-boy, a dead but preserved lizard-girl, a hunchbacked dwarf: these and others are molded from
normal germ plasm in the spirit of capitalist enterprise. Demonic love with
economic overtones appears yet again, imaginatively different from those
we have seen, but undeniably akin. Moreover, lobotomy is performed on
one of the conjoined twins and is discussed as the natural goal for all the
believers in a quasi-religious cult centering on the aqua-boy. The carnival
ends in a telepathically triggered firestorm, one more demonic mutation
of fire. Or consider Max Apple's *Propheteers*. His fictional Walt Disney
calmly electrifies a fence against which a horde of children is pressing:

> Margery saw those angelic faces contort, those pudgy fingers cling briefly
> and then fall free. It was like a scene from a concentration camp film.
> Those little bodies fell to the ground. . . . The youngest ones were on their
> feet, shaking the bewilderment from their limbs. The older children were
> now being shocked. She saw the five- and six-year-olds writhe, then rise,
> and brush themselves off. Quickly lines began to form at each of the flash-
> ing red lights. Parents were taking snapshots of their children as their gums
> rolled up in shock. (305)

Coover's electrocution as public spectacle is viciously powerful, and he
does his readers the courtesy of assuming that they can be horrified. Here
we find the minijolt as Disneyfied fun for the whole family, and Disney's
calmness encourages reduced reaction from readers. Margery realizes—and
we sighingly accept—that "he was giving them what they wanted" (306).
Demonic fire in a truly degenerate America does not even need to kill,
because everyone is already lobotomized.

chapter seven

Liberating *the Land of Freedom*

Anarchy has a popular and a technical meaning. In common parlance, anarchy signifies chaos, but only one of the texts this chapter will consider operates on that understanding. For the major anarchist thinkers—Godwin, Proudhon, Bakunin, and Kropotkin—and for the novelists discussed here, anarchy means the absence of centralized, coercive power, and they picture this existence as rational, harmonious, and peaceful, the opposite of violent or random disorder.[1] To these writers, Americans are not a free people, and anarchic fiction proffers plans for liberating them.

Theoretically, rational anarchy might have resulted had the communist state withered away, but the collapse of the U.S.S.R. produced no such results. Historically, anarchy existed in Spain in the 1930s as a cooperative organization of factories without a central authority. In America, anarchism has not enjoyed a high profile since the Sacco and Vanzetti case and cannot be called a political presence today; however, its major tenets have found sympathetic exponents in recent fiction. These writers feel excessively controlled by America's intensifying lust for law and order. As a group, they are hostile to the Christian, Republican, or capitalist right for its invasions of their moral liberties and destruction of the natural world, or they are hostile to liberals for their positive legislation and attempts to compel political correctness. However, the assumptions of any one writer may be green, leftish, libertarian, spiritual, or religious. These literary anarchists wish to tear down rules—or some of them—and enlarge our liberties. Liberal and conservative writers fear that America is plunging into chaos, but those who look beyond the immediate dangers and discomforts of the plunge are trying to make us understand that desirable liberties may come from such a change *if* we are mentally prepared to deal with them. They are trying to educate us for those new freedoms.

Creative anarchist thought undoes hierarchies, insists that values must be negotiated, and reminds us that elements of a system, like words in a language, are defined in relation to other elements but cannot be established in absolute terms. When we look at these novels, we can usefully ask, What center do the authors pick as the source of political oppression? How thoroughly do the authors manage to remove it in their fictional world? How do they envision decentered systems working? Do they reinstate centralized order in a disguised form? Do they view the annihilation of the center as a devolution, revolution, evolution, or reversal?

The novels considered in this chapter cluster about three images for anarchy: riot in the city; the trickster creating vortices of disorder; and utopia. We find two attitudes toward anarchy in the city. Richard Brautigan finds such anarchy appalling though very American, and his *Sombrero Fallout: A Japanese Novel* illustrates the negative and middle-class attitude toward anarchy. The other city novels look to the chaos for some kind of liberation. In *Dhalgren,* Samuel R. Delany is prepared to see a burned-out city as the place to discover who and what one really is away from America's rules, which are based on class, color, and sexual orientation. As we shall also see, cyberpunk writers view the ungoverned city as a proving ground for new technologies, a working system without a center. Tricksters are another way of introducing chaos into orderly systems. The Chinese monkey king is the trickster tool that both Maxine Hong Kingston and Gerald Vizenor use to break tyrannical laws and oppressive customs. Utopian anarchists present anarchy in its most orderly sense. Ursula Le Guin, Marge Piercy, and Starhawk draw variously on European anarcho-syndicalism, Native American tribal life, Israeli kibbutzim, Wiccan beliefs, and feminist theory. A lot of recent utopian writing shows values of the sort labeled culturally "female" and "relational" by Carol Gilligan. Those values imply resistance to centralization and dominance structures, so one test for a well-planned utopia is its method for altering male patterns or incorporating them within the female system, a problem not acknowledged or taken up in classical anarchist thought.

Anarchy appeals to Americans of many ethnic, racial, and sexual backgrounds. Delany has African, Latino, and Euro-American ancestors and is himself bisexual. Kingston has Chinese ancestors. Vizenor's mixed blood includes French and Anishinaabe, and he likes to portray unusual sexualities. Le Guin is a Euro-American influenced by California Indian tribes and the anthropological study of their cultures. Brautigan, a Euro-American, is the only one to be noticeably bothered by the breakdown of the present order, but he casts the problem in terms of the relationship between an American man and an Asian woman; behind his distress lurk echoes of the Vietnam War. The cyberpunk authors, though also from the white, male middle class, welcome some breaks in the current system and usually imagine a good deal of ethnic, cultural, and sexual mixing in their future worlds. Marge Piercy uses protagonists who are Chicana and Jewish and thus both outsiders to the mainstream of her imagined futures, and her future cultures are comfortable with hetero-, homo-, and bisexual orientations. America may lack an anarchist party in its presidential elections, but anarchist thought is not trivial in the politics explored by literature. Changing the nature of power and community is at the heart of anarchist and some feminist and Native American thinking, so America's problems understandably call forth imagined futures concerned with such issues.

Anarchic Cities: Brautigan, Delany, and the Cyberworld Writers

Sombrero Fallout: A Japanese Novel (1976)

Sombrero Fallout is a haunting dirge for a lost relationship, or so I would argue, though Edward Halsey Foster sees it instead as bleakly narcissistic, the dark side of the individualism celebrated by the American Bicentennial; he calls it "perhaps the least of all Brautigan's novels" (103). I freely admit that politics were probably not foremost in Brautigan's mind when he wrote this. He may not even have been consciously thinking about the Vietnam War or the inner-city riots of the last decade. Nevertheless, Brautigan portrays so deftly an American town wracked by violent frenzies that readers must wonder what connection he saw between the agony of disappointed love and social violence. The relationship is not one-to-one. The riot takes place because a lovelorn writer (whose books sound very much like Brautigan's own) has torn up the first page of a new story, and its characters decide to carry on living in the wastebasket, a literary trick made famous by Flann O'Brien and Gilbert Sorrentino. In one narrative strand, the writer endures one crisis-wracked hour of extreme distress. In another, we watch his ex-lover sleep serenely in her distant flat while her cat purrs and eats. In the third, the wastebasket-level riot runs its course, its excesses sometimes obviously related to the writer's frenzies but sometimes not.

Brautigan literalizes his metaphors. The wastebasket characters are "torn up" emotionally, and their town becomes "torn up" physically. The violence starts "at the drop of a hat" when a sombrero falls from the skies and lands near three men in this subworld. Two of the men unaccountably start crying as they vie for the mayor's attention, and the mayor and spectators lose their heads over these disturbing tears. This small town, like Bradbury's Green Town, is the idyllic community redolent with America's supposed innocence. The citizens' actions cause them to lose their innocence, even as the writer loses his Adamic idyll with his Japanese lover, Yukiko. She supplied the peace and reason necessary to balance the writer's frenetic mood swings; she not only kept him going, she was the exotic other, the Asian woman who met his sexual wants with extraordinary talent. In this Bicentennial fantasia, the white American male mourns lost innocence, a loss connected to violence, weapons associated with Vietnam, and an Asian other.

The international media within the wastebasket world force us to consider the riot to be peculiarly American: "unfortunate but American," "AN AMERICAN TRAGEDY," and "YANKS DO IT AGAIN" appear in editorials and headlines around the world (170). The very American uneasiness over men crying spills over into a cascade of little reasons for blows being exchanged. One woman shouts that the mayor is crazy, and this prompts someone who voted for the mayor to punch her, and someone then slugs her attacker for hitting a woman. Slogans emerge. The unhinged mayor screams an old license-plate number—"AZ 1492"—a formula with no precise meaning, like many slogans, but with a broad suggestiveness: the A to Z of the alphabet and the date of Europeans' arrival in the New World. Later, we hear "guns for killing" (132) and "death to all outsiders" (125). Those guns are "the finest collection of hardware outside of Indo-China during the great Vietnam War days" (132). Logic cannot penetrate the berserk fury of the townspeople, who "responded with withering gunfire in the direction of anyplace they thought there might be a loudspeaker" (171). The violence becomes convoluted and provides moments of hapless grotesquerie that haunt the memory: the librarian has both her ears shot off, for instance. Throughout the tank attack, Norman Mailer serves as a war correspondent, and "that evening 100 million Americans saw Norman Mailer covered with blood say, 'Hell. There is no other word for it. Hell'" (174).

When discussing the enigmatic, subzero black sombrero, Brautigan remarks, "Everybody passed by the sombrero as if it were invisible. The sombrero of course was not invisible. It was as plain as the nose on your face. You couldn't miss it. The sombrero was in plain sight for the whole world to see" (137). So too are big, obvious causes like poverty or the lack of meaningful jobs ignored when the evening news talks about city riots. Brautigan mildly acknowledges the sexually stimulating nature of the violence when noting that early in the riot, sexual couplings were going on in the street. Violence begets sexual arousal and aggression, which may feed back into violence. The sexual component is another of those obvious factors not discussed when a riot is covered on television.

This civic cyclone is laid to rest so crassly as to set one's teeth on edge. The president gushes gooey clichés: "We are on the edge of a great future together. Let us go hand-in-hand into that future with God's glory lighting the way like a torch and His mercy and forgiveness will be the path we walk on" (181). The town's huge cemetery, with a statue of the mayor, becomes a tourist shrine "featured on millions of postcards" (182), becoming more popular than the Grand Canyon. The mayor, now called General License Plate, had committed suicide rather than yield to the forces of the U.S. government. Brautigan writes, "He had fought his hardest. What

else can you say? He was an American" (176). In the midst of this com-
mercialization and ideological decontamination, the sombrero turns white,
a transformation smacking of the inauthentic and artificial. The hat takes
on the color of the "good guy" hats of cowboy iconography. Like the mon-
umentalized mayor, the whitewashed sombrero fits a picture that lets
America feel proud of itself in the aftermath of a pointless, horrendous
massacre. The massacre is recast in the heroic mold, as the Vietnam War
later was in postwar films like *The Deer Hunter* and *Rambo*, where individual American heroics overshadow moral issues and the American defeat. The town has experienced the full fury of a civil riot and the breakdown of all conventional controlling structures; no attempt to learn from
this takes place. Instead, Americans turn it into self-congratulation, commercial kitsch, and emotional pabulum as quickly as possible.

Similarly, the protagonist turns his private agony into a country-and-western song, imagining it sung by Waylon Jennings. The protagonist's pellu-
cid erotic recollections of his first encounter with Yukiko and Brautigan's
hauntingly lyrical description of Yukiko's sleeping and dreaming, his loving tribute to her long black hair and her cat are all overwhelmingly effective, evincing Brautigan's writing at its best. These passages' evocation of
desire is stunning. The bathetic descent into lame country-and-western
lyrics produces an aesthetic dissonance. Brautigan may not welcome the
pain of separation any more than he would welcome a riot. If such acts must
take place, though, he seems to ask, Why do we so trivialize them?

Were Brautigan only concerned with the quality of art to be made from
the riot, he might seem a heartless aesthete. He does, however, seem to
be saying something more about the sources of such violence, and he treats
them as particularly American. A generalized loss of love is one source:
the protagonist loses his girlfriend through his selfish obsessions and his
inability to fill most of her needs. One of the weeping men is unemployed
and starving, a victim of America's loss of love for *all* of its citizens, and
those at the bottom have lost their belief in America's demonstration of
love, the American Dream. Why should anyone go hungry in this, the rich-
est country of the world? The ethnic identity of the lost love may also be
relevant. To the writer, the woman's being Japanese is important; her black
hair and thoughtful silences are attractively alien. In details of personality, she is no stereotyped Madame Butterfly, but her ministering to his
unstable ego does fit stereotypes concerning Asia. White Americans, as
Toni Morrison argues in *Playing in the Dark*, need the ethnic other to create a positive image of themselves. When the writer's world fragments
through the loss of this prop, anarchy cascades down to the wastebasket
world and riot ensues. When faced with the bottomless grief of the starving man, a grief shared by the perennially poor in the land, or with those
oppressed on racial grounds, the white citizens become restless and dis-

turbed, exploding in mindless anger rather than facing the sources and nature of their discomfort. The violence just beneath the surface in this "gunfighter nation" (as Richard Slotkin calls it) erupts. These connections are not explicit in the novel; Brautigan does not seem to have been writing an allegory about the roots of civil violence or our loss of innocence in Vietnam. However, he sets up parallel worlds of love and riot, and the two suggest related themes involving the nature of grief, violence, and the sense of loss on both the personal and the national level.

Brautigan interprets anarchy in the commonplace way as threatening and bad, as a devolution or falling off from a desirable status quo, a conclusion slightly unexpected in the author of *The Confederate General from Big Sur*, a very tricksterish novel. However, Brautigan may feel that riots killing people are not as amusing as hippie hijinks; he does see why the eruption of anarchy in this town is foreseeable, even justifiable, and he exhibits sympathy for the rioters. Similarly, his primary identification lies with the writer, but his sympathies do not blind him to the justice of Yukiko's cause or to the commercialized, kitschy, spiritually nugatory nature of what America now offers its citizens.

Dhalgren (1974)

The city destroyed by riots also represents anarchy for Samuel Delany. Unlike Brautigan, though, Delany is prepared to argue that anarchy is enabling and nurturing. He is reacting to the oppressive rules governing sexual behavior and racial identity in America and rebelling against the need to play roles, against middle-class values, against Du Boisian double consciousness. The setting for his thought experiment is Bellona, once a city of two million in the center of the United States, now partly ruined and inhabited by only a thousand people. This anarchy, like many utopias, demands a low population, but Delany's is exceptionally small. There are no services, no government, no rules, and no connection between Bellona and the outside world. People eat what they loot from stores. Money has disappeared because it is meaningless. Everything is free. A few individuals provide services, apparently because they want to structure their time that way. A bartender serves free beer while a transvestite continues to dance for the bar patrons. A bus driver drives one route. A woman bakes bread and gives it to anyone who wants it. Lanya decides to run a school for children. Roger Calkins runs a newspaper for Bellona. Its dates vary whimsically: 1795 may appear on one issue and 1995 on the next, while days of the week may read Sunday three days in a row.

Not only is the urban infrastructure lacking, so too is the ordinary consistency supplied to life by nature. The sky is so smoky that the sun, moon, and stars are rarely visible. During the protagonist's stay, a second moon appears briefly, perhaps invoking the two moons of Mars, suitable for a city named Bellona, a goddess of war. The sun rises unreliably in different quarters of the compass, and one day, a huge sun fills half the sky. The landscape apparently shifts, for the river is two blocks from a building one time but half a mile at another. There are no seasons.

The protagonist cannot remember his own name, so he is called the Kid, Kidd, or Kydd. He remembers that he is half Cherokee and half white—but he has bouts of amnesia such that he loses several days at a time. He has panic attacks. He apparently writes poetry during the times lost to amnesia; but when challenged with a charge of plagiarism, he cannot actually remember writing the piece, though he remembers revising it. The sequences that may be a dream or reality are his, and he cannot tell us which is the case. He wonders at times if he is going insane, and he has spent time in a mental hospital in the past. In other words, the protagonist himself suffers from inner chaos.

With chaos, however, comes freedom. Delany writes that such a state results in "no laws: to break, or to follow. Do anything you want. Which does funny things to you. Very quickly, surprisingly quickly, you become . . . exactly who you are" (23). Or, as Lanya tells Kid, "I want to try out some things I'm afraid of. That's the only reason to be here" (71). People explore their sexuality. Lanya analyzes her own feelings when she exchanges sex for money (even though the money is worthless) because the transaction goes against her class and gender taboos. Kid explores his bisexual feelings. When he gets off the bus one day on an impulse and lands in a dangerous situation, he wonders why he had gotten off and discovers that "it had been in response to some un-named embryo feeling, and he had leapt out of the bus, following it to term. But now it was born; and was terror" (368). In other words, without articulating a Maileresque code, Kid learns to push himself into situations that frighten him. His responses under such pressure help to make him a leader. He soon learns that there is a logic underlying all the violence: "People just don't get beat up for nothing at all" (95). Hence, Kid's success amid the chaos rests on his ability to assimilate unwritten rules quickly.

Delany dissects such violence. The scorpion gangs enjoy a reputation for mindless assaults, but most of their hours are spent lazing around, and their "runs" chiefly involve letting off steam by breaking things. In a ruined city, a few more broken windows hardly matter. The scorpions get into an abandoned bank during one run and into a house chosen at random on another. While breaking into the house, somebody is killed, but that is quite upsetting to most of the scorpions. The killer is the least stable (and least favorite) scorpion: he is white and has racial hang-ups, and the victim was somebody who did not behave according to the unstated rules governing

violence. That one death is the only violence with irreversible consequences chalked up by the scorpions during the course of the novel;[2] meanwhile, two or three white snipers regularly use the bank building as a place
for picking off blacks with their guns. American newspapers condition us
to respond with horror to the death of an "innocent bystander" in a "gang
spree"; "defense" of a bank might well make the outside papers as a species of heroism, yet money is useless in Bellona, as is the bank.

Rape is another kind of violence somewhat altered by contextualization.
Apparently, the initial riot that trashed the city was fueled by the rape of
a seventeen-year-old white girl named June Richards by a black man named
George Harrison. This symbolic act, so feared and fantasized by whites, is
rendered more complex by George's discussion of sexuality and his liking
for a certain kind of resistance, by his discussion of the various kinds of
actions punished as rape by the law, and by the fact that George is generally a very nice person who is well-liked in the community. When a fire
breaks out in their neighborhood, George rescues children from a burning
building. George models for posters that feature him naked, and these
posters are admired by heterosexual women and homosexual men. When
the second moon appears in the sky, the community spontaneously names
it after George. The Kid meets the white girl who was victim of the initial "rape" and is puzzled by her stubbornly, if timidly, seeking George out.
Her sexual attraction toward George is such that she may half-deliberate-
ly have pushed her brother to his death in a squabble over the famous
poster. George himself boasts that when she finds him, their second coupling will bring on the apocalypse, and the cosmological violence that ends
the book—earthquakes and noises as if the sky were falling—seems to stem
from that second meeting. In Bellona, rape is not a simple concept, nor is
it a common occurrence.

When there is no centralized power, what customs develop? One is a new
kind of hospitality. When someone shows up, the host automatically offers that person food. Virtually taboo as a topic for discussion or argument
is sexual practice. In the nest, anything goes. If one does not like it, then
that person does not have to join in, but that person cannot interfere.
Another form of politeness has to do with one's claims for personal space.
June is a bourgeois girl. When visiting a scorpion nest, she is standoffish,
and this is felt to be an insult: "the isolation she demands about her destroys our concept of human space. That their hostility comes out in sexual leers and sexual jibes . . . is a generic response to something far more
personal than her gender" (625). Politeness when on the territory of others is another rule. The nest accompanies Kid to a party at the Calkins
mansion. They talk with Roger's middle-class guests in a civilized fashion, and they keep an eye on their own to make sure that the less stable

members do not drink too much or pick fights. They prove much politer than the middle-class guests, whose racist and classist comments can be overheard all too easily.

Another development when all the old rules are gone is a fine, descriptive discrimination of skin tones. Sometimes blacks and whites are referred to, but more often, characters note someone's skin as copper, a light coffee color, brown, or freckled white. The color and texture of hair are specified with equal precision. The terms become descriptive rather than pejorative or discriminatory. This is a world of mixed blood, and while remnants of American racism remain as part of everyone's background, only a few unstable scorpions cling to outmoded racist stereotypes.

Delany takes a softer line than Norman Mailer in "The White Negro." Mailer believes that when the racial revolution comes, there will be a lot of violence, and everyone *should* act out repressed impulses. Ultimately, he hopes that humans will prove more creative than destructive and holds out hope on that basis. Delany seems to feel that less violence will be necessary as long as sufficient food is available, and he suggests through the snipers and the scorpion named Dollar that the real lust for violence is found among whites, not blacks. Rational behavior will emerge from below; it need not be enforced from above. In this, he is unexpectedly close in spirit (if not detail) to Robert A. Heinlein in *The Moon Is a Harsh Mistress*. Delany seems to see most people as wanting a life that meets a minimum standard of comfort, in which they can laze and talk and enjoy sex. Some want a sense of belonging and direction, and they join a nest. For those people, a very local form of centralized power exists in the nest leader, so Delany does not totally exclude all forms of center, but he does limit them. A few people want more sense of purpose; not content to "be," they want to "do," and they bake bread or teach children or write poetry. Far from being a bad thing, anarchy in circumstances that do not make survival a cutthroat issue offers humans the shortest route to precisely that sort of life. "Being" rather than "becoming" and time rather than money govern such an existence. The artificial barriers of race, class, and sexual preference evaporate.

Delany does not deal with what will happen when stockpiles of food disappear. The apocalyptic sounds near the end may signal the end of this thought experiment. As he sets it up, his world is a testing ground for personalities and ideas. Outside of time and normal space, he envisions a new equality. Delany evidently wants to show us what it might look like rather than worry about the problem of bringing it into reality in the here and now. Like the cyberpunk writers who were to come later, however, he invites us to look at slums with something other than middle-class revulsion.

◎ ◎ ◎

For contrast, look at the vision of cities in cyperpunk fiction. William
Gibson's *Neuromancer*, Marge Piercy's *He, She and It*, and Neal Stephenson's *Snow Crash* figure cityscapes in which most conventional civil organization has disappeared.[3] The cities may be the BAMA (Boston Atlanta Metropolitan Axis) Sprawl of Gibson, the Glop of Piercy (which seems
to cover large areas of North America), or the West Coast of Stephenson.
Roads have deteriorated, though vehicles still exist. Mail service appears
to be spotty or nonexistent. Parcel delivery is handled by independent
courier systems. Food mostly consists of doctored algae and is often produced locally so that denizens need not rely on nonfunctioning distribution systems. Contagious diseases have outstripped medicine's capacity to
tame them. Drugs, information, pirated videos or stimmies, software,
transplant organs, and sex are the main items of exchange. Neighborhoods
are the tightly controlled territories of gangs, descendants of the Crips and
the Bloods, the mafia, and the Asian Tong, Triad, and Yakuza groups. Rich
people live in protected enclaves and sometimes even in orbit. Those enclaves derive their identity and orderliness from multinational corporations, the new units that have replaced nation-states.
    The worlds of Gibson, Piercy, and Stephenson differ significantly, but
all three tackle the problem of how we might live in a world lacking an
order-enforcing center. Physical survival in their cities is the most obvious problem, and the tendency of these authors to write about heroic characters makes them take an insufficiently Hobbesian view of the brutality
that would probably follow total deregulation. Metaphorically, however,
they equate such a decentered city with the idealized, bodiless, uncentered
world of the Internet, and they actually show us much more about electronic life than about living in such a city.[4] In the Net world, even individuals are decentered, and the vision is distinctly antihumanist.[5] Users
of the Net can assume any identity they wish: they may choose to be male,
female, or alternate; choose their age; and program their appearance and
change it often if that sort of virtual reality is part of the author's idea of
the Net. Gender, age, and race cease to be meaningful distinctions; in this
sense, the Net realizes the dreams of utopia. Gibson's male protagonist and,
to some extent, Piercy's female protagonist deal with this disembodied
world by becoming outlaw hackers, whereas Stephenson's "Hiro Protagonist" is one of the creators of the virtual reality that is part game-world,
although it is real enough that players can be mentally disabled by a computer virus. City and Net are not completely equivalent, but the life possible in a decentered Net is meant to awaken in us the belief that life in a
decentered realm is possible and may even have its attractions.

Violence in the city, the home of citizens and civilized practices, makes many readers feel threatened, especially those who live in safe suburbs or ritzy sectors of downtown. Violence on the mythic frontier is one thing; the city, especially in its better parts, is supposed to be safe. In *Welcome to Hard Times*, E. L. Doctorow plays on our assumptions about frontier and civilization when he shows how an incident of violence in a town struggling to come into existence is enough to destroy that town.[6] The denizens cannot bear being betrayed by their hoped-for refuge from lawlessness. America suffers collectively from a sense of being betrayed by its cities (never mind the reasons for such civic and urban decay). Some cyberworld creators accept that the old "safe" city is no more, but their imaginations do not simply flee to the suburbs. They try to reinvent city life. Some underplay the greed and violence of city gangs, but those authors seem to feel that open greed and violence are no worse than the hidden forms of capitalist tyranny currently oppressing the poor. What can be said for their thought experiments is that these writers and Delany are trying to go against the middle-class hand wringing over dying cities. They wish to reimagine human relationships with cities in this increasingly chaotic state. Finding positive values in anarchy may set readers up for living with it successfully, something not possible if they view slums and riots only through the conservative perspective of Saul Bellow or even the sympathy of Richard Brautigan. The cyberwriters are also, curiously, supporting a picture of life that escapes American materialism. Power, money, and sex have relatively little attraction in the Net world. We are being invited instead to base life on challenge, on using our wits, on developing expertise, on cultivating highs of all sorts and not for "making a killing." They offer a high-tech form of life for the sake of "being" moment by moment instead of "becoming."

Trickster Anarchism: Kingston and Vizenor

Tripmaster Monkey: His Fake Book (1989) and *Griever: An American Monkey King in China* (1987)

Chaos may operate either on a grand scale or very locally. Characters who deliberately create small pockets of chaos are, or can be, tricksters. In novelistic literature, tricksters resemble picaresque heroes, but while picaros are disrespectful of social order, they simply want enough pelf to join it on more advantageous terms. Nor are tricksters quite like the beats of *On the Road.* Sal Paradise and Dean Moriarty seek nirvana, not just free play. Jerzy Kosinski produces a grim and sometimes deadly figure with a trickster's propensities in *Cockpit.* The protagonist's adventure with phony uniforms, his terrorizing the aggravating child on the airplane, his picking locks on mailboxes to read mail, and some of the novel's sexual sequences could be part of a trickster story. My own squirming over the mailbox episode made me realize the degree to which middle-class values were his target. His protagonist does not really try to overthrow social order or create chaos, however. He liberates himself from middle-class strictures out of Nietzschean motives and uses his freedom to punish those he feels to have wronged him and to manipulate people for his own satisfaction. His punishments are vicious and lack any element of the high good humor that is often associated with tricksters.

The term trickster enters Western intellectual jargon with Paul Radin's studies of Winnebago myths. Jung identified the trickster as an archetype. We learned to apply that label to Brer Rabbit and Reynard the Fox. I could quote anthropological studies of the phenomenon, but Gerald Vizenor, a Native American specialist in Amerindian tricksters, cites and makes fun of anthropological analyses in a couple of his essays on the subject.[7] One of his own definitions states that "the trickster is a chance, a comic holotrope in a postmodern language game that uncovers the distinctions and ironies between narrative voices; a semiotic sign for 'social antagonism' and 'aesthetic activism' in postmodern criticism and the avant-garde, but not 'presence' or ideal cultural completion in narratives" ("Trickster Discourse" 192). Quite so. Vizenor is very hard on non-Indians who try to define or discuss tricksters. For instance, he takes Andrew Wiget to task for calling tricksters scandalous: "the use of the word *scandalous* . . . would prescribe a neocolonial moral presence in tribal stories. Wiget is sincere, to be sure, but he has undermined the creative power of tribal literature with his use of structuralism and other social-science theories."[8] Whatever I say is likewise open to censure since it derives from reading rather than from stories told by tribal elders on a reservation. However, I am focusing on novelistic figures with trickster propensities, not the traditional beings of oral legend. My comments concern how these trickster figures—already adapted to a Western form—seem to function in these two novels for a white, middle-class reader. That a Euro-American audience is, for the corrective part of these satires at least, the targeted group is clear, because whites' bad behavior and the social constructions of nonwhites are one of the main objects of attack.

Legendary tricksters often enjoy divine or semidivine status and are sometimes powerful or at least prodigal contributors to the creation of the world, not just marginal troublemakers. They may have carnivalesque characteristics reflected in their abundance of sexual and scatological activities. They can be killed, yet they return. When moving among humans, they care nothing for human rules. This figure is largely absent from the biblical tradition and appears relatively trivially in classical and Norse myths as Hermes and Loki. As an exotic mythical import into the Western tradition, however, the idea of a trickster attracts a mainstream writer like Donald Barthelme. He catches the whirlwind energies of this divine cultural progenitor in *The Dead Father* when his title character reminisces about fathering the poker chip, the juice extractor, the rubber pretzel, the punching bag, the inkblot, the midget Bible, and thousands of ordinary children (49). After fathering the Pool Table of Ballambangjang and finding himself having to play against Evil itself, the Dead Father describes his predicament:

> I realized instantly that I was on the wrong side of the Styx. However I was not lacking in wit, even in this extremity. Uncoiling my penis, then in the dejected state, I made a long cast across the river, sixty-five meters I would say, where it snagged most conveniently in the cleft of a rock on the farther shore. Thereupon I hauled myself hand-over-hand 'midst excruciating pain as you can imagine through the raging torrent to the other bank. . . . and on that bank of the river there stands to this day a Savings & Loan Association. A thing I fathered. (51)

In illo tempore, the Dead Father was more than a bit of a trickster, but the novel is not a trickster story, because the Dead Father has become a tyrant, the embodiment of social order in its most deadening and oppressive forms. Barthelme's trickster grew up to become a patriarch.

The novels by Maxine Hong Kingston and Gerald Vizenor declare their trickster intents by invoking the Chinese legend of the Mind Monkey or Monkey King. Kingston draws loosely on Chinese legends and embodies them in an American of ethnic Chinese background.[9] Vizenor spent several months in China as a teacher; from those experiences, he distills a carnivalesque story about Griever de Hocus, an American Indian who plays the Monkey King in China. Vizenor's novel was first published in 1986 and Kingston's in 1989, but bits of hers appeared in the previous two years. Both seem to be opposing the reactionary developments of the Reagan years, and Kingston's novel is objecting to the Vietnam War as well, for she sets her novel in the 1960s.

Kingston's Monkey King is Wittman Ah Sing (Whitman "I Sing . . ."). Like Andrea Dworkin's protagonist, this "Whitman" with Chinese ancestors longs for the open, oceanic America hymned by Walt Whitman. Instead, he feels so overwhelmed by all the social constructions of his identity inimical to his essence that he contemplates suicide as his story opens. One such construction by whites is the assumption that his Asian features mean he is not American. People ask, "Are you Japanese, Chinese, or Korean?" or "How do you like this country?" or "Where's a good Chinese restaurant here?" They say, "You people are good with figures." He condemns the facile write-off that Asians are inscrutable and writhes when interlocutors assume that while at the University of California at Berkeley he must have majored in science or engineering and not in English.[10]

Others' demands on his identity include the requirement that he take a disgusting job simply to be respectable. Even his family wants to alter his identity, blaming him for not becoming an engineer or doctor. Another regulation about to enter his life at any moment is the draft; the government wishes to send him to Vietnam to murder Asians who have done him no harm. On a whim, he marries someone he has known for less than twenty-four hours and finds himself up against stereotypes of married life. He assumes that a wife should clean up cups and ashtrays and is shocked when his wife says that she will not be a wife and wants him to be the "wife" instead. The worst pressure he faces is that of his life's work. He is not lazy and would be happy with a job that let him be a playwright or work to preserve the world from the bomb, but the unemployment bureau does not recognize such positions.

Wittman's little rebellions involve deliberately shocking middle-class, law-abiding citizens, making them feel uncomfortable because Wittman is breaking rules. When on a bus, he starts reading aloud, thus rupturing conventions of being quiet in public. When entertaining his dream date, he knowingly makes her uncomfortable by forcing her to listen to his poems and then exploding when he does not like her reaction. Monkey-like, he lopes about on his knuckles, leaping up and down and throwing papers around. If she were the right sort of person (he feels), she would feel protective and maternal rather than horrified, expectations that show his childish streak. When bored by his job selling toys and irritated by the bad manners of the buying public, Wittman winds up a jumping monkey doll and wraps a Barbie doll's legs around its waist, thus producing a sexual tableau that gets him fired. Kingston differentiates Wittman from the traveling gang in Kerouac's *On the Road* by involving him in a three-day community happening. Wittman sketches a scenario based on the Chinese *Romance of the Three Kingdoms;* through it, he hopes to let people with Chinese features exercise their star qualities, since usually they are relegated to bit parts and villains. Unexpectedly, the participants take over the show and evolve a drama in which the line between spectator and actor blurs, and nobody really knows what will come next until it happens. The end of the third night emerges as a monologue by Wittman, who exhorts his audience about racial stereotypes and marital roles. It turns into a community celebration of his emphatically nonromantic marriage.

With his happening, Wittman settles several problems in his mind. His play about war convinces him that he must be a pacifist and resist the American government's sending him to kill the Vietnamese. He rejects capitalism, having realized that one's life can be devoted to gaining time or money, and he prefers time. He rejects romantic marriage and its emphasis on physical beauty. Instead, he proclaims, "We're going to prove that any two random people can get together and learn to care for one another. . . . The superior man loves anyone he sets his mind to. Otherwise we're fucked" (337). In other words, if American society were to encourage rational attitudes, politeness, and caring rather than unreasonable expectations of glamour and one type of racial beauty, some irrational hatreds would not choke us as they do. Wittman's anarchy is very local, but what started as personal rebellion ends as a cooperative effort involving peoples of several racial backgrounds having a good time. Wittman even wins for himself some recognition by the community as a trickster and playwright rather than being considered a failed engineer or doctor.

In *Griever: An American Monkey King in China,* Vizenor's Griever de Hocus operates on a somewhat larger scale when he strews his chaos. He is practically a one-man invasion of China, and while China is not America and this not a direct literary attack on the United States, the second sentence of the book calls China "an enormous reservation" (13). Griever sets up various parallels between his Chinese and American experiences. The chickens remind him of a high school escapade with frogs. He discovers that some Chinese groups, like many Native American groups, recognize bears as totem animals. He comes across Chinese scrolls that have shamanistic pictures and markings much like some he knows among tribes at home. Simply reading China as a metaphor for the United States is not a balanced reading; I am doing that here, however, because China lets Vizenor explore kinds of oppression. When displayed in China, these acts are visible to Euro-Americans. In America, the oppressions of Native Americans are less visible to white middle-class readers because they are on the giving rather than the receiving end. Simply by being in China, Griever is read primarily as an American and only secondarily as a Native American.

Griever, like Wittman, resists social pressures to conform. He insists on keeping a cock in a dormitory in which pets are not allowed, despite its crowing at dawn. He presses against all barriers erected to keep him from speaking to Chinese people. He refuses to conform to dress codes when going to Maxim's of Beijing. He flagrantly transgresses Chinese sexual rules by sleeping with two women who are technically both daughters of the man who administers the foreigners' compound, and he gets one of them pregnant. Whereas society shuns people of mixed ancestry, Griever seeks them out. Like Wittman, he refuses to rein in his emotions to be respectable by middle-class standards. He expresses himself freely and ferociously (insofar as language will permit), and the emotions that do not get blown off in front of others are screamed into "panic holes" that he digs down by the lake.

He frees some chickens in the market; this proves to be a dry run for freeing prisoners going to their executions. Were this a demonic vision, more would be made of public execution; here, the event is merely a shadowy reminder of the state's ultimate weapon in enforcing conformity to its narrow standards of acceptable behavior. Griever, in monkey face-paint, dances around the trucks of prisoners. He hops up on top of the cab of one truck and demands the prisoners' release. Titters and laughter follow the production of his identification, which shows him with monkey king makeup. As the caravan sets off, he manages to open one truck, toss out the driver, and lose the soldiers with some fast swerves. Once the pursuit has been shaken, he tries to free the prisoners. The rapists, heroin dealer, and murderer take off happily enough, but the prostitute, robber, and art historian stay, convinced that no one is free in their world and that there is no point to running. Soldiers shoot some of the escapees, and the monkey king has to go into hiding.

Griever's sexual escapades seem thoroughly tricksterish. Hester Hua Dan is rendered pregnant, and shortly after her father learns of it, she is found dead in the pond near the compound where unwanted infants are often drowned. Griever takes no responsibility for birth control and thereby shows a trickster's callousness toward second parties that might be hurt by his fun; perhaps, too, he values the mixed-blood fetus because of its unusual mixture more than the life of the mother.

Griever finds himself outraging everyone in China who identifies with social rules and conventions. His frustration finds an appropriate outlet in his soaring aloft and vanishing in a microlight airplane, carrying one of his mixed-blood loves and his rooster with him. He rises above the troubles below and finds a more divine perspective as he heads for Macao and freedom. However, an enigmatic reference buried at the beginning of the book states that Griever "vanished" in his microlight, implying that he was never heard from again. Readers never learn whether this is a modern-day assumption into heaven or a fatal crash.

"Wild" is an obviously strange and much valued word to Vizenor, as it is for Kathy Acker; to both of them, "wild" is positive and desirable, an aspect of liberation. When first having sex with Hester (a Chinese Hester Prynne?), Griever inhales her "wild humors"; a "wild ichor burst from her sheath"; and he whispers "the wild moon" to her (105, 106). He does this although she is hardly a wild figure like himself; what governs her is "her fear, resignation to paternal power, and her dedication to the nation" (200). Moments free from time are wild, and stories labeled histories are usually called wild. The word expresses the chaos valued by tricksters, the activities represented when "he talked backward, and he disturbed common manners in the world" (128).

Vizenor looks at China, the country that spawned the monkey king legends, and notes the degree to which the trickster's freedom is totally absent. His other books make plain that he sees much of the same rigidity and oppression in the United States. Certainly, that is so for Native Americans, who, like the Chinese, cherish trickster legends. Because of white social pressures and rules, they find liberating chaos difficult to achieve. China is a reservation, and reservations are all too much like China. In both, and anywhere, one should liberate oneself from identities constructed and enforced by the opinions of others. In both Kingston and Vizenor, the trickster situation—involving the trickster and the rules being flouted— seems to link anarchy to authenticity, though authenticity is something to be sought for the sake of the process of seeking and not a presence guaranteeing something absolute.

Whatever tricksters may be in myths, in these two novels, they seem to represent individual liberation. They work by example and occasional direct action to help others liberate themselves. They do not aim seriously at the governmental level of orderly control. Trickster government is not their aim, it being a contradiction in terms. For thinkers who try to envision the United States totally refashioned according to anarchist principles, we have to turn to utopian writers. Tricksters operate only in opposition—at least in their novelistic roles. They are not the creators of a new, more liberated order—if there is to be any order—because order itself is anathema to them.

Utopian Anarchies: Le Guin, Piercy, and Starhawk

Behind each sunny utopia lies a shadowland, the unsatisfactory world that the novelist wishes to reform, to reshape nearer his or her heart's desire. In a fish's heaven, there will be no land (as Rupert Brooke points out). In the utopias of the three writers discussed here, there will be no more thoughtless industrial ravaging of the Earth and no more racism or sexism, all seen as prime characteristics of America, as the ways in which America has failed most spectacularly. All the authors are convinced that even if the American pattern were more equitable than it seems to them, it *must* be abandoned because it cannot be sustained. Cataclysmic breakdown awaits us in the future, the mass annihilations so cheerfully foreseen by Leslie Marmon Silko and Gerald Vizenor in chapter 6. Since at present land still exists, the piscine desire for a watery heaven can be dismissed as escapist, and utopias usually are so dismissed. However, far too few groups of thinkers, let alone government agencies, ask themselves in a platonic fashion, "What is *good* government? What would be *better* than what we have?" Good needs to be attached to a morality, though not necessarily to a religion. These writers are asking what a true morality of right living might be.

The five utopias to be discussed agree on many features that they consider part of the desirable life. None is as stress-free as the life shown in Morris's *News from Nowhere* or Bellamy's *Looking Backward;* all of these societies are under pressure from hierarchically organized rivals or suffer from natural disasters that strain life and force value decisions challenging their very existence. Each writer brings different concerns to these studies of the human condition, though all might be labeled leftist for their anticapitalistic, antiracist, pan- or nontheistic, and generally multicultural values. Ursula K. Le Guin works on the social institutions needed to make a government that truly works upward rather than downward; she also asks what the nature of human life should be, particularly if no afterlife is posited and no materialist answers are deemed adequate. Marge Piercy focuses on essentialist barriers to equality and removes the distinctions between man and woman and between human and machine. Starhawk, an eco-feminist and theologian of Wiccan practice, removes barriers between humans and nature. To create their utopias, these novelists excise those core practices that they see as damaging the world we inhabit, and they imagine what would happen once that tumor has been removed. They vary in the degree to which they criticize America directly, but all the narratives except Le Guin's *Dispossessed* are set in future Americas and tackle issues visible in our country today. As Le Guin points out in several of her critical writings, all fantasy is metaphor; it may talk about the future or an elsewhere, but it cannot help but be a response to the here and now. On that basis, I slant my reading toward the implicit critiques of America, even if the authors themselves may cast the story in terms of problems like human versus machine or see the trouble as global rather than exclusively American.

Whereas the extreme individualism of right-wing libertarian anarchists derives from Max Stirner and German thought, the collectivist side of anarchist utopian thought owes much to Native American tribes.[11] Early reports of the eastern American tribes worked their way into European intellectual thought. The observers were fascinated with the way the tribes lived without king or money and enjoyed considerable freedom and equality. Rousseau's noble savage is one reflection of these accounts. Marx studied Lewis Henry Morgan's *League of the Iroquois,* and when Engels rewrote Marx's notes after Marx's death, the piece emerged as *The Origin of the Family, Private Property, and the State: In the Light of the Researches of Lewis H. Morgan.* When contemporary Native American writers describe tribal life, they often consciously offer a society that is noncapitalist, that displays kinds of freedom lacking in white America, and that has no true centralized power but that offers consensus, checks and balances, and the right of individuals to refuse a majority decision. James Welch portrays such a society in *Fools Crow;* to a lesser degree, we see such cultures in Leslie Marmon Silko's *Ceremony* or Louise Erdrich's *Tracks.* Recent utopian writers derive their models and values from four main sources: European socialist and anarchist thought; Native American cultural practices; collectivist practices of Israeli kibbutzim; and values identified as relational and culturally feminine by theorists like Carol Gilligan. The European and Israeli models carry traces of American Indian tribal patterns (as understood and misunderstood by European Marxists) but reflect their own urban, agricultural, or religious styles. Only the feminist pattern seems initially independent of Native American roots; in practice, though, it reaches similar conclusions about how life should be led.

Always Coming Home (1985) and *The Dispossessed* (1974)

Ursula K. Le Guin has been a major ideologue expounding political anarchism for a quarter century.[12] She takes anarchy seriously as a viable mode of living and as a realizable alternative to capitalism. She explores the social scale on which it can operate; she considers the implications of various levels of technology to be preserved or created or done away with. She has constructed detailed anarchic societies in two quite different styles: one based directly on Native American modes of life, the other modeled on European anarcho-syndicalism and an urban lifestyle. She uses her fictional powers to make contemporary Americans from the mainstream culture understand the spiritual reorientation that would be necessary for such a mode of existence. She is no star-dazed dreamer. The people in her societies are not implausibly happy all the livelong day; a few in *Always Coming Home* clearly made mistakes in choosing spouses, and the protagonist of *The Dispossessed* may not survive his homecoming because many of his countrymen are furious at him. Le Guin rigorously explores the theoretical weaknesses of her two systems and shows us what such societies have most to fear as the seeds of their own destruction. She sums up what anarchism is all about in her short story "The Day before the Revolution," in which the ideologue, Odo, now an old woman close to death, is musing on what the coming revolution must be: "Though in those days, before she and the others had thought it through, it had been a very green and puerile revolution. Strikes for better wages, representation for women. Votes and wages—Power and Money, for the love of God! Well, one does learn a little, after all, in fifty years" (397). A writer who can elaborate societies that operate with neither power nor money is performing an impressive act of imagination, one that deserves more recognition.

The America that Le Guin reacts against is one whose natural landscape has been damaged by unchecked industrialism. She excoriates our excessive standard of living, which relies on such industrialism and on nonrenewable resources. She notes the connection to our war-based economy; after all, the proportion of the Gross National Product (GNP) spent on the military during the cold war has been very similar to that of World War II. She points to the necessity of greatly reducing our population both for our own health and that of the natural landscape consisting of plants and other living creatures. For her, the current pattern is not sustainable, and disastrous breakdown will ensue. The question is how to create something sustainable that is not a minimalist, rigid hell, the Terra described by the Terran ambassador in *The Dispossessed*. She also deplores the lack of any nurturing spiritual dimension to our lives. The traditional Judeo-Christian religions supply some spirituality for some Americans but do not produce a cherishing attitude toward the land, toward the animals, or even toward other people if they do not belong to the same sect. She finds American culture lacking in close personal relationships and considers it twisted and deformed by its preference for rivalry over cooperation. Although her two utopias differ markedly from one another, the problems they fight against are much the same.

Always Coming Home illustrates its lesson in anarchy even in its structure. Readers are invited to choose different possible sequences for reading the diverse materials. North Owl's account of leaving the Kesh village is broken into several parts. We are given the option of reading it straight through or taking the parts as they come, mixed in with many shorter personal narratives, an anthropological analysis of the Kesh culture, poems, descriptions of dances, scripts for little plays or pageants or rites, accounts of music, and maps and pictures. Anarchy, therefore, involves active choice on the part of the participants; it also reminds us as readers of our own mind-set, our resistance to such apparent randomness. However, we will better understand the nature of what North Owl leaves, and we will understand how it looks to her when she comes back after several years in a very different culture if we read the interspersed anthropological material as well.

This anarchic community of the future comes about after ecological and geomorphic cataclysms, for California's great valley is now an inland sea. The effects of America's twentieth-century ecological profligacy still linger in birth defects caused by industrial pollutants. Indestructible plastic pellets float in great masses on the ocean even centuries after the disaster. We are told that a computer network still exists, accessible throughout the world and in remaining space installations. Its function is to collect data, which is available to anyone through terminals. The Keshian villages and towns in an area north of the San Francisco Bay area can access this information in one of their towns; more settlements are eligible for terminals but have refused, seeing no need. Here, however, Le Guin gives us (as desirable) a bulwark against reversion to prescientific superstition, which would include the irrational fear of the deformed or abnormal and the practice of making scapegoats of such individuals. Various kinds of scientific information are available should they be needed.

Within the village of Shinshan, we find a version of tribal life. Everyone is born into one of five "houses" (Obsidian, Blue Clay, Serpentine,

Yellow Adobe, and Red Adobe). These offer basic cosmological identifi-
cations and define one kind of affinity considered so close that sexual
contact between coinhabitants of the house would be incest. As children
grow older and develop interests, they become members of various lodges,
societies, and arts. Lodges include hunters, fishers, salt gatherers, doctors,
planters, and two having to do with death and history. Societies include
several clown lodges and cults. Finally, the arts include glassmaking, tan-
ning, cloth production, potting, tending the village's water systems, book-
making, woodwork, musical instruments, winemaking, smithwork, and
milling, which includes not only all sorts of wind and water mills but also
doing things with the electricity they generate. We find no central government, only a balance among the five "Houses of Earth" with their
cosmological orientation.

No money as such is mentioned. Families contribute to a common ware-
house of the goods they produce and take from it according to need. Those
families considered wealthy are those who give much, and the words for
giving and rich are the same. Therefore, no family piles up goods through
hoarding or accumulation over generations. Without wealth as we define
it, there is little to quarrel over and little reason to lust for power. Power
to do what? When we look to see what can be collected, we find not goods
but intangibles. Individuals own chants and songs and can as a favor or gift
teach these to other individuals. To be the guardian of several such songs
makes one well endowed in this community.

As is visible in Silko's *Ceremony*, Welch's *Fools Crow*, Momaday's
House Made of Dawn, and numerous other Native American novels, life
in *Always Coming Home* has a strong spiritual dimension, including rituals, chants, and kinship to all nature. Those who live in Shinshan call
all creatures "people"; they specify *human* people or *coyote* people when
a particular group is intended. Considerate spiritual attitudes are fostered,
including a generous and logical attitude toward emotions. When North
Owl, renamed Woman Coming Home, tries to untangle her feelings for a
Keshian suitor, she sums it up in this way: "I was still the Condor's daughter and the Condor's wife, ignorant, poor of mind, only beginning to be a
person. I was raw, and needed a lot of cooking yet. Though I had lived
twenty-six years, I had lived only nineteen of them in the Valley. Nineteen is young to marry. I told Alder these thoughts. He listened carefully,
without answering" (397). Eventually, Alder says, "I am taking your
strength. What I have to give you, you don't want or need" (397). He does
not see his need as a claim on her and does not exalt romantic love as all-
important in life. Generosity to her is more important than his own lusts
and demands a logical weighing up of the forces at work. Their calm logic allows them eventually to work out a satisfying, if not particularly
romantic, life between them.

In a series of fascinating explosions of key metaphors into their social implications, Le Guin gives us one for "house," which she considers central to Kesh life:

The Metaphor: THE HOUSE.
What it generates: STABILITY.
Universe as house: Rooms in one mansion.
Society as household: Division within unity; inclusion/exclusion.
Person as householder: Selfhood.
Medicine as protection.
Mind as householder: Belonging.
Language as self-domestication.
The Relationship of human with other beings in the house: Inside/Outside.
Images of the House: Doors, windows, hearth, home, the town. (521)

She parses war, the central feature of the contrasting Condor society, as follows:

The Metaphor: THE WAR.
What it generates: STRUGGLE.
Universe as war: The triumph of being over nothingness. The battlefield.
Society as war: The subjection of weak to strong.
Person as warrior: Courage; the hero.
Medicine as victory over death.
Mind as warrior: Conquistador.
Language as control.
The relationship of human with other beings in war: Enmity.
Images of the War: Victory, defeat, loot, ruin, the army. (519)

She also discusses "machine" and "lord" as metaphors, and their concern for control and hierarchy dovetail tightly with the metaphors generated by war. Those values, masculine in contrast to the feminine values of Keshian society, are embodied in the neighboring Condor society.

The Condors' devotion to war and conquest may well reflect the Strategic Defense Initiative debates and the cold war crisis of November 1983 that were taking place while the book was written. Our upping the portion of the GNP to develop that weaponry would have forced us yet closer to the war specialization of Condor society. Le Guin explains the interrelationship of warrior values and dominance-defined masculinity: "True Condor warriors were to be one thing only, reflections of One, setting themselves apart from all the rest of existence, washing it from their minds and souls, killing the world, so that they could remain perfectly pure. That is why my father was named Kills. He was to live outside the world, killing it, to show the glory of One" (213–14). Such a warrior would never sully himself by helping with agricultural labor, and he believes that drudges, women, and foreigners have no souls. Here we see the separation between self and world produced by a monotheistic cult and the gnostic exaltation of soul at the expense of all material existence that leads so easily to the destruction of the world. The separation of the masculine self from the feminine is possibly the first step in that cascade reaction. Not surprisingly, Le Guin shows the Condor empire, like other great military powers, over-reaching itself, overextending economically with its attempt at high-tech weapons to expand conquests over lands the Condors do not have the in-frastructure to control.[13]

If the point of Condor life is to reflect the One and separate the spirit from the dross of the world, what is the point of Keshian life? Nothing that simple. To live life with enhanced awareness of its complexities, perhaps. People prepare themselves for life as a series of stages, to which belong particular rites and behaviors. They do not privilege any one stage: not youth, not mature wisdom, not death. All must be in balance. They enjoy the many-leveled appreciation of their relationships to human people, nonhuman people, and plants. They develop skills such as pottery mak-ing and think of them as work of the mind and body, seeing that as a very satisfactory outlet for human impulses. They are conditioned to get plea-sure from giving rather than from hoarding. Money and efficiency in an industrial sense are meaningless, so instead they have time and awareness. Like Kingston's monkey king or Delany's inhabitants of Bellona, they strive for time rather than money or its equivalent. Nothing is wasted or thrown away: "Here / is no away to throw to. / A way with no away" (523). They are saved from the drawbacks of a prescientific outlook by the remnants of the previous world-culture. Le Guin has, though, found a level of exis-tence that demands relatively little technology yet provides conditions for comfort (if not luxury) derived from renewable resources. Its every feature reproaches mainstream American society.

The Dispossessed, Le Guin's other anarchy, creates a society not based on tribal living—with its spiritual ties to nature—but on the European, urban model. The theorist of this revolution, Odo, focused her plans for society on a form of decentralization that would maintain an urban world:

> She had no intention of trying to de-urbanize civilization. Though she suggested that the natural limit to the size of a community lay in its de-pendence on its own immediate region for essential food and power, she intended that all communities be connected by communication and trans-portation networks, so that goods and ideas could get where they were wanted. . . . But the network was not to be run from the top down. There was to be no controlling center, no capital, no establishment for the self-

perpetuating machinery of bureaucracy and the dominance drive of individuals seeking to become captains, bosses, chiefs of state. . . . They cut back very hard indeed, but to a minimum beneath which they would not go; they would not regress to pre-urban, pre-technological tribalism. They knew that their anarchism was the product of a very high civilization, of a complex diversified culture, of a stable economy and a highly industrialized technology that could maintain high production and rapid transportation of goods. However vast the distances separating settlements, they held to the ideal of complex organicism. (77–78)

Their communities have "workshops, factories, domiciles, dormitories, learning centers, meeting halls, distributories, depots, refectories" (79), all of which are built in cellular fashion around squares. Labor assignments are parceled out by a computer, but one has the freedom to refuse: "One's own pleasure, and the respect of one's fellows" (121) are what govern individual behavior. Individuals are encouraged to value what the community values through their education, through the deliberate conditioning to think collectively, and through sharing. Possessive pronouns and adjectives do not exist.

Whereas utopian communities are usually located in lush, tropical locations so that living takes little hard work and less fuel (e.g., Huxley's *Island*), Le Guin gives her anarchists no such easy break. Anarres is a moon that is dusty, water-starved, and possessed of a very minimal ecology; the living conditions are adequate only as long as nature offers no surprises. When several years of drought ravage the land, the freedoms of anarchism shrivel. People no longer feel free to turn down labor postings even if these tear families or friends apart. Social patterns rigidify and tolerance for variation dies.

Le Guin's image for the threat to her anarchy is "the wall." Whenever the protagonist, Shevek, is frustrated by others, he dreams of coming up against a wall or of walls closing in on him in a prison. When Shevek decides to act against the will of most Anarresti and go to Urras, the planet orbited by their moon Anarres, he describes his mission in terms of walls. "Here in A-Io [equivalent to the United States and other first-world countries] they fear me less because they have forgotten the revolution. They don't believe in it any more. They think if people can possess enough things they will be content to live in prison. But I will not believe that. I want the walls down. I want solidarity, human solidarity. I want free exchange between Urras and Anarres" (112). Such barriers divide culture from culture, class from class, one form of physics from another, and family member from family member. Walls make property possible, destroying the freedoms of movement and exchange that should characterize anarchy.

All such walls are the basis for life on the Earth-like planet, and Shevek explores this way of living that is so different from his own preferred mode. Ultimately, he wants to dismantle such barriers, and most of all, he wishes to destroy the barrier between Urras and Anarres—not to mention the barriers that have grown up within Anarresti society. His professional lucubrations as a physicist are devoted to a theory that would help remove barriers by making instantaneous communication across many light-years possible. Not only does he succeed, but he broadcasts his equations so that no one society can own the power over communication and thus fence others off from its benefits.

Shevek at one point takes refuge in the Terran embassy after participating in a peace demonstration over a foreign war similar to the Vietnam War of the late 1960s and early 1970s, and he talks to the out-world ambassador from what is our planet. Shevek tells her that Urras (where the riots are being brutally squelched) is hell, and she responds that to her it seems paradise: "My world, my Earth, is a ruin. . . . There are no forests left on my Earth. The air is grey, the sky is grey, it is always hot. . . . Well, we had saved what could be saved, and made a kind of life in the ruins, on Terra, in the only way it could be done: by total centralization. Total control over the use of every acre of land, every scrap of metal, every ounce of fuel. Total rationing, birth control, euthanasia, universal conscription into the labor force" (279–80). Shevek considers Urras hellish because of its spiritual state; the ambassador thinks it paradisal for its ecological richness and the vast variety of lifestyles. The same double view can be taken of America. By implication, Urras and America are both headed in the Terran direction. Hence, Le Guin's urge to find an alternative to capitalism.

The Anarresti life is not luxurious—excess is excrement, as one of their cultural truisms puts it—but this nonluxurious life nevertheless offers many chances for self-realization. Shevek does his physics, either living hermit-like when he feels like it or joining in the community. He does the tenth-day drudge labor that everyone has to do, the unpleasant work like processing shit. He accepts occasional postings that take him to other parts of the country and expose him to new kinds of physical labor such as planting trees. Teaching a class does not mean forcing reluctant students to learn something they do not want; in an anarchist institution, a class is offered when students band together and ask for it. He chooses to take a permanent partner but is under no obligation to. When opposed by his physics colleague, he and friends set up a printing syndicate to print his work. They also open radio communication with Urras, an act that is much against the wishes of the official bodies that normally handle such communication, but Shevek and his friends are within their rights to do so. Once Shevek's society has hardened, his goal is to bring back the perpetual revolution that makes anarchy possible. We are left to feel that he probably will succeed either by direct example or by his own martyrdom. The inherent weakness of such an anarchy is the hardening of custom into rule. Le Guin's ideal is the perpetual, flexible revolution, an ideal more akin to Jeffersonian democracy, with its openness to revolutions, than to the America that actually developed.[14]

Woman on the Edge of Time (1976) and He, She and It (1991)

Marge Piercy shares Le Guin's anger at America's ecological profligacy, and both her utopias show future Americans dealing with serious damage to the ecosphere. That damage, however, merely serves as a correlative to her chief worry, the incompatibility between our institutions and the needs of people. Woman on the Edge of Time shows how poverty, the welfare system, and a mental hospital damage the potential of an intelligent, well-meaning person and keep her from being productive, happy, or fulfilled. Chapter 6 of this study dealt with the demonic vision embedded in the dystopian half of the plot; this chapter's discussion of Woman on the Edge of Time concerns the utopian half. He, She and It, set in a cyberpunk future, shows how multinational companies, so hymned by Bruce Sterling in Islands in the Net, are more likely to develop into callous institutions that are intolerant toward cultural difference, coldly manipulative, and greedy. Her alternative world is a Jewish kibbutz-like anarchy that maintains autonomy within a world of multinational dominance by marketing computer defenses. Both utopias show small-scale communities governing themselves through open meetings—sometimes through elected representatives but sometimes via a town meeting that comprises whomever cares or is free to attend. Anarchy is not quite as complete as in Le Guin's Dispossessed. Some laws, such as a prohibition against creating cyborgs, are held to bind individuals, so those who contravene this law are not really within their rights. Le Guin's two utopias seem content to stick to humans and deal with their imperfections, simply encouraging education that would reduce the dominance drive and encourage cooperation. Piercy wants more; in Woman on the Edge of Time, she wants to do away with essentialist gender identities; in He, She and It, she explores what might happen if humanity were to be enlarged to include cyborgs.

In Woman on the Edge of Time, we find an anarchist world in which organization and governance are entirely handled through consensus. The village, Mattapoisett, has a council (chosen by lot or, in the case of Earth and animal advocates, by dream) and sends a representative to a grand council. Decisions are only finalized when all parties agree, and "winners" must provide a feast and entertainment for the "losers." We do not learn much about any higher planning body (such as the one that runs the war being fought against some unregenerate nonutopian country), but any such body presumably works in this same fashion. As much as possible, one does what one wishes in life. People serve on defense in the war only if they wish; however, since everyone understands the threatened status of their life, many volunteer. The notion of a draft strikes them as bizarre; as one member of the community puts it, who would wish to serve with the unwilling? Such a soldier might not do his or her best. They choose whether and with whom to become co-mothers, though some planning council prevents overpopulation. People can change professions. Even the self is not strongly centered: people change their names at their rite of passage into adulthood and, thereafter, at will. Self-realization and contribution to community life are the aims of this society.

In keeping with an anarchist attempt to do away with hierarchies and fixed centers, Piercy does her best to visualize a world in which gender and race as we know them would genuinely not be of much interest to anyone. Children are gestated in artificial wombs and nursed by three "mothers"—including medically altered, lactating males as well as females, all of different racial background and none genetically related to the infant.[15] Piercy thus does away with gendered patterns of power. Both sexes are encouraged to nourish the young, and when fighting must be done, weaponry makes female physique no disadvantage, so fighting is performed by both genders.

Racial patterns are changed through the technology of artificial wombs. The world of the future is organized by village. Each village has an ethnic model: Hasidic Jewish, Chinese country village, African-American Harlem, and Wamponaug Native American are the ones named. Genetically, however, each living group is a total mixture. The computer determines the racial mix of any infant, and every form of pure and mixed blood exists, with emphasis on darker skins, and no one type has any majority anywhere. Thus, the Chinese village has people of every skin color and genetic background. "Chinese" has cultural, but not a racial, meaning. Prejudices about sexual orientation have similarly been worked on; many inhabitants are bisexual, and a variety of emotional relationships are shown, from polymorphous sexuality to chosen chastity.

Other hierarchies are destroyed. Rudimentary communication has been established with higher animals, so humans cannot cut themselves off so easily from other animals; as a result, the community is mostly vegetarian. The relations between the First World and the Third World are changed. Not only is the future community doing what it can to repair the ravages of the past on nature; it is also doing what it can to repay colonized third-world countries for the loss of raw materials taken by more advanced countries. Technology is permitted to replace humans for jobs that are boring or dangerous. Technology is also used for the artificial wombs and is thus a necessary element in creating Piercy's vision of equality. For most situations, however, human labor is considered more appropriate. In many respects, members of Mattapoisett could take a one-way ticket to Anarres or a Kesh village and would feel at home.

In her cyberpunk novel *He, She and It,* Piercy goes a step further, opening the barriers between biological humans and non- or semibiological personalities that might claim the same rights as humans and exploring what that would mean. For this to be possible, she again chooses an anarchist setting. She recasts the Jewish golem legend as a cyborg story that centers on the fusion of machine, computer, and biological components into a human-looking being with a personality. The setting is a kibbutz-like town, Tikva, that is located in the United States on the Northeast Coast, but the greenhouse effect makes that a hot location. As a free town, Tikva precariously maintains its independence from the multinationals (or "multis") because, like the Internet itself, it supplies services that all parties want. Shira, the protagonist, is involved in training a cyborg, Yod, to pass as human. In one of the multis, he would have remained only a machine to be used, but in Tikva, people instantly explore his possible personhood. Since he has been trained as a Jew, can his presence help to make up a minyan? (The need to argue through that issue sent the six rabbis off extremely happy!) Should he be paid for his work? Since he was designed for defense and has an explosive self-destruct mechanism built in that can be triggered against his will, does the community have the right to send him to his death? He has, after all, developed love relationships, free will, and ties to life that make him want to live.

Yod's and Shira's problems are the main plot. As a critique of America, the book looks more at ecological profligacy and at technological privilege as opposed to life in the slums in the Glop, from which no escape is possible. In Tikva, Piercy shows how a society might avoid that split, which is so characteristic of America today. Her ideal culture here is ecologically oriented, and sexual equality has been achieved, even though that involved changes in Jewish tradition. This village-style group limits the amount of labor that it turns over to machines, so people remain relatively close to the processes that produce everyday life. High technology exists in some still-computerized areas but not in all. To achieve such a community, the size of the population must be kept low. As with Le Guin's *Always Coming Home,* the unit is the village. In this, we find an attack on America's love of gigantism and a return to the nostalgic small town—but this time, the model of the small town is predicated on the rational basis of the correct size for an ideal anarchic government. Given the degree of decentralization that the Internet allows, one need not feel that one is hopelessly rusticated if one lives in a small community. Not everything is possible in such a small enclave that would be in large cities or corporate enclaves, but one may enjoy many of the advantages of Green Town with a reduced number of the disadvantages.[16]

The Fifth Sacred Thing (1993)

In an essay titled "A Cyborg Manifesto" Donna Haraway says of cyborg imagery that "it means both building and destroying machines, identities, categories, relationships, spaces, stories. Although both are bound in the spiral dance, I would rather be a cyborg than a goddess" (181). In *He, She and It*, Piercy seems to agree with that, but Starhawk, the author of *The Fifth Sacred Thing*, makes the opposite choice. At this point in discussing recent utopias, another relatively anarchic society that has done away with sexism, ecological insanity, dominance structures, and racism is of interest only for what is different from the others. Starhawk's novel serves as a showcase for Wiccan beliefs, and her emphasis on goddess worship clarifies the elements in all these utopian visions that make them compatible with or traceable to feminist thought. The anarchic mode of social organization as these women writers have envisioned it is also a feminist mode of behavior. In her study *In a Different Voice*, Carol Gilligan outlined what she found to be distinct modes of masculine and feminine behavior, though she emphasizes that the gendering of behavior is not absolute and that many men think in the "feminine" mode and many women in the "masculine." In simple terms, the masculine or hierarchical pattern solves problems by deciding what the rules are and who has the status to do what to whom, whereas the feminine tries to smooth over the problem and prevent damage to the social network. The masculine-minded person might steal a frightfully expensive drug to save a spouse's life because saving life is more important (i.e., higher in the moral hierarchy) than breaking the rule against theft. The feminine (or "relational") response is to get the community involved—to use radio appeals for funds, for instance.

Shinshan, Mattapoisett, Tikva, Starhawk's San Francisco, and, to a degree, Le Guin's Anarres all cultivate the feminine rather than the masculine pattern. They have done away with central authority and hierarchy and dominance of a structural sort. They want as few universal and constraining rules as possible and prefer ways of accommodating the individual's needs. All of these societies have men as well as women, unlike some thought experiments that eliminate men (e.g., Joanna Russ's "When It Changed"; James Tiptree Jr.'s [Alice B. Sheldon] "Houston, Houston, Do You Read?"). What all such utopias need to face is the problem of adapting masculine-patterned thinkers to a feminine-patterned mode of life. Le Guin's Kesh shows outlets for aggressive impulses but does not explore the problem in depth. Men lactating and nurturing children may through those activities learn some feminine patterns. Piercy also offers them involvement in aesthetic projects as a harmless outlet for competitive urges. Starhawk does even less to adapt men to the pattern; she assumes willingness to adapt, even as she shows Jews willing to invoke Asherah and the four sacred things, along with the Lord and Elijah, at a Passover Seder. All one can say is that she does offer men as well as women the spiritual benefits of being witches. Like the healer Madrona, the musician Bird is able to tap into ch'i force, to produce effects on the world around, and to heal others, though she is much more talented in healing, while his superior abilities lie in music. Starhawk possibly feels that winning gratitude and recognition through these skills is enough to compensate for a lack of other sorts of power.

Readers can respond to Starhawk's Wiccan practices (healing, trancing and communicating in dreams, using mental power to affect electronic circuits) in several ways. They can accept them enthusiastically as desirable fantasies or as truths. They can react in Christian horror to the idea of Wicca itself. Curiously, Starhawk and Pat Robertson (in *The End of the Age*) imagine a very similar dystopian society governing most of this country. However, he sees her new-age spirituality as one of the forces that contributes to the loathed New World Order, while to her, his brand of Christianity is the force behind the millennialist hypocrisy governing the dystopian society. Yet another position involves a suspension of disbelief. For the purposes of her proselytizing, Starhawk shows what she feels to be possible if we adopt a different spiritual mind-set. Readers not willing to believe can distance themselves from the claim by noting that the powers she shows operate mostly as a matter of healing and that healing does not follow totally rational rules anyway, as is well known. One can read the novel and consider its political argument for nonviolence without being a Wiccan believer.

಄ ಄ ಄

Civics classes insist that this is the land of liberty and that Americans are a free people. The anarchist writers discussed in this chapter say that much of our freedom is illusory and that we damage ourselves with our unexamined assumptions. They see in future collapses of social order a valuable potential for a much freer society; from their very different perspectives, they try to educate us to live with such new freedoms.

We might ask what the point is of living in these various forms of anarchy? Not to become a relentless consumer; not to build up wealth, whether for your own pleasures or to be handed on to children; not to found a dynasty; not even to create a visible monument, inanimate but imposing. Nor is the point simply to be entertained.

All of the novels focus on the quality of individual experience in the here and now rather than on the production of artifacts that will last indefinitely, and they expect their characters to generate some of their own experience or to collaborate to produce worthwhile entertainment and not passively be fed it. Time and money take on un-American and noncapitalist values in anarchic fiction, with time becoming the valuable commodity. If we look at tribal examples of the uncentralized life, as in James Welch's *Fools Crow* or Le Guin's *Always Coming Home*, we find that some historical perspective tells tribal members how a life is to be led, but the tie to the moment is still paramount. If one achieves the right balance between one's mind and the surrounding world, and part of maintaining that balance is the constant little adjustments to changes, then, in fact, one is living very much in the present. When one escapes the present, one is more likely to move into the sacred realm rather than simply into a realm of daydreaming, future planning, or nostalgia for an unreachable past. When we get to the future anarchies, we find this same orientation to the present—and to the sacred—in *Always Coming Home* and *The Fifth Sacred Thing*.

The Dispossessed is a bit different because we are following the life of someone seriously critical of the system. Once Shevek comes to oppose the developments on his home world, he has to think in terms of the past and future. Likewise, as he finishes his major scientific work, he has to worry about future developments and implications. Despite this linear orientation toward time, however, Shevek is not bound by the fear of death that so influences our culture's attitudes toward time and encourages us to control events, to build up wealth, and to create monuments in the hope of delaying death or winning some kind of immortality. Shevek remains very much centered on this life and on assimilating his experiences of the moment.

The anarchy-as-chaos stories concern themselves with achieving liberty, giving it to others, and using it to find one's authentic self. The anarchy-as-living-without-central-government stories are concerned with developing and maintaining a spiritual attitude. Most of these also rebel against certain culturally sanctioned patterns that are associated with the masculine. Maxine Hong Kingston's monkey king suffers from not being considered a true man; his unwillingness to define himself in terms of professional work and his refusal to devote his life to steady productivity are adjudged not just social choices but weakness in his gender makeup. Samuel Delany's Kid violates masculine stereotypes by exploring his bisexuality. The riot in *Sombrero Fallout* began, in part, from the crowd's discomfort over unmanly tears. The utopias try to form societies that rely more on the feminine than the masculine pattern. Ideally, the authors would have given us more specifics of how the dominance drive can be modified rather than just repressed, for, as Le Guin points out regarding repression of their feminine side by Urrasti males, "they . . . contained a woman, a suppressed, silenced, bestialized woman, a fury in a cage. . . . They knew no relation but possession. They were possessed" (*Dispossessed* 60). Most of the male characters we see in the utopias are happy in their productive lives and work cooperatively. Le Guin gives us a partial sketch of how it might be achieved by showing us Shevek's education at various stages, but one wishes the other writers had faced the problem adapting men to this pattern. They could do worse than study Huxley's *Island*, a utopia where all manner of exercises to redirect aggression are practiced.

If we stand back from the various sorts of anarchic fiction, we find them all urging fluidity, openness to change, and multiplicity as politically useful qualities. Rigidity is the enemy of our minds, of society, and of ultimate human survival. So is too narrow a span of values. If all we can respect is the efficiency that permits us to make more money, then we will be unable to make changes that will permit long-term survival, because survival might dictate short-term inefficiency or monetary loss. Rigidity shows itself in definitions of gender; in organizing life about private property; in the social uses of male courage; in the tendency of society to become hierarchical: these are all to be actively resisted. These authors, ideologues of anarchy, are looking to the very long-term. Perhaps the most sobering feature of their thought is the recognition that anarchy probably works best on a relatively small political scale, whether imagined as a village or city-state. That being the case, the development of such anarchies can only be tied to terrific cataclysms, which might themselves prove terminal to life on Earth.

chapter eight

Small *Is Beautiful*

The utopias discussed in the last chapter show ideal small communities in moderately favorable circumstances. These anarchist images of the good life permit their authors to attack the nature of American government and American notions of a satisfying, productive life. None of those communities, of course, exists. Several novels in the present chapter feature fictional counterparts to extant enclaves—village, tribal encampment, rural shantytown, or urban neighborhood. These enclaves suffer many kinds of stress, including acute poverty, and are far from perfect. Nonetheless, they are defiantly offered as alternatives to one form of the American Dream: middle-class life in the suburb or city. In the wake of World War II, the suburb seemed utopia enough, but inhabitants now lament the loss of community. According to the writers who are the focus of this chapter— whether of African-American, Native American, or Euro-American descent—most moderately well-off citizens no longer identify with a local community, no longer feel any duty toward the commonweal, and no longer participate in a social network that helps its own members.[1] America, they claim, has lost not only its humanity but also everything (apart from material goods) that makes life worth living. Furthermore, the middle-class life is actively to be resisted because those who enjoy it are regrettably prone to trying to destroy those who organize their lives around different values.

The visions to be discussed here represent alternatives to suburban life. African-American writers have been passionate celebrants of their communities' invisible bonds. Toni Morrison's analyses of community have won international acclaim, and her novel *Sula* illustrates several kinds of community interaction. Her novels make us wonder what we can do to recover the closeness destroyed by, among other things, the television and telephone. Several of John Wideman's novels develop an image of neighborhood that he locates in the Homewood section of Pittsburgh, and he raises the issue of how one should feel about someone who leaves such a community for personal advancement. The enemies of these communities are the surrounding, mostly white city and middle-class values. Native Americans have striven for more than two centuries to protect their tribal communities from outside encroachments. Louise Erdrich's *Tracks* and *Love Medicine* and Leslie Marmon Silko's *Ceremony* argue that the enemies of these noncapitalist tribes are lumber companies, ranchers, the U.S. government, and Christianity. In her three books concerning the denizens of Egypt, Maine, Carolyn Chute maintains that the rural poor, even when white, are just as threatened by middle-class America. These pictures of community all look to the past for patterns to be upheld. But what of the suburbs and those who live there? Kurt Vonnegut asks this question and tries to find an answer to it in *Slapstick*. For those who embrace high-tech life, new forms of electronic community are emerging, and Bruce Sterling's *Islands in the Net* portrays electronic community mingling with corporate identity to replace all community functions. Whether looking to the past or future for their inspiration, all of these writers are excoriating America's present lack of communal identification. In their critique of America, this lack is no trivial concern, for the absence of community spirit contributes to a sense of the loss of soul, the loss of innocence, the loss of ethnic identity, and the failure of democracy. As I shall argue in chapter 9, community is central to the thinking of writers who wish to get beyond a lament for inadequacies and find a place to start changing America for the better.

Because these novelists come from a variety of ethnic backgrounds, they do not value the same elements in community life, and they disagree on what is desirable. To understand these fictional social systems and how they criticize middle-class America, we should note several problems that communities must solve one way or another. How does the community view violence and death? How does it deal with difference in behavior, such as madness, or the difference represented by mixed blood? How do the inhabitants deal with a member who is handicapped or with one who is willfully unproductive? Most of this literature is Janus-faced. Partly, this sort of writing addresses itself to people like those described as local inhabitants. Partly, though, it is bought by middle-class readers who subscribe to the *New York Times Book Review* or by college students taking literature courses.[2] How are the latter readers supposed to respond to pictures of community that may have little to do with their own background and that may seem impractical in a huge, high-tech society? If these novels are not to be seen as simply nostalgia or a form of lament for lost authenticity and innocence, what do they have to say about living today?

The Strengths of Beleaguered Community: Morrison and Wideman

Sula (1973)

Toni Morrison's portrayal of black communities at times of historical stress[3] is overwhelmingly vivid, in part because she acknowledges problems as well as virtues, and partly because her main characters are not idealized. Morrison's sympathies are broad; as she makes plain in an interview with Nellie McKay, she loves all her characters, though she does not identify with them.[4] She certainly shows us *why* Milkman Dead in *Song of Solomon* starts out as such a spoiled and selfish creature: he is the man his family created. In *Beloved,* Sethe murders her own baby. Unattractive in different ways, Sula is guilty of causing the death of a playmate, and she destroys the marriage of her only friend. Morrison thus puts the community under strain with her characters and shows us how the enclave reacts to a problematic person. In the meantime, readers experience the community through troublemakers like these, feel the limits of what is permitted or frowned on, and feel support or rejection through their treatment.

Sula focuses on the Bottom, the black section of Medallion, Ohio. The Bottom in the 1920s and 1930s is a neighborhood; however, from the standpoint of the narrative voice, which is speaking in 1965, that community has disappeared. Things might seem better: "You could go downtown and see colored people working in the dime store behind the counters, even handling money with cash-register keys around their necks. And a colored man taught mathematics at the junior high school" (163). But Nel (who seems to be the focalizing viewpoint if not the actual narrator) finds the young people reminding her of the feckless, permanently immature, narcissistic "Deweys" she had known back in the 1940s. In this brave new world of the 1960s, she keeps seeing new homes for old folks being built. It is not that people live longer; they just get put away sooner. The narrator states that "it was sad, because the Bottom had been a real place. These young ones kept talking about the community, but they left the hills to the poor, the old, the stubborn—and the rich white folks. Maybe it hadn't been a community, but it had been a place. Now there weren't any places left, just separate houses with separate televisions and separate telephones and less and less dropping by" (166). In the 1920s, 1930s, and 1940s, though, back before the television and telephone, we find a very different sort of community. The concern of living, aside from getting enough food and heat, is to understand each other. "They were mightily preoccupied with earthly things—and each other, wondering even as early as 1920 what Shadrack was all about, what that little girl Sula who grew into a woman in their town was all about, and what they themselves were all about" (6). Before World War I, Shadrack had been "a young man of hardly twenty, his head full of nothing and his mouth recalling the taste of lipstick" (7); then he encountered the horrors of trench warfare in France and became unhinged. After time in a hospital, he returned home: "They knew Shadrack was crazy, but that did not mean that he didn't have any sense or, even more important, that he had no power" (15). The narrator states that "on Tuesday and Friday he sold the fish he had caught that morning, the rest of the week he was drunk, loud, obscene, funny and outrageous. But he never touched anybody, never fought, never caressed. Once the people understood the boundaries and nature of his madness, they could fit him, so to speak, into the scheme of things" (15). Like the war-damaged veterans in Silko's *Ceremony*, Shadrack is allowed to work out his own destiny within the community. His fellow citizens do not feel the need to lock him up for his obscenities, and his "National Suicide Day" demonstrations eventually become a civic parade. Difference can thus be tolerated, dealt with, and even celebrated.[5]

When a plague of robins hits town, we see the community attitude toward "evil days":

> What was taken by outsiders to be slackness, slovenliness or even generosity was in fact a full recognition of the legitimacy of forces other than good ones. . . . They did not believe Nature was ever askew—only inconvenient. Plague and drought were as "natural" as springtime. . . . The purpose of evil was to survive it and they determined . . . to survive floods, white people, tuberculosis, famine and ignorance. They knew anger well but not despair, and they didn't stone sinners for the same reason they didn't commit suicide—it was beneath them. (90)

When Sula returns to town, promiscuous and obviously changed by her ten years out in the world, the residents of the Bottom "looked at evil stony-eyed and let it run" (113). Sula's being shunned actually affects the local people in positive ways. "They began to cherish their husbands and wives, protect their children, repair their homes and in general band together against the devil in their midst" (117–18). While Sula lives, mothers keep their children from going near her; they become better mothers to spite her contempt for them. Once she dies, they find themselves cuffing their children again and no longer feeling the need to massage the egos of their men to keep them from straying in Sula's direction. Sula's putting her grandmother in a home for the elderly had prompted them to care for their own elderly in a more loving fashion, but that impulse lapses and the inevitable resentments resurface.

Most of this novel teases out the relationship between Sula and Nel, and much of the criticism on the novel addresses the ways they complement and balance each other.[6] However, what concerns me here is Morrison's portrayal of an enclave on the edge of a white city. From Morrison's description, everyone would have known everyone else within the Bottom, at least by sight. We see that the community can handle a fairly advanced form of mental illness without having to institutionalize the person, as long as he can support himself. Older people may be seen as a burden, but most of them are cared for within the community, and Sula's sending Eva away while Eva was peculiar but still made sense was one of the acts that was viewed as evincing Sula's evil. Most of the violence within the community takes place within Sula's family, and their anomalous living arrangements may point to their being an irritant within the group from the beginning. Eva kills her own son when he becomes a drug addict content to drift toward death in a drugged haze.[7] Hannah dies when her clothes catch fire while she burns trash in the yard. A girl when this occurred, Sula watched, entranced, doing nothing. Sula as a child whirls another child into the river, where he drowns. Hannah sleeps with many men; and, in a more insulting fashion, so does Sula. The community tolerates this waywardness until Sula returns and is felt to transgress basic boundaries. However, she is not driven off or killed, just shunned; her lonely death is handled by county officials and white folks, not friends and family. She knows what the consequences of her behavior will be and does not seem to mind; rather, she courts these repercussions, and thus she cannot be said to be unfairly hurt by this treatment. And while she is still alive, a neighbor or a churchwoman doing good fetches her medicine. In the background, the community is supporting its members, helping them deal with joblessness, racism, natural disasters like the plague of robins or the exceptionally cold winter.

In the 1960s, when young people have moved away, and when telephones and televisions isolate inhabitants of houses from each other, the community withers and disappears. The shade trees and fruit trees have been cut down. "They are going to raze the Time and a Half Pool Hall. . . . A steel ball will knock to dust Irene's Palace of Cosmetology, where women used to lean their heads back on sink trays and doze while Irene lathered Nu Nile into their hair. Men in khaki work clothes will pry loose the slats of Reba's Grill, where the owner cooked in her hat because she couldn't remember the ingredients without it" (3). What was once a place that people lived in and where they tried to figure each other out will soon be a golf course for rich whites. Sula enjoys a moment of postmortem consciousness in which her spirit, looking down at her body, says, "It didn't even hurt. Wait'll I tell Nel" (149). The death of the community, accompanied as it is by apparent improvements in employment and integration, does not hurt enough, Morrison insists. The people of the Bottom led hard lives, but they lived and mused on what each one of them meant. The black saleswomen in the Medallion of the 1960s merely want consumer goods. Morrison offers no direct answer to what people might do to prevent that

community from being destroyed by "success" and "progress." One senses from the fiercely cherishing tone of her story that she is not merely
indulging in nostalgia. However, televisions, telephones, and more advanced forms of technology are ubiquitous now. If readers (coming from
such a neighborhood) have any chance of retaining it, or if middle-class
readers wish any chance to construct something like such a community,
they will need to think about the pressures for dissolution that Morrison
articulates. They will also need to find ways to include community values in their individual lives: lots of face-to-face contact; a different attitude toward disasters and evil; and a greater sense of belonging to each
other. And for black readers, Morrison implies but does not state the pref-
erability of staying in a natal community if possible and contributing to
its general renovation rather than decamping to an integrated suburb.

Hiding Place (1981), *Damballah* (1981), and
Sent for You Yesterday (1983)

John Edgar Wideman's novels celebrate life in the Homewood area of Pittsburgh, but it is a Homewood of his own creation and not merely a rendition of the place he lived in until he was twelve. As Wideman says in an
interview with Jessica Lustig, "Those elements of Philadelphia that I came
to appreciate and enjoy, and the same with Laramie, I plug into Homewood.
They're in there, although they're kind of disguised. . . . It's not like there's
this well of Homewood experiences that I keep drawing from; it's stuff in
the future that I'm also locating there. It has to happen that way, or else
the work would become static, a moldy thing, nostalgic. The neighborhood,
the place, is an artistic contrivance for capturing *all* kinds of experience"
(456). The community thus exists as a kind of personal myth, a fact that
makes his purposiveness in describing the workings of a true community
all the clearer.[8] The people of Homewood

> created it through their sense of values and the way they treated one an-
> other, and the way they treated the place. That's *crucial* to the strength
> of Homewood, and it's something very basic about African American cul-
> ture. Africans couldn't bring African buildings, ecology, languages whole-
> sale, in the material sense, to the New World. But they brought the invis-
> ible dimensions of their society, of our culture, to this land. That's what
> you have to recognize: This world that's carried around in people's heads
> overlays and transcends and transforms whatever the people happen to be.
> (Lustig 454)

That invisible world is, of course, unrecognized by planning commissions
with bulldozers.

Though most of Wideman's linked stories cover events since 1900, his characters' family history stretches back to the 1840s, to slavery times and the ancestress who made the break for freedom with her master's son. In *Sent for You Yesterday*, references to urban renewal (23) make clear that various city and state authorities are the community's worst enemy. Homewood may not seem appealing to a suburbanite, but it is home to its inhabitants, and their roots run deep and wide. Everyone is related. The man selling ices to children tells them anecdotes about their parents' childhoods on the same street. Family stories—such as Lizabeth's being put in a snowdrift just after birth to shock her into breathing and living—get retold and refashioned for her descendants (*Damballah* 30). The shade of skin, the look of the eyes, the hair straight or nappy are all family traits and are accepted as links to those ancestors.

The community embraces variety. Individuality and eccentricity are accepted as a matter of course. When old Bess in *Hiding Place* says she does not like electricity and is criticized for it, she snaps, "I suppose that's my business" (81). And indeed it is. Similarly, men who have succumbed to liquor or who have taken up illegal hustles are nonetheless accepted—they are scolded by their womenfolk, yes, but their right to make their own choices is recognized. Bess formalizes this recognition of the irregular: "You give the white folks the evens. They likes things neat. Two-four-six-eight-ten. Two by fours and ten little Indins [*sic*] all in a row. They like things with corners, things you can break in half, things that got a nature you can tame" (142). Bess prefers betting on odd numbers and wins. Bess explains this to Clement, himself an irregularity, being a retarded boy without parents; he is tolerated and indeed nurtured in the community. He is sent on errands, protected from getting into trouble, and taught to be polite. As Miss Claudine explains it to him, "A little etiquette don't cost a cent. A little respect for people don't cost a thin dime and it can make a person feel like a million dollars" (17).

Bess is an eccentric recluse living on family land that may be forfeit for back taxes. No one knows exactly. To all of the Homewood family, Bruston Hill is sacred because it is where Sybela Owens, their slavery-era ancestress, settled with Charlie Owens, the master's son, when they ran away from the South and settled in a free state. All Sybela's various descendants have their own money troubles, however, so no one has paid attention to the demands for tax payments. Bess is the oldest of the clan, and the hut she lives in on Bruston Hill is hardly better than slave quarters, but it is her own, and she is content. Things balance out: her water is strongly flavored, mineralized and rusty; as she notes, though, that flavor is needed to cut the burning flavor of her cheap whiskey. Were the tax authorities to eject Bess from her cabin, they would damage the symbolic heart of the community. Wideman, however, is not chronicling the destruction of Homewood. The ending to *Hiding Place* is phantasmagoric, but evidently Bess walks down to join the community again so she can testify for Tommy.

As in much of this fiction—and hence in the Homewood community—there is a fair amount of violence. In *Hiding Place,* Tommy is on the run, his partner in a crime having shot someone. Tommy himself did not kill anyone, but the police are not likely to make fine distinctions, and Tommy is afraid they will kill him. In the matter of how violence is viewed, we see that Tommy is specifically defined as *not* a killer, and overall Wideman seems more concerned with how people deal with death rather than with defining man as a killer (as, say, Mailer or Bellow do, though their generic "man" is white). In Wideman's world, a lot of babies die. Older generations die, and we learn about John French's death in his bathroom, the funeral of Grandfather Lawson, and the long wait for death by Faun and the bedridden Freeda. Being killed by the police is a real enough terror, but it is seen as very different from violent deaths within the community: "Fighting is different. Long as two men stand up and beat on each other ain't nobody else's business. Fighting ain't gon hurt nobody. Even if it kill a nigger every now and then" (*Damballah* 39). Killing in a fair fight is not murder, evidently, and such a fighter is not seen as being naturally a killer. White men may be killers at heart—as the white authors just mentioned claim (or the cultures that some of them come from may condone more violence)—but the death most folk in Homewood face is not murder but various forms of disease, bodily breakdown, or accident.

We also find ecstasy in life possible within this community. Rocking in the church provides rapture for some, and hearing the singing of Reba Love Jackson transports others, but the most interesting instance of ecstasy is perhaps Bess's vision of an angel at Kaleesha's funeral. She "watched an angel pick apart a cobweb stuck to the roof of the chapel. . . . Only a cellophane-winged angel in a blue-eyed gown would have the patience to pick those dust threads apart one by one and wind each one up into a ball and tuck the balls into her blue-eyed gown without snapping one thread. Angels don't hurt things" (*Hiding Place* 52). That an angel should be winding up threads at a child's funeral (tidying up the loose ends, as it were) elevates this picture of community as a web. That same angel returns to Bess and sets her shanty on fire, and she thanks it as she pulls herself together to descend the hill and testify that Tommy had not killed anybody. Whether in fact she is walking away from the shanty or hallucinates this while burning to death is unclear in *Hiding Place,* since her long-dead husband accompanies her on this walk. In *Damballah,* however, we learn that she did survive the fire. Moreover, Tommy was not shot by the police but did go to jail. That angel in *Hiding Place* makes Bess very happy, because she realizes she has a mission and possesses a knowledge needed by others. Even a woman as old and cantankerous as Bess has a place in this network.

The crucial question that Wideman raises but does not answer concerns individuals leaving the beleaguered community. If the human network is so valuable, does anyone have the right to abandon it, especially for financial and social gain? In real life, Wideman's parents took him away at the age of twelve, so he had no choice.[9] In his fiction, his alter ego, John Lawson, goes to college and then moves on to a middle-class job as a professor of creative writing in Wyoming. The import of that decision is not discussed, although it—like the acquisition of telephones and televisions in *Sula*—embodies a pattern that contributes to the destruction of such a community by leeching away its ambitious and intelligent young people. Morrison is more obviously negative toward the character of Jadine in *Tar Baby*, who similarly gains an education and the trappings of a higher class and goes on to reject her background. Wideman does not specifically reject Homewood, and his alter ego does return with his family on visits. The author's refusal to address this problem is disappointing, because the issue is so crucial to a critique of suburban America's lack of community. In a sense, Wideman *has* to support his alter ego's living elsewhere, since the perspective on Homewood that permits him to write comes in part from having left the community. Analytic vision may come more readily to one who gains distance from the home community by experiencing an alternative. The paradox of celebrating community may be that one must leave it to realize its value, and in leaving, one may contribute to its demise. The fiction is a gift back to the community, but what is given and what is taken are incommensurable.

Preservation and the Reservation: Erdrich and Silko

Tracks (1988) and *Love Medicine* (1984)

Louise Erdrich portrays the woodland tribal community variously called the Anishinaabe, Ojibwe, or Chippewa. *Tracks* concerns one generation between 1912 and 1924; *Love Medicine* follows the many descendants at important crossings of paths in their lives between 1934 and 1984. The older community is much closer to traditional Native American ways of life. Some members of the group still believe in the old religion and place their dead up in trees. Some spend their winters nearly starved and then crawl back to life in the spring. Some still know how to hunt and how to call up paranormal powers such as clairvoyance and out-of-body travel to help in such hunting. A few see visions. Ghosts are real and are experienced at different levels of belief and concern.[10]

Erdrich's community is characterized by complex, sprawling families. Surprisingly few of her major characters are raised by their genetic parents.[11] Both Pauline (later Sister Leopolda) and Pauline's unacknowledged illegitimate daughter, Marie, are treated as though they were Morriseys or Lazarres, though they are not. Marie herself adopts several abandoned children, including June Morrisey and then June's out-of-wedlock son, Lipsha. The paternity of Lulu is in doubt. Eli seems the most likely, but the father could be Misshepeshu or one of the men who raped Fleur; ultimately, Nanapush's name goes on the government birth certificate as the father. Lulu's eight boys and her girl are all by different fathers, although she is legally married. Bloodlines grow in all directions, like a rhizome, and official family structures matter less than the ways in which true blood tells.[12] The Pillager line is first known for magic in general, then for the ability to escape jail and for power manifested in the hands. That power may be healing by the laying on of hands, or it may show itself in winning at cards, even though that winning is partly a matter of marking the cards and cheating. When we see Lipsha Morrisey's healing and card-dealing powers, we know them from variants seen in his father, Gerry; in his father's mother, Lulu; in his genetic grandfather, Moses Pillager; and in his genetic great-grandmother, Fleur Pillager, who was once seen in a vision playing cards in the land of the dead, trying to win the life of her prematurely born infant. Lipsha also sees his flat nose in Lulu, and both Lipsha and Gerry have curiously feminine characteristics that echo Lulu.[13] The Kashpaws have luck with making money, and Nector Kashpaw's unacknowledged son by Lulu inherits his sire's moneymaking abilities. Margaret Kashpaw and her son Nector both prove somewhat treacherous when it comes to land belonging to others. Nector's grandson, King, betrays a fellow prison inmate, and King's son, Howard, betrays his father. The various families have reputations for shiftlessness or dangerous dealings, and one first sizes up a member of such a family in terms of the family reputation. Nector assumes that Marie "Lazarre" (actually not of their blood, though Nector does not know that) is living up to her family reputation by stealing linen from the convent. Nanapush warns Lulu what marrying a no-good Morrisey will mean in terms of her life, and he is right.

  Tracks sets the tribe up against the U.S. government and the lumber companies. To force the Native Americans to give up their seminomadic tribal life and become farmers, the government transforms homeland into personal property through the Indian Allotment Act of 1904.[14] Once the government forces the distribution of tribal lands to individuals, people can be separated from the land permanently and "legally." The government simply charges an annual fee on the property thus distributed. To a people living subsistence lives in largely precapitalist ways, a money fee is an almost unbearable burden. They possess little to trade or sell and have few ways of making money. Those who fail to come up with this sum find their land confiscated and auctioned out from under them, usually to the lumber companies. No matter that their ancestors died there; no matter that this tribe's patterns presuppose one family living near each lake and that to take that lake means removing a major source of food as well as destroying a center of spiritual significance. In Fleur Pillager's lake resides the manitou Misshepeshu: "Pillager land was not ordinary land to buy and sell. When that family came here, driven from the east, Misshepeshu had appeared because of the Old Man's connection. But the water thing was not a dog to follow at our heels" (*Tracks* 175). Tribal councils can be pressured or bribed to push auctions along, thus handing the land over to lumber companies, because some members have become Christian and are eager to eradicate traces of the old religion. Men are forced to work for those lumber companies for the money needed to protect their own land from those same companies while cutting the timber on the land of friends and relatives. The more frequently that the men sign up for labor as tree-cutters or harvest workers, the less time they have to hunt or practice their hunting skills. They and their sons lose the ability to live from the land.

What Erdrich shows is a community struggling with decaying circumstances and forced to change to a less tribal and more agricultural and urban form of life. In *Love Medicine,* Albertine can study to be a nurse or doctor; Lulu can move to a retirement home. The more obvious signs of belief in the old religion have disappeared; the dead are no longer tied in tree branches, though some people still avoid mentioning the deceased by name. People attend mass and serve in the convent. As a girl, Marie can dream of becoming a saint.[15] The tribe plans to build a factory for making plastic Indian souvenirs to sell to tourists. Alcohol drags down melancholics and misfits. Many families have battered cars, televisions, and other appliances made possible by the family members working at money-producing jobs or by some member of the family having had life insurance. Young men can become as fixated on automobiles as their white counterparts. People still feel themselves to be a group apart from white society, but Indianness now is more a matter of family relationships than it is a way of life. Many members of the tribe live like the poor whites in the region. As Native Americans, they still give each other some support (as seen in their adoption of others' children), but they are just as likely to get into wrangles over land or tribal council matters. They are forced to live close to one another, which is not the Chippewa way. They can do relatively little for one another, given that so many pressures upon them are financial, and none of them has much money. They have entered capitalist society at the bottom level, without enough farming land to support them, without access to city factories, and without access to unexploited forests for hunting; as a result, they are another group of the rural poor who are not permitted to be what some would still like to be. Most are too ignorant of their past to go back to the old ways, even if that were possible.

The characters maintain a strong moral code on some issues, and violence is one such issue. Unlike the Euro-American community in Carolyn Chute's Maine, the Chippewa community does not look to murder or
violence to solve problems. In the earlier generation of *Tracks*, Nanapush
is greatly provoked but cannot bring himself to kill two men in cold blood.
In *Love Medicine*, Lipsha really wants to know whether his father, Gerry,
actually killed a state trooper or whether the white police had told lies.
We sense that he would neither reject his father were the deed real nor
rejoice if it were; however, he would not think of his father in the same
way, and he certainly does not consider the answer trivial. As far as violence goes, the women are more dangerous than the men. Pauline locked
three rapists in a freezer during a tornado and strangled the man who impregnated her. The community suspects her act of violence but has no
evidence; she is treated as mentally ill and not very welcome, but she is
not totally shunned.

Erdrich does not oversimplify the clash between the old ways of the
Chippewa and the new, and she does not suggest that her characters could
or should wish to go back. The new world has many ugly elements, and
suicide is a common reaction to those (Henry Lamartine Sr., June, and
Henry Lamartine Jr. all take their own lives), but Lulu, as the sprightly
queen of the retirement home, would hardly relish the living conditions
she experienced as a young girl. Indeed, her promiscuity might have gotten her into serious trouble in really old tribal days. In *Love Medicine*,
Erdrich returns to Native American forms of storytelling, to circular movements out from and returning to the center; in social terms, though, her
characters have fallen into Western linearity and have no hope of going
back.[16] At best, they can try to conserve parts of the past as a conscious
choice: "'My girl's an *Indian*,' Zelda emphasized. 'I raised her an Indian'"
(*Love Medicine* 23). Zelda declares this even though the child's father had
been of Swedish descent. That their "whitened" form of life in shabby trail-
ers still permits community is suggested by the content of *Love Medicine*.
June walks out into a blizzard and dies in the first episode; the other episodes all show her relationships to other members of the group, the effect
of her life on theirs, and the effects of her suicide as well. Instead of Wideman's spiderweb image, the image here is of a stone tossed into a lake; the
ripples spread over the whole surface.[17] Erdrich is showing readers that the
tribal communal experience is still real and valuable, even though changes
might mislead us into thinking it lost.

Ceremony (1977)

Leslie Marmon Silko's *Ceremony* shows a community noticeably different from others discussed so far because of Silko's stress on that commu-

nity's exclusionary practices. Morrison and Wideman insist that the black community embraces rather than excludes and that it certainly shows its tolerance regarding personality variants. Nor is mixed blood a major issue for them, although a lack of spiritual identification as an African American can be seen as "white," self-oriented behavior. Tribal people show more readiness to exclude, at least if one judges by the many novels regarding the suffering of mixed-blood characters who would like to be accepted as members of the tribe. The protagonist of *Ceremony*, Tayo, endures tribal rejection because his father was an unknown white man while his mother was a Laguna woman who had become a prostitute. Hence, although raised on the reservation, Tayo was ignored by the men in the tribe and never taught native ceremonies, wisdom, or ways. They chose to ignore him and leave him to the not very tender mercies of his Christian aunt, who abusively made him feel unwelcome and inferior to her own son, Rocky. Luckily for Tayo, his uncle, Josiah, taught him to appreciate the sights and sounds of nature and animals and exposed him to Native American values concerning life. When Tayo returns from the Pacific after World War II, he desperately needs those memories of positive experiences to help him cling to sanity.

In this community, as in the others previously discussed, we see how dysfunctional members are handled. Tayo's fellow veterans have all failed to fit back into reservation life since coming home after the war. The tribe does care for them but not in coercive or forcible ways. They are still free to act as they see fit, even if that is to drink or even to do evil. Evidently, one must not be restrained for one's own good but must control oneself or deal with the consequences—which can include shunning or banishment, as happens to Emo. Even more than in black communities, there is a taboo on violence here. Tayo's not having killed anyone in the war as far as he knows is very important to his self-respect. His nearly lethal attack with a broken bottle on his tormenter in the bar counts heavily against him locally. His climactic temptation is to save a former friend by killing the men who are torturing the friend, but driving a screwdriver into Emo's skull would only forward the powers of witchery by giving way to violence and confirm Tayo's own alienation from the culture. The veterans who do not succeed in returning to tribal values are those who took pleasure in killing Japanese; Emo carries a bag of teeth he has knocked out of the mouths of men he fought.

Despite the initial rejection of Tayo by the tribal traditionalists, community in this novel is defined more by shared knowledge than by blood. Tayo lacks knowledge of traditional myths, wisdom, and rites. Old Ku'oosh tries to help, but he speaks in "the old dialect full of sentences that were involuted with explanations of their own origins" (34), and vocabulary remains a problem. Old Ku'oosh calls the world "fragile": "The word he chose to express 'fragile' was filled with the intricacies of a continuing process, and with a strength inherent in spider webs woven across paths through sand hills where early in the morning the sun becomes entangled in each filament of web. It took a long time to explain the fragility and intricacy because no word exists alone, and the reasons for choosing each word had to be explained with a story about why it must be said this certain way" (35). Ku'oosh helps Tayo, though not enough. The solution for Tayo is found by a medicine man from a neighboring tribe, the Navaho Betonie, who has extensive experience in the white world as well as a creative relationship with native traditions. He can see the sort of project that Tayo needs to tackle while coming to terms with his experiences.

Much has been made of Tayo's reclaiming a feminine side to his nature through his dealings with Night Swan, Ts'eh, and mythically with Thought Woman/Spider Woman, the creator of all, whose web symbolizes the interconnectedness of everything.[18] Much has also been made of the meaning-giving properties of the landscape and of the way in which the myths of place unify the tribal community.[19] Also important are the discussions of healing and its imagery in this novel and of the cycles and hoops and returns to the center.[20] In different fashions, these concerns all point to the way in which the community creates insiders and outsiders through shared knowledge and belief. For Tayo to win acceptance, he has to reject the white world and its beliefs.[21]

Tayo is much like the protagonists of N. Scott Momaday's *House Made of Dawn* and James Welch's *Winter in the Blood* in going back to a modified tribal life.[22] Although Silko does not engage here in the radical politics that appear in her later *Almanac of the Dead,* her talk of adapting tribal ways to the current world seems mostly dictated by the necessity of dealing with invidious manipulations and invasions by whites and not by a desire to find a compromise cultural position. Silko grew up on a reservation and finds the life thoroughly livable. The community she describes works better the less it is diluted by white values and concerns. One cannot live in balance with the land and seek to maximize financial profit.

Poor, Rural Whites: Chute

The Beans of Egypt, Maine (1985), *Letourneau's Used Auto Parts* (1988), and *Merry Men* (1994)

In these three novels, Carolyn Chute offers us populist fiction. She writes very much from within the community she describes. She has sorted potatoes, worked in a chicken factory and shoe factory, and scrubbed hospital floors. Her husband is illiterate. She ran out of funds before she could get very far in college. Before *The Beans of Egypt, Maine* came out, she says in an interview with Ellen Lesser, she was poorer than the characters described (169–70). Nonetheless, she has managed to acquire enough perspective to see the community from the outside as well as from the inside. Her populism, or that of her characters, involves distrust of big government or big business and resists creeping liberalism in all forms. She is angry at reviewers who make an equation between poor and bad and talks in the Lesser interview of how poverty can make people cease to worry about good or bad behavior. She does not, however, want to turn her stories into sociological studies. Instead, she sticks close to the perspective of her characters; we as readers have to make our own assessments and judgments. We are positioned to join Chute in her view of big business through her use of vivid details and her lyrical vocabulary that harshly cherishes this world.

Life is wearing and ugly in *The Beans of Egypt, Maine* and *Letourneau's Used Auto Parts.* Work is exhausting, rough, and dirty, whether it involves potato harvesting, timber felling, factory work, or stripping hulks for auto parts. Those who do it come back covered with bar oil or auto grease or pine pitch or factory lint. Deerflies, blackflies, mosquitoes, and ticks infest these workers, sometimes all over their bodies. Injuries not given medical attention fester, producing their own stink and lasting physical problems. Stomach ailments produce excrement-soiled clothes. Pregnancies result in endless morning sickness, and a covered bucket is always available for more vomit since someone—whether wife, mistress, hanger-on, or charity case—is always pregnant. Dogs and cats live with the families, and the stench of dog coats is often remarked on.

Screaming is a way of life. Children scream at each other and their mothers; their mothers scream at them and at their fathers, if they have a resident father. People scream at their dogs, neighbors, landlords, or county officials. When quiet folk take over neighboring land and build a real house with windows, this is bad news for the tar-paper shacks. Quiet folk complain, report to authorities, and disdain the noisy.

Violence is endemic. Everyone has guns and uses them. Some take out their impulses on game. Crowe Bovey slaughters thousands of crows and small animals, though not to eat them; he just hates them. Reuben Bean is approached by a reasonably sympathetic game warden who says, "It ain't what's hangin' in your shed, Rubie. That isn't why I'm here. It's what's strewed all over the power line, drawin' flies. . . . I can understand bein' a glutton for meat, Rubie, but what you left on the power line isn't meat . . . it's a friggin' holocaust. Haven't you got a sprig o' conscience?" (*Beans* 117). The warden tries to take Bean quietly, without handcuffs; for his pains, he is battered nearly to death and left lying by the road. The housing-code officer in *Letourneau's Used Auto Parts* is closer than he realizes to a similar fate. Violence is also familial. A blow to the head is the usual cure for female behavior that does not fit male value patterns. Some women try to resist: "I'll call the deputy if you touch me. . . . This is not the old days. . . . Go maul your new sweetie pie" (*Beans* 83). By and large, however, these women accept the patterns and pass them on by hitting their own children.

The enemies to this society are game wardens, housing-code officers, landlords, welfare officers, teachers, and employers. Work is mostly resented for its unreliability and unpleasantness; all three books show the effects of being laid off on families already living well below the poverty line. Earlene and Beal's baby does not have milk for five days when Beal cannot work because of an injury. When she begs him to let her apply for food stamps, he threatens to beat her. Much of his work has been illegal—outside the regulations of minimum wage, insurance, social security, and the like—and he fears that the government would prevent such employment if nosy welfare officers started asking questions (*Beans* 195). Teachers seem like bullies forcing monstrous irrelevancies on the children. What they learn in school has no connection to their home lives. As Lloyd Barrington of *Merry Men* puts it in one of his boyish poems: "School is weerd. You sit for hours. But it is the law that you do it" (47). Naturally, most of the children wish to leave as soon as they can. Furthermore, teachers make demands on the parents that those parents cannot meet; Earlene frets at a note from school that her daughter has gum disease. Dental work is out of the question since the family does not even have enough money to put food on the table.

What makes the community function as a community is poverty, blood connections, and, for some, religion. The Letourneaus are French and Catholic; Earlene Pomerleau and E. Blackstone Babbidge are Baptist fundamentalists.[23] Babbidge came by his religion after serving in Vietnam. He is an interesting testament to the cohesive powers of the community, despite the community's not being as attractively nurturing as Morrison's or Wideman's, because he did experience another life. Babbidge mixed with hippies, used drugs, and must have known about the pill. However, he has returned, accepted Christ as his personal savior, and has ten children by his first wife and more by his second spouse and by her daughter. He was exposed to other possibilities but returned to a hard, underpaid life as an auto-salvage crewman.

Continuity is also furnished by blood, as is also the case in Wideman's and Erdrich's communities. Chute stresses this by making her families very distinct physically. Beans are fox-eyed, always broad-shouldered, and the Bean men let their beards grow and never cut them. Letourneaus have penny-colored eyes and thick lower lips and suck in their left cheeks when in doubt; Babbidges have icy blue eyes and black hair. The progenitors always breed true, and their unofficial offspring proclaim their paternity as loudly as their official children. Chute describes loose, extended families. In *Merry Men*, Lloyd tells a yuppie stranger, "My father's sister, my aunt

Hoover . . . real name of Marjorie, married this little gal's father's mother's brother . . . so we're related that way, too" (647; ellipses in original). Big Lucien Letourneau has been married—with various degrees of legality—to several women and has children by at least four women, not all of whom enjoy even semiofficial status. Contraceptives in the form of condoms are known but little used. Women simply assume that having children is their life; unless they are religious, they do not seem to feel that having a husband makes that much difference. All the marriages shown start with pregnancies, and romantic love plays no part in this life. People adapt phrases and ideas from television, but romantic love is not one of them.

Chute's attitude toward this community is complex. She understands the many aspects of her characters' lives that revolt middle-class readers. She sees the effect of grinding poverty, the degree to which much unattractive filth cannot be readily avoided. At the same time, she offers no pity. Her characters feel no self-pity and are proud of themselves, feeling at no disadvantage with regard to the rest of the world. Their bumper stickers read GOD BLESS AMERICA, GOD BLESS PRESIDENT REAGAN, and MORE NUKES, LESS KOOKS (*Letourneau* 242). Public radio is "commie radio" (*Letourneau* 100), and someone who comes with West Virginia mine-union experience to talk about organizing is met with extreme distrust, for fear that such talk is "commie" talk (*Merry Men* 616). Their attitudes are those of many rural populist groups: they are proud of being American and see themselves as the best kind of American: they are anticommunist without having any notion of what communism is; and they do not want interference from outside, from city slickers, from the government. Their way may be poverty-stricken by middle-class standards, but it is theirs, and they feel no great ambition to change it. Even television does not give them unassuageable longings for luxuries or refinement. They would like steady work and can imagine better shacks or clothes, but they are not yet caught up in consumerist patterns of thought. They recognize hardships but do not expect to remedy dissatisfactions; thus, they do not spend time longing for acquisitions. By the time he was eight years old, "Lloyd would never whine, 'Gimme this' or 'I want that, pleeeeeeeeeeeeeeze!' Lloyd knows sodas are out there in the world. Deep in the gurgling cold water of the coolers. Some red. Some pale green. Some orange. They are there in the world to admire. Like sunsets" (*Merry Men* 52).

What bear hardest on Chute's characters, particularly those of *Letourneau's Used Auto Parts*, are the rules and regulations spawned in cities. Many of those originated in liberal desires to prevent people from living in squalor and to force landlords to improve premises; by the time the rules are applied, though, they function as a weapon for battering the poor. Big Lucien Letourneau lets people squat for free on his land in a shantytown called Miracle City. Nowhere else is that possible. Their shacks are illegal, built from scrap and unable to meet any code, but they offer shelter of sorts. If the shack does not meet standards, the county can force the inhabitants to move out—but where can they go to? Chute dedicates this book to "all the Bleeding Hearts and Hearts of Gold. Any bird, bug, or animal including the human animal can be self-serving, cool, and steely-hearted. It is only the superhuman who can rise to Compassion." When chased out of their minimal domicile by coldhearted regulators, Severin, his wife, and their two children sleep in his truck all night with the motor running to keep themselves from freezing. They have no money whatever. The selectmen of Egypt, Maine, want codes passed that would permit them to wipe Big Lucien's eyesore camp out. He takes in waifs and strays and tries to give them someplace to stay and some work, providing practical help that the county refuses to undertake. What happens to those driven out is of no interest to the selectmen. For those evicted, like Severin, the result may be freezing or starvation; clearly, the selectmen face those outcomes with indifference. Severin asks one of the older members of the community what he can do: "'In the old days, somebody tried to take your home, you'd put one of these inside their head.' He holds one of the shells toward the light. 'But nowadays . . .' He sighs, his clear green eye fixed to Severin. 'Nowadays when they come to make you go, you take a shell like this one here . . .' He rolls it between his fingers. '. . . and you put it in your own head'" (228). Three such suicides are mentioned in passing in this book. In the old days—partly frontier, partly mythical—one could defend oneself. One could literally fight for survival and kill to achieve it. Now, all the advantages are on the side of the government, and individuals cannot defend themselves, nor can the community defend itself by refusing to acknowledge federal or county rules or by physically assaulting code officers. Even welfare can damage people if it gets them punished for the only kinds of work they can find, which happen to be technically illegal.

What Chute's characters want is the freedom to live their own way and work. Education does not help them in their hardships. One of the proselytes for union organization in *Merry Men* points out that the people of Maine suffer from "impractical schooling" (622) as well as from capitalism and consumerism. She specifies that "there's been no interest thus far on the part of educators to teach our kids *self*-discipline, interdependence, and a sense of responsibility to others . . . certainly not any working together. Only competition" (624). Nor do they have what is crucially necessary for rural independence: land to farm. Furthermore, some of the functioning members of the Egypt community are of low intelligence; others, less functional, are half-wits. Some of the sprawling Bean clan are dyslexic. This limits their options. Most of the men understand the innards of cars and chain saws, and those in *Merry Men* know their big trucks, but their technological expertise stretches no further, and their abilities to deal with book learning or bookkeeping are not well developed. They are a rural under-class trying to survive in old ways—but without the necessary land. They are squeezed by a society that does not want them and wishes they would disappear.

One of the major events in *Merry Men* is the birth of a dead baby (per-haps echoing *The Grapes of Wrath*). The child is three weeks overdue, and then the mother suffers from nonprogressive labor for two further weeks, but the hospital will not take her in because the labor is not progressive. This grotesque labor parallels the labor of these lives and the unfairness of the powers that control those lives. The doctors know the child will be dead but do not warn the parents. They evidently do not want to do a ce-sarean section because the woman has no health insurance. The baby's father, Carroll, is deaf and depressive. His life was enormously improved by an antidepressant drug, but it costs half his wife's weekly wages per bottle, and they have been unable to afford it for months. A hospital secu-rity policeman forcefully wrests the dead child from its father's arms, say-ing words that Carroll cannot hear. In his frustrated desire to hold and love his child, Carroll responds to the policeman's violence by throttling him and ends up in jail, where he is kept from living but prevented from kill-ing himself.

As Lloyd Barrington—one of the few to get a college education—muses on the future, he pictures "camps" for all the people who cannot keep up payments and cannot keep up with high technology, those who are driv-en to petty crime by the larger crimes against them committed legally by corporations. Like Ishmael Reed (*The Terrible Twos* and *The Terrible Threes*) and Thomas Pynchon (*Vineland*), Chute sees such detention camps as part of our future, when the world is run by such multinationals as "MATRIX BANKCORP ENERGY INTERNATIONAL" (686).

Chute does not make glowing claims for community solidarity and nurturing human networks, but readers do see the occasional helping hand when someone is tossed out for failure to pay rent. We see children taken on by relatives and friends because of parents ill or in jail. As the labor organizer points out, however, these people have not learned to cooperate much beyond the extended family circle, and their cultural background inclines them to value rugged independence over community spirit. They tend to cherish the gratification of personal desires over community needs. When a group of women protest the dangers to themselves and their chil-dren posed by hunters, the hunters would very much like to shoot the women and certainly do nothing to curb their illegal hunting near dwell-ings and roads. Despite the lack of mutuality, Chute maintains the desir-ability of a life so different from suburban values. Throughout history and prehistory, humans were farmers and hunters. All of a sudden, those with a natural affinity for that life find themselves targeted for annihilation by society. Her middle-class white readers may disdain the rural lifestyle and cringe at its nastiness. African-American, Native American, and Chicano readers might see her characters as rural rednecks whose attitudes are those that have done so much damage to race relationships in this country, for these rural men are temperamentally as eager as any frontiersman to settle disputes with guns or physical violence. Chute upholds the validity of difference, however, and its right to exist and its right not to be killed off through liberal "pity."

ⓞ ⓞ ⓞ

In setting up the lives of poor, local groups as alternatives to suburban values, the African-American and Native American writers are also setting their ethnic groups up against what they perceive to be white patterns. Not surprisingly, they stress the virtues of their own group and the vices of whites. Violence is an issue that brings out basic assumptions regarding difference in these portraits of community. In *Song of Solomon*, Morrison's characters talk of whites' unnatural liking for violence that they themselves could never share, but she says nothing about the violence common to black as well as Latino and white city gangs. Nor does she mention the violence, including torture and tactical rape, that has been commonplace in the civil wars in Africa—Nigeria, Rwanda, and the Sudan, for instance. Morrison's characters simply assert the humane nature of African-descended people in their own community. Native American writers similarly stress white violence and American Indian restraint as if these were genetic differences. Silko admits that Aztecs were "destroyers" (as are whites) in *Almanac of the Dead* but pays no attention to the fact that some woodland tribes went in for elaborate, extended torture or that some tribes were fiercely warlike, even if others were peaceable. If these writers are underestimating their people's capacity for violence, however, they do not seem to exaggerate their picture of inclination on the part of some whites to use brute force. Chute, who is not concerned with nonwhite groups, and who is not ideologically constrained to distinguish her characters from white culture, in fact supports Native American and African-American claims by showing the violence of her Maine denizens. Disagreements usually involve severely beating the transgressor. Moreover, Chute admits that underneath the violence, for some part of the population, lies an enjoyment of cruelty.

One might contrast three episodes involving large mountain cats. Toni Morrison's lynx-hunters in *Song of Solomon* are businesslike but respectful of their prey, and Silko's Tayo is astonished and worshipful when he sees a mountain lion's tracks, saying a prayer in its honor; he traces with his finger "the delicate edges of dust the paw prints had made, deep round imprints, each toe a distinctive swirl" (*Ceremony* 196) and sprinkles pollen on them. In *Merry Men,* Chute represents a conversation heard at the corner lunch counter:

> Tim Gowen shows how you show a lynx who's boss. Tim Gowan describes the paw that's crushed in the trap . . . and now the three paws that are "pulped." Tim Gowan tells how he said to his boy, "You want to ride him? I'll let you ride him before I put him down." No, the boy had said. He's still got teeth. "Well, let's smash out his mouth for you," Tim had said. "Not every day you get to ride a wildcat." So Tim Gowen tells how he got a bigger limb and smashed that lynx's mouth in and all that critter could do now was bang his head on you. But still the boy didn't want to ride the cat. So Tim Gowen had said to his boy, "What is it you scared of now?" That cat *lookin'* at you? You don't like the way he's watchin' you with those scary eyes?" So Tim laughs at this and then explains how he took care of the eyes. (271; ellipses in original)

Artificial Extended Families: Vonnegut

Slapstick; or, Lonesome No More! (1976)

So far in this chapter, the suburbs have fared badly in analyses of community. Kurt Vonnegut, a writer whose characters are frequently suburban, asks where they can go to find what they are lacking.[24] His family background as a German-American made him aware of how his people had lost their sense of community, and graduate work in anthropology made him aware that black American culture was considered more successful in maintaining community spirit than were contemporary Euro-American communities. In *Breakfast of Champions* and *Slapstick,* he investigates the problem anthropologically.

Anthropology taught him about kinship groups and about how people without writing depended on memory for their information. In *Breakfast of Champions,* he links memory and kinship twice, using the number 600 to make us see the connection between the two systems. Cyprian Ukwende is an Indaro from Nigeria living in Midwest City, and we are told that he knows 600 living relatives by name. His African-American ambulance driver, Eddie Key, has been the member of his family to memorize family history, and he knew names and anecdotes concerning 600 ancestors: "Eddie Key, because he knew so much by heart, was able to have deep, nourishing feelings about Dwayne Hoover, for instance, and about Dr. Cyprian Ukwende, too. Dwayne was a man whose family had taken over Bluebird Farm [which once belonged to Eddie's family]. Ukwende, an Indaro, was a man whose ancestors had kidnapped an ancestor of Key's on the West Coast of Africa, a man named Ojumwa" (271). With so complex a set of personal pigeonholes, Eddie can relate many things and the people he sees to himself and his family.

Slapstick came out three years after *Breakfast of Champions*, and Vonnegut was still chewing on this notion that extended family could be a solution to our rootless and emotionally numb existence. He talks about his own family prior to the First World War, German-Americans who could speak German and who admired German music, literature, and science. The extended family lived within a few blocks of each other, so children could always find refuge if things became tense at home, and those in need of sympathy could find a shoulder to cry on. Because of the hostility to Germany generated by the world wars, members of the family ceased speaking German or identifying with German culture. When Vonnegut and his siblings left what had once been a German enclave in Indianapolis, none of their relatives "could think of a reason why we should come home again. We didn't belong anywhere in particular any more. We were interchangeable parts in the American machine" (*Slapstick* 7).

In *Slapstick*, Vonnegut sets out to create a sense of community that will work in the suburbs as well as in city neighborhoods or small towns. Furthermore, he wants to make it work nationwide, not just locally. Wilbur Swain, his protagonist, uses his power as president of the United States to create artificial families. The country is disintegrating through a lack of fuel plus two plagues; however, despite shortages, Wilbur has a computer distribute names to everyone on a random basis. The name consists of an animal, plant, or mineral and a number. Wilbur Swain's middle name becomes Daffodil-11. He is a brother to every other Daffodil-11 and a cousin to Daffodils of other numbers. Family newspapers spring up, and so do family insurance schemes. One does not need to love all one's relatives—far from it—but they are there. Individuals can call on them when they travel and maybe even stay with them. Wilbur points out that under his new scheme, if a beggar approaches you, you can ask his name; and if the beggar says Hollyhock-13, you can tell him that you are a Uranium-3 and that he has 190,000 cousins and 10,000 brothers and sisters and that he should turn to one of them for help. Opposition mostly comes from people like Wilbur's wife, who was a Rothschild and who wanted nothing to do with other people named Peanut-3. As the country disintegrates and Michigan, for instance, becomes a kingdom, local low-tech wars happen, but Wilbur notices a difference. Having witnessed one such conflict, he reports, "And thank God that there's no such thing as a battle between strangers any more. I don't care who fights who—everybody will have relatives on the other side. . . . I saw several people killed. I also saw many people embracing, and there seemed to be a great deal of deserting and surrendering going on. This much news I can bring you from the Battle of

Lake Maxinkuckee. . . . It is no massacre" (220–21). Massacres are a sore subject to a survivor of Dresden, and rendering them impossible is something Vonnegut devoutly desires. Community and therefore a sense of the enemy's humanity are fostered by his system.

Vonnegut ends this novel with the traditional *Märchen* signal, labeling this a fairy tale; and in many respects, this is a satiric solution aimed to point out what contemporary America lacks. Vonnegut, though, seems very serious on the desirability of finding something that would function as extended families once did, even if it is achieved in an artificial manner. Morrison and Wideman would presumably find this system lacking in the blood ties that produce visible family traits and equally lacking in the need to show humanity to everyone in the neighborhood. Silko would find such a community devoid of the kinds of knowledge and beliefs that produce meaningful coherence for her characters and would reject it as extraneous to the reservation. Chute would probably find the scheme without any true means of bridging the class gap between her characters and suburbanites with the same artificial names. These are legitimate objections, but Vonnegut's solution has the advantage that it could be made available to everyone and is not invalidated by telephones, television, or drastic economic collapse. A simulacrum of extended family may for many be better than none at all. As a thought experiment, at least, it is interesting, if only semiserious.

Electronic Community: Sterling

Islands in the Net (1988)

Bruce Sterling's novel *Islands in the Net* beautifully exemplifies the late imperial romance pattern, albeit in a futuristic guise.[25] The powers represented by the computer network correspond to the imperium of Kipling or Conrad. With the globe largely united through the Net, and with information rather than raw materials and cheap labor being what the multinationals seek, there are few territorial equivalents to India or Africa to be claimed by imperial powers. A late imperial romancer must therefore find ways to re-enchant pockets of the world within the empire, places where danger, exotic mystery, and intense experience are possible. Sterling does this through his "islands" in the Net, small communities that do not belong to the one Net but instead steal data from it and try to live by different standards. Another major aim he pursues, however, is to conceptualize community in a high-tech world. At first glance, the realm of electronic communication is as far as one can get from the neighborhood enclave so valued by other novelists in this chapter. Videophones, e-mail, and fax machines are not the same as dropping by of an evening to sit on the porch and chat. Sterling shows what kinds of relationships can be developed through these media, however, and looks to one's job for the definition of community. He takes his model from Japanese corporations and modifies it to improve democratic input. In doing this, he is creating a community quite different from the youth- and self-oriented black-market world found in William Gibson's *Neuromancer* or in the rigidly hierarchical multinationals in Marge Piercy's *He, She and It*. Both of these novels also look to Japan but use what they take dystopically. Sterling's multinational, Rizome, practices consensus decision making. Negotiation is the modus operandi in all things. Members of Rizome self-consciously nurture democracy. After someone has served as chief executive officer for a term, he or she spends time doing unskilled tasks in a hospital to cultivate new perspectives and to interrupt habits of self-importance. Members of this economic democracy all try to cultivate the right attitude and praise each other when they see such an outlook maintained under pressure.

After the murder of an envoy who was under Rizome's protection, we see the company's rituals for handling the resultant trouble:

> You could tell the importance of this meeting by the elaborate informality of their dress. Normal problems they would have run through in Atlanta, standard boardroom stuff, but this Grenada situation was a genuine crisis. Therefore, the whole Committee were wearing their Backslapping Hick look, a kind of Honest Abe the Rail-Splitter image. Frayed denim jeans, flannel work shirts rolled up to the elbow. . . . Garcia-Meza, a hefty Mexican industrialist who looked like he could bite tenpenny nails in half, was carrying a big straw picnic basket. (68; ellipses in original)

> They joined hands and sang a Rizome anthem. Then they ate.
> It was fascinating to watch. The Committee really worked at it, at that sense of community. They'd made a practice of living together for weeks on end. Doing each other's laundry, tending each other's kids. (69)

Sometimes this cultivated group mentality is called *Gemeineschaft* (*sic*) after German antecedents, and the protagonist, Laura, notes an equivalent cultivation of group spirit based on military or revolutionary models in some of the "islands" antagonistic to the Net, but Rizome's basic source of inspiration is Japanese.

Laura sees the corporate world as supportive because it can allow her to work and make professional progress while raising a small child. Laura and David had taken on the building and running of a retreat hotel for Rizome, which was their project for the years of their child's infancy. Laura can run the hotel and feed a baby, something not always easy to do with an office job. Rizome makes such job reassignments possible, and Laura glories in the fact that she is not dropping out. Her mother reminds her that power is where the action is, but Laura rejoins, "Mother, the action's everywhere now. That's why we have the Net" (28). The electronic connections keep her a part of her community.

Sterling's world allows for a future generation in a way that the black-market worlds of William Gibson or Thomas Pynchon do not. While Sterling is aware that the Net has little to offer the illiterate, the not very bright, the dyslexic, and the very poor, he has produced a model for community that would work without demanding a return to village life. Attempts to conserve an extant pattern in a city enclave or a pueblo are vulnerable to technology, prosperity, and middle-class education. Most utopian attempts to reestablish community demand regression to modified village conditions. That some technology may be preserved helps prevent the worst problems of village life, but that vision of a future certainly assumes a drastic drop in population and a hitherto unmanaged combination of low-tech and high-tech life. Sterling does not try for such a seemingly contradictory combination. He looks to the high-tech future and defines community in corporate terms and in terms of communications only somewhat better than those today. Fewer changes would be necessary for his world to come into being than is true of the utopian communities in Marge Piercy's *Woman on the Edge of Time* and Ursula Le Guin's *Always Coming Home*, and far fewer changes would be demanded than by modeling life on Silko's pueblo existence.

This vision of community seems to me much more important than the story. Our present middle-class world is one in which people define themselves in terms of their work, so Sterling looks to the workplace as the site where our sense of community logically should operate. Physical, face-to-face dealings, deliberately introduced into Rizome's activities, are augmented by constant electronic communication, in which video screen permits you electronic face-to-face communication as well. Piercy's critique of quasi-Japanese structures is compelling, and so is Chute's disbelief in any corporation's working for good ends, but their corporations are rigidly stratified in terms of top and middle management and workers; Sterling anticipates such problems by prominently featuring the consensus-making ethos and a kind of membership that prevents class stratification.

୭ ୭ ୭

Once upon a time in Western civilization, the New Jerusalem, the City of God, the Greek city-state, or the center of empire in Rome were the idealized images of community. At later times, Paris, London, and Moscow were the centers of their respective countries with a degree of intensity that no American city has enjoyed (except, perhaps, New York City). Late twentieth-century experience with decayed inner cities has reduced America's already weak affinity for that archetypal image.[26] The small town or village or even just the small, well-defined neighborhood in a city seem more attractive to most writers. Where everyone knows everyone else through the third generation, unexpected dangers are rare. Of course, this mythical village is just that. People have willingly been leaving real villages for cities for centuries; small-town attractions when one has no alternatives are being overrated by several of these authors. Indeed, such attractions are mostly felt by inhabitants who have been elsewhere: Tayo has suffered in the Pacific theater of war; Nel looks back on the Bottom from the perspective of one who has outlived the community she remembers; John Lawson, in the Homewood novels, comes back for visits, having become a professor of creative writing in Wyoming. Chute does not pretty up the picture of rural Maine, but she is unusual in not trying to make her readers feel personally attracted to her realm. She seems more to uphold her characters' right to exist and not be reduced to welfare subsistence by an unfeeling government bureaucracy. She also makes admirable if not likable the toughness necessary to survive.

From any pastoral, one can deduce the flaws of the city whose poet hymned the shepherds. Similarly, these hymns to small communities point to what is perceived as a major flaw in American society. Families have been reduced to a temporary cohabitance of parents and children. As family awareness shrinks to the immediate, so does the sense of the shared humanity of others. Without a firm conviction of humanity, we do dreadful things to other people. Personal interaction becomes attenuated by the telephone, and time spent in each other's company loses its cohesive power if the television dominates such meetings. Return to a lower-technology agricultural past is no answer unless we can contemplate with equanimity the annihilation of much of the world's population; and such a return would merely bring us up against the problems of primitive life ignored by these writers. Japanese consensus procedures may look more mature and calmly rational than the black-market world of William Gibson; however, even their believer, Laura, admits that they smother creativity. That postmodern black-market Zone, established by Pynchon and battened on by many cyberwriters, is a world of ebullient electronic and biological novelty, but it is ultimately unsupportive and unnurturing. None of these writers offers a clearly satisfying solution to middle-class America's loss of community. None of these novelists has written a fictional exposition of communitarian theory, and theorists like Amitai Etzione have made no headway in the broader political world. By showing functioning enclaves from past and present, however, these writers sharpen readers' sense of what is missing in many contemporary lives and invite consideration of how to gain or retain such ties to other people. As seen by these and similar writers, our lack of community is not just an important flaw in American life, it is one problem that might admit of solutions.

chapter nine

The Failure *of the Dream in Fiction*

Between approximately 1960 and 1990, we find an odd disagreement in American cultural attitudes. Novelists, as we have seen, frequently respond with anger or disillusion to the gap between the America they experience or see and the ideal America enshrined in founding documents and the American Dream. Outside of fiction, the attitude is much more mixed, and we find grateful and enthusiastic testimonials as well as the same disenchanted anguish. This dichotomy between a large body of literature and the rest of the culture is worth considering for a moment before going on to look at the effects that disillusionment with the American Dream has had on literary form.

Among the enthusiasts, one certainly finds some immigrants. Legal and illegal, they still stream into the country. Those with good English language skills and educations can often get jobs that pay them many times what they might have made in their native countries, and their attitudes are understandably enthusiastic. Those with little English doing less-skilled labor may not reach prosperity within their own lifetimes, although some Mexican crop pickers are able to build expensive homes back in Mexico. Many Cubans have flourished, and Vietnamese names are common in the winners' list each year for the Annual Westinghouse Science Talent Search for high school students, which suggests that the second and third generations are excelling through education. Another group of enthusiasts consists of people with some start-up capital who prove skillful at making money in the stock market. Even if they do not specialize in junk bonds, currency speculation, and other high-risk activities, they can hope to make millions, and those who have done so laud America happily when they serve as consultants on television financial shows. Those who finish a long period of training and get a good job despite a poor job market are likely to feel that the country has done well by them. Many people, particularly of the pre–Vietnam War generation, are patriotic even if they are not flourishing economically. The life that is possible here looks wonderful to many peoples inside the country and out of it. Why then does this generation of fiction writers view the subject so sourly, especially since many of those discussed in this study are successful enough to be prosperous?

Novelists are not uniquely gloomy. Numerous journalists and social thinkers trumpet their conviction that the United States has fallen very short of turning assorted versions of the American Dream into reality. Each month, the *New York Times Book Review* pulls more such negative rabbits out of the popular sociology or political science hats. Consider some titles: *America: What Went Wrong?* (Donald L. Barlett and James B. Steele); *Declining Fortunes: The Withering of the American Dream* (Katherine S. Newman); *Who Will Tell the People: The Betrayal of American Democracy* (William Greider); *Breaking the News: How the Media Undermine American Democracy* (James Fallows).[1] Republicans and Democrats both make campaign boasts that they will restore the American Dream, but that very phrasing implies the Dream's moribund state.[2] Moreover, this promise applies only to the personal finances of voters and implies nothing about curbing the media and industry forces that are said to turn democracy into an empty simulacrum of itself. Many Americans in the 1970s and 1980s fear they will not achieve their parents' prosperity. Those who have suffered from constricted job possibilities and straitened finances mostly feel betrayed; their long years of hard work seem to them to have been for nothing. That, in brief, is the uneven and contradictory state of cultural attitudes toward the American Dream. That novelists so consistently entertain the disenchanted vision suggests that they deliberately function as society's conscience or that they involuntarily respond (like canaries in mines) to some poison in the atmosphere—or, possibly, they do both.

Now that so many novels have been identified as sharing an element of attitude, what kinds of conclusions can be drawn about them? What are their shared perceptions of America? What hopes do they offer for improvements in the future? What effects does the negative vision have on literary structures? Why would readers bother to wade through dismal visions? Why is it that so many writers who are themselves comfortably off can only think in terms of anguish? And, finally, what does this study suggest about reading books from this roughly thirty-year period after 1960?

The Absence at the Heart of Recent American Fiction

Given the great diversity found among these dreamscapes, the point of summing up anything beyond what has already been said is to clarify our sense of what the fiction agrees on. The most obvious shared element is a glaring absence. In most of these books, we find *no sense of a desirable future.* Let us look at the books in terms of how they chart the everyday concerns of their characters. How do characters fill their time and gauge success? What makes life worthwhile?

Where Are the Children?

Where in these novels is the birth of a child a triumph and cause for fam-' ily celebration and expression of hope? If children bring no such lift, at least temporarily, what are the reasons? What are the attitudes toward the next generation? A chronological and highly selective list offers us the follow- ing treatments of children. I could easily double or triple the examples for each decade. In the 1960s, a newborn infant is drowned in John Updike's *Rabbit, Run;* and the remaining child, in the last of the Rabbit books, will be a cocaine addict who destroys the family business to support his habit. Children are eaten in Ishmael Reed's *Free-Lance Pallbearers.* Insofar as D.J. is his father's child in Norman Mailer's *Why Are We in Vietnam?,* we see how that relationship warps him toward becoming a killer. Pecola of Toni Morrison's *Bluest Eye* is incestuously abused by her father and bears a still- born child.

Fiction from the 1970s shows us more of the same. Adult children of Saul Bellow's Mr. Sammler and Elya Gruner behave in ways that seem freak- ish and irresponsible to their parents. Tom More's child in Walker Percy's *Love in the Ruins* dies of cancer. The children in E. L. Doctorow's *Book of Daniel* are badly damaged by their heritage. Sula is castigated by her grand- mother for not having children; and while Morrison upholds having chil- dren as a necessary duty and the point of life, she is honest in showing what hardships children mean to the very poor in that novel. The children in Thomas Pynchon's *Gravity's Rainbow* may survive, although we do not know this for sure. Meanwhile, they keep alive by finding the fate worse than death negotiable, as Pynchon puts it: Ludwig eats cock, and Bianca turns nymphet. Various forms of abuse are found in Kurt Vonnegut's *Slap- stick,* Leslie Marmon Silko's *Ceremony,* Morrison's *Song of Solomon,* and Kathy Acker's *Blood and Guts in High School.* Twin fetuses, the product of rape, are poisoned with their mother in Gerald Vizenor's *Bearheart: The Heirship Chronicles.*

Nor do things look better in the 1980s. The children of three of the main characters in Lisa Alther's *Original Sins* destroy their parents' chance of going to college and thereby escaping their economic and social niche. Reed's *Terrible Twos* uses the impossibly irritating behavior of two-year- olds to say something about the narcissism and greed of America in gen- eral. Richard Brautigan's and Vonnegut's tales of boys with guns show moderately unhappy children rendered neurotically unhappy by their own actions. William Kennedy's *Ironweed* turns on the protagonist's acciden- tally breaking his infant son's neck. In *Love Medicine,* Louise Erdrich fea-

tures many children peripherally; arguably, the most vivid portrayal involves the girl June trying to manipulate others into hanging her, and the
book revolves around her adult suicide. A dead baby at Christmastime lies
at the heart of Naylor's *Linden Hills*. In *Continental Drift*, Russell Banks
shows Bob Dubois's girls becoming psychologically disturbed, and Vanise's
nephew is drowned after suffering the modern Middle Passage. Carolyn
Chute shows children as part of the picture of poverty: yelling, hating
school, starving for five days when the father cannot work. Most survive
and grow up, but they represent at best a life of suffering and endurance
and not anything more enjoyable. Acker's *Don Quixote*, a dark-night-of-
the-soul quest, centers on an abortion. James Welch's *Fools Crow* shows
conventional pleasure over a child, but Fools Crow knows from a vision
that his child has no future in a white world. Vizenor's American monkey
king in China begets a fetus that drowns with its suiciding or murdered
mother. Anne McCaffrey's *Crystal Singer* makes sterility a condition for
adapting to the crystal-bearing planet. Octavia Butler's futuristic vision of
humans and aliens mingling cultures and genes does uphold the value and
individuality of the children even while regretting the alien admixture. In
The Thanatos Syndrome, Walker Percy shows children being sexually
abused. Morrison's *Beloved* portrays a mother trying to kill her children
and living with the remorse and confusion afterward. Laura loses her child
to divorce in Bruce Sterling's *Islands in the Net*, and daughters are seriously estranged from mothers in Amy Tan's *Joy Luck Club*, Lee Harvey
Oswald's child is ironically celebrated in Don DeLillo's *Libra*, and Bharati Mukherjee's *Jasmine* ends with a happy pregnancy for Jasmine, though
this presumably results in a terrible loss for the paralyzed Bud.

The books from the start of the 1990s carry on in the same general vein.
Patrick Bateman murders a child in Bret Easton Ellis's *American Psycho*
and is disappointed that a child is so trivial a being that the act can produce little response in himself. Silko's *Almanac of the Dead* figures a kidnapped boy, probably murdered, and characters in this novel enjoy intra-
uterine films of abortion as snuff films. Julia Alvarez's García girls suffer
from their relationship to a King Lear-like father. This list of destructive
and damaged children represents less than half of my original list of in-
jured offspring. The number of such portrayals is a literary symptom, not
a set of social statistics. Most readers and most of the authors will have
experienced the traditional triumph and pleasure of a wanted child's birth,
and many readers know children who have not been abused or starved and
who have grown into cheerful and self-supporting members of society.
Despite this, the literary construction of America provides us with no link
to the future.

Just as I started writing this chapter, I read two novels that gave special
prominence to births: Chute's *Merry Men* and Gloria Naylor's *Bailey's*

Cafe. Chute's characters tend to marry because the girl gets pregnant, not out of romantic love, but Anneka falls for a depressive, virtually deaf parolee, goes to the trouble of learning American Sign Language, and proposes to him by signing in the lunch bar, nobody else knowing what they are saying. Her heart medicine and his antidepressant drugs cost them most of their income, but they feel hope at the improvement in his state of mind, and both long passionately for the child. After a grotesque, two-week labor, the child is born dead. The grieving father's deafness keeps him from understanding the overbearing policeman who tries to take the corpse from him, and in the struggle, the officer gets killed. So much for the future of that strange but loving marriage; and as those two lose their future, so symbolically does that community in Maine.

In *Bailey's Cafe,* Naylor sets up a birth that is met with rejoicing, but she feels that she must go to narrative extremes to create such an atmosphere. The life stories that make up this novel all concern people who have suffered and reached a dead end. They eat at the café or live in a boardinghouse that is also a selective bordello. One of the sufferers, in a magic-realist story, is a feeble-minded black Jewish girl from a primitive, isolated community in Ethiopia who finds herself pregnant without any man having slept with her. Through magic, she finds herself in this New York neighborhood. As this infibulated virgin named Mariam gives birth, the inhabitants manage to celebrate the only child born into their little society. As his first cry is heard, they go wild, dancing and singing and breaking out champagne. Through magic-realist sleight of hand, the mother apparently drowns herself in a wall of water in a back garden, but the boy lives, and we gather that he will become the George who marries Cocoa and dies for her in *Mama Day.* Naylor creates a welcomed birth only by making it mythic, Christ-like, and more than a bit ironic (in Northrop Frye's sense). In this community, there is no place for an ordinary birth—let alone a happy one. As the narrator points out, they cannot raise a child on this street.

Children are no longer their own reward in many novels, except in some fiction by members of racial groups who are determined not to conform to white, Euro-American pressures and die out and for whom multiplying is a sacred responsibility. In past centuries and in agricultural societies, the more children, the more workers for the family and thus the better off that family would be. Now, in urban and suburban life, children are a serious drain on parental time, money, and professional advancement, even when their number is controlled. Those same children are unlikely to reciprocate by lavishing time and money on parents when parents grow old. The children will be in other parts of the country, and, like as not, daughters as well as sons will be working all day. An unacknowledged reaction to this unidirectional flow shows up in the attitudes toward children in the fiction studied here. Perhaps the lack of reciprocity darkens the sense of future and produces so many families with no future at all.

What Happened to Love?

Brian McHale cites John Bayley as saying that "it has become difficult to imagine literature without love" (*Postmodernist Fiction* 222). McHale sees love circulating everywhere in fiction. When I look at these novels, however, I see few, if any, long-lasting, loving relationships; indeed, there are few short but incandescent relationships either. Romantic love is not a universal cultural value or practice, and Toni Morrison can shrewdly call it as pernicious as the cult of personal beauty: "Both originated in envy, thrived in insecurity, and ended in disillusion" (*Bluest Eye* 97). Nonetheless, the idea that such a relationship is important has been central to Western literature since the troubadours, and somewhere in the nineteenth century, people began to expect to live according to its tenets and not just read about them and daydream. In various developed countries, marriage for financial gain or familial alliances gave way, for better or worse, to marriage based on hormonal attractions. Popular novels, such as Robert James Waller's *Bridges of Madison County* and Erich Segal's *Acts of Faith*, still count on the love story to sell. The detective story and serious science fiction have avoided love in favor of logic and scientific method, but science fantasy and other forms of speculative fiction are perfectly willing to use this emotional material to shape the story, if only to provide a convenient ending. But where are the loves of our recent yesteryears in the mainstream?

We find a rather silly passion in Norman Mailer's *American Dream*; the sophisticated and experienced Rojack falls in love at first sight with a nightclub singer. However, Cherry is murdered, and their embryo dies with her. Again, somewhat shallowly, the Native American monkey king in China claims he loves an interpreter, but she and their unborn scion drown. We do find love in a second marriage in *Love in the Ruins*, although the romantic element is undercut by Tom More's pursuing three women at once, and he marries one only because of his inability to bed her without a wedding band. Love is given a place in utopias, as we see in Ursula Le Guin's *Dispossessed* and Ernest Callenbach's *Ecotopia*; however, in Marge Piercy's *Woman on the Edge of Time*, we find that everyone lives single while developing loving relationships, often bisexual, with several people. No sort of exclusive passion is seen or expected. There is some hope for the loves at the end of *Beloved* and *Mama Day*. As Morrison would doubtless point out, the love of Paul D for Sethe is not a romantic passion but a human desire to help and cherish the partner, a feeling for someone who matters felt by people who have suffered all their lives. In *Mama Day*, Cocoa marries after George's death, and much of the point of that marriage seems to be to have children, for many African-American authors like Naylor still give traditional weight to procreation. Cocoa is sensible and down-to-earth about what she wants from this relationship; perhaps the marriage will be the less troubled for that unromantic practicality.

The conventions of love can be negated in many ways in this fiction. The love may simply be absent (as in the Rabbit tetralogy), or, if present, it is thwarted (as in Richard Brautigan's *Sombrero Fallout*). Of course, since romantic love need not be the only kind, we might note that several of these books explore alternatives to that narrow, exclusive, often jealous relationship. The line marriage in Robert Heinlein's *Moon Is a Harsh Mistress* is an arrangement for consolidating family power and caring for children. The open, flexible, changing relationships, all publicly known and unresented, in *Woman on the Edge of Time* are another solution to the drawbacks of conventional marriage. Parenting agreements are limited contracts, and children live a communal life from early on, thus freeing parents from confining obligations and letting them pursue professional concerns. The same lack of permanent conjugality exists in Starhawk's *Fifth Sacred Thing* and Le Guin's *Dispossessed*. In their ways, these futuristic fantasies reshape marriage as we know it to fit the demands of careers that take mothers away from full-time parenting. Naylor and Morrison uphold conventional mothering but do wish to see sounder bases for marriages than the hormonal reactions that govern behavior now. That is a positive interpretation of what happens in a few of the books that discount romantic love. In the others, a lack of love seems more in tune with a lack of point to living.[3]

Where Is the Work That Satisfies?

Jobs, not surprisingly, seem to be little respected, welcomed only when the alternative is unemployment. In *World's End*, Walter Van Brunt feels no sense of achievement when alienated from the product of his labor as a hand in a noisy factory. Similarly, work without its fruits brought no satisfaction to his indentured Dutch ancestors. His response is to drink, do drugs, and ride recklessly on his motorcycle. Ken Kesey's Randle McMurphy has no use for the unskilled jobs he can get; he works to make a bit of money, but his pleasure comes from gambling, cardsharping, and brawling. The jobs he has when free are much the same as those he does when in low-security jails. Hence, his fatal mistake is assuming that the mental institution's routines would be just a lark and a change but not a threat. In Heinlein's lunar prison society, Mannie's work as a computer repairman is more job than profession until the computer becomes sentient; the pleasure he gets from work is not consciousness of duty done or pleasure at exercising a skill but enjoyment over cheating the prison authorities. Andrea Dworkin's Andrea hates the work she does typing at four dollars an hour. The dangers and hardships of laying the railroad are graphically displayed in Kingston's *China Men*, and while the men can take pride in what they have accomplished—a tunnel or bridge is an enduring sign of their labor—their only reason for doing this is the money. The pleasures are far too few to do it for the work's sake. In *Continental Drift*, Bob Dubois gives up on his skilled but badly paid job as a furnace repairman, and when he gets in trouble running a liquor store, he agrees to do illegal work, but none of these jobs offers him any satisfaction. Kingston's Wittman Ah Sing hates working in a department store and takes unemployment compensation whenever he can get it. In De Lillo's *Libra*, Oswald hates his various low-level jobs; he wants to feel more important. When jobs do provide psychic satisfactions, they can be damaging: in Morrison's *Bluest Eye*, Pauline Breedlove's work as a maid for a white family teaches her to prefer the white child to her own children.

Professions offer more satisfaction in some novels but not much. In the utopias, professional work (indeed all work) is portrayed as rewarding. In nonutopian worlds, the best one can hope for is a profession that absorbs one without becoming an obsession. Mama Day may not have university degrees, but her work as an herb doctor to a small community is professional work, and she derives much pleasure from her own competence in health care. Most professions, however, are portrayed as demanding too much. In *Islands in the Net*, Laura derives her sense of self from her professional competence, but her devotion to her employer destroys her marriage. Music is the profession for Oscar Hijuelos's Mambo Kings, but it does not seem to be a calling; Nestor's death causes Cesar to drop out of the music world rather than discipline himself to develop musically. In *Linden Hills*, several successful African Americans commit suicide (or seem headed in that direction) because their devotion to white professional styles vitiates all that is authentic in them. Another such professional gone awry is Luther Nedeed in the same novel. His work as an undertaker appropriately reflects his role in overseeing the death-oriented lives of his tenants. Perhaps the ultimate in unsatisfactory professionals is Patrick Bateman, the American psycho. His mergers and acquisitions gruesomely connect in his mind to his true vocation, murder.

At first glance, vocations seem absent from these novels, but closer examination shows numerous unconventional vocations, all of them being essentially different from the character's means of earning a living and frequently inimical to it. Ebenezer Cooke in John Barth's *Sot-Weed Factor* feels called to be a poet; the fact that he is not a good poet is irrelevant. Mr. Sammler is called to be learned to the point that he sponges off others rather than support himself. Kilgore Trout in Vonnegut's *Breakfast of Champions* writes his stories despite the fact that he makes no money and his devotion to his writing and his pessimism have combined to destroy his marriages and estrange him from his son. Bellow's Dean Corde is an academic by profession, but he seems to be a moralist with a calling when he writes his articles on Chicago (despite severe damage to his career). He insists on talking in terms of the soul, evil, redemption, and other such concepts that his professional world will not let him use to discuss the degeneration at the heart of Western civilization.

When asked at a party, most people identify themselves by their occupation, saying, "I'm a stock-broker" or "I'm a yoga teacher," with a much smaller percentage identifying themselves as "Christian," "Gemini," "homosexual," or "husband." Given this professional orientation, we would hope to find some satisfactions being expressed regarding work in a world where a higher percentage of people than ever before are working at jobs distinct from housekeeping and family care and where many more jobs demand long years of education. The days when one could get by with "people skills" and a high school diploma are gone and are nostalgically celebrated in Ray Bradbury's *Dandelion Wine*.

Significantly, authors of utopian and futurist fiction focus on the problem of job satisfaction and try to envision conditions that would let people enjoy both work and personal relationships. In *Woman on the Edge of Time*, much effort goes into plant breeding at Mattapoisett, and individuals do that on a small scale, tending their own plants. Any gardening success or mistake will be personally felt, and the small community clearly tries to celebrate successes. In *Ecotopia*, people are encouraged to make every job highly personal. The telegraph operator comments on messages sent and argues over their contents; those cleaning up in a commune kitchen chat, give back rubs, tell jokes, and engage in much physical contact, all of which diminish the sense of drudgery and disciplined devotion to unrewarding labor. Thus, even dull, unchallenging routines are made rewarding through personal interactions. Callenbach's *Ecotopia Emerging*, like *The Dispossessed*, centers on an inventive genius and celebrates the joys of political engagement. However, we as readers are being assured that even if we personally cannot invent an efficient solar cell or make instantaneous communication across the universe possible, we can at least enjoy the invention of new political attitudes and solutions to conventional problems. In *Always Coming Home*, Le Guin introduces us to "mindbody work" such as making pottery and upholds such low-tech labor as something that engages our whole being. Most members of the village pursue some such work at least part of the time. One finds even more radical solutions if one looks to science fiction and fantasy; McCaffrey's *Crystal*

Singer turns high-tech work into ecstasy, the equivalent to a prolonged drug high, but with the addictional drawbacks of drugs as well as their pleasures.

Utopian thinkers are not the norm, however, and novels set in present-day reality may show commitment to work, but they reward it with relatively few satisfactions. Characters with white-collar jobs mostly find them boring. The poor face unpleasant labor and unemployment. Some African Americans and immigrants have had to put up with jobs far below their training and ability. Very few feel genuine commitment to their life's activity.

What Does It Mean to Succeed?

If love, marriage, children, and professions are not providing much satisfaction to characters in contemporary fiction, then we are hardly surprised to find other kinds of success similarly absent. Updike's Rabbit fulfills any dream of material wealth he might have had as a boy and young man, but given the discontents of his marriage and son and his spiritual yearnings for something more, that success is never more than a temporary gratification. In *An American Dream,* Mailer declares Rojack to have done reasonably well (though not perfectly) in facing his fears and winning his freedom. However, to agree, readers must swallow a definition of acceptable behavior that includes murder as a legitimate way to terminate a marriage, even though divorce is possible. The revolution in *The Moon Is a Harsh Mistress* might seem success enough for the characters, but the lunar society plunges into red tape and restrictive laws, resulting in a total failure by the standards of the revolutionaries. Abel's return to the old ways in N. Scott Momaday's *House Made of Dawn* is a triumph from a Native American perspective; how well he will merge with his grandfather's people, having never been fully part of the society, remains to be seen. In *The Dispossessed,* Le Guin's Shevek resolves the central problem of physics but may be killed by a mob when he returns home. To have survived and faced one's fears is success in Samuel R. Delany's *Dhalgren,* but Kid does not stay in Bellona, and his future outside is not promising. Milkman Dead does find his roots and face a mortal challenge, so he may be said to have achieved his goal in *Song of Solomon;* as a social being, however, he still has a lot of growing up to do. Proude Cedarfair transcends this world for a higher spiritual level of existence in *Bearheart,* though his earthly body may well die. The protagonist of Andrew Macdonald's *Turner Diaries* is content with his crowning contribution to the Movement; for him, though, winning forgiveness and reintegration into the inner circle consists of a suicide mission. Welch's Fools Crow carries out a difficult dream quest, but it tells him that his people are doomed, and he must live with this knowledge. In *Islands in the Net,* Laura succeeds brilliantly (in company terms) for Rizome but loses her family for the same actions. The Mambo Kings appear with Desi Arnaz early in their career, but their lives run downhill from there. *Jasmine* chronicles a series of triumphs, but Mukherjee's protagonist leaves a trail of victims. Kingston's Tripmaster Monkey manages to orchestrate the community happening but is still jobless, married to a woman he scarcely knows, and no better suited to fitting into society. The movement of the dispossessed indigenes toward the north in *Almanac of the Dead* will cause millions to die, and the collapse of a high-tech society to a low-tech culture will be painful or fatal for most concerned, the poor as well as the wealthy. Of course, that may be better than the destruction of all life on Earth, which is Silko's pitiless argument.

These last few offer successes of a sort, but no success is unalloyed. A number of these characters, given their choice, might have preferred to fail than to reap the success they do, so high are the costs. In *Continental Drift,* Bob Dubois murmurs to himself that America will force the Haitians to give up more than they would have been willing to lose to try for the American Dream. Vanise proves his point: she makes it to America but loses her sanity.

Why Read Such Fiction?

If no joy is to be had from love, children, or work within these novels, and if they do not feature spiritual transcendence or philosophical enquiry, why would anyone wade through such gloom and doom? Where is the pleasure that keeps one's attention? Professional readers seeking evidence of world construction, gender performance, or postmodern flattening of history can read with theory in mind, but they constitute a very select group. What do these books do, in terms of literature, for people who pick up the book in a bookstore and decide to buy it?

Oddly enough, happy endings, at least of a sort, are not totally lacking. Some are more symbolic than substantial, meaning that the protagonists of *House Made of Dawn* and *Ceremony,* for instance, end with homecomings, a traditionally positive conclusion. What Abel or Tayo can hope for in their respective futures must be severely limited. They may or may not be fully accepted by their tribes. That they have rejected white ways is meant to be encouraging, but their lives will not be rendered especially happy by their having done so. Happy endings are also ironized or deflated from fairy-tale status; and while this form of conclusion provides little assurance, it does correspond to the tenuous and fragile improvements possible in real life. Vonnegut's finales tend to be ironized; his characters suffer various major world collapses and enjoy a moment of insight that helps explain life to them (as in *Slapstick, Breakfast of Champions, Blue-*

beard); however, Wilbur Swain, surrounded by his candles, can hardly be called a truly hopeful symbol of continuance. Kingston's *Tripmaster Monkey* finishes by celebrating a marriage so strange by current standards that it ironizes the *hieros gamos* and leaves us disturbed. *Bearheart* climaxes, apparently seriously, with Vizenor's protagonist rising to another level of existence; similar apotheoses are ironized in Ishamel Reed's *Free-Lance Pallbearers* and Donald Barthelme's *Snow White*.

Some novels hold us through suspense, but many persuade us through sheer virtuosity. An extraordinary recreation of history is one common form: Pynchon's *Gravity's Rainbow*, Robert Coover's *Public Burning*, De-Lillo's *Libra*, and many others fit this pattern. If a past historical event is not the focus for the intensity, then a world may be. Almost any kind of world qualifies. The ethnic worlds of *The Joy Luck Club* and *The Mambo Kings Play Songs of Love* are such. So is the Irish-American Albany of William Kennedy's fiction, and there is also the rural Maine world of Carolyn Chute. The intensity may come from a character (Patrick Bateman in *American Psycho* or Andrea in *Mercy*) or from the intensity of the authorial tone, as in *Blood and Guts in High School*.

Another relatively large group of titles that share a power of attraction do so through engaging with an idea—"fiction of thought" rather than of plot or character. In almost all of them, the idea is some aspect of what makes a desirable (or undesirable) community. They may explore how to bring such a community into being by means of revolution (*The Moon Is a Harsh Mistress, Almanac of the Dead*) or muse on what made the community work (*Sula*) or not work (*Linden Hills*). The utopian fiction all fits here, as does Bellow's exploration of capitalist and communist cities. As in other idea-oriented novels, many of these books are noticeably didactic, so the reader's tolerance for preachiness will determine whether the work attracts or repels.

One can, of course, enjoy negative experiences in entertainment, whether one is wrung by a tragedy or revels in the adrenaline rush of a horror film. Sophisticated readers do not need the assurance of a triumphal ending, nor do they simply identify with a character and so wish the vicarious pleasure of seeing that character finish the story in a happy state. Such pleasures do contribute to making a novel popular, though, so authors whose aim is not primarily to give pleasure must intensify their efforts in other directions.

However, identification can give other sorts of pleasure: the enjoyment of finding someone voicing your experiences when those experiences are silenced by mainstream culture; the pleasures of having unexpressed frustrations vented for you; and the complex pleasures of experiencing some culture or mind-set alien to yourself. Maxine Hong Kingston's *Woman Warrior* articulated feelings that other Chinese-American women had felt but found unacknowledged in the culture at large, even while letting Euro-American readers experience the virtually unknown Chinese culture in their midst. One may regret the exposure of healing ceremonies to profane eyes (as Paula Gunn Allen does regarding Silko's chants), but one may be reassured to see the healing properties of ceremonies taken seriously, something that does not happen in most Euro-American novels. Kesey catches frustration at the institutional power felt in the 1960s. Reed touches fears of secret powers behind the scenes in government. Banks gives voice to the sense of unfairness felt by those who work honestly yet find they cannot afford the life they believed to be rightfully theirs. The Gutenberg age may be dying, but the power of print is such for serious readers that finding their feelings mirrored and elaborated in a book still generates a frisson of pleasure.

Clearing Paths into a Trackless Future

As we have seen, the lack of a future certainly affects the narrative tone of these novels. For all this negativity, however, some authors find ways of infusing life with meaning. Three methods seem to appeal to the authors of this era: code, survival (often interconnected), and community. Codes can be religious, moral, or philosophical, and one has only to think of Stoic philosophers or of Hasidim living all the rules of the Mosaic code to see how thoroughly such a code can infuse life with meaning. An American Dream, House Made of Dawn, Mr. Sammler's Planet, The Dispossessed, Bearheart, The Turner Diaries, The Joy Luck Club (Chinese ethics for the mothers), and Billy Phelan's Greatest Game and Ironweed (the codes, respectively, of gamester and hobo)—those are the most obvious examples of a code-given meaning. The code may be more generally a spiritual outlook, as in Ceremony and Fools Crow. Aside from religion, not many such codes still exist in Euro-American culture, and most of these writers look to an idealized past, ethnic or philosophical, to find them. Survival of hardship provides coherence in The Sot-Weed Factor, China Men, Carolyn Chute's books, Jasmine, Octavia Butler's trilogy, and Mama Day. Survival associated with adhering to a code appears in Ceremony, Beloved, Neuromancer, An American Dream, House Made of Dawn, and Mr. Sammler's Planet.

Community, however, is where most of these authors look when they want to find ways of defining a worthwhile life. For the individual working alone, there are few ways of structuring life when the community is unsatisfactory. One way is to give up any hope of controlling one's life and simply follow the general pattern, ultimately becoming part of the problem rather than part of the solution. This process usually follows the pattern of marrying young (often because of a pregnancy), having children without controlling their number, not worrying about the lack of a steady job or a place to live, living from hand to mouth, and figuring that one will manage somehow. This is what some characters do in *Letourneau's Used Auto Parts, Love Medicine,* and *Rabbit, Run.* Another strategy is to try to create a niche for oneself that will make life more comfortable. PaPa La-Bas does this in Ishmael Reed's *Mumbo Jumbo;* the niche he creates through being a root man lets him live comfortably and even support some employees in a society that did not make life for African-Americans easy. Insofar as his medicine helps his clients, he does good to them as well. As a detective, block king, and gypsy-cab driver, Reed's Nance Saturday creates an unfettered life for himself and manages to help others in *The Terrible Threes.* The third strategy is to devote oneself to social and political change, but we find little belief in social action in this fiction.

Social action depends on working together as part of a community, and the American myth of individualism, reinforced by our educational emphasis on working alone rather than cooperatively, has resulted in people with a weak sense of obligation to any community and a stunted ability to work with others. The characters in these novels may not be true nonconformists, but neither are they good at serious collaboration. While few novels—except utopian fictions and revolutionary blueprints—show social action, about forty of the novels discussed in this study concern community directly or peripherally, and several others pointedly focus on the nonfunctionality of a specific community. The American Dream has often been understood in terms of one individual rising or of one family improving its lot. Within that storyline, the satisfactoriness of the community is assumed, or the individual moves elsewhere—the suburbs, the West, the Sunbelt. What I think we see in this focus on the problems of community is an important response to the failure of the American Dream. Some of these authors seem to be groping for action that might indeed change America for the better. They wish to get away from the narcissistic focus on the self—the American distortion of liberalism—and find viable ways of being part of a larger network of people. They see this change as the starting point for any improvement, for any desirable future.

The novelists define community in several fashions: family, tribe, ethnic enclave, utopia. Those who live by the same code form a community, as do those who practice the same religion, those who share the same hacker skills, and those who have meshed to live outside of mainstream society—in a criminal underworld or as part of a resistance movement, for instance. Most ethnic literature concerns community, if only to contrast the enclave favorably to the surrounding Euro-American culture, which is perceived as both hostile and sterile. Several of the futuristic texts explore new forms of human network, trying to integrate the human need for community with new electronic or evolutionary possibilities.

Among the novelists to focus on family as the chief structure for maintaining meaning, we find Saul Bellow, John Edgar Wideman, William Kennedy, Gloria Naylor, Amy Tan, Thomas Pynchon, Rudolfo Anaya, Toni Morrison, and Carolyn Chute. I do not need to list the ethnic and tribal authors who emphasize larger networks than the family yet stay small-scale. While most of the fiction lauds such groups, a few authors are able to maintain some critical distance. Naylor's *Linden Hills* is interesting in that it does not claim a seemingly successful black community to be ideal; instead, by copying white patterns, the inhabitants of this housing development have rendered themselves barren, suicidal, and pointless. Momaday's *House Made of Dawn* and Silko's *Ceremony* also make clear that mixed-bloods may suffer rejection for something they themselves could not help. Overall, writers who enjoy some of the conveniences of the high-tech world would like to see a community that can enjoy selective technology. *Always Coming Home* offers modified tribal values as the only sane choice for all people in a postcataclysmic future, but Le Guin's village can access a global net of sorts.

Utopias are by definition ideal communities, so concepts of a viable community are central to all such novels. The group may be formed by racial and ethnic cleansing (*The Turner Diaries*), or it may simply involve the creation of low-tech sustainable cultures in which people live closer to the earth yet retain some comforts of the modern world. Examples of the latter include the *Ecotopia* novels, *Woman on the Edge of Time*, Le Guin's two anarchic utopias, and *The Fifth Sacred Thing*. In all of these, the community is meant to impress readers as a great improvement over middle-class suburban alienation, the apartment-dweller's urban isolation, the housing-project inhabitant's crowding, and the collective insensibility to fellow humanity.

Less idealized are the more or less criminal communities, many of which emerge as an answer to high technology and its social structures. In *Libra* and Donald Freed's *Spymaster*, for instance, the intelligence world is a society within society. Members of this group live off secrets. The agents form a network and trade with their "enemy" opposites as much as with their co-nationalists. They help or murder each other with little concern for whose side the other party is attached to. Despite such murders, these people are legal, unlike the bootleggers of William Kennedy's *Legs*. Marcus Gorman is drawn to the illegal community by the charisma of Legs Diamond. He sees all too clearly how murders define the boundaries of that community, but he still finds it attractive because it *is* a fellowship and because its leader so entrances his followers that they lose most of their moral judgment. Another mostly illegal community is the hacker world of cyberpunk. Although everything is for sale in this world, the hackers do recognize each other as belonging to a group with occasional obligations toward other members but no obligations toward lesser mortals. The hackers consider themselves technological supermen. Thomas Pynchon's black market is a loosely cohesive group that lets its members survive the chaos of World War II. Of all these authors, Pynchon is the one who downplays violence most. His notion that an underground could be casual and noncoercive seems romantic, but his lack of realism does not negate his argument that only in small communities outside of official society is there even a chance of relatively unselfish human cooperation.

Vonnegut's *Slapstick* and Sterling's *Islands in the Net* both trace the problems with community to our high-tech world and offer technological solutions. Vonnegut issues everyone with a middle name and number so that each American citizen acquires thousands of artificial siblings and cousins. Sterling proposes that one's workplace become one's community for life. The multinational corporation, Rizome, ultimately proves more important to Laura than her family. Its patterns of consensus formation seem to her a model on which the whole world could be reformed. Sterling may be romanticizing corporations (as implied by Marge Piercy in *He, She and It*). However, like Pynchon, Sterling is trying to imagine solutions to the problems of community that do not demand a return to a fairly primitive pastoral world, for the supposedly ideal nature of that world is undoubtedly romanticized.

Finally, a small group is not looking for solutions: various members of the "brat pack" or the next wave—the Blank Generation or Generation X. For Bret Easton Ellis, Jay McInerney, and Douglas Coupland, American culture is McDonald's and Nike, Microsoft and Armani, cellular phones and the World Wide Web. This is it, we live it, and they do not think we will find anything more worthwhile by looking further, looking backward, or trying to change. Their characters are adapted—sometimes uneasily— to a life without a supportive community and without any but short-range professional goals. While they hardly celebrate this life, they do not reject it in the name of some other values.

Narrative Responses to the Lost Dream

As Richard Chase pointed out in *The American Novel and Its Tradition*, our fiction has favored the romance form, with protagonists who are intense and driven loners. Ahab is paradigmatic. In *The American Adam*, R. W. B. Lewis excavated and laid out the penchant for innocents mangled by experience, their fall often taking place against a frontier or wilderness backdrop. This story of growing up derives its structure or at least motifs from that other definition of romance, the hero monomyth. Nathaniel Hawthorne supplies several such protagonists. Ihab Hassan looked at post–World War II fiction in *Radical Innocence*, seeing the protagonist types as victim and rebel (again, driven and intense people): he deals with novels by William Styron, Norman Mailer, Bernard Malamud, J. D. Salinger, and Ralph Ellison, among others. Richard Ohmann speaks of a "sickness narrative" in which the protagonist's social malaise is presented through images of illness (Sylvia Plath's *Bell Jar*, Salinger's *Franny and Zooey*, Ken Kesey's *One Flew over the Cuckoo's Nest*, among many others). In the novels discussed in these later studies, and in the books discussed in *American Dream, American Nightmare*, we find the formal descendants of Chase's romances. Most of them lean toward individual action rather than social interaction, and many burn with intensity and moral seriousness.

The monomythic romance structure, though, is also present and gives shape to many American novels. I find no single narrative such as the sickness narrative; but within the stories told here, I do find many structural remnants or variants of the romance. They seem to suit the romance longings for individual success or for ideal social structures implicit in the American Dream itself. The romance quest plot tends to be upbeat and uplifting. Perhaps such plot structures help balance the unpleasantness and pessimism that so many of the plots convey. The experience of reading these books is not often ameliorated by the catharsis of tragedy; the suffering usually does not terminate neatly, and the unsolved problems disturb our sensibilities as we seek but fail to find any exit. Nonetheless, we read on. How do structure and content work together to present their unpalatable message?

Bildungsroman

In the hands of a novelist, the hero monomyth quest undergoes considerable displacement from myth in terms of the setting and the psychological complexifying of the human situations. One form that this takes is the drawn-out account of growing up, education, and the rites of initiation: the bildungsroman. This structure works—without irony—for a number of writers trying to define identity and culture on the margins of Euro-American culture. They can still believe passionately in the problem of entering a culture or rejecting one, as we see in Rudolfo Anaya's *Bless Me, Ultima*, Morrison's *Song of Solomon*, Welch's *Fools Crow*, Octavia Butler's *Imago*, Mukherjee's *Jasmine*, and Naylor's *Mama Day* (regarding Cocoa's part in the plot). These stories draw readers from the same ethnic group as the protagonist through giving voice to their story; they draw readers from other ethnic groups by the attractions of the little-known culture and by the comforting sameness of any bildung-patterned plot. Publishers consider stories of growing up and coming of age safe and attractive, commercially speaking. When Vonnegut, however, uses it in *Deadeye Dick*, he cannot find a point at which his protagonist has "grown up." That story meanders on, and Rudy Waltz never really develops any higher level of vision. By the end, he is much older than the twenty- or thirty-year-old protagonists of the other novels mentioned. Vonnegut's *Bluebeard* is a *Künstlerroman* and as such is expected to go much further into the artist's life and development, but Karabekian is portrayed as a man of very little artistic output until his final painting, so the same delay, the same difficulty in finding any wisdom, remains apparent. Similarly, the artist in William Kennedy's *Very Old Bones* has trouble reaching any humane wisdom, even if his artistic vision garners admiration. That novel tells two stories, one the *Künstlerroman* of Peter Phelan, the other the bildung story concerning Orson Purcell, the illegitimate son of the artist. Orson's development is maimed, manic-depressive, and generally less than promising. His being integrated into his family may help, but he shows less groundedness in some inner self than Tayo of Silko's *Ceremony* or even Abel in Momaday's *House Made of Dawn*. If one were teaching the bildungsroman, one could make something of this unsureness of what education and culture should add up to. A Euro-American lack of assurance here emerges clearly in the Vonnegut and Kennedy novels and contrasts with the ethnic versions of the story that appeal to the marketplace.

Two Worlds; or, There and Back Again

Another variation on the quest story, called (in J. R. R. Tolkien's subtitle to *The Hobbit*) "there and back again," becomes in novelistic hands a contrast of two (or more) worlds. Among these stories, we find *The Dispossessed* (Le Guin), *Woman on the Edge of Time* (Piercy), *The Dean's December* (Bellow; literally a tale of two cities), *Always Coming Home* (Le Guin), *Adulthood Rites* (Octavia Butler), *Islands in the Net* (Sterling), and (with little journeying but strong contrasts) *The Mambo Kings Play Songs of Love* (Hijuelos), *World's End* (Boyle), and *The Tokyo-Montana Express* (Brautigan). Whereas the romance form of such a story found in most popular fiction would emphasize the protagonist's development, these novels do more with setting and cultural contrasts than with character. Arguably the most sophisticated of these, *The Dean's December*, also proves to be the closest to the romance form. Dean Corde, like Shevek in *The Dispossessed*, has faced certain moral challenges, decides what stances he must take, and takes them, knowing that the results may be professionally catastrophic. The background is more complicated than that of *The Dispossessed*, but the trajectory of the plot and the attraction of contrasting two worlds are much the same. All of these, whether set in the past, present, or future, challenge the values of American culture, and they hold our attention through combining the unknown (particularly for the futuristic stories) with the world we know (or with its metaphoric equivalent).

Descent and Return

Yet another trajectory related to the quest is descent and return. The protagonist descends (in mythic terms) into the land of the dead or of spirits or of dark forces, be they of chaos, depression, despair, or madness. That pattern guides seventeen or so of the novels, and they range from fairly traditional romances like Delany's *Dhalgren*, where return is as substantial as descent, through a number of ambiguous liminal texts, to those which simply descend into a dark vortex and end bleakly. The traditional novels include William Kennedy's *Billy Phelan's Greatest Game* and *Legs*, Saul Bellow's *Mr. Sammler's Planet*, Norman Mailer's *American Dream*, and Leslie Marmon Silko's *Ceremony*. All but the first, though they finish with a return, give us scant cause to rejoice. Sammler has reaffirmed his family ties but to a semi-insane daughter who will bear him no grandchildren. Mailer's Rojack has braved some fears but remains a murderer whose violence seems unwarranted to many readers. And Silko's Tayo identifies himself with his mother's people, even if they show only grudging willingness to accept him.

The crossover texts call the possibility of true return into question. John Barth's *Sot-Weed Factor* ends with conventional equilibrium, but so much has happened to produce such extremely modest happiness that we feel only a token impulse to rejoice. Thomas Pynchon ends *The Crying of Lot 49* with Oedipa Maas hoping she will learn whether she is mad or the conspiracy exists; sinister hints also suggest that she is in danger. The novel ends before any questions are answered. Her leaving the room, let alone returning to a "sane" world, is very far from assured, though we do learn in Pynchon's *Vineland* that she survived. Kathy Acker's *Don Quixote* ends with an affirmation of awakening from the dark night, but that affirmation is so slender, and the darkness and madness of the night so vast, that any talk of hope seems almost laughable. Norman Mailer's *Why Are We in Vietnam?* ends with a rite of initiation, but the hero dedicates himself to becoming a killer in service to a dark god. *Sombrero Fallout* shows Richard Brautigan's protagonist emerging from an hour's madness by turning his extravagant and beautifully described grief into a banal ballad, even as the town that erupts into civil strife quiets down into the tedious kitsch of tourism. Are we to feel relieved at this escape from darker forces? I think not altogether. The vulgarity is too grating to grant much sense of rescue. Freed's *Spymaster* ends with Prescott contemplating suicide in part because he is unable to tell the world what he knows about the CIA's illegal acts that have altered history. He is likely to be assassinated if he does not blow his own brains out first. The body of the story is pure thriller, but the ending breaks out of that romance mold to offer a stricken lament for America in the hands of its own spooks.

The texts that make no bones about descending to the nether depths include Morrisons's *Bluest Eye,* Vonnegut's *Breakfast of Champions,* Brautigan's *So the Wind Won't Blow It Away,* Naylor's *Linden Hills,* Kesey's *One Flew over the Cuckoo's Nest,* and Banks's *Continental Drift.* Our only hope as readers comes from the figure of the onlooker who comments on the madness enfolding the focal character. Morrison's Pecola goes mad, but Claudia can learn and even be enlightened by what she learns. The inhabitants of Linden Hills go mad to varying degrees, except for the street poet. Dwayne Hoover goes insane, but the "Kurt Vonnegut" character reaches illumination about what is sacred and what matters in life. Kesey's McMurphy is lobotomized, but Chief Bromden escapes. No such relief offers itself in *Continental Drift,* however. Readers follow the downfall of someone betrayed by the American Dream; that victim in turn betrays others betrayed by the Dream. Death, madness, and a next generation bound up in the same life-blighting disappointments and poverty are what result. Readers are carried along this downward trajectory to the degree that they share Bob Dubois's or Vanise Dorsinville's ambitions to prosper more than their natal situation allows.

Other Forms

Some narrative forms have already been discussed because they overlap with thematic content in chapters: utopias, apocalypses, and demonic and satiric visions. Aside from some of the genre fiction, which simply follows pure hero monomyth patterns, the last group worth considering is the set of novels that invert their forms with irony and thus make a straight response virtually impossible. I have already mentioned some in the groups that they ironically distort: *The Sot-Weed Factor, Why Are We in Vietnam?, Legs, One Flew over the Cuckoo's Nest.* Others, however, are harder to place. John Updike's *Rabbit, Run* follows a "there and back again" trajectory, but Rabbit himself only goes in circles. The ironic distance between his glimpses of meaning and his life are enough to rob any literary pattern of its traditional meaning. Barthelme's *Snow White* ironizes the fairy tale; all its promises of living happily ever after end in the dust. We can enjoy the glittering humor with which this is done but can rejoice neither in Snow White's apotheosis nor in the dwarves' determination to carry on. Ishmael Reed's *Mumbo Jumbo* and some of his other novels are parody detective stories as well as satires, and they tend to leave us epistemologically humbled and not at all sure that we have followed the logic of events or know what really happened. *Original Sins* is a multifocus bildungsroman whose characters do not mesh with their old society after a sojourn elsewhere. They ask how one can grow up and what an adult should be in our society, but they find no satisfying answers. This book offers a paradigmatic unresolved ending in which old verities have collapsed under scrutiny and no solutions have emerged, while humor and satire jostle with queasy uncertainty and disillusionment. William Kennedy's *Ironweed,* Octavia Butler's *Dawn,* Carolyn Chute's *Letourneau's Used Auto Parts,* and Julia Alvarez's *How the García Girls Lost Their Accents* are others that twist and therefore affect our formal expectations. By the time we have finished *Ironweed,* we are not sure whether we are dealing with Odysseus or a saint in the form of Francis Phelan, a murderous hobo who may be dying, leaving town on a boxcar, rising into some mystic state, or merely coming home. Somehow, we find ourselves seeing Phelan as all of these, and we feel a very contradictory set of responses to the end of that novel.

Grouping novels according to their basic narrative trajectories like this reminds us that novelists from different cultural backgrounds may nonetheless use the same literary building blocks and create works with a certain shared tone or shared concern with the sanity of life in America. Native Americans and African Americans find descent into madness, with or without return, as necessary a metaphor as do Euro-American writers. The bildungsroman is, if anything, a stronger form for those who feel marginalized by mainstream Euro-American culture. The satire and apocalypse likewise appeal to all groups. And, of course, all can ironize conventional patterns to meet the harsher needs of this fiction. Formally and pedagogically, the combinations are intriguingly varied.

Of course, we can easily find novelists not centrally concerned with America: writers asking metafictional questions about the limits of meaning in plot or language. When Robert Coover writes about Nixon, whether in *The Public Burning* or *Whatever Happened to Gloomy Gus of the Chicago Bears?,* he can hardly help criticizing the system, but his *Spanking the Maid* or *Gerald's Party* or *Pinocchio in Venice* concern fiction, philosophy, and literary theory and tradition. Metafiction has enjoyed an international boom, and most authors producing it work in apolitical modes. Italo Calvino's *Castle of Crossed Destinies* or De Botton's *On Love* have little to say about Italian or English or European politics.

A form of plot that has burgeoned recently, the search for and recreation of the past, can likewise ignore America's problems if the author so wishes. Cynthia Ozick's *Messiah of Stockholm* is a fascinating hunt for a manuscript that is comparable in its literary quest to A. S. Byatt's later and more famous *Possession.* Ozick's passion to recuperate a lost work of Bruno Schultz leaves no space for concern with America, however, Schultz having been central European, the novel's setting being Scandinavian. Richard Powers's *Gold Bug Variations* also reconstructs a past, even an American past, but the focus seems much more psychological and philosophical than national. In *Pinball* or *Passion Play,* whether Jerzy Kosinski deals with erotics or barbarities, he welcomes certain freedoms that are possible in America. He ignores the country's social problems in most of his novels, he being apparently unsympathetic toward people who need help to survive or rise socially. Philip Roth's *Counterlife* shows life in America, England, and Israel, but the novel seems less interested in comparing those three societies as systems than in the inner life of its characters. Even though the American books listed here are not politically concerned with America, they show many of the same traits discussed: few children, a dissatisfaction with work, and little sense of why life is worth living. Although not directly critical of America as a political entity, these novels show little imaginative sense of possible futures.

While it is hardly fair to look at a single book for contrast, consider A. S. Byatt's *Possession*, the winner of England's Booker Prize in 1990. Several of the characters are strongly engaged in their work; they hunt passionately for the truth of a historical event, for varying reasons of scholarship, detective ardor, sentiment, avarice, collector's mania, and possessiveness. The fervent quest brings some of these scholars together in physical pairings that are likely and unlikely. The story concerns a child who, although illegitimate, is cherished, cared for, and of central importance to the narrative. She is the object of concern during her own life and in the later period. Her marriage is cause for cheer, and her child is cause for rejoicing. The romance of the two Victorian poets and of Maud and Roland is handled with an erotic power that makes a claim for such congress mattering deeply. Roots in the past are important to several of these characters; at least academically, some are building for the future as they assemble collections, establish a women's studies center, or look for jobs. None of the American novels discussed in this book have these elements in such profusion. Powers's *Gold Bug Variations* is similar in scale and inventiveness and revels in the pleasures of the historical quest, but a child who was *not* conceived is at the heart of the earlier crisis, and the novel's modern romance is severely damaged by the woman's having chosen to be sterilized. When Andrea Dworkin looks back to the nineteenth century, she stumbles over Walt Whitman and despairs over the contrast between Whitman's America and hers: *Mercy* is a furious complaint directed in part at Whitman for raising her expectations as to what America should be. Likewise, the protagonist of Maxine Hong Kingston's *Tripmaster Monkey*, Wittman Ah Sing, tries to adapt Whitman's spontaneity to contemporary America but finds the going difficult. Byatt is not driven to castigate her poets—evocative of Robert Browning and Christina Rossetti—for the woes of contemporary Britain. She sees them as contributing positively to a literary tradition that she can still comfortably call great. She feels herself to be part of an ongoing literary community, and her characters also feel comfortably situated within their literary and scholarly circles.

Mourning the Death of the Dream

When we look for bedrock agreements among these texts, we find one that is shared by many novels radically different in their subjects and ideologies: distress over the diminution of local community ties. Writers from identifiable communities are deeply worried by the threat to the nuclear (let alone the extended) family offered by the mobility of our technology- and job-oriented culture. Writers from suburban culture ruefully seek some kind of belonging and look nostalgically to the small-town past or tentatively to an electronic future for succor. They agree that loss of community is terribly important and vitally damaging to this country, even though they and their characters are frequently the beneficiaries of the mobility and job orientation that cause the problem. Over one-third of the books considered in this study deal with community one way or another, and insofar as any of the authors see some way of bettering the future, they believe that creating or recreating a sense of community is the starting point. If the writers come out of a liberal or leftist tradition, they are likely to think in terms of improving community spirit, collaborative mentality, and supportiveness. If they come from a conservative tradition, they are likely to define community as a place of shared traditional beliefs and of harmonious collaboration and subordination within a supposedly natural hierarchy and through natural gender roles. Or they may, like Carolyn Chute, have found that left and right have been replaced by up and down, by big business versus rural workers and farmers. Her real-life activism embraces a "People's Army," apparently a form of militia group. Within the group, Marxists and libertarians work together. The ideology resembles that of European folk fascism before World War II.

Also at the bedrock level for this group of novels, we find discomfort at the lack of an envisioned future, whether for America or for a specific group. Because the future is empty, the past and present lose their shaping telos and become unformed as well. The authors themselves are distressed at being unable to imagine a plausible future for America. There are no children, no joy in work, no sense of success, and no loving relationships. The tally of damaged and dead children in these novels flies in the face of actual statistics, but the image is compelling and an appalling telltale of morale. Happy families may all be alike and hence not make good story material, but the pileup of unhappy families and individuals goes beyond mere narrative convenience. The American Dream had promised an expansive future, and what we now find is a melancholy loss of faith in America's exceptionalism, a sense of tarnished morality at odds with the official propaganda upholding America's innocence and good will. Or, as Walker Percy phrases the sentiment, "All this time we were not really different from Ecuador and Bosnia-Herzegovina, just richer" (*Love in the Ruins* 48).

The more liberal writers are obsessed with America's loss of goodness and righteousness, a claim that stemmed from the promise of liberty and justice for all and that had always seemed to justify America's prosperity. Many of these writers were children in the 1950s (as I was) and were bombarded in grade school with statements that our national fairness, honesty, prosperity, and good will made America the best nation in the world, a utopian state realized rather than something needing to be striven for. Even writers from nonwhite and non-middle-class backgrounds had cause during the late 1950s and 1960s to think that what was wrong with their lives might be improving. Whereas political leftists from before the war gave up on utopian dreams when they rejected Stalin and communism, the later generation of liberals invested some of their utopian hopes in America. With the economic shifts of the 1970s, people all around the political compass felt their hope and faith diminish.

Such literary mourning resulting from the loss of a myth is not unprecedented. Two literary groups that were similarly obsessed are the British Romantics and the writers of the postbellum American South. The Romantics, as D. G. James pointed out over half a century ago, tried to replace what they saw as the failed truths of a worn-out religion with transcendent truths reachable through art. When they pushed their philosophy and aesthetic theory to the limit and failed to find the bridge between the material world and anything higher, Wordsworth and Coleridge virtually ceased to write, and Keats died, knowing that what he hoped from literature was proving impossible. In the next literary generation, Matthew Arnold likewise wished to pierce the mundane to touch a higher reality, since Christianity no longer provided him with a sense of transcendent meaning. In "Stanzas from the Grande Chartreuse," he laments his liminal state: "Wandering between two worlds, one dead, / The other powerless to be born" (85–86). He too ceased to write poetry when it became clear that it could not aspire to higher truth. The anguish of these writers stems from the defeat of passionate spiritual cravings. Someone whose belief was never strong would suffer less trauma—and less sense of betrayal—at vanished certitude. Later literary generations, more exposed to doubts about Christianity and more used to the possibility of a godless world, may take up the issues—as does Updike—but with a less searing sense of loss.

Another analogue to the current obsession with a mythological loss occurs in fiction emerging from the American South after the War between the States. For a century, Southern writers could hardly escape writing about the effects of that conflict. Its unfinished business rendered every other subject secondary. By now, that is ceasing to be true. Some teenagers grow up in Virginia yet do not know who Robert E. Lee or Ulysses S. Grant were (Hirsch, *Cultural Literacy* 8). They do not care who won or lost that war, and they are used to living in a relatively racially integrated world. They go to integrated schools. What they know about Civil War battles will be what children in the West and North learn, mostly from television specials or films like *Gettysburg*. Hearing the story from a grandfather who took part is one thing; such a personal application disappears when one sees it on television. Given the movement of Northerners to the sunbelt, a current Southerner's ancestor may well have worn blue or may still have been living in Italy or Vietnam, thus reducing familial interest in a war concluded in 1865. Thousands of Civil War buffs reenact the battles and fanatically adhere to original uniforms and equipment, but their commitment seems to stem more from what some of them call the time-travel high rather than from ideological attachment to the issues fought over. Tony Horwitz's *Confederates in the Attic* makes much of these Southern reenactors of battles, but the North also has its share of battle buffs. The obsession of Southern writers has not entirely vanished, but it will continue to weaken as new sustaining myths and new problems develop; presumably, the same will happen for later generations of writers who have not been raised on bedazzled dreams of rising prosperity and America's ideal nature.

౿ ౿ ౿

In the 1950s, the canon for American literature was primarily white and male. Now it has broadened to the point that the syllabus for a course in contemporary American fiction has rather few items by such authors. To my mind, the enlargement of the canon is wonderfully enriching and energizing, but while broadening the field, we have created regrettably rigid subcategories.[4] By not organizing the chapters of this study around ethnic and gender issues, I have tried to show that all the novels considered here (radically diverse in many ways) share important common ground. Their concerns and techniques mark them as part of a generation. A great many authors in the last thirty to forty years have written about their sense that this country is failing its citizens. Classroom practice and marketing strategies have divided the novels into categories in a fashion that reduces the visibility of common concerns. The ethnic and gender contexts are vital but are not the only ones possible or worth discussing. By pulling the novels together and letting the texts talk to each other across those conventional borders, I have tried to dismantle barriers and the blinkered thought that they produce. For instance, courses in contemporary literature (and scholarly articles) tend to read a book by a Native American author as a Native American text and compare it to other Native American texts. Louise Erdrich is compared to Leslie Marmon Silko, Silko is compared to N. Scott

Momaday. Gerald Vizenor causes much shaking of heads because his work is unlike that of other Native American novelists. However, we can also read these Native American books as American fiction, as sharing a set of problems and outlooks. Vizenor's *Bearheart* might be read against Max Apple's *Propheteers* or Ishmael Reed's *Yellow Back Radio Broke-Down* or even Vonnegut's *Sirens of Titan.* All achieve eerie shock effects through zany unpredictability, black humor, grotesquerie, and a spacey sense of motion. In Reed's novel, we even find another shaman to compare to Vizenor's. One might match Tim O'Brien's *Things They Carried* with Gloria Naylor's *Women of Brewster Place* rather than just refer it to Mailer's *Naked and the Dead* or other war fiction. Such a comparison would bring out the ways in which Naylor's African-American women are on a sort of front line and point to the differences between male and female bonding. Naylor's *Linden Hills* contrasts handsomely in the classroom with *The Dean's December* by Bellow: they share a subtext of Dante's *Inferno,* and both present arguments over the nature of civilized and nurturing life. All these novels share territory, a fact that does not communicate itself well when they are segregated into ethnic contexts. Even books not openly critical of the country reflect the failure of the American Dream in their handling of the themes of love, children, jobs, and success. The most fantastic space opera may be asking questions about failures in current American patterns of marriage and community by projecting them onto the future. Books published since 1960 have much to say to each other.

No matter what political backgrounds writers come from, many of them show concern for community and the support systems possible in a neighborhood. One can no longer better one's conditions by heading west. Indeed, given water shortages in the Southwest, northerners are creating serious problems by migrating to the Sunbelt to escape decaying northern cities. Instead, these authors argue, we must improve the social context where we live now, however unappealing it looks at present. If these writers are to be believed, we *want* group values, and we *want* to share group belief. Part of this drive may be pure nostalgia; but in the political arena, we are so driven to create that conformity that we are losing all tolerance for dissent, as one can see on issues like abortion. What politics, public morality, and education offer now seems unsatisfactory to most interest groups. Where writers differ from politicians is that some of them are telling middle-class readers that the well-to-do, and not just the welfare cheat or the child abuser, are socially dysfunctional when it comes to contributing to a local community. They are not what they have thought they were, and the golden future based on individualist economic ambition is a delusion for most dreamers of that dream. The novelistic result is distress, confusion, dismay, and uncertainty as to where we—individually or nationally—go from here. Politicians still promise to restore the American Dream, and voters may wish to believe politicians' rhetoric, but a broad spectrum of novelists—apparently agreeing with Vonnegut that they are canaries in a coal mine—warn us not to expect improvement from above. Very often, these authors do not appear to be consciously making such a political pronouncement. However, their urging us to model our expectations in some other fashion seems to be a major implication that emerges from the emotional core of these books.

Many writers feel anger and helplessness at the death of a myth that has sustained several generations. Much of the idealism may never have been plausible or logical, but that does not mean that Americans were not deeply influenced by its assumptions. Reasonable or not, they find their disappointment devastating. New sustaining myths have not yet manifested themselves, except insofar as reconstructing or maintaining an ethnic identity apart from the mainstream is becoming such a myth, complete with belief in sustaining ethnic social structures. How can we make ourselves forget the congeries of assumptions that made up the American Dream so that something new may take its place? How can we escape the American Dream's siren song of plenty, its ego-stroking belief in exceptionalism, and even the mission it gave America as the challenger of the Soviet empire? And how can we assure ourselves that what emerges is worthy of our best aspirations?[5] Given the totalitarian assumptions that govern most utopias and the grassroots fascism and militias springing up in real life, the feel-good claims of improved community are not necessarily innocent.

The First World War was a turning point for Western culture, and writers exposed to its unassimilable horrors became the Lost Generation. The current generation of American writers—from 1960 into the 1990s—can usefully be characterized as the Generation of the Lost Dream. A great deal—though not all—of what they write expresses acute distress at the failure of a vision and a sense of future. As regards this country, their fiction offers no answers. Indeed, what characterizes their novels is the honesty with which the writers acknowledge that they intuit no grand answers, no replacement for the lost vision. Rather frighteningly, the utopian fantasists insist narratively that America must be destroyed before anything better can be created. What intensifies this writerly generation's frustration is a sense of helplessness. Their imaginative faculties provide no inkling of where we might look for solutions. Some retain hopes for local community, but most of the writers in this generation no longer feel that they can dream for the whole nation.

Notes

Introduction

1. Chénetier, *Beyond Suspicion*, 48.

2. See this and other invocations or denials of the American Dream in the introduction to Madden's *American Dreams* (xv). For discussion of the ways the Dream has changed over time, see Wilson, *After Affluence*, 139–42. For analyses of the American Dream and its component strands, see Fossum and Roth, *American Dream*; Hearn, *American Dream*; Parrington, *American Dreams*; essays by Busby and Mogen in Mogen et al., *Frontier Experience*; and Sugiura, "Collapse." The term gained its currency rather late in America's history. Adams is credited with popularizing it in 1931 in *Epic of America*. However, the idea was present long before. According to Fossum and Roth (*American Dream* 5), Hugh Swinton Legaré made a famous early formulation of the American Dream in 1823.

3. Schaub, *American Fiction*, 4, 137.

4. Henriksen locates the start of the critical attitude toward America during the 1950s in *Dr. Strangelove's America*. However, her descriptions reveal that any subversiveness or criticism is contained and largely negated by happy, upbeat, and patriotic endings. The impetus for criticizing the country that she traces comes from America's use of the atomic bomb.

5. For the parallel losses of moral certainty in Europe and America, see Friedman and Squire, *Morality USA*, 45–46. Their analysis is partly based on that in West, *American Evasion*, 235–39.

6. For fantasy as the repressed side of bourgeois literature, see Jackson, *Fantasy*; for science fiction, see Suvin, *Metamorphoses*.

Chapter 1: The Shocks of Transplantation

1. I look at these immigration novels for their critiques of America rather than for their ethnic traditions. For discussion of specific traditions, see Paredes, "Evolution of Chicano Literature"; Guttmann, *Jewish Writer*; Kim, *Asian American Literature*; Lim and Ling, *Reading the Literatures* (on various Asian

immigrant traditions); and Skårdal, *Divided Heart* (on the Scandinavian experience), as well as books that deal with several traditions, such as Ferraro, *Ethnic Passages*. This is a highly selective list, and much that concerns specifically female immigrant novels is discussed in feminist collections.

2. The three-generations-to-assimilation model of immigration was propounded in 1933 and popularized in 1951 by Handlin in *The Uprooted*. Sollors discusses the evolution and adequacy of the paradigm in *Beyond Ethnicity* (208–36). In the twentieth century, assimilation as ideal has given way to the conscious cultivation of ethnicity. The melting pot metaphor was declared inadequate in Glazer and Moynihan's *Beyond the Melting Pot* and has made way for the image of the salad bowl, mixed but separate (see D'Innocenzo and Sirefman, *Immigration and Ethnicity*). For familial and autobiographical accounts of "the anguish of becoming American" by a variety of well-known writers, see Wheeler, *Immigrant Experience*.

3. Reilly stresses the need to remember the literariness of ethnic fiction in "Criticism of Ethnic Literature."

4. Schueller's "Theorizing Ethnicity" analyzes the ways in which the mothers are right and talks about the complicated currents that result from one daughter's atonement with her dead mother when meeting the mother's two Chinese daughters. In "Generational Differences," Shear differentiates helpfully among the Chinese narrators. Xu challenges Tan's belief that the mothers' histories can help the daughters in "Memory and the Ethnic Self," which foregrounds ways in which identity construction necessarily happens differently for those who come from China and those who do not.

5. My analysis of *China Men* was written before I read Goellnicht's "Tang Ao in America." Given that he sees everything about gender that I saw and more, I would have dropped this novel from the chapter were there another that covered the territory as well. In *Donald Duk*, Chin takes up the issue of American cultural diminution of Chinese masculinity but in a less complex way than Kingston's indictment of both Chinese and American patterns. Other views of Kingston's challenges to Chinese and American gender constructions include Rabine's "No Lost Paradise" and Fichtelberg's "Poet and Patriarch."

6. Li's *"China Men"* and Wu's "Chinese Reader's Response" give us illuminating background materials for understanding Kingston's use of the Tang Ao story and her use of other Chinese or Western tales that have made their way into Chinese consciousness. In "Exile and Intertextuality," Shih discusses Kingston's variations on the Chinese attitudes to exile.

7. Butler's choice of heroine clashed with white marketing pressures. Publishers refused to show a black woman on the cover, so one early edition shows a purple woman, and the standard paperback used in universities today displays Lilith as a dark-haired, porcelain-skinned, Irish-looking beauty.

8. In "Erotics of Becoming," White argues that the Oankali consume difference with "a death-driven desire to totalize within themselves the sum biotic

potential of the universe" (405). He sees their consensus as something more like enforced uniformity. In "'There Goes the Neighborhood,'" Green calls the trilogy a "scathing condemnation of the tendency of human beings to hate, repress, and attack differences they do not understand" (166). In *Simians, Cyborgs, and Women,* Haraway stresses the mythic component in a chapter titled "The Biopolitics of Postmodern Bodies." Lilith rather than Eve is first mother to the race, and "these humanoid serpent people speak to the woman and urge her to touch them in an intimacy that would lead humanity to a monstrous metamorphosis. Multiply stripped, Lilith fights for survival, agency, and choice on the shifting boundaries that shape the possibility of meaning" (227).

9. In "'We Murder Who We Were,'" Carter-Sanborn notes the fable classification (583) and also sets up an interesting contrast with *Jane Eyre,* a novel mentioned early in *Jasmine,* in which Jane's care-giver's role toward a maimed husband is a glamorized version of what Jasmine refuses to take on. Wickramagamage's "Relocation as Positive Act" relates Jasmine's metamorphoses to Hindu attitudes toward the self.

10. Quoted in Carter-Sanborn, "'We Murder Who We Were,'" 573.

Chapter 2: Mythical Innocence

1. Lewis has analyzed the Euro-American archetype in *The American Adam,* and Noble adds more recent authors to the canonical list in *The Eternal Adam.* Jones (*O Strange New World*) and Marx (*Machine in the Garden*) discuss some of the uses to which paradisal images are put in white America's system of myths. Hassan's *Radical Innocence* takes up transformations undergone by the American Adam in modern literature. Karl's *American Fictions* identifies the presence of a related theme, the pastoral, in a wide range of recent fiction by authors like Cheever, Morris, Gass, Matthiessen, Kesey, Gardner, and most novels featuring baseball.

2. In "Ray Bradbury's *Dandelion Wine,*" Mengeling insists that the novel is not nostalgic. I disagree but admit that Bradbury was aware of the dangerous power of that idealized image of the small town, which telepathic Martians use to lure humans to their deaths in *The Martian Chronicles.*

3. In *Tar Baby,* Morrison declares Valerian Street to be "guilty . . . of innocence" and continues, "An innocent man is a sin before God. Inhuman and therefore unworthy" (243). For Morrison's emphasis on community existence rather than romantic (white) individualism, see Rubenstein's chapter on Morrison in *Boundaries of the Self.* For the forces that combine to destroy authentic black self-image, see Kuenz, *"Bluest Eye"*; and Willis, "I Shop."

4. All of Morrison's novels focus on historical cusps of black history. These women left their southern homes to migrate to more northerly cities in the 1940s. For a tally of these cusps, see Willis, "Eruptions of Funk."

5. Harding and Martin offer an elaborate reading of this passage in "Reading

at the Cultural Interface."

6. As Whalen-Bridge points out in *Political Fiction*, "this victim position has had great power in generating what might be called 'relative innocence,' . . . even when that character does something awful" (132).

7. The ghost is more than the dead child; she also represents someone who endured the Middle Passage. For discussions of these and further elaborations on the meaning of *Beloved*, see Osagie, "Is Morrison Also"; Broad, "Giving Blood"; Mathieson, "Memory and Mother Love"; and Jessee, "'Tell me your earrings.'"

8. My concern with innocence dictates this particular reading. Obviously, many other emphases are possible within this complexly plotted and mysterious novel. For a sense of how this novel resonates with other major works in the American tradition (each such comparison yielding a somewhat different reading), see Askeland, "Remodeling"; Lewis, "Ironic Romance"; Mayer, "'You Like Huckleberries?'"; Moreland, "'He Wants to Put His Story Next to Hers'"; and Woidat, "Talking Back." Phelan uses the multiplicitous nature of the novel to illustrate problems with standard academic interpretation in "Toward a Rhetorical Reader-Response Criticism."

9. White feminist readers tend to admire Pilate extravagantly for her ability to go her own way—indeed, for a kind of rugged individualism. However, Bakerman points out in "Failures of Love" that Pilate's female initiation is a partial failure and that the life she leads as a bootlegger is marginal to the community in ways that Morrison does not consider desirable or healthy.

10. In "The Ornamentations of Old Ideas," Saunders emphasizes the degree to which the novel is a dialogue with the dead.

11. George is sympathetically portrayed but apparently is more attractive to Euro-American than to African-American readers. His daydreams of self as romantic hero rather than member of a community help to explain why he does not survive in a female-patterned world of magic. For an extremely convincing analysis of the clash between white and black values in the novel, see Meisenhelder, "'Whole Picture.'" Likewise, and in her own terms, Cocoa appeals more to black than to white readers. Naylor analyzes styles of female sexuality in "Love and Sex." For a similar view of George as embodying white and masculinist values, but with the addendum that Cocoa also has too many white values to find authenticity easily, see Warren, "Cocoa and George."

12. Traub's "Rainbows of Darkness" tries to make sense of Naylor's very problematic use of Miranda (a sorceress), a tempest, and a character named Ophelia. The significance of these invocations to Shakespeare is never as clear as those to Dante in *Linden Hills*. Having taught *Mama Day* and *The Tempest* together, I can attest that what emerged was the overwhelmingly male construction of magic and hierarchy in the Renaissance text, whereas the modern is just as passionately female in kinds of magic and the relative lack of hierarchy.

13. Not much has been written on *Original Sins*, but in "Lisa Alther," Ferguson calls the novel postmodern for its presentation of competing visions of reality, and she stresses its grim hopelessness, downplaying its humor.

14. A film like *Rambo: First Blood, Part II* (1985) ignores the morality of Americans being in Vietnam to begin with and upholds the rights of soldiers to be thanked by their country for what they suffered. This Conan-with-helicopters sort of hunk heroism does not lend itself to moral thought but does insist on individual innocence as possible. Within the frame of the film, Rambo is meant to seem justified in killing so many people with bullets, fire, arrows, and explosions. Any blame belongs to politicians who betrayed soldiers.

15. Sexuality and gender roles do not operate only as markers of innocence. Smith's "'The Things Men Do'" talks about the masculine rituals of homosocial bonding and the patriarchal assumptions in the novel.

16. This reworking of *Heart of Darkness* differs from *Apocalypse Now* in its more innocent tone. The girl falls for the excitement of the hunt, whereas Coppola's Kurtz goes off because he despises the idiocy of the army and wants a free hand to do the fighting and killing thoroughly, to win by any means.

17. Some of the redemptive powers of storytelling in O'Brien's work are discussed by Bonn in "Can Stories Save Us?"

18. He seems to have been as traumatized by this as were Steve and Nick in *The Deer Hunter* when they were forced to play Russian roulette. Nick indeed is so horrified by all he has seen and done that he feels he cannot go home, and he keeps testing himself against that roulette experience (and seeking death) by continuing to face the roulette bullet for money.

19. "*Invisible Man* and the Comic Tradition" by Andreas analyzes a great deal of the novel's humor, treating the material as universal rather than color-coded, which Ellison might have preferred, given his own denial of black influences. Rovit relates the humor to Emerson and Melville in "Ralph Ellison." Lyne provides a good analysis of laughter and Ellison's many "signifying critiques of nineteenth-century canonical American authors like Melville, Emerson, and Twain or of African American figures like Booker T. Washington and Wright" ("Signifying Modernist" 321). In *Visible Ellison*, Schor discusses the fashion in which readers can laugh, but the Invisible Man cannot until he has gone underground and gained perspective on himself (71–72).

20. O'Meally presents an overview of Ellison criticism in his introduction to *New Essays on "Invisible Man"* (1–23). In "The Conscious Hero," John Wright focuses on the mythic structures of the novel. For the rhetorical and narrative structures, see Smith, "Meaning of Narration"; Austin Wright, *Formal Principle*. Moses ("Novel"), Lee ("Ellison's *Invisible Man*"), and Schaub ("Ellison's Masks") identify precursor texts. For politics, see the chapter on Ellison in Schaub, *American Fiction*. O'Meally analyzes folk materials in *The Craft of Ralph Ellison*, as does Kent in "Ralph Ellison." Nadel provides a fine in-depth study in *Invisible Criticism*.

21. Martin's *"Invisible Man"* points out that early criticism tended to assume that the narrator's innocence merely makes him a victim and is not something for which he should be deemed culpable.

22. In "Roadblocks and Relatives," Awkward offers a feminist analysis of the Trueblood episode that challenges the masculinist values I have just described. Among other things, Trueblood drives away the rest of the community, thus isolating himself and his family from community support or censure. He turns his experience into a commercially valuable commodity, telling the story for support, and feels good about the way he is better off now than ever before—despite the fact that his wife and daughter will not speak to him. Awkward sees Pecola's rape by her father in *The Bluest Eye* as a feminist revision of *Invisible Man*'s depiction of incest.

23. In "'What Marvelous Plot,'" Holder congratulates Barth for choosing that portion of the colonies that are less well known than any other and less mythologized. Maryland was, in fact, sexually very different from other colonies. In *Intimate Matters*, D'Emilio and Freedman point out that men outnumbered women four to one in the Chesapeake (9–14). As a result, "single women may have been less concerned about guarding their virginity than women in England or the Puritan settlements. Even women who bore illegitimate children might marry respectably in this region" (11). Among the lawsuits they cite to illustrate sexual mores is one against Captain William Mitchell, "an influential Marylander who served on the governor's council [and] not only impregnated Mrs. Susan Warren and gave her a 'physic' to abort the child, but . . . also 'lived in fornication' with his pretended wife, Joan Toaste" (12).

24. Dippie discusses the Indian elements in this revision of history in "'His Visage Wild.'"

25. In *History and the Contemporary Novel*, Cowart offers an excellent reading of the novel in terms of history, and he also has interesting things to say about innocence (53–75).

26. Tharpe's *John Barth* makes the point that "perhaps the most unpleasant conclusion of the action is that nothing is accomplished when Ebenezer becomes aware. His life is done; whatever his accomplishment, it was made in his ignorance, in the process of getting whatever knowledge he acquired. The end is anonymity—neither responsibility nor contribution" (45).

Chapter 3: Yearning for Lost Civilization

1. Such a stance characterizes Bloom's *Closing of the American Mind* and garnered much appreciation from readers distressed by the aimlessness of much higher education. In *Cultural Literacy*, Hirsch also upheld the centrality of Western civilization to what the educated person should know.

2. See Weatherford's *Indian Givers* and *Native Roots* for discussions of Native American agricultural experimentation.

3. For details of Welch's biography and reference to his library sources, see

Welch et al., "Conversation with James Welch." Sands analyzes Welch's uses of local landscape in "Closing the Distance"; Westrum uses Welch's historical novel to help explain Welch's other novels in "James Welch's *Fools Crow*."

4. In "Dialogue with James Welch," Bevis notes that "the way Europeans have separated themselves from animals and nature is exotic to most of the world" (181).

5. Ranching is a fact of life for current Native Americans in Montana, as Bovey ("Whitehorns and Blackhorns") makes plain, and Welch does not wallow in nostalgia for the days before the European arrivals.

6. Welch does not draw solely on anthropology. To find language that would let him cross borders of reality easily, Welch found some inspiration in Latin American writers and in Vittorini's *Conversations in Sicily*. See Bevis, "Dialogue with James Welch," for such literary influences. In "Quaternity," Berner discusses the Native American symbolism defining Welch's world in *Fools Crow*. Nora Barry notes in "'A Myth to Be Alive'" the way in which the Feather Woman episode helps transform the problem from a personal and local situation to a cosmic level that is beyond individual responsibility.

7. In Bevis ("Dialogue with James Welch"), Welch discusses the American Indian pattern of clamming up and being stone-faced around whites but behaving differently among themselves: "It's incredible to be in a roomful of Indians. The stories and, as you said, the wit is incredible. They just are very quick minds. When I'm in a room with Indians I'm just laughing constantly. It's just one witty word-play joke after another. They're very verbal" (168). For a discussion of the various fashions of portraying the Indian as noble, savage, victim of massacre, and dying, see Truettner, *West as America*.

8. In "The Holocaust," Kremer analyzes the insane behaviors as the ravages of Holocaust experience on survivors.

9. In *"The Dean's December,"* Goldman also points out that Sammler is an eastern European Jew viewing America while Corde is a Protestant American viewing eastern Europe.

10. Minna's doubts are easy to overlook, given the basically favorable portrait of Corde, but in "Bellow and Nihilism," Judie Newman teases out all the references to Corde as a womanizer, to the way in which "debased images of murder and of love as low sexuality pollute Corde's higher feelings" (114). Corde's period of visiting red-light areas of Chicago with Maxie Detillion may justify uneasiness.

11. In "Bellow's Dire Prophecy," Chavkin and Chavkin analyze this underclass and Bellow's portrayal of it in *The Dean's December*. They rely on Glasgow's *Black Underclass* for definitions of this new phenomenon.

12. In "Communication," Weinstein analyzes the problem with language as the media having so infected people with dead categories of intellect and words that they can no longer deal with social problems or even personal communication. Cronin's "Through a Glass Brightly" sees the problem more generally

as Corde being Bellow's tool for resolving the dichotomy between "empirical and mystical modes of apprehension" (25).

13. In "Living Your Own Experience," Booth interprets the gendering of this novel in terms of Corde's own psychology. By writing in a fashion that draws on feeling, Corde has disqualified himself from the Western male pattern, and the novel concludes with his blending "traditional male and female characteristics, not to achieve a non-gendered being, but to construct a whole being" (15). Nilsen's "New Kind of Male-Female Relationship" interprets the shift in simpler terms, seeing the Bellow hero becoming less misogynistic and more sensitive to women. Kiernan, however, feels that Corde shows "a philanderer's contempt for women" (*Saul Bellow* 181).

14. Miller argues that the inner city images in *The Dean's December* actually represent mainly "Bellow's heart, his spirit, his soul." She goes on: "To miss this dimension of the novel is to miss the insight Bellow offers on Bellow, for what he thinks of his wife and family, his friends and fellow writers, his own career and his art, is as important as Bellow's attitude toward Chicago and the United States and Russia, toward society and politics and science and history and culture" (*Saul Bellow* 270).

15. Bellow's portrayal of an Eastern Bloc country has been challenged. Igor Maver of Ljubljana sees this rendition of Bucharest as grotesque, filtered through Kafka. In "The Delicate Balance of Tension," he writes, "It is by far exaggerated, which shows that Corde, or for that matter also Bellow, does not have a clue about what is going on there" (110). In *"The Dean's December,"* Levine relates Bellow's portrait of the city to several accounts of Communist Bloc cities by both Eastern and American writers. Bach agrees that *The Dean's December* somewhat resembles *The Spy Who Came in from the Cold* in its vision of communist areas. However, Bach insists that the Eastern material mostly exists to comment on the failure of America and that the novel is really a "running commentary on the present state of America, its cultural disorientation and tortured, smug pharisaical *Selbstbild*" ("Dean" 105).

16. In *"The Dean's December,"* Hall sees the options offered for organizing life as the old Rumanian way—Macedonian, Roman, Eastern—as being based on concepts of justice and loyalty; the Darwinian jungle warfare of Zaehner; and the science of Minna.

17. Despite the fallen state of his protagonist, Percy has been credited with a wide range of theological interests. See Brooks ("Walker Percy") on Gnosticism; Lawson ("Tom More: Cartesian Physician") on Gnosticism, Harvey Cox, and Jacques Maritain; Eubanks ("Walker Percy") on Grace; Hayward ("Walker Percy's Vision") on spiritual death and Percy as prophet; Hughes ("Walker Percy's Comedy") on salvific comedy; Kennedy ("Sundered Self") on all forms of schism and dividedness; LeClair ("Walker Percy's Devil"); and Luschei (*Sovereign Wayfarer*) on "why does humanism lead to beastliness?" (170).

18. In *The Fiction of Walker Percy,* Hardy argues that the novels are prima-

rily satires, so More's analysis here is being satirized; instead of the particular inhumanity of slavery, America has failed to the extent that people of any race, gender, ethnic group, or the like are inhumane to those of other groups.

19. Johnson's "Virgin and the Cooling Tower" declares that Tom represents "the familiar, liberal humanistic line" (24).

20. In *Walker Percy*, Allen argues that More, like Quentin Compson, is torn between identifying with his father (in More's case, a drunk and suicide) and rejecting that father and the southern heritage. As Allen traces the mental maneuvers, More manages to reject his bad father (Art Immelmann) by invoking his good father, Sir Thomas More (88–89).

21. Lawson ("Tom More and Sigmund Freud") identifies Moira as goddess of rotation and More as Don Giovanni, wanting to know women through many women; Lola is goddess of nostalgia (aesthetic repetition) and makes More feel like Faust, learning women through one exhaustively.

22. Godshalk argues in *"Love in the Ruins"* that More is highly unreliable as a narrator, far more so than the example of the vines suggests. Godshalk teases out numerous inconsistencies and falsities and sees them as part of the very heavy satire on More. By contrast, Hardy notes other instances of contradictory details in *The Fiction of Walker Percy* but interprets them as forgetfulness or carelessness on Percy's part.

23. Gottfried and Fleming, *Conservative Movement*, 95.

24. In "Donald Barthelme's *Snow White*," Morace focuses on this problem of surrendering to contemporary culture or criticizing it, and he summarizes other critics on the point. Larry McCaffery ("Donald Barthelme") and Jonathan Culler ("Junk and Rubbish") deal with trash theory.

25. On the relationship between the novel and the fairy tale, see Gilman, "Barthelme's Fairy Tale."

26. In "Neo-HooDoo," Schmitz elucidates this text in terms of its signifying on *Invisible Man*; Fabre deals with the excremental vision in "Ishmael Reed's *Freelance Pallbearers*"; and La Polla analyzes its multilevel attack on the classical bourgeois novel in *"The Free-Lance Pallbearers."* (Note that the American edition of Reed's book and the cover of the British edition use "Free-lance" but the title page and spine of the British edition omit the hyphen. I follow American usage and retain the hyphen throughout the text.)

27. Emphasis on the Arthurian material is only one avenue of approach to this novel. In "The Gods Must Be Angry," Harris discusses Reed's concern with spirituality and the ability to respond to the unseen as well as the seen. Weixlmann elaborates on the Poe subtext in both "Politics" and "Ishmael Reed's Raven" and discusses Reed's sense that a people's culture is its most valuable spiritual capital and is not to be exploited by others. Rushdy's "Ishmael Reed's Neo-HooDoo Slave Narrative" sees the entire novel as generated by Reed's "Neo-HooDoo" aesthetic. In "'Riding Bareback,'" Schöpp reads it against the background of the fugitive slave narrative.

28. Anaya uses this myth to essentialize Anglo culture in his essay "An American Chicano in King Arthur's Court." He is more willing than Reed to enjoy the Arthurian tales, as long as Anglos are willing to learn about Spanish and Indian tales in exchange.

29. For a serious historical analysis of the antebellum South and its relationship to various medieval models, see Genovese, "Southern Slaveholders' View."

Chapter 4: Seeking Spiritual Reality

1. Chase's *American Novel* establishes the importance of this nonrealistic strain in the American literary imagination. In "A Theory of Genre," Post analyzes the definitions of realism and romance offered by Perry Miller, F. O. Matthiessen, Terrence Martin, Joel Porte, Daniel Hoffman, and Nicolaus Mills; Post argues that romance seeks to articulate what he calls moral reality. In "The Melodramatic Imagination," Brooks analyzes this tradition as that melodramatic mindset in search of the moral occult.

2. Allen expounds the positive qualities of the decision from an Indian point of view in *The Sacred Hoop* (144–46). Bevis, in "Native American Novels," also points to such twofold interpretations. Similarly, Ruppert (in "Mediation and Multiple Narrative in Contemporary Native American Fiction") argues that, read on a psychological level, Momaday's Abel is a failure; read on a ceremonial or other Indian level, though, the interpretation would have to be different.

3. In "Momaday, Welch, and Silko," Antell argues that these authors create functionally motherless heroes to embody alienation from Indian identity; as Allen argues in *The Sacred Hoop*, one's mother locates one in Indian cultures. Mothers are also the conveyors of cultural knowledge.

4. In "The Killing," Evers gives the Anglo newspaper account and then looks at three similar fictional murders, some of which involve an element of witchery. Abel's murder of the albino is one; the other two examples are stories by Silko and Ortiz.

5. For the Native American male bildungsroman pattern, which relies on this return to the old ways, see Bevis, "Native American Novels." For the positive functions of landscape in this novel, see Nelson, *Place and Vision*; and for material on Native American attitudes toward medicine, see Scarberry-García, *Landmarks of Healing*.

6. For an analysis of some of these folk traditions as they fed into the development of Mormonism, see Brooke, *Refiner's Fire*.

7. In "'Middling, Hidden, Troubled America,'" Campbell focuses on Rabbit's typicality and supplies useful historical context and relevant theories of American individualism. A different view of individualism in these novels is offered in Wilson, "Rabbit Tetralogy." Mazurek ("'Bringing the Corners Forward'") dislikes Rabbit and Updike for seeing as natural a view of social troubles that is contingent and historical, so he berates their lack of deliberate and leftist

theorizing. A similarly hostile view of Rabbit and Updike is supplied by Clausen ("Native Fathers"), who contrasts *Rabbit at Rest* with John Edgar Wideman's *Philadelphia Fire* as both showing deadbeats; however, Clausen views Updike as doing so in a fashion that does not show the suffering caused by Rabbit's behavior. Olster's "Rabbit Rerun" and "Rabbit Is Redundant" supply a great deal of useful context on the economic state of America and on popular culture as those phenomena saturate the novels. Ristoff discusses Updike's use of American history in *Updike's America*; Hicks focuses on Updike's sense of morality in "Updike's Rabbit Novels"; and Horvath ("Failure") shows how Rabbit's erotic questing follows the shifts in popular culture's views on love.

8. The elaborate equation between the women Rabbit has sex with and death or nothingness is well analyzed by Mazurek in "'Bringing the Corners Forward.'" For the transcendent elements, and for the interplay of religion, sport, and sex, see Wright, "Mapless Motion."

9. In "From Babbit to Rabbit," Porter outlines the many parallels between these two—intentional, since Babbit is invoked in an epigraph—and also the intertextual relationship to Willy Loman.

10. Sanders analyzes the magic in "Southwestern Gothic" as follows: "Because her power is not coercive, Ultima cannot triumph over Tenorio; she can only thwart his evil acts and hope that he will stop trying to control destiny. But he insists on pursuing her. Ultima can cancel Tenorio's evil only in an equation that balances her fate with his: they must both die" (45).

11. In "The 'Horror of Darkness'" and "The Quest," Lattin insists that Antonio is rejecting Christianity and accepting the Indian metaphysic as his religion. Less extreme interpretations and analyses are offered by Lamadrid ("Myth" and "Dynamics of Myth") and Tonn (*"Bless Me, Ultima"*).

12. Liam Kennedy rejects the term magic realist in "Memory and Hearsay" except insofar as it signifies "interactions of realism and romance, and of historical and mythical vision" (79). In addition to magic realism, I would note the postmodern gesture of moving off-center. As Hutcheon puts it, we see such authors contesting the "centralization of culture through the valuing of the local and peripheral: not New York . . . but William Kennedy's Albany" (*Poetics* 61).

13. Walter Benjamin calls an aura the persistence of the sacred into the secularized world and says that auratic intensity is driven out of that world by machines and technology. Jameson summarizes Benjamin's scattered references to aura in *Marxism and Form*, 76–77.

14. Rosenberg traces the very Arthurian popular belief that John F. Kennedy had been spirited away to some hidden place, frequently an island, where he would recuperate and return when his country needed him ("Kennedy in Camelot" 57).

15. The multitude of Homeric and Joycean references in *Ironweed* and *Billy Phelan's Greatest Game* are expounded by Tierce in "William Kennedy's

Odyssey." In "Francis Phelan," Novelli points out many parallels between Francis and Heracles.

16. Taylor creates an elaborate argument that Francis Phelan, in his travels to the land of the dead, is a shaman. She notes that the novels give "a picture of a Celtic, male, tribal group, whose lives, violent and vengeful, are governed by a code of shame, and whose laws are self-generated. . . . Pride in the magical power of the dominant male pervades the trilogy. . . . Women appear as goddesses, often in triplicate . . . as in the threesome of Katrina/Annie/mother in *Ironweed*" ("*Ironweed*, Alcohol, and Celtic Heroism" 114).

17. One difference between the film *Ironweed* (1987) and the novel is this issue of ghosts and magic. The visible ghosts appear on-screen, all too obviously material actors, while the nonvisible ghosts belonging to this sensed dimension of life are not even attempted on-screen. Francis merely talks to the headstone; the gruesome and grotesque specificity of his mother's eating bitter dandelion roots is entirely absent. As Giamo points out in "*Ironweed* and the Snows of Reduction," what gets lost is the magic.

18. Murtaugh explicates the strange tone of the ending as follows: "Everything that really happens is conveyed to us in conditional verbs. Everything that is merely a dream is conveyed with indicative verbs. What really happens is that Francis hops a freight out of town" ("Fathers and Their Sons" 302). The comments about Danny's room are only wishful might-have-beens.

19. The cultural move to privatize morality is analyzed by Friedman and Squire in *Morality USA*.

20. Wenke's *Mailer's America* details Mailer's attempts to come to terms with the American Dream.

21. In "Existential Aesthetics," Adams quotes Mailer describing his experience with Rojack's type of magical thought projections.

22. Gerson has explicated Mailer's theology and its relationship to Sabbatian mysticism in "An American Dream"; in "Norman Mailer," she deals with his overall concepts of creativity and bravery. Finholt explores Mailer's metaphysic in *American Visionary Fiction* but ties it more to the Elizabethan great chain of being than to Jewish traditions. Bernstein ("Heart of the Nation") relates Mailer's values to those of the Puritans as well as to the Jewish tradition.

23. Mailer makes this argument in "The White Negro." For discussions of Mailer's metaphysic, particularly as it relates to his views of America, see Wenke.

24. This unrealistically meteoric rise through academic ranks was partly dictated by revisions made to the serial version of the text in *Esquire* when it was brought out in the Dial edition. Just as Mailer launched the first installment, Kennedy was assassinated, which necessitated changing the whole Kennedy element in the novel and resetting the scenario some months earlier than planned originally, since Kennedy is still alive in the novel. For analysis of this time shift and other modifications, see Parker, *Flawed Texts*.

25. In "Pynchon's Angels," McLaughlin links such beings to the earthly hierarchy of "Them" as the next step higher; in "'Beasts Vaulting,'" Caesar looks at the variety of monstrous entities looming above Pynchon's world.

26. See Hume, "Views from Above."

Chapter 5: The Fragility of Democracy

1. For American paranoia, see Hofstadter, *Paranoid Style*; Pinsker, "America's Conspiratorial Imagination"; and Fulcher, "American Conspiracy."

2. In *War Stars*, Franklin lists as feared invaders Britain, Spain, China, Japan, Czarist Russia, Germany, France, Italy, Mexico, and Africa. His second chapter is devoted to these "Fantasies of War: 1880–1917."

3. Vankin's *Conspiracies, Cover-Ups and Crimes* analyzes these groups. This conspiratorial mindset is not an exclusively American paranoia. Eco's *Foucault's Pendulum* shows us a highly intellectual and philosophically humorous European version of such a mania focused on the Knights Templars, the Masons, and the Kabbalah (to mention only three of the novel's interlocking sources of secret power).

4. In *Postmodernist Allegories*, Madsen writes about Pynchon but does not deal with historical referents of this sort in her discussion of *Crying of Lot 49*.

5. My emphasizing the similarities to the world of the Kennedy conspiracy is not meant to deny broader interpretations. In "Decoding the Trystero," Kermode sees Oedipa's effort to interpret conspiracies as a reflection on hermeneutic problems in general. O'Donnell ("Engendering Paranoia") treats the conspiratorial air as part of a larger cultural phenomenon and looks at other examples from Mailer, DeLillo, and McElroy. More specific readings include those of Mendelson ("The Sacred, the Profane") and Nohrnberg ("Pynchon's Paraclete"), which look at the quest as a religious search for transcendent meaning, and Hite (*Ideas of Order*), who stresses the escape from commodified life to true humanity. In "The Romance of the '60s," Farrell considers Oedipa as working through paradigms of self versus community, and in "Existential Subjectivity," Tyson offers a Lacanian reading of Oedipa's quest. Gleason shows the multiplication of mazes in "The Postmodern Labyrinths."

6. Issues aside from guilt or innocence are taken up in the novel. In "Genealogy/Narrative/Power," Reed sees the book as a study of "the fifties and the sixties, in particular between two generations of radicals, the Old and the New Left" (289). Cooper's "Cutting Both Ways" labels the book Doctorow's critique of the left.

7. Lorsch ("Doctorow's *The Book of Daniel*") and Estrin ("Surviving McCarthyism") comment at greater length on parallels to the Biblical Daniel.

8. Saltzman discusses the moral and aesthetic dimensions of this uncertainty in "The Aesthetic of Doubt."

9. Harpham argues that in this novel, electricity is the "master principle of narrative" that joins such concepts as desire, production, and resistance. "Con-

ceived in this way, the entire novel—in fact, all novels, all narratives—could be said to be portraits of 'electric currents . . . moving through a field of resistance'" ("E. L. Doctorow" 88). Gross ("Tales of Obscene Power") notes the role of electricity in the Disneyland scene and thus relates its uses to Disneyland's position as a symbol for contemporary American culture. Friedl sees that for Doctorow, metaphysical reality "seems to be inextricably contained in the concept of power and its temporal realization as degradation" ("Power and Degradation" 20).

10. In the interview with DeCurtis, DeLillo says, "If I make an extended argument in the book it's not that the assassination necessarily happened this way. The argument is that this is an interesting way to write fiction about a significant event that happens to have these general contours and these agreed-upon characters" ("'Outsider'" 50). He says later in the same interview, "I think that the book is an exploration of what variations we might take on an actual event rather than an argument that this is what really happened in Dallas" (57). For an overall analysis of the novel, see Keesey, *Don DeLillo.*

11. Quoted by Mott (*"Libra"* 131). Mott calls *Libra* "an investigation of the episteme born in the slow-motion bloodspray of the Zapruder film" (131).

12. Branch represents the writer of realistic novels or traditional histories; he expects cause and effect and wants truth to emerge. See Civello ("Undoing the Naturalistic Novel") on the conspiracy as an open system and Branch's account as a closed system. In *"Libra* and the Assassination," Kronick treats John F. Kennedy's death as a text and gives it a linguistic reading; in "Superlinear Fiction," Johnston focuses on the multiplicity of Oswalds—real, imagined, constructed by him and others.

13. Michael ("Political Paradox") stresses the harsh conditions of Lee's boyhood that can be extracted from Marguerite Oswald's account.

14. Hutcheon analyzes this parody of Dickens's *Christmas Carol* in *A Poetics of Postmodernism* (130–31).

15. Analyses of the Heart of Whiteness in various of Reed's novels are found in Fox, *Conscientious Sorcerers;* Gates, "Ishmael Reed" and "Blackness"; and Schmitz, "Neo-HooDoo."

16. My comments on *The Turner Diaries* were already written when the Oklahoma City bombing took place. I owe the information on the relationship between that bombing and the book to Philip Jenkins of Penn State's history department. The *New York Times* discusses *The Turner Diaries* in the Oklahoma City bombing context on 5 July 1995, A1, A18–19. The nature of the far-right conspiratorial beliefs is analyzed in the *New York Times,* 6 July 1995, 1, B9.

17. Although hostile to the One-World ideal (because that united world might be run by Jews), Macdonald does not seem to fear this emerging all-white world. Other writers from the far right fear the One-World scenario; see presidential

candidate Pat Robertson's *End of the Age* (1995) and John Milius's film *Red Dawn* (1984).

18. Tschachler ("Despotic Reason") still feels that Callenbach's vision is somewhat childish or at least that he makes childhood the ideal state, stressing emotional interactions over reason and argument. Tschachler also calls to our attention the elided totalitarian elements in the vision. In "Ernest Callenbach," he relates the spirit of Ecotopia to the American Revolution and the New Deal and notes that its pastoral mythos is not a return to the past but an attempt to envision a postindustrial future.

19. For an analysis of Heinlein's politics throughout his career, see Franklin (*Robert A. Heinlein*) and Nicholls ("Robert A. Heinlein"). For an interesting comparison between Heinlein's lunar anarchy and that of Ursula Le Guin in *The Dispossessed*, see Williams, "Moons."

20. In "Harlan Ellison and Robert A. Heinlein," Sullivan argues that Heinlein establishes the positive paradigm for humanity's relationships to computers in this novel; I suggest that his killing the computer off, functionally speaking, suggests unease with his own vision.

21. *Vineland* is also a complex critique of popular culture. I do not take up those issues here; for considerations of them, see McHale (*Constructing Postmodernism*), Cowart ("Attenuated Postmodernism"), and Booker ("America and Its Discontents"). Booker notes that one of *Vineland*'s critiques of popular culture involves "its tendency to freeze its consumers in the cultural world of the past, a world which no longer corresponds to the present. Our conceptions of popular culture are thus formed principally in childhood and tend to remain perpetually naive, whereas effective political resistance requires a sense of history that is diametrically opposed to such nostalgic visions of the times of one's own youth" (98). The combination of complicity and critique of popular culture is also well analyzed by Wilde, "Love and Death."

22. Pynchon's use of the left of both 1984 and the 1930s is discussed by Solomon ("Argument by Anachronism") and Pittman ("'Dangerously Absent Dreamers'").

23. Pynchon's treatment of adoration of those in uniform is analyzed in Freudian terms by Booker in "America and Its Discontents." He does not note Pynchon's previous engagement with a related concern in *The Crying of Lot 49*. He does look at other novelists' hopes that sexual rebellion might have political consequences (e.g., *1984*) and argues that such a hope by the sexually liberated is false.

24. In analyzing what Pynchon does with the media in *Vineland*, Slade points out that "Ronald Reagan was an important figure in the labor racketeering and corporate machinations that suppressed diversity in the movie industry" and that this "allows Pynchon to suggest the dimensions of establishment power" ("Communication" 128).

Chapter 6: Demonic Visions

1. A version of this material on Reed appears in Hume, "Ishmael Reed." Reed's signifying on the Invisible Man's journey to the Heart of Whiteness is discussed by Fox (*Conscientious Sorcerers*), Gates ("Ishmael Reed" and "Blackness"), and Schmitz ("Neo-HooDoo").

2. Satire is famously concerned with upholding norms. Hence, any deviancy is treated as aberrant, as the action of knaves and fools. However, neither HARRY SAM's actions in *The Free-Lance Pallbearers* nor Uncle Sam's in *The Public Burning* seem motivated by homoeroticism; their anal rapes function as metaphors for abuse of power.

3. For a discussion of the stercoraceous strain in contemporary literature, see Pops, "Metamorphoses of Shit"; for Reed's anal material, see Fabre, "Ishmael Reed's *Freelance Pallbearers*."

4. Mazurek's "Metafiction" discusses how *The Public Burning* relates to history; Chénetier (*Beyond Suspicion* 145–46) and Hutcheon (*Poetics* 194) take up historical consciousness and historical truth, respectively; Orlov's "Fiction of Politically Fantastic 'Facts'" also focuses on history as fact and introduces FBI files that were unavailable when Coover was writing. For an analysis of the take on history as seen in terms of changing scientific perspective, see the chapter on Coover in Strehle's *Fiction in the Quantum Universe*. In addition to his excellent analysis of *The Public Burning* as a political novel, LeClair ("Robert Coover") clarifies the circus structure. The three rings consist of panoramic chapters featuring Uncle Sam as ringmaster, melodramatic interludes featuring the acrobatic Rosenbergs, and sections narrated by the clown, Nixon. In *Robert Coover's Fictions*, Cope explores the novel's Bakhtinian dimensions. In "The Clown," Viereck also analyzes the circus and carnivalesque elements. Estes introduces us to the folk elements in "American Folk Laughter." Reitz ("Reconstruction") analyzes the differing modes of constructing the 1950s in *The Public Burning* and *The Book of Daniel*.

5. If one takes the rite as "intended magically to preserve the American dream and our manifest destiny," then it fails in part because Uncle Sam "will not submit to the dissolutions necessary to the re-creation of the psyche"; thus, "the only birth we seem to get is a periodic 'New Nixon'" (Ramage, "Myth and Monomyth" 63, 66).

6. For an elaborate analysis of this moviegoer, see Gallo, "Nixon."

7. In "Coover's *The Public Burning*," Guzlowski analyzes the portrayal of Nixon as embodying theories by R. D. Laing on the modern sense of estrangement. The essay discusses the emphasis in America on performance, on acting a part, on deriving one's sense of self only from the reactions of others.

8. For various analyses of this distrust of institutions, see Gerberding and Smith, *Radical Left*. My focus on the demonic vision makes me treat McMurphy as the protagonist and accept a positive valuation of him. For a different

approach, see Madden's "Sanity and Responsibility," in which Chief Bromden is central and McMurphy starts as a free spirit but becomes victim to the will of the other inmates and loses his sanity to their group pressure. In this reading, one is under no obligation to overlook McMurphy's racism, sexism, and paternalism, as one tends to do if he must be redemptive.

9. As critics have argued, McMurphy and Nurse Ratched are each other's doubles: both are big to the point of mythic dimensionality; both are bossy, manipulative, determined to challenge each other and win. See Hague ("Gendered Irony") for the most detailed comparison of the two. The frontier-related nature of the myths involved and the Melvillian intertexts are analyzed by Morey-Gaines in "Of Menace and Men." Larson ("Stories Sacred and Profane") carefully analyzes the religious myths. The childish qualities of the patients come out in "Big Mama, Big Papa and Little Sons," a Ruth Sullivan essay that utilizes Freudian analysis. By removing Chief Bromden's narrative perspective, the film makes the confrontation even more childish and simplistic. For analyses of the film, see Leeds ("One Flew"), Safer ("'It's the Truth'"), and Zubizarreta ("Disparity").

10. The parallels between institution and society are brought out by McGrath in "Kesey and Vonnegut," whom McGrath studies as critics of liberal democracy. For a standard analysis of the Bakhtinian carnivalesque elements, see Goluboff, "Carnival Artist."

11. Dix talks about her "embarking on a nomadic line of flight, attempting to break out of the social segmentations of her society through her own molecular becomings" ("Kathy Acker's *Don Quixote*" 57) and generally ties her project to that of Deleuze and Guattari's *Thousand Plateaus*. Acker and her personae cannot escape society or change it but can change themselves to the nomadic pattern, which disrupts hegemonic control.

12. For masochistic themes in Acker's writing in general, see Redding, "Bruises, Roses."

13. For an analysis of the "plagiarisms," see Jacobs, "Kathy Acker."

14. Irmer assumes that it is a satire and that we must bring obvious moral standards to the story; he argues that throughout *American Psycho* Ellis is showing the repression of the liberational values of the 1960s by the greed of the 1980s and that those repressed impulses, in Bateman, come out violently. Bateman's denial of his own past—"The past isn't real. . . . Don't mention the past"—"holds true for the whole novel in an even more challenging way concerning the 1960s and its meaning in the Reagan era" ("Bret Easton Ellis's *American Psycho*" 352).

15. In 1989, four years after Ellis's *Less than Zero* and two years before his *American Psycho*, Winter wrote a catchy parody of the first novel called "Less Than Zombie," in which the aimless West Coast teens show the capacity for violence of a sort that prefigures *American Psycho*. One of those teens he called Bret. As Irmer points out, critics were not sensitive to the potential for vio-

lence visible in Ellis's first book ("Bret Easton Ellis's *American Pscho*" 352);
only Winter, through his parody, showed us what was there.

16. See Jenkins's *Using Murder* (27) for actual numbers killed by major serial killers, only one of which is as high as forty-nine; since the alleged perpetrator has not been apprehended, the dead attributed to that killer may be the
victims of more than one person.

17. Gordon vividly and persuasively analyzes Mailer's intestinal imagery in
"*Why Are We in Vietnam?*" The fears of sodomy and disembowelment that
Gordon contextualizes make interesting reading in conjunction with anal and
excremental materials in *The Free-Lance Pallbearers* and *The Public Burning*.
Gordon's comments on the magic thinking behind the fantasies of disembow-
eling suggest parallels between the psychology of Patrick Bateman and that of
D.J. One very challenging psychological point is made by Ramsey, however,
who points out that D.J. claims a wide range of sexual encounters but describes
none, which, as he says, "might raise the question of D.J.'s virginity" ("Current and Recurrent" 419).

18. Hassan beautifully pays tribute to this love of America, and defends the
stylistic elements reviled by early readers of the novel, but obliquely takes
Mailer to task for his philosophy ("Focus on Norman Mailer's *Why Are We in
Vietnam?*").

19. However, as Wenke points out regarding this action, "there is no true
community of hunters that the boys can enter" (127) and Luke is neither their
teacher nor surrogate father. Thus, Wenke argues, "the true values the boys
do learn must be essentially private rather than communal" (*Mailer's America* 127). For further discussion of the frontier myths that attract Mailer, see
Witt, "Bad Man."

20. Gerson's "Norman Mailer" on the Jewish and specifically Kabbalistic
bases for Mailer's sexual and philosophical outlook does much to make sense
of his values. Pearce analyzes Mailer's deconstruction of frontier myths and
argues that the homosexual moment (first celebrated by Leslie Fiedler) "is the
benign expression of the frontier myth" ("Norman Mailer's *Why Are We in
Vietnam?*" 413)—though it takes malign form in the corporation infighting.
Other commentators, including Ramsey ("Current and Recurrent") and Wenke
(*Mailer's America*) have argued that D.J.'s failure to explore that impulse and
act on it, his repressing it out of fear, is a failure. His failure to face this fear is
what will send him down the wrong path and make him a killer rather than
let him enter into a more creative relationship with the world. For other discussions of Mailer's evolving cosmology, see Finholt (*American Visionary Fiction*) and Lennon ("Mailer's Cosmology").

21. Robinson's *American Apocalypses* argues that recent American writers
have tried to restrict the American apocalyptic vision and limit the cataclysm
(xiii). In that Vizenor does not show almost all the population dead, his is a

restricted vision; clearly, people will be dying in swarms, and if humanity survives in the hypothetical future of his novel, it will be in small groups, run by dictatorial hardliners, and a life worth living will be difficult or impossible to come by.

22. Owens looks at Vizenor's attacks on the invention of Indianness in "'Grinning Aboriginal Demons'" and in the "Afterword" to *Bearheart*. He notes that Vizenor's gothicism makes the structures of white civilization the new wilderness and revises the traditional push toward the western frontier. Hochbruck analyzes Vizenor's narrative originality in "Breaking Away." In "Gerald Vizenor's Indian Gothic," Velie also analyzes this as a Native American variation on frontier gothic.

23. Not only do we find the dog-lover motif transposed to the human realm, we find the great gambler story given a setting in this world. See Barry's "Chance and Ritual" for Vizenor's use of the gambler.

24. For analyses of the trickster element in this and other Vizenor fiction, see Velie, "Trickster Novel"; Vizenor, "Tricksters and Transvaluations"; and idem, "Trickster Discourse."

25. Hochbruck makes the following interesting point in "Breaking Away": "There is a numeric problem here with mythological worlds, for to several Native peoples the present world is already the fourth. Within the context of *Bearheart*, however, the pilgrims' progress (of course, this is one of the intertexts) into the fourth world makes the one they leave the third, which is what tribal politicians have claimed on several occasions: that their reservations are actually part of the Third World" (274).

26. The African-American/Native American element is strong enough in one of the many subplots for it to gain analysis as such by Holland in "'If You Know I Have a History.'"

27. Sexual relations with animal-form lovers, including dog-form, have special resonance for some Native American cultures. One of Proude Cedarfair's followers enjoys sex with her two boxers, and "dog-lover" is an insult in Welch's *Fools Crow*. The Plains Indians had a myth about a woman and her supernatural dog-shaped lover; their children were were-dogs, humans capable of changing shape. When culture heroes transgress taboos, they establish their superhuman status, but Silko does not seem to imply a valid mythic dimension to this act as carried out by an ordinary white human. Linton, in "'Person' in Postmodern Fiction," argues that Vizenor's use of the motif is positive. She quotes Vizenor as saying that the scene is not pornographic or bestial because animals are not inferior to humans in the Native American vision of nature (9). She goes on: "By offering myth as reality, Vizenor challenges readers' certainties about who is a person and who is not, what is fitting and what is not" (9). Silko's use seems more unequivocally negative.

Chapter 7: Liberating the Land of Freedom

1. See Crowder's *Classical Anarchism* for the basics about this political stance.

2. Bray sees the scorpions in a much more negative light, simply as a "gang of marauders," so Kid's association with them undercuts any evidence of growing maturity. She does make the interesting argument that the novel parodies the American quest of the innocent exposed to sex and death: "Kid is an American dreamer who winds up at the symbolic center of American dreams. Only in *Dhalgren*, such dreams do not have archetypally American results" ("Rites of Reversal" 58).

3. Bukatman discusses the postmodernity of this cityscape in "The Cybernetic (City) State." Olsen invokes Toffler's *Third Wave* to say that the first wave of civilization was agricultural, the second was industrial, and the third "embraces the antithesis of 'indust-reality': customization, decentralization, demassification, diversification, and globalization. Rather than thinking in terms of specialized hierarchy, it thinks in terms of integrative network" ("Shadow of Spirit" 279).

4. For a view of cyberpunk that conflates the two worlds to some extent and sees in this subgenre a new kind of "becoming," see Stivale, "Mille/Punks/Cyber/Plateaus."

5. Hollinger ("Cybernetic Deconstructions") and Rosenthal ("Jacked In") both discuss the antihumanism. In "Cyberpunk," Nixon analyzes claims of cyberpunk's radicalism and deflates them devastatingly. She deconstructs the imagery of *Neuromancer* as that of rape; however, Olsen sees it as the fusion of opposites, and Grant sees it as the urge to transcend ("Transcendence through Detournement"). Chénetier (*Beyond Suspicion*) calls attention to the way *Neuromancer* "subjects language to distortions comparable to those of spatiotemporal categories" (118).

6. Doctorow alters most of the clichés of the western to create this serious interrogation of gunslinging violence; furthermore, as Shelton points out, Doctorow explodes the great American hope that "man can begin again, begin afresh and forget the past." Shelton continues: "The novel embodies Doctorow's vision of the unreality, yet the persistence, of the American dream" ("E. L. Doctorow's *Welcome to Hard Times*" 16, 17). Hutcheon reads it rather as showing the "power of money, greed, and force on the frontier," and she goes on to point out that some noble myths (the frontier) have "capitalistic exploitation at their core" (*Poetics* 134).

7. See Vizenor, "Tricksters and Transvaluations" and "Trickster Discourse."

8. Vizenor, "Native American Indian Literature," 224.

9. Kingston discusses her Americanization of other Chinese legends in "Cultural Mis-readings." In "Maxine Hong Kingston's Fake Books," Shostak catalogs the extensive range of works, Western and Eastern, that are adapted by Kingston.

10. In "Theorizing Ethnicity," Schueller reads *Tripmaster Monkey* primarily in terms of this attack on ethnic stereotypes. In "Clashing Constructs," Lin stresses instead Wittman's effort at self-retrieval.

11. For the genealogy of various branches of anarchism, see Woodcock, *Anarchism*; for the Iroquois influence on Marx and Engels, see Weatherford, *Indian Givers*.

12. For a vision of the utopian movement as heavily influenced by anarchism, see Sargent's "New Anarchism." In "Anarchism and Utopian Tradition," Brennan and Downes discuss anarchism's place in *The Dispossessed*. Smith ("Unbuilding Walls") tallies details of Le Guin's borrowings from Kropotkin. In "Turn from Utopia," Fitting analyzes the dystopic elements that to some extent counter the rosy anarchist picture.

13. Kennedy's *Rise and Fall of the Great Powers* came out after Le Guin's novel but she works on the same theory that empires fall through military overexpansion.

14. Philmus, in his unusual and well-argued analysis of *The Dispossessed* ("Ursula Le Guin"), treats Anarres as far more deeply and significantly flawed and hypocritical than I have here, and he sees Shevek as sharing these flaws. Shevek's breaking free from these past mistakes is in doubt until the very end; only when he accepts his responsibility does he become again what an anarchist should be and worthy to be the "hero."

15. As Drake points out in "Two Utopias," "there are no 'fathers' in Mattapoisett. Men and women alike may be 'mothers'" (113). However, given the communal nature of the society, there is no need for a breadwinner or protector of the hearth. For a detailed analysis of the various levels of meaning attached to motherhood in this novel, see Orr, "Mothering as Good Fiction."

16. In "Woman on the Edge of a Genre," Booker notes that *He, She and It* is influenced by Haraway's essay titled "A Cyborg Manifesto" (in *Simians, Cyborgs, and Women*), in which she attacks feminists for ceding technology to men and retreating to pastoral utopias. Haraway argues that technology is too powerful to be thus handed over to the enemy, as it were. In *He, She and It*, Tikva and many of its inhabitants, female and male, are cutting-edge computer people, and their cyborg goes beyond anything created by the multis.

Chapter 8: Small Is Beautiful

1. Lasch analyzes the withdrawal from any sense of public duty by the elites in *The Culture of Narcissism*; the communitarian Etzioni, in *An Immodest Agenda*, suggests ways that sectors of a community could develop mutualism by attending better to each other's interests—industry and education, for example. Perin's *Belonging in America* looks at how Americans define neighborhoods and belonging through exclusion and prohibition rather than affirmation of common concerns.

2. Wiget points out that the main audience for Native American novels is Anglo-American. Those Indians who read Silko and Momaday "can do so pre-

cisely because they, like the authors who satisfy them, are marginalized sufficiently from their own communities to read complex literary forms and comprehend an elaborate structure of allusion to those structures of knowledge (economics, psychology, physical science, literary criticism) that undergird contemporary Euro-American life" ("Identity, Voice, and Authority" 260).

3. In "Eruptions of Funk," Willis places Morrison's various novels at the cusps of change in black American history, the 1920s, 1940s, 1960s, and 1980s, and she analyzes the relevance of shifts from farming to wage labor.

4. Morrison can even admire some aspects of those black men who leave their families, a fact that should make us wary of imposing white, middle-class assumptions on her various complicated uses of flight and leaving. See Krumholz ("Dead Teachers") for Morrison's savoring black men's willingness to "split in a minute" (555). Her many uses and moral evaluations of flying are discussed by Hovet and Lounsberry in "Flying as Symbol and Legend," and further subtleties are pointed out by Guth in "A Blessing and a Burden."

5. Willis analyzes Morrison's concept of community. Regarding Shadrack, she writes, "When Morrison remarks that the black community tolerates difference while the white bourgeois world shuts difference out, she underscores the fact that for the white world, under capitalism, difference, because it articulates a form of freedom, is a threat and therefore must be institutionalized or jailed" ("Eruptions of Funk" 276).

6. These issues are important in the analyses by Abel ("(E)merging Identities"), Bakerman ("Failures of Love"), Banyiwa-Horne ("Scary Face of the Self"), Coleman ("One and One"), Lee ("Missing Peace"), Montgomery ("Pilgrimage"), and Rubenstein (*Boundaries of the Self* 125-63).

7. In *Boundaries of the Self*, Rubenstein points out the dubiousness of Eva's stated motive; she reads this as Eva projecting her own incest wish on Plum rather than any such desire on his part (147).

8. Other readings concerned with structure and theme include Rushdy, "Fraternal Blues" (on the musical variations played on narrative, story, song, and letter), and Berben, "Promised Land and Wasteland" (on that imagery). In *Afro-American Novel*, Bell points out that Wideman's education was entirely "white"—Fielding, Sterne, Joyce, and Eliot were important influences on his writing (307). Only when asked to teach African-American literature did he make himself acquainted with that tradition.

9. See Rowell, "Interview with John Edgar Wideman," for a discussion of Wideman's family's departure from Homewood and for references to Wideman's time at the University of Pennsylvania and Oxford, which would do something to separate him from the Homewood ethos.

10. In "Of Cars, Time, and the River," Magalaner offers useful information on traditional Ojibwe life.

11. Wong raises this issue in "Adoptive Mothers and Thrown-Away Chil-

dren." Rainwater also comments on the nonbiological families in "Reading between Worlds."

12. Towery analyzes the interconnections from one book to another in "Continuity and Connection."

13. For the oddly feminine patterns in Lipsha and Gerry, see Barry and Prescott, "Triumph of the Brave."

14. Non-Indian readers can remedy some of their ignorance about government dealings concerning Native American lands and the effects on the American Indians in *Tracks* in Larson's "Fragmentation" and Peterson's "History, Postmodernism."

15. Flavin ("Louise Erdrich's *Love Medicine*") indeed argues that she really is saintly in her taking in orphans, making her husband into something, taking him back when he strays, and so forth.

16. Berner ("Trying to Be Round") and Lutz ("Circle") analyze the cyclical structures of Native American narration. For discussion of oral elements and the unusual structure of *Love Medicine*, see Flavin ("Novel as Performance"), Sergi ("Storytelling"), and Ruppert ("Mediation and Multiple Narrative in *Love Medicine*"). When characters have mythic overtones, they may not be able to go back to the old ways, but they can be shown to head for a different spiritual realm (as happens in Vizenor's *Bearheart*). Ruppert shows Gerry as a trickster heading for another spiritual plane of existence.

17. That the novel starts with June's death does not prevent it from being a homecoming novel of the sort described by Bevis in "Native American Novels." For that kind of reading, see Silberman, "Opening the Text."

18. Allen ("Feminine Landscape" in *Sacred Hoop* 118–26), Flores ("Claiming and Making"), Rubenstein (*Boundaries of the Self* 190–208), and Swan ("Feminine Perspectives at Laguna Pueblo") discuss the reclaimed feminine as necessary to Tayo's cure.

19. See García ("Senses of Place"), Nelson ("Place and Vision"), and Silko ("Landscape, History, and the Pueblo Imagination"). Schweninger discusses Silko and other Native Americans as nature writers in "Writing Nature."

20. Allen (*Sacred Hoop*), Coltelli ("Re-enacting Myths"), Evasdaughter ("Leslie Marmon Silko's *Ceremony*"), St. Andrews ("Healing the Witchery"), and Swan ("Healing via the Sunwise Cycle") analyze the healing process.

21. As Bird puts it in "Towards a Decolonization of the Mind," Tayo has to shed imposed white patterns, and Bird considers this the best Native American novel on that subject. Hobbs treats Tayo's Indian-leaning reinterpretations of the elements in his life as a form of radical reading ("Living In-Between").

22. In "Native American Novels," Bevis lays out the Native American male bildungsroman pattern in fascinating detail. In "Culture of 'Internal Colonialism,'" Wald insists that *Ceremony* does not advocate an impossible return to pretechnological existence.

23. Wright ("Of Pomerleaus and Pumpkins") argues that the Christian patterns of the Pomerleaus are "dead," while the pagan patterns of the Beans celebrate life.

24. Cowart looks at themes of community in Vonnegut's work, seeing it as emerging tentatively in *Happy Birthday, Wanda June*. Cowart writes of Vonnegut, "In *Jailbird* . . . he sets out to record the history of the twentieth-century American Left, the history, that is, of those in this country who . . . advocate treating all citizens—not just those who have money or other forms of privilege—as family members" ("Culture and Anarchy" 171). Cowart also charts the theme in *Deadeye Dick, Slapstick,* and *Galápagos.*

25. See McClure's *Late Imperial Romance* for an exciting analysis of this subgenre.

26. Oscar Handlin, in *The Uprooted,* talks about the unimaginable importance of the natal village to many of the central European immigrants to America.

Chapter 9: The Failure of the Dream in Fiction

1. Other such studies include Galbraith's *Culture of Contentment,* which shows how the materially well-to-do prevent all reform, even though deficits rise and the underclasses find themselves farther from improvement than ever before. In *The True and Only Heaven,* Lasch points out that most Americans believe in endless material progress, despite evidence regarding the Earth's finite resources and the growing number of people in impoverished, underdeveloped populations. In keeping with these criticisms of America is the title of a previous study by Lasch, *The Culture of Narcissism: American Life in an Age of Diminishing Expectations.*

2. See Thompson's "Restoring the American Dream" for the Republicans' version of this promise.

3. In "Marriage," Coale argues that one finds very little true attention to marriage in recent literature, and what there is consists of "the mismatched marriages of manichean minds" (119). In "Marriage," Heilbrun points out that fiction spent a long time showing courtship but not marriage (especially not from a woman's viewpoint) and notes that what intrigues female authors now is not the achievement of marriage but the achievement of divorce and the establishment of an independent self.

4. Writers themselves rail against publishers' demands that they conform to generic expectation. Chénetier helpfully resists such ghettoization when looking for what Clarence Major and Alice Walker say about their art and its relationship to language, rather than focusing on ethnic issues (72, 276).

5. In *The Twilight of Common Dreams,* Gitlin articulates what has happened to American political thought. The left, once the repository of theories stressing the universality of human needs and desires, has fragmented into special-

interest enclaves that deny any common culture. Meanwhile, the right, once concerned with the upper, middle, and lower classes being separate and deserving different treatment, is now claiming to be the repository of universal values. Gitlin places any hope for a better future in the left's turning not to community but to ensuring fairness for all.

Bibliography

Abel, Elizabeth. "(E)Merging Identities: The Dynamics of Female Friendship in Contemporary Fiction by Women." *Signs* 6.3 (1981): 413–35.

Acker, Kathy. *Blood and Guts in High School.* 1978. New York: Grove Weidenfeld, 1989.

———. *Don Quixote.* New York: Grove Press, 1986.

Adams, James Truslow. *The Epic of America.* Boston: Little, Brown, 1931.

Adams, Laura. "Existential Aesthetics: An Interview with Norman Mailer." *Partisan Review* 2 42.2 (1975): 197–214.

Allen, Paula Gunn. *The Sacred Hoop: Recovering the Feminine in American Indian Traditions.* Boston: Beacon Press, 1986.

Allen, William Rodney. *Walker Percy: A Southern Wayfarer.* Jackson: University Press of Mississippi, 1986.

Alther, Lisa. *Original Sins.* 1981. New York: Signet, 1982.

Alvarez, Julia. *How the García Girls Lost Their Accents.* 1991. New York: Plume, 1992.

Anaya, Rudolfo. "An American Chicano in King Arthur's Court." In *The Frontier Experience and the American Dream: Essays on American Literature.* Ed. David Mogen, Mark Busby, and Paul Bryant. College Station: Texas A&M University Press, 1989. 180–85.

———. "Aztlán: A Homeland without Boundaries." In *Aztlán: Essays on the Chicano Homeland.* Ed. Rudolfo A. Anaya and Francisco A. Lomeli. Albuquerque, N.Mex.: Academia/El Norte Publications, 1989. 230–41.

———. *Bless Me, Ultima.* 1972. New York: Warner, 1994.

Andreas, James R. "*Invisible Man* and the Comic Tradition." In *Approaches to Teaching Ellison's "Invisible Man."* Ed. Susan Resneck Parr and Pancho Savery. New York: Modern Language Association of America, 1989. 102–6.

Antell, Judith A. "Momaday, Welch, and Silko: Expressing the Feminine Principle through Male Alienation." *American Indian Quarterly* 12.3 (1988): 213–20.

Apple, Max. *The Propheteers.* New York: Harper and Row, 1987.

Askeland, Lori. "Remodeling the Model Home in *Uncle Tom's Cabin* and *Beloved.*" *American Literature* 64.4 (1992): 785–805.

Awkward, Michael. "Roadblocks and Relatives: Critical Revision in Toni Morrison's *The Bluest Eye.*" In *Critical Essays on Toni Morrison.* Ed. Nellie Y. McKay. Boston: G. K. Hall, 1988. 57–68.

Bach, Gerhard. "The Dean Who Came in from the Cold: Saul Bellow's America of the 1980s." *Studies in American Jewish Literature* 8.1 (1989): 104–14.

Bakerman, Jane S. "Failures of Love: Female Initiation in the Novels of Toni Morrison." *American Literature* 52.4 (1981): 541–63.

Baldwin, James. "Sonny's Blues" (1957). In *Going to Meet the Man.* New York: Vintage, 1995. 101–41.

Banks, Russell. *Continental Drift.* 1985. New York: Ballantine, 1986.

Banyiwa-Horne, Naana. "The Scary Face of the Self: An Analysis of the Character of Sula in Toni Morrison's *Sula.*" *SAGE* 2.1 (1985): 28–31.

Barlett, Donald L., and James B. Steele. *America: What Went Wrong?* Kansas City, Kans.: Andrews and McMeel, 1992.

Barry, Nora. "Chance and Ritual: The Gambler in the Texts of Gerald Vizenor." *Studies in American Indian Literatures* ser. 2, 5.3 (1993): 13–22.

———. "'A Myth to Be Alive': James Welch's *Fools Crow.*" *MELUS* 17.1 (1991–92): 3–20.

Barry, Nora, and Mary Prescott. "The Triumph of the Brave: *Love Medicine*'s Holistic Vision." *Critique* 30.2 (1989): 123–38.

Barth, John. *The Sot-Weed Factor.* 1960. Rev. ed., Garden City, N.Y.: Anchor, 1987.

Barthelme, Donald. *The Dead Father.* 1975. New York: Pocket, 1976.

———. *Snow White.* 1967. New York: Atheneum, 1972.

Bell, Bernard W. *The Afro-American Novel and Its Tradition.* Amherst: University of Massachusetts Press, 1987.

Bellow, Saul. *The Dean's December.* London: Penguin, 1982.

———. *Mr. Sammler's Planet.* 1970. London: Penguin, 1972.

Bennett, David H. *The Party of Fear: From Nativist Movements to the New Right in American History.* 1988. New York: Vintage, 1990.

Berben, Jacqueline. "Promised Land and Wasteland in John Wideman's Recent Fiction." *Revue française d'études américaines* 16.48–49 (1991): 259–70.

Berner, Robert L. "Quaternity in James Welch's *Fools Crow.*" In *Entering the 90s: The North American Experience.* Ed. Thomas E. Shirer. Sault Ste. Marie, Mich.: Lake Superior State University Press, 1991. 108–13.

———. "Trying to Be Round: Three American Indian Novels." *World Literature Today* 58.3 (1984): 341–44.

Bernstein, Mashey. "The Heart of the Nation: Jewish Values in the Fiction of Norman Mailer." *Studies in American Jewish Literature* 2 (1982): 115–25.

Bevis, Bill. "Dialogue with James Welch." *Northwest Review* 20.2–3 (1982): 163–85.

Bevis, William. "Native American Novels: Homing In." In *Recovering the Word: Essays on Native American Literature.* Ed. Brian Swann and Arnold Krupat. Berkeley: University of California Press, 1987. 580–620.

Bird, Gloria. "Towards a Decolonization of the Mind and Text 1: Leslie Marmon Silko's *Ceremony.*" *Wicazo SA Review* 9.2 (1993): 1–8.

Bloom, Allan. *The Closing of the American Mind.* New York: Simon and Schuster, 1987.

Bonn, Maria S. "Can Stories Save Us? Tim O'Brien and the Efficacy of the Text." *Critique* 36.1 (1994): 2–15.

Booker, M. Keith. "America and Its Discontents: The Failure of Leftist Politics in Pynchon's *Vineland.*" *Literature, Interpretation, Theory* 4.2 (1993): 87–99.

———. "Woman on the Edge of a Genre: The Feminist Dystopias of Marge Piercy." *Science-Fiction Studies* 21.3 (1994): 337–50.

Booth, Sherryl. "Living Your Own Experience: The Role of Communities in Saul Bellow's *The Dean's December.*" *Saul Bellow Journal* 10.1 (1991): 13–24.

Bovey, Seth. "Whitehorns and Blackhorns: Images of Cattle Ranching in the Novels of James Welch." *South Dakota Review* 29.1 (1991): 129–39.

Boyle, T. Coraghessan. *World's End.* 1987. New York: Penguin, 1988.

Bradbury, Ray. *Dandelion Wine.* 1957. Rev. ed., New York: Bantam, 1976.

Brautigan, Richard. *Sombrero Fallout: A Japanese Novel.* New York: Touchstone, 1976.

———. *So the Wind Won't Blow It All Away.* 1982. New York: Delta, 1984.

———. *The Tokyo-Montana Express.* 1980. New York: Delta, 1981.

Bray, Mary Kay. "Rites of Reversal: Double Consciousness in Delany's *Dhalgren.*" *Black American Literature Forum* 18.2 (1984): 57–61.

Brennan, John P., and Michael C. Downs. "Anarchism and Utopian Tradition in *The Dispossessed.*" In *Ursula K. Le Guin.* Ed. Joseph D. Olander and Martin Harry Greenberg. New York: Taplinger, 1979. 116–52.

Broad, Robert L. "Giving Blood to the Scraps: Haints, History, and Hosea in *Beloved.*" *African American Review* 28.2 (1994): 189–96.

Brooke, John L. *The Refiner's Fire: The Making of Mormon Cosmology, 1644–1844.* New York: Cambridge University Press, 1994.

Brooks, Cleanth. "Walker Percy and Modern Gnosticism." In *The Art of Walker Percy: Stratagems for Being.* Ed. Panthea Reid Broughton. Baton Rouge: Louisiana State University Press, 1979. 260–72.

Brooks, Peter. "The Melodramatic Imagination." *Partisan Review* 2 39.2 (1972): 195–212.

Bukatman, Scott. "The Cybernetic (City) State: Terminal Space Becomes Phenomenal." *Journal of the Fantastic in the Arts* 2.2 (1989): 43–63.

Burroughs, William S. *Cities of the Red Night*. 1981. New York: Holt, Rinehart and Winston, 1982.

Busby, Mark. "The Significance of the Frontier in Contemporary American Fiction." In *The Frontier Experience and the American Dream: Essays on American Literature*. Ed. David Mogen, Mark Busby, and Paul Bryant. College Station: Texas A&M University Press, 1989. 95–103.

Butler, Octavia. *Adulthood Rites*. New York: Warner, 1988.

———. *Dawn*. New York: Warner, 1987.

———. *Imago*. 1989. New York: Popular Library, 1990.

Butler-Evans, Elliott. *Race, Gender, and Desire: Narrative Strategies in the Fiction of Toni Cade Bambara, Toni Morrison, and Alice Walker*. Philadelphia: Temple University Press, 1989.

Byatt, A. S. *Possession: A Romance*. 1990. New York: Vintage International, 1991.

Caesar, Terry P. "'Beasts Vaulting among the Earthworks': Monstrosity in *Gravity's Rainbow*." *Novel* 17.2 (1984): 158–70.

Callenbach, Ernest. *Ecotopia*. 1975. New York: Bantam, 1977.

———. *Ecotopia Emerging*. 1981. New York: Bantam, 1982.

Campbell, Jeff. "'Middling, Hidden, Troubled America': John Updike's Rabbit Tetralogy." *Journal of the American Studies Association of Texas* 24 (1993): 26–45.

Caramello, Charles. *Silverless Mirrors: Book, Self, and Postmodern American Fiction*. Tallahassee: University Presses of Florida, 1983.

Carter-Sanborn, Kristin. "'We Murder Who We Were': *Jasmine* and the Violence of Identity." *American Literature* 66.3 (1994): 573–93.

Chase, Richard. *The American Novel and Its Tradition*. 1957. Baltimore, Md.: Johns Hopkins University Press, 1980.

Chavkin, Allan, and Nancy Feyl Chavkin. "Bellow's Dire Prophecy." *Centennial Review* 33.2 (1989): 93–107.

Chénetier, Marc. *Beyond Suspicion: New American Fiction since 1960*. Trans. Elizabeth A. Houlding. 1989 (in French). Philadelphia: University of Pennsylvania Press, 1996.

Chin, Frank. *Donald Duk*. Minneapolis: Coffee House Press, 1991.

Chute, Carolyn. *The Beans of Egypt, Maine*. 1985. New York: Warner, 1986.

———. *Letourneau's Used Auto Parts*. 1988. London: Minerva, 1990.

———. *Merry Men*. New York: Harcourt Brace, 1994.

Civello, Paul. "Undoing the Naturalistic Novel: Don DeLillo's *Libra*." *Arizona Quarterly* 48.2 (1992): 33–56.

Clausen, Jan. "Native Fathers." *Kenyon Review* n.s. 14.2 (1992): 44–55.

Coale, Samuel C. "Marriage in Contemporary American Literature: The Mismatched Marriages of Manichean Minds." *Thought* 58.228 (Mar. 1983): 111–21.

Coleman, Alisha R. "One and One Make One: A Metacritical and Psychoanalytic Reading of Friendship in Toni Morrison's *Sula*." *College Language Association Journal* 37.2 (1993): 145–55.

Coltelli, Laura. "Re-enacting Myths and Stories: Tradition and Renewal in *Ceremony*." In *Native American Literatures*. Ed. Laura Coltelli. Pisa, Italy: Servizio Editoriale Universitario, 1989. 173–83.

Cooper, Stephen. "Cutting Both Ways: E. L. Doctorow's Critique of the Left." *South Atlantic Review* 58.2 (1993): 111–25.

Coover, Robert. *The Public Burning*. New York: Viking, 1977.

Cope, Jackson I. *Robert Coover's Fictions*. Baltimore, Md.: Johns Hopkins University Press, 1986.

Coupland, Douglas. *Generation X: Tales for an Accelerated Culture*. New York: St. Martin's, 1991.

Cowart, David. "Attenuated Postmodernism: Pynchon's *Vineland*." *Critique* 32.2 (1990): 67–76.

———. "Culture and Anarchy: Vonnegut's Later Career." In *Critical Essays on Kurt Vonnegut*. Ed. Robert Merrill. Boston: G. K. Hall, 1990. 170–88.

———. *History and the Contemporary Novel*. Carbondale: Southern Illinois University Press, 1989.

Cronin, Gloria L. "Through a Glass Brightly: Corde's Escape from History in *The Dean's December*." *Saul Bellow Journal* 5.1 (1986): 24–33.

Crowder, George. *Classical Anarchism: The Political Thought of Godwin, Proudhon, Bakunin, and Kropotkin*. Oxford: Clarendon Press, 1991.

Culler, Jonathan. "Junk and Rubbish: A Semiotic Approach." *Diacritics* 15.3 (1985): 2–12.

Davis, Walter T., Jr. *Shattered Dream: America's Search for Its Soul*. Valley Forge, Pa.: Trinity Press, 1994.

DeCurtis, Anthony. "'An Outsider in This Society': An Interview with Don DeLillo." In *Introducing Don DeLillo*. Ed. Frank Lentricchia. Durham, N.C.: Duke University Press, 1991. 281–304.

Delany, Samuel R. *Dhalgren*. 1974. New York: Bantam, 1975.

Deleuze, Gilles, and Félix Guattari. *A Thousand Plateaus: Capitalism and Schizophrenia*. Trans. Brian Massumi. 1980 (in French). Minneapolis: University of Minnesota Press, 1987.

DeLillo, Don. *Libra*. 1988. New York: Penguin, 1989.

D'Emilio, John, and Estelle B. Freedman. *Intimate Matters: A History of Sexuality in America*. 1988. New York: Perennial Library, 1989.

D'Innocenzo, Michael, and Josef P. Sirefman. *Immigration and Ethnicity: American Society— "Melting Pot" or "Salad Bowl"?* Westport, Conn.: Greenwood Press, 1992.

Dippie, Brian W. "'His Visage Wild; His Form Exotick': Indian Themes and Cultural Guilt in John Barth's *The Sot-Weed Factor*." *American Quarterly* 21.1 (1969): 113–21.

Dix, Douglas Shields. "Kathy Acker's *Don Quixote:* Nomad Writing." *Review of Contemporary Fiction* 9.3 (1989): 56–62.

Doctorow, E. L. *The Book of Daniel.* 1971. New York: Ballantine, 1987.

———. *Ragtime.* 1975. New York: Bantam, 1976.

———. *Welcome to Hard Times.* 1960. New York: Vintage, 1992.

Drake, Barbara. "Two Utopias: Marge Piercy's *Woman on the Edge of Time* and Ursula Le Guin's *The Dispossessed.*" In *Still the Frame Holds: Essays on Women Poets and Writers.* Ed. Sheila Roberts. San Bernardino, Calif.: Borgo Press, 1993. 109–27.

Dunn, Katherine. *Geek Love.* 1989. New York: Warner, 1990.

Dworkin, Andrea. *Mercy.* 1990. New York: Four Walls Eight Windows, 1992.

Eco, Umberto. *Foucault's Pendulum.* Trans. William Weaver. 1988 (in Italian). New York: Harcourt Brace Jovanovich, 1989.

Ellis, Bret Easton. *American Psycho.* New York: Vintage, 1991.

Ellison, Ralph. *Invisible Man.* 1952. New York: Vintage, 1989.

Engels, Friedrich. *The Origin of the Family, Private Property and the State: In the Light of the Researches of Lewis H. Morgan.* 1884 (in German). New York: International Publishers, 1942.

Erdrich, Louise. *Love Medicine.* 1984. New York: Bantam, 1985.

———. *Tracks.* New York: Henry Holt, 1988.

Estes, David C. "American Folk Laughter in Robert Coover's *The Public Burning.*" *Contemporary Literature* 28.2 (1987): 239–56.

Estrin, Barbara L. "Surviving McCarthyism: E. L. Doctorow's *The Book of Daniel.*" *Massachusetts Review* 16.3 (1975): 577–87.

Etzioni, Amitai. *An Immodest Agenda: Rebuilding America before the Twenty-first Century.* New York: McGraw-Hill, 1983.

Eubanks, Cecil L. "Walker Percy: Eschatology and the Politics of Grace." *Southern Quarterly* 18.3 (1980): 121–36.

Evasdaughter, Elizabeth N. "Leslie Marmon Silko's *Ceremony:* Healing Ethnic Hatred by Mixed-Breed Laughter." *MELUS* 15.1 (1988): 83–95.

Evers, Lawrence J. "The Killing of a New Mexican State Trooper: Ways of Telling an Historical Event." In *Critical Essays on Native American Literature.* Ed. Andrew Wiget. Boston: G. K. Hall, 1985. 246–61.

Fabre, Michel. "Ishmael Reed's *Freelance Pallbearers;* or, the Dialectics of Shit." *Obsidian* 3.3 (1977): 5–19.

Fallows, James. *Breaking the News: How the Media Undermine American Democracy.* New York: Pantheon, 1996.

Farrell, John. "The Romance of the '60s: Self, Community, and the Ethical in *The Crying of Lot 49.*" *Pynchon Notes* 30–31 (1992): 139–56.

Ferguson, Mary Anne. "Lisa Alther: The Irony of Return?" *Southern Quarterly* 21.4 (1983): 103–15.

Ferraro, Thomas J. *Ethnic Passages: Literary Immigrants in Twentieth-Century America.* Chicago: University of Chicago Press, 1993.

Fichtelberg, Joseph. "Poet and Patriarch in Maxine Hong Kingston's *China Men.*" In *Autobiography and Questions of Gender.* Ed. Shirley Neuman. Portland, Oreg.: Frank Cass, 1991. 166–85.

Fiedler, Leslie A. *Love and Death in the American Novel.* 1960. Rev. ed., New York: Stein and Day, 1966.

Finholt, Richard. *American Visionary Fiction: Mad Metaphysics as Salvation Psychology.* Port Washington, N.Y.: Kennikat Press, 1978.

Fitting, Peter. "The Turn from Utopia in Recent Feminist Fiction." In *Feminism, Utopia, and Narrative.* Ed. Libby Falk Jones and Sarah Webster Goodwin. Knoxville: University of Tennessee Press, 1990. 141–58.

Flavin, James. "The Novel as Performance: Communication in Louise Erdrich's *Tracks.*" *Studies in American Indian Literatures* ser. 2, 3.4 (1991): 1–12.

Flavin, Louise. "Louise Erdrich's *Love Medicine:* Loving over Time and Distance." *Critique* 31.1 (1989): 55–64.

Flores, Toni. "Claiming and Making: Ethnicity, Gender, and the Common Sense in Leslie Marmon Silko's *Ceremony* and Zora Neale Hurston's *Their Eyes Were Watching God.*" *Frontiers* 10.3 (1989): 52–58.

Fossum, Robert H., and John K. Roth. *The American Dream.* London: British Association for American Studies, 1981.

Foster, Edward Halsey. *Richard Brautigan.* Boston: Twayne, 1983.

Fox, Robert Elliot. *Conscientious Sorcerers: The Black Postmodernist Fiction of LeRoi Jones/Amiri Baraka, Ishmael Reed, and Samuel P. Delany.* Westport, Conn.: Greenwood Press, 1987.

Franklin, H. Bruce. *Robert A. Heinlein: America as Science Fiction.* New York: Oxford University Press, 1980.

———. *War Stars: The Superweapon and the American Imagination.* New York: Oxford University Press, 1988.

Freed, Donald. *The Spymaster.* 1980. New York: Bantam, 1981.

Friedl, Herwig. "Power and Degradation: Patterns of Historical Process in the Novels of E. L. Doctorow." In *E. L. Doctorow: A Democracy of Perception.* Ed. Herwig Friedl and Dieter Schulz. Essen, Germany: Die Blaue Eule, 1988. 19–44.

Friedman, Ellen G., and Corinne Squire. *Morality USA.* Minneapolis: University of Minnesota Press, 1998.

Frye, Northrop. *Anatomy of Criticism: Four Essays.* Princeton, N.J.: Princeton University Press, 1957.

Fulcher, James. "American Conspiracy: Formula in Popular Fiction." *Midwest Quarterly* 24.2 (1983): 152–64.

Galbraith, John Kenneth. *The Culture of Contentment.* Boston: Houghton Mifflin, 1992.

Gallo, Louis. "Nixon and the 'House of Wax': An Emblematic Episode in Coover's *The Public Burning.*" *Critique* 23.3 (1982): 43–51.

García, Reyes. "Senses of Place in *Ceremony.*" *MELUS* 10.4 (1983): 37–48.

Gates, Henry Louis, Jr. "The 'Blackness of Blackness': A Critique of the Sign and the Signifying Monkey." *Critical Inquiry* 9 (1983): 685–723.

———. "Ishmael Reed." In *Dictionary of Literary Biography*, vol. 33. Detroit: Gale, 1984. 219–32.

Genovese, Eugene D. "The Southern Slaveholders' View of the Middle Ages." In *Medievalism in American Culture*. Ed. Bernard Rosenthal and Paul E. Szarmach. Binghamton, N.Y.: Center for Medieval and Early Renaissance Studies, 1989. 31–52.

Gerberding, William P., and Duane E. Smith. *The Radical Left: The Abuse of Discontent*. Boston: Houghton Mifflin, 1970.

Gerson, Jessica. "An American Dream: Mailer's Walpurgisnacht." *Studies in American Jewish Literature* 2 (1982): 126–31.

———. "Norman Mailer: Sex, Creativity, and God." *Mosaic* 15.2 (1982): 1–16.

Giamo, Benedict. "*Ironweed* and the Snows of Reduction." In *Take Two: Adapting the Contemporary American Novel to Film*. Ed. Barbara Tepa Lupack. Bowling Green, Ohio: Bowling Green State University Popular Press, 1994. 131–53.

Gibson, William. *Neuromancer*. New York: Ace, 1984.

Gilligan, Carol. *In a Different Voice: Psychological Theory and Women's Development*. Cambridge, Mass.: Harvard University Press, 1982.

Gilman, Richard. "Barthelme's Fairy Tale." In *Critical Essays on Donald Barthelme*. Ed. Richard F. Patteson. New York: G. K. Hall, 1992. 29–35.

Gitlin, Todd. *The Twilight of Common Dreams: Why America Is Wracked by Culture Wars*. New York: Henry Holt, 1995.

Glasgow, Douglas G. *The Black Underclass: Poverty, Unemployment, and Entrapment of Ghetto Youth*. San Francisco: Jossey-Bass Publications, 1980.

Glazer, Nathan, and Daniel Patrick Moynihan. *Beyond the Melting Pot: The Negroes, Puerto Ricans, Jews, Italians, and Irish of New York City*. Cambridge, Mass.: MIT Press and Harvard University Press, 1963.

Gleason, William. "The Postmodern Labyrinths of *Lot 49*." *Critique* 34.2 (1993): 83–99.

Glickman, Susan. "The World as Will and Idea: A Comparative Study of *An American Dream* and *Mr. Sammler's Planet*." *Modern Fiction Studies* 28.4 (1982–83): 569–82.

Godschalk, William Leigh. "*Love in the Ruins*: Thomas More's Distorted Vision." In *The Art of Walker Percy: Stratagems for Being*. Ed. Panthea Reid Broughton. Baton Rouge: Louisiana State University Press, 1979. 137–56.

Goellnicht, Donald C. "Tang Ao in America: Male Subject Positions in *China Men*." In *Reading the Literatures of Asian America*. Ed. Shirley Geok-lin Lim and Amy Ling. Philadelphia: Temple University Press, 1992. 191–212.

Goldman, L. H. "*The Dean's December*: 'A Companion Piece to *Mr. Sammler's Planet*.'" *Saul Bellow Journal* 5.2 (1986): 36–45.

Goluboff, Benjamin. "The Carnival Artist in the Cuckoo's Nest." *Northwest Review* 29.3 (1991): 109–22.

Gordon, Andrew. "The Modern Dream-Vision: Freud's *The Interpretation of Dreams* and Mailer's *An American Dream.*" *Literature and Psychology* 27.3 (1977): 100–105.

———. "*Why Are We in Vietnam?*: Deep in the Bowels of Texas." *Literature and Psychology* 24.2 (1974): 55–65.

Gottfried, Paul, and Thomas Fleming. *The Conservative Movement.* Boston: Twayne, 1988.

Grant, Glenn. "Transcendence through Detournement in William Gibson's *Neuromancer.*" *Science-Fiction Studies* 17.1 (1990): 41–49.

Green, Michelle Erica. "'There Goes the Neighborhood': Octavia Butler's Demand for Diversity in Utopias." In *Utopian and Science Fiction by Women: Worlds of Difference.* Ed. Jane L. Donawerth and Carol A. Kolmerten. Syracuse, N.Y.: Syracuse University Press, 1994. 166–89.

Greider, William. *Who Will Tell the People: The Betrayal of American Democracy.* New York: Simon and Schuster, 1992.

Gross, David S. "Tales of Obscene Power: Money and Culture, Modernism and History in the Fiction of E. L. Doctorow." In *E. L. Doctorow: Essays and Conversations.* Ed. Richard Trenner. Princeton, N.J.: Ontario Review Press, 1983. 120–50.

Guth, Deborah. "A Blessing and a Burden: The Relation to the Past in *Sula, Song of Solomon,* and *Beloved.*" *Modern Fiction Studies* 39.3–4 (1993): 575–96.

Guttmann, Allen. *The Jewish Writer in America: Assimilation and the Crisis of Identity.* New York: Oxford University Press, 1971.

Guzlowski, John Z. "Coover's *The Public Burning:* Richard Nixon and the Politics of Experience." *Critique* 29 (1987): 57–71.

Hague, Theodora-Ann. "Gendered Irony in Ken Kesey's *One Flew over the Cuckoo's Nest.*" *Cithara* 33 (1993): 27–34.

Haldeman, Joe. *The Forever War.* 1974. New York: Ballantine, 1976.

———. *1986: A Novel.* 1994. London: Hodder and Stoughton, 1995.

Hall, Joe. "*The Dean's December:* A Separate Account of a Separate Account." *Saul Bellow Journal* 5.2 (1986): 22–31.

Handlin, Oscar. *The Uprooted: The Epic Story of the Great Migrations That Made the American People.* Boston: Little, Brown, 1951.

Haraway, Donna J. *Simians, Cyborgs, and Women: The Reinvention of Nature.* London: Free Association Books, 1991. 223–30.

Harding, Wendy, and Jacky Martin. "Reading at the Cultural Interface: The Corn Symbolism of *Beloved.*" *MELUS* 19.2 (1994): 85–97.

Hardy, John Edward. *The Fiction of Walker Percy.* Urbana: University of Illinois Press, 1987.

Harpham, Geoffrey Galt. "E. L. Doctorow and the Technology of Narrative." *PMLA* 100.1 (1985): 81–95.

Harris, Norman. "The Gods Must Be Angry: *Flight to Canada* as Political History." *Modern Fiction Studies* 34.1 (1988): 111–23.

Hassan, Ihab. "Focus on Norman Mailer's *Why Are We in Vietnam?*" In *American Dreams, American Nightmares*. Ed. David Madden. Carbondale: Southern Illinois University Press, 1970. 197–203.

———. *Radical Innocence: Studies in the Contemporary American Novel*. Princeton, N.J.: Princeton University Press, 1961.

Hawthorne, Nathaniel. *The House of Seven Gables*. Vol. 2, Centenary Edition of the Works of Nathaniel Hawthorne. Ed. Fredson Bowers. Columbus: Ohio State University Press, 1965.

Hayles, N. Katherine. *The Cosmic Web: Scientific Field Models and Literary Strategies in the Twentieth Century*. Ithaca, N.Y.: Cornell University Press, 1984.

Hayward, Nancy. "Walker Percy's Vision: A Study of Thanatos." *Notes on Mississippi Writers* 20.2 (1988): 49–61.

Hearn, Charles R. *The American Dream in the Great Depression*. Westport, Conn.: Greenwood Press, 1977.

Heilbrun, Carolyn G. "Marriage and Contemporary Fiction." *Critical Inquiry* 5.2 (Winter 1978): 309–22.

Heinlein, Robert A. *The Moon Is a Harsh Mistress*. 1966. New York: Berkley, 1968.

Heller, Joseph. *Something Happened*. 1974. New York: Ballantine, 1975.

Henriksen, Margot A. *Dr. Strangelove's America: Society and Culture in the Atomic Age*. Berkeley: University of California Press, 1997.

Hicks, Thomas H. "Updike's Rabbit Novels: An American Epic." *Sacred Heart University Review* 13.1–2 (1992–93): 65–70.

Hijuelos, Oscar. *The Mambo Kings Play Songs of Love*. 1989. New York: Perennial Library, 1990.

Hirsch, E. D., Jr. *Cultural Literacy: What Every American Needs to Know*. 1987. New York: Vintage, 1988.

Hite, Molly. *Ideas of Order in the Novels of Thomas Pynchon*. Columbus: Ohio State University Press, 1983.

Hobbs, Michael. "Living In-Between: Tayo as Radical Reader in Leslie Marmon Silko's *Ceremony*." *Western American Literature* 28.4 (1994): 301–12.

Hochbruck, Wolfgang. "Breaking Away: The Novels of Gerald Vizenor." *World Literature Today* 66.2 (1992): 274–78.

Hofstadter, Richard. *The Paranoid Style in American Politics and Other Essays*. New York: Knopf, 1966.

Holder, Alan. "'What Marvelous Plot . . . Was Afoot?' History in Barth's *The Sot-Weed Factor*." *American Quarterly* 20.3 (1968): 596–604.

Holland, Sharon P. "'If You Know I Have a History, You Will Respect Me': A Perspective on Afro–Native American Literature." *Callaloo* 17.1 (1994): 334–50.

Hollinger, Veronica. "Cybernetic Deconstructions: Cyberpunk and Postmodernism." *Mosaic* 23.2 (1990): 29–44.

Horvath, Brooke. "The Failure of Erotic Questing in John Updike's Rabbit Novels." *Denver Quarterly* 23.2 (1988): 70–89.

Horwitz, Tony. *Confederates in the Attic: Dispatches from the Unfinished Civil War.* New York: Pantheon, 1998.

Hovet, Grace Ann, and Barbara Lounsberry. "Flying as Symbol and Legend in Toni Morrison's *The Bluest Eye, Sula,* and *Song of Solomon.*" *College Language Association Journal* 27.2 (1983): 119–40.

Hughes, Robert. "Walker Percy's Comedy and *The Thanatos Syndrome.*" *Southern Literary Journal* 22.1 (1989): 3–16.

Hume, Kathryn. "Ishmael Reed and the Problematics of Control." *PMLA* 108.3 (1993): 506–18.

———. *Pynchon's Mythography: An Approach to "Gravity's Rainbow."* Carbondale: Southern Illinois University Press, 1987.

———. "Views from Above, Views from Below: A Perspectival Subtext in *Gravity's Rainbow.*" *American Literature* 60.4 (1988): 625–42.

Hutcheon, Linda. *A Poetics of Postmodernism: History, Theory, Fiction.* New York: Routledge, 1988.

Irmer, Thomas. "Bret Easton Ellis's *American Psycho* and Its Submerged References to the 1960s." *Zeitschrift für Anglistik und Amerikanistik* 41.4 (1993): 349–56.

Jackson, Rosemary. *Fantasy: The Literature of Subversion.* London: Methuen, 1981.

Jacobs, Naomi. "Kathy Acker and the Plagiarized Self." *Review of Contemporary Fiction* 9.3 (1989): 50–55.

James, D. G. *Skepticism and Poetry: An Essay on the Poetic Imagination.* London: George Allen and Unwin, 1937.

Jameson, Fredric. *Marxism and Form: Twentieth-Century Dialectical Theories of Literature.* 1971. Princeton, N.J.: Princeton University Press, 1974.

Jaynes, Julian. *The Origin of Consciousness in the Breakdown of the Bicameral Mind.* Boston: Houghton Mifflin, 1976.

Jenkins, Philip. *Using Murder: The Social Construction of Serial Homicide.* Hawthorne, N.Y.: Aldine De Gruyter, 1994.

Jessee, Sharon. "'Tell Me Your Earrings': Time and the Marvelous in Toni Morrison's *Beloved.*" In *Memory, Narrative, and Identity: New Essays in Ethnic American Literatures.* Ed. Amritjit Singh, Joseph T. Skerrett Jr., and Robert E. Hogan. Boston: Northeastern University Press, 1994. 198–211.

Johnson, Mark. "The Virgin and the Cooling Tower: Literature as Science in

Percy's The Thanatos Syndrome." New Orleans Review 16.4 (1989): 22–26.

Johnston, John. "Superlinear Fiction or Historical Diagram?: Don DeLillo's Libra." Modern Fiction Studies 40.2 (1994): 319–42.

Jones, Howard Mumford. O Strange New World: American Culture—The Formative Years. New York: Viking, 1964.

Karl, Frederick R. American Fictions, 1940–1980: A Comprehensive History and Critical Evaluation. 1983. New York: Harper Colophon, 1985.

Keesey, Douglas. Don DeLillo. New York: Twayne, 1993.

Kennedy, J. Gerald. "The Sundered Self and the Riven World: Love in the Ruins." In The Art of Walker Percy: Stratagems for Being. Ed. Panthea Reid Broughton. Baton Rouge: Louisiana State University Press, 1979. 115–36.

Kennedy, Liam. "Memory and Hearsay: Ethnic History and Identity in Billy Phelan's Greatest Game and Ironweed." MELUS 18.1 (1993): 71–82.

Kennedy, Paul M. The Rise and Fall of the Great Powers: Economic Change and Military Conflict from 1500 to 2000. New York: Random House, 1987.

Kennedy, William. Billy Phelan's Greatest Game. 1978. New York: Penguin, 1983.

———. Ironweed. 1983. New York: Penguin, 1984.

———. Legs. 1975. New York: Penguin, 1983.

———. Very Old Bones. 1992. New York: Penguin, 1993.

Kent, George E. "Ralph Ellison and Afro-American Folk and Cultural Tradition" (1970). In Ralph Ellison: A Collection of Critical Essays. Ed. John Hersey. Englewood Cliffs, N.J.: Prentice Hall, 1974. 160–70.

Kermode, Frank. "Decoding the Trystero." In Pynchon: A Collection of Critical Essays. Ed. Edward Mendelson. Englewood Cliffs, N.J.: Prentice Hall, 1978. 162–66.

Kesey, Ken. One Flew over the Cuckoo's Nest. New York: NAL Signet, 1962.

Kiernan, Robert F. Saul Bellow. New York: Continuum, 1989.

Kim, Elaine H. Asian American Literature: An Introduction to the Writings and Their Social Context. Philadelphia: Temple University Press, 1982.

Kingston, Maxine Hong. China Men. 1980. New York: Vintage, 1989.

———. "Cultural Mis-Readings by American Reviewers." In Asian and Western Writers in Dialogue: New Cultural Identities. Ed. Guy Amirthanayagam. London: Macmillan, 1982. 55–65.

———. Tripmaster Monkey: His Fake Book. 1989. New York: Vintage, 1990.

———. The Woman Warrior: Memoirs of a Girlhood among Ghosts. 1976. New York: Vintage, 1989.

Klinkowitz, Jerome. Literary Disruptions: The Making of a Post-Contemporary American Fiction. 2d ed. Urbana: University of Illinois Press, 1980.

Kosinski, Jerzy. Cockpit. 1975. New York: Bantam, 1976.

———. Passion Play. 1979. New York: Bantam, 1980.

———. Pinball. 1982. New York: Bantam, 1983.

Kremer, S. Lillian. "The Holocaust in *Mr. Sammler's Planet.*" *Saul Bellow Journal* 4.1 (1985): 19–32.

Kronick, Joseph. "*Libra* and the Assassination of JFK: A Textbook Operation." *Arizona Quarterly* 50.1 (1994): 109–32.

Krumholz, Linda. "Dead Teachers: Rituals of Manhood and Rituals of Reading in *Song of Solomon.*" *Modern Fiction Studies* 39.3–4 (1993): 551–74.

Kuenz, Jane. "*The Bluest Eye:* Notes on History, Community, and Black Female Subjectivity." *African American Review* 27.3 (1993): 421–31.

Lamadrid, Enrique R. "The Dynamics of Myth in the Creative Vision of Rudolfo Anaya." In *Pasó por Aquí: Critical Essays on the New Mexican Literary Tradition, 1542–1988.* Ed. Erlinda Gonzales-Berry. Albuquerque: University of New Mexico Press, 1989. 243–54.

———. "Myth as the Cognitive Process of Popular Culture in Rudolfo Anaya's *Bless Me, Ultima:* The Dialectics of Knowledge." *Hispania* 68.3 (1985): 496–501.

La Polla, Franco. "*The Free-Lance Pallbearers;* or, No More Proscenium Arch." *Review of Contemporary Fiction* 4.2 (1984): 188–95.

Larson, Janet. "Stories Sacred and Profane: Narrative in *One Flew over the Cuckoo's Nest.*" *Religion and Literature* 16.2 (1984): 25–42.

Larson, Sidner. "The Fragmentation of a Tribal People in Louise Erdrich's *Tracks.*" *American Indian Culture and Research Journal* 17.2 (1993): 1–13.

Lasch, Christopher. *The Culture of Narcissism: American Life in an Age of Diminishing Expectations.* New York: W. W. Norton, 1979.

———. *The True and Only Heaven: Progress and Its Critics.* New York: W. W. Norton, 1991.

Lattin, Vernon E. "The 'Horror of Darkness': Meaning and Structure in Anaya's *Bless Me, Ultima.*" *Revista Chicano-Requeña* 6.2 (1978): 50–57.

———. "The Quest for Mythic Vision in Contemporary Native American and Chicano Fiction." *American Literature* 50.4 (1979): 625–40.

Lawson, Lewis A. "Tom More: Cartesian Physician." *Delta* 13 (1981): 67–82.

———. "Tom More and Sigmund Freud." *New Orleans Review* 16.4 (1989): 27–31.

LeClair, Tom. *The Art of Excess: Mastery in Contemporary American Fiction.* Urbana: University of Illinois Press, 1989.

———. "Robert Coover, *The Public Burning,* and the Art of Excess." *Critique* 23.3 (1992): 5–28.

———. "Walker Percy's Devil." In *The Art of Walker Percy: Stratagems for Being.* Ed. Panthea Reid Broughton. Baton Rouge: Louisiana State University Press, 1979. 157–68.

Lee, Kun Jong. "Ellison's *Invisible Man:* Emersonianism Revised." *PMLA* 107.2 (1992): 331–44.

Lee, Rachel. "Missing Peace in Toni Morrison's *Sula* and *Beloved.*" *African American Review* 28.4 (1994): 571–83.

Leeds, Barry H. "One Flew, Two Followed: Stage and Screen Adaptations of *Cuckoo's Nest.*" In *Take Two: Adapting the Contemporary American Novel to Film.* Ed. Barbara Tepa Lupack. Bowling Green, Ohio: Bowling Green State University Popular Press, 1994. 36–50.

Le Guin, Ursula. *Always Coming Home.* 1985. New York: Bantam, 1986.

———. "The Day before the Revolution" (1974). In *The Best of the Nebulas.* Ed. Ben Bova. New York: Tor, 1989. 390–401.

———. *The Dispossessed.* 1974. New York: Avon, 1975.

Lennon, John Michael. "Mailer's Cosmology." *Modern Language Studies* 12.3 (1982): 18–29.

Lentricchia, Frank. "*Libra* as Postmodern Critique." In *Introducing Don DeLillo.* Ed. Frank Lentricchia. Durham, N.C.: Duke University Press, 1991. 193–215.

Lesser, Ellen. "An Interview with Carolyn Chute." *New England Review and Bread Loaf Quarterly* 8.2 (1985): 158–77.

Levine, Paul. "*The Dean's December:* Between the Observatory and the Crematorium." In *Saul Bellow at Seventy-five: A Collection of Critical Essays.* Ed. Gerhard Bach. Tübingen, Germany: Gunter Narr Verlag, 1991. 125–36.

Lewis, Charles. "The Ironic Romance of New Historicism: *The Scarlet Letter* and *Beloved* Standing in Side by Side." *Arizona Quarterly* 51.1 (1995): 33–60.

Lewis, R. W. B. *The American Adam: Innocence, Tragedy, and Tradition in the Nineteenth Century.* Chicago: University of Chicago Press, 1955.

Li, David Leiwei. "*China Men:* Maxine Hong Kingston and the American Canon." *American Literary History* 2.3 (1990): 482–502.

Lim, Shirley Geok-lin, and Amy Ling, eds. *Reading the Literatures of Asian America.* Philadelphia: Temple University Press, 1992.

Lin, Patricia. "Clashing Constructs of Reality: Reading Maxine Hong Kingston's *Tripmaster Monkey: His Fake Book* as Indigenous Ethnography." In *Reading the Literatures of Asian America.* Ed. Shirley Geok-lin Lim and Amy Ling. Philadelphia: Temple University Press, 1992. 333–48.

Linton, Patricia. "The 'Person' in Postmodern Fiction: Gibson, Le Guin, and Vizenor." *Studies in American Indian Literatures* ser. 2, 5.3 (1993): 3–11.

Lorsch, Susan E. "Doctorow's *The Book of Daniel* as *Künstlerroman:* The Politics of Art." *Papers on Language and Literature* 18.4 (1982): 384–97.

Luschei, Martin. *The Sovereign Wayfarer: Walker Percy's Diagnosis of the Malaise.* Baton Rouge: Louisiana State University Press, 1972.

Lustig, Jessica. "Home: An Interview with John Edgar Wideman." *African American Review* 26.3 (1992): 453–57.

Lutz, Hartmut. "The Circle as Philosophical and Structural Concept in Native American Fiction Today." In *Native American Literatures.* Ed. Laura Coltelli. Pisa, Italy: Servizio Editoriale Universitario, 1989. 85–100.

Lyne, William. "The Signifying Modernist: Ralph Ellison and the Limits of the Double Consciousness." *PMLA* 107.2 (1992): 319–30.

Macdonald, Andrew (pseud. for William L. Pierce). *The Turner Diaries.* (Serialized in 1975.) 2d ed. Hillsboro, W.Va.: National Vanguard Books, 1980.

Madden, David, ed. *American Dreams, American Nightmares.* Carbondale: Southern Illinois University Press, 1970.

Madden, Fred. "Sanity and Responsibility: Big Chief as Narrator and Executioner." *Modern Fiction Studies* 32.2 (1986): 203–17.

Madsen, Deborah L. *The Postmodernist Allegories of Thomas Pynchon.* Leicester, England: Leicester University Press, 1991.

Magalaner, Marvin. "Of Cars, Time, and the River." In *American Women Writing Fiction: Memory, Identity, Family, Space.* Ed. Mickey Pearlman. Lexington: University Press of Kentucky, 1989. 94–109.

Mailer, Norman. *Advertisements for Myself.* 1959. New York: Signet, 1960.

———. *An American Dream.* London: Andre Deutsch, 1965.

———. *The Naked and the Dead.* 1948. New York: Signet, n.d.

———. *Why Are We in Vietnam?* 1967. New York: Holt, Rinehart and Winston, 1982.

Martin, Mike W. "*Invisible Man* and the Indictment of Innocence." *College Language Association Journal* 25.3 (1982): 288–302.

Marx, Leo. *The Machine in the Garden: Technology and the Pastoral Ideal in America.* 1964. New York: Oxford University Press, 1967.

Mathieson, Barbara Offutt. "Memory and Mother Love: Toni Morrison's Dyad." In *Memory, Narrative, and Identity: New Essays in Ethnic American Literatures.* Ed. Amritjit Singh, Joseph T. Skerrett Jr., and Robert E. Hogan. Boston: Northeastern University Press, 1994. 212–32.

Maver, Igor. "The Delicate Balance of Tension in Saul Bellow's *The Dean's December:* An Attempt at Interpretation from a European Perspective." In *Cross-Cultural Studies: American, Canadian, and European Literatures, 1945–1985.* Ed. Mirko Jurak. Ljubljana, Yugoslavia: Učne Delavnice, 1988. 107–13.

Mayer, Sylvia. "'You Like Huckleberries?' Toni Morrison's *Beloved* and Mark Twain's *Adventures of Huckleberry Finn.*" In *The Black Columbiad: Defining Moments in African American Literature and Culture.* Ed. Werner Sollors and Maria Diedrich. Cambridge, Mass.: Harvard University Press, 1994. 337–46.

Mazurek, Raymond A. "'Bringing the Corners Forward': Ideology and Representation in Updike's Rabbit Trilogy." In *Politics and the Muse: Studies in the Politics of Recent American Literature.* Ed. Adam J. Sorkin. Bowling Green, Ohio: Bowling Green State University Popular Press, 1989. 142–60.

———. "Metafiction, the Historical Novel, and Coover's *The Public Burning.*" *Critique* 23.3 (1982): 29–41.

McCaffery, Larry. "Donald Barthelme: The Aesthetics of Trash (*Snow White*)." In *Critical Essays on Donald Barthelme*. Ed. Richard F. Patteson. New York: G. K. Hall, 1992. 153–63.

McCaffrey, Anne. *Crystal Singer.* Garden City, N.Y.: Doubleday, 1982.

McClure, John. *Late Imperial Romance.* London: Verso, 1994.

McGrath, Michael J. Gargas. "Kesey and Vonnegut: The Critique of Liberal Democracy in Contemporary Literature." In *The Artist and Political Vision.* Ed. Benjamin R. Barber and Michael J. Gargas McGrath. New Brunswick, N.J.: Transaction Books, 1982. 363–83.

McHale, Brian. *Constructing Postmodernism.* London: Routledge, 1992.

———. *Postmodernist Fiction.* New York: Methuen, 1987.

McInerney, Jay. *Bright Lights, Big City.* 1984. New York: Vintage, 1987.

McKay, Nellie. "An Interview with Toni Morrison." *Contemporary Literature* 24.4 (1983): 413–29.

McLaughlin, Robert L. "Pynchon's Angels and Supernatural Sytems in *Gravity's Rainbow.*" *Pynchon Notes* 22–23 (1988): 25–33.

Meisenhelder, Susan. "'The Whole Picture' in Gloria Naylor's *Mama Day.*" *African American Review* 27.3 (1993): 405–19.

Mellard, James M. *The Exploded Form: The Modernist Novel in America.* Urbana: University of Illinois Press, 1980.

Mendelson, Edward. "The Sacred, the Profane, and *The Crying of Lot 49.*" In *Pynchon: A Collection of Critical Essays.* Ed. Edward Mendelson. Englewood Cliffs, N.J.: Prentice Hall, 1978. 112–46.

Mengeling, Marvin E. "Ray Bradbury's *Dandelion Wine:* Themes, Sources, and Style." *English Journal* 60.7 (1971): 877–87.

Michael, Magali Cornier. "The Political Paradox within Don DeLillo's *Libra.*" *Critique* 35.3 (1994): 146–56.

Miller, Ruth. *Saul Bellow: A Biography of the Imagination.* New York: St. Martin's Press, 1991.

Mogen, David. "The Frontier Archetype and the Myth of America: Patterns That Shape the American Dream." In *The Frontier Experience and the American Dream: Essays on American Literature.* Ed. David Mogen, Mark Busby, and Paul Bryant. College Station: Texas A&M University Press, 1989. 15–30.

Mogen, David, Mark Busby, and Paul Bryant, eds. *The Frontier Experience and the American Dream: Essays on American Literature.* College Station: Texas A&M University Press, 1989.

Momaday, N. Scott. *House Made of Dawn.* 1968. New York: Harper and Row Perennial, 1977.

Montgomery, Maxine Lavon. "A Pilgrimage to the Origins: The Apocalypse as Structure and Theme in Toni Morrison's *Sula.*" *Black American Literature Forum* 23.1 (1989): 127–37.

Morace, Robert A. "Donald Barthelme's *Snow White:* The Novel, the Critics, and the Culture." In *Critical Essays on Donald Barthelme.* Ed. Richard F. Patteson. New York: G. K. Hall, 1992. 164–72.

Moreland, Richard C. "'He Wants to Put His Story Next to Hers': Putting Twain's Story Next to Hers in Morrison's *Beloved.*" *Modern Fiction Studies* 39.3–4 (1993): 501–25.

Morey-Gaines, Ann-Janine. "Of Menace and Men: The Sexual Tensions of the American Frontier Metaphor." *Soundings* 64.2 (1981): 132–49.

Morrison, Toni. *Beloved.* 1987. New York: Plume, 1988.

———. *The Bluest Eye.* 1970. New York: Washington Square Press/Pocket Books, 1972.

———. *Playing in the Dark: Whiteness and the Literary Imagination.* Cambridge, Mass.: Harvard University Press, 1992.

———. *Song of Solomon.* 1977. New York: Signet, 1978.

———. *Sula.* 1973. New York: Plume, 1982.

———. *Tar Baby.* 1981. New York: Plume, 1982.

Moses, Wilson J. "The Novel and Its Afro-American, American, and European Traditions: *Invisible Man* and the American Way of Intellectual History." In *Approaches to Teaching Ellison's "Invisible Man."* Ed. Susan Resneck Parr and Pancho Savery. New York: Modern Language Association of America, 1989. 58–64.

Mott, Christopher M. "*Libra* and the Subject of History." *Critique* 35.3 (1994): 131–45.

Mukherjee, Bharati. *Jasmine.* 1989. New York: Ballantine, 1991.

Murtaugh, Daniel M. "Fathers and Their Sons: William Kennedy's Hero-Transgressors." *Commonweal,* 19 May 1989, 298–302.

Nadeau, Robert. *Readings from the New Book on Nature: Physics and Metaphysics in the Modern Novel.* Amherst: University of Massachusetts Press, 1981.

Nadel, Alan. *Invisible Criticism: Ralph Ellison and the American Canon.* Iowa City: University of Iowa Press, 1988.

Naylor, Gloria. *Bailey's Cafe.* 1992. New York: Vintage, 1993.

———. *Linden Hills.* 1985. New York: Penguin, 1986.

———. "Love and Sex in the Afro-American Novel." *Yale Review* 78.1 (1989): 19–31.

———. *Mama Day.* 1988. New York: Vintage, 1989.

———. *The Women of Brewster Place.* 1982. New York: Penguin, 1983.

Nelson, Robert M. "Place and Vision: The Function of Landscape in *Ceremony.*" *Journal of the Southwest* 30.3 (1988): 281–316.

———. *Place and Vision: The Function of Landscape in Native American Fiction.* New York: Peter Lang, 1993.

Newman, Judie. "Bellow and Nihilism: *The Dean's December.*" *Studies in the Literary Imagination* 17.2 (1984): 111–22.

Newman, Katherine S. *Declining Fortunes: The Withering of the American Dream.* New York: Basic Books, 1993.

Nicholls, Peter. "Robert A. Heinlein." In *Science Fiction Writers: Critical Studies of the Major Authors from the Early Nineteenth Century to the Present Day.* Ed. E. F. Bleiler. New York: Scribners, 1982. 185–96.

Nilsen, Helge Normann. "A New Kind of Male-Female Relationship: A Note on Saul Bellow's *The Dean's December.*" *International Fiction Review* 13.2 (1986): 89–92.

Nixon, Nicola. "Cyberpunk: Preparing the Ground for Revolution or Keeping the Boys Satisfied?" *Science-Fiction Studies* 19 (1992): 219–35.

Noble, David W. *The Eternal Adam and the New World Garden: The Central Myth in the American Novel since 1830.* 1968. New York: Universal Library, 1971.

Nohrnberg, James. "Pynchon's Paraclete." In *Pynchon: A Collection of Critical Essays.* Ed. Edward Mendelson. Englewood Cliffs, N.J.: Prentice Hall, 1978. 147–61.

Novelli, Cornelius. "Francis Phelan and the Hands of Heracles: Hero and City in William Kennedy's *Ironweed.*" *Classical and Modern Literature* 12.2 (1992): 119–26.

O'Brien, Tim. *The Things They Carried.* 1990. New York: Penguin, 1991.

O'Donnell, Patrick. "Engendering Paranoia in Contemporary Narrative." *boundary 2* 19.1 (1992): 181–204.

Ohmann, Richard. "The Shaping of a Canon: U.S. Fiction, 1960–1975." *Critical Inquiry* 10.1 (1983): 199–223.

Olsen, Lance. "The Shadow of Spirit in William Gibson's Matrix Trilogy." *Extrapolation* 32.3 (1991): 278–89.

Olster, Stacy. "Rabbit Rerun: Updike's Replay of Popular Culture in *Rabbit at Rest.*" *Modern Fiction Studies* 37.1 (1991): 45–59.

———. "Rabbit Is Redundant: Updike's End of an American Epoch." In *Neo-Realism in Contemporary American Fiction.* Ed. Kristiaan Versluys. Amsterdam, The Netherlands: Rodopi, 1992. 111–29.

O'Meally, Robert G. *The Craft of Ralph Ellison.* Cambridge, Mass.: Harvard University Press, 1980.

———. "Introduction." In *New Essays on "Invisible Man."* Ed. Robert O'Meally. Cambridge: Cambridge University Press, 1988. 1–23.

Orlov, Paul A. "A Fiction of Politically Fantastic 'Facts': Robert Coover's *The Public Burning.*" In *Politics and The Muse: Studies in the Politics of Recent American Literature.* Ed. Adam J. Sorkin. Bowling Green, Ohio: Bowling Green State University Popular Press, 1989. 111–23.

Orr, Elaine. "Mothering as Good Fiction: Instances from Marge Piercy's *Woman on the Edge of Time.*" *Journal of Narrative Technique* 23.2 (1993): 61–79.

Osagie, Iyunolu. "Is Morrison Also among the Prophets? 'Psychoanalytic' Strategies in *Beloved.*" *African American Review* 28.3 (1994): 423–40.

Owens, Louis. "Afterword." In *Bearheart: The Heirship Chronicles* by Gerald Vizenor. 1978. Minneapolis: University of Minneapolis Press, 1990. 247–54.
———. "'Grinning Aboriginal Demons': Gerald Vizenor's *Bearheart* and the Indian's Escape From Gothic." In *Frontier Gothic: Terror and Wonder at the Frontier in American Literature*. Ed. David Mogen, Scott P. Sanders, and Joanne B. Karpinski. Cranbury, N.J.: Associated University Presses, 1993. 71–83.
Ozick, Cynthia. *The Messiah of Stockholm*. 1987. New York: Vintage, 1988.
Paredes, Raymund A. "The Evolution of Chicano Literature." In *Three American Literatures*. Ed. Houston A. Baker Jr. New York: Modern Language Association of America, 1982. 33–79.
Parker, Hershel. *Flawed Texts and Verbal Icons: Literary Authority in American Fiction*. Evanston, Ill.: Northwestern University Press, 1984.
Parrington, Vernon Louis, Jr. *American Dreams: A Study of American Utopias*. 2d ed. New York: Russell and Russell, 1964.
Paulson, Ronald. *The Fictions of Satire*. Baltimore, Md.: Johns Hopkins University Press, 1967.
Pearce, Richard. "Norman Mailer's *Why Are We in Vietnam?*: A Radical Critique of Frontier Values." *Modern Fiction Studies* 17.3 (1971): 409–14.
Percy, Walker. *Love in the Ruins*. 1971. New York: Ballantine, 1989.
———. *The Thanatos Syndrome*. 1987. New York: Ballantine, 1988.
Perin, Constance. *Belonging in America: Reading between the Lines*. Madison: University of Wisconsin Press, 1988.
Peterson, Nancy J. "History, Postmodernism, and Louise Erdrich's *Tracks*." *PMLA* 109.5 (1994): 982–94.
Phelan, James. "Toward a Rhetorical Reader-Response Criticism: The Difficult, the Stubborn, and the Ending of *Beloved*." *Modern Fiction Studies* 39.3–4 (1993): 709–28.
Philmus, Robert M. "Ursula Le Guin and Time's Dispossession." In *Science Fiction Roots and Branches: Contemporary Critical Approaches*. Ed. Rhys Garnett and R. J. Ellis. New York: St. Martin's Press, 1990. 125–50.
Piercy, Marge. *He, She and It*. 1991. New York: Ballantine, 1993.
———. *Woman on the Edge of Time*. New York: Fawcett Crest, 1976.
Pinsker, Sanford. "America's Conspiratorial Imagination." *Virginia Quarterly Review* 68.4 (1992): 605–25.
Pittman, Barbara L. "'Dangerously Absent Dreamers': Genealogy, History, and the Political Left in *Vineland*." *Pynchon Notes* 30–31 (1992): 39–51.
Pops, Martin. "The Metamorphoses of Shit." *Salmagundi* 56 (1982): 26–61.
Porter, M. Gilbert. "From Babbit to Rabbit: The American Materialist in Search of a Soul." *Costerus* 66 (1988): 185–96.
Porush, David. *The Soft Machine: Cybernetic Fiction*. New York: Methuen, 1985.
Post, Robert C. "A Theory of Genre: Romance, Realism, and Moral Reality."

American Quarterly 33.4 (1981): 367–90.

Powers, Richard. *The Gold Bug Variations.* 1991. New York: Harper Perennial, 1992.

Pynchon, Thomas. *The Crying of Lot 49.* 1966. New York: Bantam, 1967.

———. *Gravity's Rainbow.* New York: Viking, 1973.

———. *Vineland.* Boston: Little, Brown, 1990.

Rabine, Leslie W. "No Lost Paradise: Social Gender and Symbolic Gender in
the Writings of Maxine Hong Kingston." *Signs* 12.3 (1987): 471–92.

Radin, Paul. *The Trickster: A Study in American Indian Mythology.* New York:
Philosophical Library, 1956.

———. *Winnebago Hero Cycles: A Study in Aboriginal Literature.* Baltimore,
Md.: Waverly Press, 1948.

Rainwater, Catherine. "Reading between Worlds: Narrativity in the Fiction of
Louise Erdrich." *American Literature* 62.3 (1990): 405–22.

Ramage, John. "Myth and Monomyth in Coover's *The Public Burning.*" *Critique* 23.3 (1982): 52–68.

Ramsey, Roger. "Current and Recurrent: The Vietnam Novel." *Modern Fiction Studies* 17.3 (1971): 415–31.

Redding, Arthur F. "Bruises, Roses: Masochism and the Writing of Kathy Acker." *Contemporary Literature* 35.2 (1994): 281–304.

Reed, Ishmael. *Flight to Canada.* 1976. New York: Atheneum, 1989.

———. *The Freelance Pallbearers.* 1967. London: Allison and Busby, 1990.

———. *Mumbo Jumbo.* 1972. New York: Atheneum, 1988.

———. *The Terrible Threes.* 1989. New York: Atheneum, 1990.

———. *The Terrible Twos.* 1982. New York: Atheneum, 1988.

———. *Yellow Back Radio Broke-Down.* 1969. London: Allison and Busby,
1971.

Reed, T. V. "Genealogy/Narrative/Power: Questions of Postmodernity in Doctorow's *The Book of Daniel.*" *American Literary History* 4.2 (1992): 288–304.

Reilly, John M. "Criticism of Ethnic Literature: Seeing the Whole Story."
MELUS 5.1 (1978): 2–13.

Reitz, Bernhard. "The Reconstruction of the Fifties in E. L. Doctorow's *The
Book of Daniel* and Robert Coover's *The Public Burning.*" In *Historiographic
Metafiction in Modern American and Canadian Literature.* Ed. Bernd Engler and Kurt Müller. Paderborn, Germany: Ferdinand Schöningh, 1994. 223–
40.

Ristoff, Dilvo I. *Updike's America: The Presence of Contemporary American
History in John Updike's Rabbit Trilogy.* New York: Peter Lang, 1988.

Robertson, Pat. *The End of the Age.* Dallas, Tex.: Word Publishing, 1995.

Robinson, Douglas. *American Apocalypses: The Image of the End of the World
in American Literature.* Baltimore, Md.: Johns Hopkins University Press,
1985.

Rölvaag, O. E. *Giants in the Earth.* 1927. New York: Harper and Brothers, 1929.

Rosenberg, Bruce A. "Kennedy in Camelot: The Arthurian Legend in America." *Western Folklore* 35.1 (1976): 52–59.
Rosenthal, Pam. "Jacked In: Fordism, Cyberpunk, Marxism." *Socialist Review* 21.1 (1991): 79–103.
Roth, Philip. *The Counterlife.* 1986. New York: Penguin, 1988.
Rovit, Earl H. "Ralph Ellison and the American Comic Tradition" (1960). In *Ralph Ellison: A Collection of Critical Essays.* Ed. John Hersey. Englewood Cliffs, N.J.: Prentice Hall, 1974. 151–59.
Rowell, Charles H. "An Interview with John Edgar Wideman." *Callaloo* 13.1 (1990): 47–61.
Rubenstein, Roberta. *Boundaries of the Self: Gender, Culture, Fiction.* Urbana: University of Illinois Press, 1987.
Ruppert, James. "Mediation and Multiple Narrative in Contemporary Native American Fiction." *Texas Studies in Literature and Language* 28.2 (1986): 209–25.
———. "Mediation and Multiple Narrative in *Love Medicine.*" *North Dakota Quarterly* 59.4 (1991): 229–41.
Rushdy, Ashraf H. A. "Fraternal Blues: John Edgar Wideman's Homewood Trilogy." *Contemporary Literature* 32.3 (1991): 312–45.
———. "Ishmael Reed's Neo-HooDoo Slave Narrative." *Narrative* 2.3 (1994): 112–39.
Russ, Joanna. "When It Changed" (1972). In *The Best of the Nebulas.* Ed. Ben Bova. New York: Tor, 1989. 304–10.
Safer, Elaine B. "'It's the Truth Even If It Didn't Happen': Ken Kesey's *One Flew over the Cuckoo's Nest*" (1977). In *A Casebook on Ken Kesey's "One Flew over the Cuckoo's Nest."* Ed. George J. Searles. Albuquerque: University of New Mexico Press, 1992. 151–61.
Saltzman, Arthur M. "The Aesthetic of Doubt in Recent Fiction." *University of Denver Quarterly* 20.1 (1985): 89–106.
Sanders, Scott P. "Southwestern Gothic: Alienation, Integration, and Rebirth in the Works of Richard Shelton, Rudolfo Anaya, and Leslie Silko." *Weber Studies* 4.2 (1987): 36–53.
Sands, Kathleen Mullen. "Closing the Distance: Critic, Reader, and the Works of James Welch." *MELUS* 14.2 (1987): 73–85.
Sargent, Lyman Tower. "A New Anarchism: Social and Political Ideas in Some Recent Feminist Eutopias." In *Women and Utopia: Critical Interpretations.* Ed. Marleen Barr and Nicholas D. Smith. Lanham, Md.: University Press of America, 1983. 3–33.
Saunders, James Robert. "The Ornamentations of Old Ideas: Gloria Naylor's First Three Novels." *Hollins Critic* 27.2 (1990): 1–11.
Scarberry-García, Susan. *Landmarks of Healing: A Study of "House Made of Dawn."* Albuquerque: University of New Mexico Press, 1990.
Schaub, Thomas. "Ellison's Masks and the Novel of Reality." In *New Essays*

on *"Invisible Man."* Ed. Robert O'Meally. Cambridge: Cambridge University Press, 1988. 123–56.

Schaub, Thomas Hill. *American Fiction in the Cold War.* Madison: University of Wisconsin Press, 1991.

Schmitz, Neil. "Neo-HooDoo: The Experimental Fiction of Ishmael Reed." *Twentieth Century Literature* 20 (1974): 126–40.

Schöpp, Joseph C. "'Riding Bareback, Backwards through a Wood of Words': Ishmael Reed's Revision of the Slave Narrative." In *Historiographic Metafiction in Modern American and Canadian Literature.* Ed. Bernd Engler and Kurt Müller. Paderborn, Germany: Ferdinand Schöningh, 1994. 267–78.

Schor, Edith. *Visible Ellison: A Study of Ralph Ellison's Fiction.* Westport, Conn.: Greenwood Press, 1993.

Schueller, Malini Johar. "Theorizing Ethnicity and Subjectivity: Maxine Hong Kingston's *Tripmaster Monkey* and Amy Tan's *The Joy Luck Club.*" *Genders* 15 (1992): 72–85.

Schweninger, Lee. "Writing Nature: Silko and Native Americans as Nature Writers." *MELUS* 18.2 (1993): 47–60.

Segal, Erich. *Acts of Faith.* New York: Bantam, 1992.

Sergi, Jennifer. "Storytelling: Tradition and Preservation in Louise Erdrich's *Tracks.*" *World Literature Today* 66.2 (1992): 279–82.

Shear, Walter. "Generational Differences and the Diaspora in *The Joy Luck Club.*" *Critique* 34.3 (1993): 193–99.

Shelton, Frank W. "E. L. Doctorow's *Welcome to Hard Times:* The Western and the American Dream." *Midwest Quarterly* 25.1 (1983): 7–17.

Shih, Shu-mei. "Exile and Intertextuality in Maxine Hong Kingston's *China Men.*" In *The Literature of Emigration and Exile.* Ed. James Whitlark and Wendell Aycock. Lubbock: Texas Tech University Press, 1992. 65–77.

Shostak, Debra. "Maxine Hong Kingston's Fake Books." In *Memory, Narrative, and Identity: New Essays in Ethnic American Literatures.* Ed. Amritjit Singh, Joseph T. Skerrett Jr., and Robert E. Hogan. Boston: Northeastern University Press, 1994. 233–60.

Siegle, Robert. *Suburban Ambush: Downtown Writing and the Fiction of Insurgency.* Baltimore, Md.: Johns Hopkins University Press, 1989.

Silberman, Robert. "Opening the Text: *Love Medicine* and the Return of the Native American Woman." In *Narrative Chance: Postmodern Discourse on Native American Indian Literatures.* Ed. Gerald Vizenor. Albuquerque: University of New Mexico Press, 1989. 101–20.

Silko, Leslie Marmon. *Almanac of the Dead.* 1991. New York: Penguin, 1992.

———. *Ceremony.* 1977. New York: Penguin, 1986.

———. "Landscape, History, and the Pueblo Imagination." *Antæus* 57 (1986): 83–94.

Skårdal, Dorothy Burton. *The Divided Heart: Scandinavian Immigrant Experience through Literary Sources.* Lincoln: University of Nebraska Press, 1974.

Slade, Joseph W. "Communication, Group Theory, and Perception in *Vineland.*" *Critique* 32.2 (1990): 126–44.

Slotkin, Richard. *Gunfighter Nation: The Myth of the Frontier in Twentieth-Century America.* 1992. New York: Harper Perennial, 1993.

Smith, Lorrie N. "'The Things Men Do': The Gendered Subtext in Tim O'Brien's *Esquire* Stories." *Critique* 36.1 (1994): 16–40.

Smith, Philip E., II. "Unbuilding Walls: Human Nature and the Nature of Evolutionary and Political Theory in *The Dispossessed.*" In *Ursula K. Le Guin.* Ed. Joseph D. Olander and Martin Harry Greenberg. New York: Taplinger, 1979. 77–96.

Smith, Valerie. "The Meaning of Narration in *Invisible Man.*" In *New Essays on "Invisible Man."* Ed. Robert O'Meally. Cambridge: Cambridge University Press, 1988. 25–53.

Sollors, Werner, ed. *Beyond Ethnicity: Consent and Descent in American Culture.* New York: Oxford University Press, 1986.

Solomon, Eric. "Argument by Anachronism: The Presence of the 1930s in *Vineland.*" In *The "Vineland" Papers: Critical Takes on Pynchon's Novel.* Ed. Geoffrey Green, Donald J. Greiner, and Larry McCaffery. Normal, Ill.: Dalkey Archive Press, 1994. 161–66.

St. Andrews, B. A. "Healing the Witchery: Medicine in Silko's *Ceremony.*" *Arizona Quarterly* 44.1 (1988): 86–94.

Starhawk. *The Fifth Sacred Thing.* 1993. New York: Bantam, 1994.

Stephenson, Neal. *Snow Crash.* 1992. New York: Bantam, 1993.

Sterling, Bruce. *Islands in the Net.* 1988. New York: Ace, 1989.

Stivale, Charles J. "Mille/Punks/Cyber/Plateaus: Science Fiction and Deleuzo-Guattarian 'Becomings.'" *SubStance* 66 (1991): 66–84.

Stoppard, Tom. *Rosencrantz and Guildenstern Are Dead.* 1967. New York: Grove, 1968.

Strehle, Susan. *Fiction in the Quantum Universe.* Chapel Hill: University of North Carolina Press, 1992.

Sugiura, Ginsaku. "The Collapse of the American Dream and Contemporary Fiction." In *The Traditional and the Anti-Traditional: Studies in Contemporary American Literature.* Ed. Kenzaburo Ohashi. Tokyo: American Literature Society of Japan, 1980. 17–29.

Sullivan, Charles William, III. "Harlan Ellison and Robert A. Heinlein: The Paradigm Makers." In *Clockwork Worlds: Mechanized Environments in SF.* Ed. Richard D. Erlich and Thomas P. Dunn. Westport, Conn.: Greenwood Press, 1983. 97–103.

Sullivan, Ruth. "Big Mama, Big Papa, and Little Sons in Ken Kesey's *One Flew over the Cuckoo's Nest*" (1975). In *A Casebook on Ken Kesey's "One Flew over the Cuckoo's Nest.*" Ed. George J. Searles. Albuquerque: University of New Mexico Press, 1992. 49–66.

Suvin, Darko. *Metamorphoses of Science Fiction: On the Poetics and History of a Literary Genre.* New Haven, Conn.: Yale University Press, 1979.

Swan, Edith. "Feminine Perspectives at Laguna Pueblo: Silko's *Ceremony.*" *Tulsa Studies in Women's Literature* 11.2 (1992): 309–28.

———. "Healing via the Sunwise Cycle in Silko's *Ceremony.*" *American Indian Quarterly* 12.4 (1988): 313–28.

Tan, Amy. *The Joy Luck Club.* New York: Ivy Books, 1989.

Tanner, Tony. *City of Words: American Fiction, 1950–1970.* 1971. London: Jonathan Cape, 1976.

Taylor, Anya. "*Ironweed,* Alcohol, and Celtic Heroism." *Critique* 33.2 (1992): 107–20.

Tharpe, Jac. *John Barth: The Comic Sublimity of Paradox.* Carbondale: Southern Illinois University Press, 1974.

Thompson, Roger. "Restoring the American Dream." *Nation's Business,* May 1995, 18–24.

Tierce, Michael. "William Kennedy's Odyssey: The Travels of Francis Phelan." *Classical and Modern Literature* 8.4 (1988): 247–63.

Tiptree, James, Jr. (pseud. for Alice B. Sheldon). "Houston, Houston, Do You Read?" (1976). In *The Best of the Nebulas.* Ed. Ben Bova. New York: Tor, 1989. 420–60.

Tonn, Horst. "*Bless Me, Ultima:* A Fictional Response to Times of Transition." *Aztlan* 18.1 (1987): 59–68.

Towery, Margie. "Continuity and Connection: Characters in Louise Erdrich's Fiction." *American Indian Culture and Research Journal* 16.4 (1992): 99–115.

Traub, Valerie. "Rainbows of Darkness: Deconstructing Shakespeare in the Work of Gloria Naylor and Zora Neale Hurston." *Cross-Cultural Performances: Differences in Women's Re-Visions of Shakespeare.* Ed. Marianne Novy. Urbana: University of Illinois Press, 1993. 150–64.

Truettner, William H. *The West as America: Reinterpreting Images of the Frontier, 1820–1920.* Washington, D.C.: Smithsonian Institution Press, 1991.

Tschachler, Heinz. "Despotic Reason in Arcadia? Ernest Callenbach's Ecological Utopias." *Science-Fiction Studies* 11.3 (1984): 304–17.

———. "Ernest Callenbach: Ecotopia—A Novel about Ecology, People, and Politics in 1999" (1975). In *Die Utopie in der Angloamerikanischen Literatur: Interpretationen.* Ed. Hartmut Heuermann and Bernd-Peter Lange. Düsseldorf, Germany: Bagel, 1984. 328–48.

Turner, Patricia A. *I Heard It through the Grapevine: Rumor in African-American Culture.* Berkeley: University of California Press, 1993.

Tyson, Lois. "Existential Subjectivity on Trial: *The Crying of Lot 49* and the Politics of Despair." *Pynchon Notes* 28–29 (1991): 5–25.

Updike, John. *Rabbit at Rest.* 1990. New York: Fawcett Crest, 1991.

———. *Rabbit Is Rich*. New York: Knopf, 1981.

———. *Rabbit Redux*. 1971. New York: Fawcett Crest, 1972.

———. *Rabbit, Run*. 1960. New York: Fawcett, 1966.

Vankin, Jonathan. *Conspiracies, Cover-Ups and Crimes: From JFK to the CIA Terrorist Connection*. New York: Dell, 1992.

Velie, Alan. "Gerald Vizenor's Indian Gothic." *MELUS* 17.1 (1991–92): 75–85.

———. "The Trickster Novel." In *Narrative Chance: Postmodern Discourse on Native American Indian Literatures*. Ed. Gerald Vizenor. Albuquerque: University of New Mexico Press, 1989. 121–39.

Viereck, Elisabeth. "The Clown Knew It All Along: The Medium Was the Message." *Delta* 28 (1989): 63–81.

Vizenor, Gerald. *Bearheart: The Heirship Chronicles*. 1978. Minneapolis: University of Minnesota Press, 1990.

———. *Griever: An American Monkey King in China*. 1987. Minneapolis: University of Minnesota Press, 1990.

———. "Native American Indian Literature: Critical Metaphors of the Ghost Dance." *World Literature Today* 66.2 (1992): 223–27.

———. "Trickster Discourse: Comic Holotropes and Language Games." In *Narrative Chance: Postmodern Discourse on Native American Indian Literatures*. Ed. Gerald Vizenor. Albuquerque: University of New Mexico Press, 1989. 187–211.

———. "Tricksters and Transvaluations." In *The Trickster of Liberty: Tribal Heirs to a Wild Baronage*. Minneapolis: University of Minnesota Press, 1988. ix–xviii.

Vonnegut, Kurt. *Bluebeard*. New York: Delacorte Press, 1987.

———. *Breakfast of Champions*. New York: Delta, 1973.

———. *Deadeye Dick*. New York: Delacorte Press, 1982.

———. *Galápagos*. New York: Delacorte Press, 1985.

———. *The Sirens of Titan*. 1959. New York: Dell, 1970.

———. *Slapstick; or, Lonesome No More!* 1976. New York: Delta, 1977.

———. *Slaughterhouse-Five*. New York: Delta, 1969.

Wagenheim, Allan J. "Square's Progress: *An American Dream*." *Critique* 10.1 (1967): 45–68.

Wald, Alan. "The Culture of 'Internal Colonialism': A Marxist Perspective." *MELUS* 8.3 (1981): 18–27.

Waller, Robert James. *The Bridges of Madison County*. New York: Warner, 1992.

Warren, Nagueyalti. "Cocoa and George: A Love Dialectic." *SAGE* 7.2 (1990): 19–25.

Weatherford, Jack. *Indian Givers: How the Indians of the Americas Transformed the World*. New York: Fawcett Columbine, 1988.

———. *Native Roots: How the Indians Enriched America*. New York: Fawcett Columbine, 1991.

Weinstein, Mark. "Communication in *The Dean's December.*" *Saul Bellow Journal* 5.1 (1986): 63–74.

Weixlmann, Joe. "Ishmael Reed's Raven." *Review of Contemporary Fiction* 4.2 (1984): 205–8.

———. "Politics, Piracy, and Other Games: Slavery and Liberation in *Flight to Canada.*" *MELUS* 6.3 (1979): 41–50.

Welch, James. *The Death of Jim Loney.* 1979. New York: Penguin, 1987.

———. *Fools Crow.* 1986. New York: Penguin, 1987.

———. *Winter in the Blood.* 1974. New York: Penguin, 1986.

Welch, James, et al. "A Conversation with James Welch." *South Dakota Review* 28.1 (1990): 103–10.

Wenke, Joseph. *Mailer's America.* Hanover, N.H.: University Press of New England, 1987.

West, Cornel. *The American Evasion of Philosophy: A Genealogy of Pragmatism.* Madison: University of Wisconsin Press, 1989.

Westrum, Dexter. "James Welch's *Fools Crow:* Back to the Future." *San José Studies* 14.2 (1988): 49–58.

Whalen-Bridge, John. *Political Fiction and the American Self.* Urbana: University of Illinois Press, 1998.

Wheeler, Thomas C. *The Immigrant Experience: The Anguish of Becoming American.* New York: Dial Press, 1971.

White, Eric. "The Erotics of Becoming: XENOGENESIS and *The Thing.*" *Science-Fiction Studies* 20 (1993): 394–408.

Wickramagamage, Carmen. "Relocation as Positive Act: The Immigrant Experience in Bharati Mukherjee's Novels." *Diaspora* 2.2 (1992): 171–200.

Wideman, John Edgar. *Damballah.* 1981. New York: Vintage, 1988.

———. *Hiding Place.* 1981. New York: Vintage, 1988.

———. *Sent for You Yesterday.* 1983. New York: Vintage, 1988.

Wiget, Andrew. "Identity, Voice, and Authority: Artist-Audience Relations in Native American Literature." *World Literature Today* 66.2 (1992): 258–63.

Wilde, Alan. "Love and Death in and around Vineland, U.S.A." *boundary 2* 18.2 (1991): 166–80.

———. *Middle Grounds: Studies in Contemporary American Fiction.* Philadelphia: University of Pennsylvania Press, 1987.

Williams, Donna Glee. "The Moons of Le Guin and Heinlein." *Science-Fiction Studies* 21.2 (1994): 164–72.

Willis, Susan. "Eruptions of Funk: Historicizing Toni Morrison." In *Black Literature and Literary Theory.* Ed. Henry Louis Gates Jr. New York: Methuen, 1987. 263–83.

———. "I Shop Therefore I Am: Is There a Place for Afro-American Culture in Commodity Culture?" In *Changing Our Own Words: Essays on Criticism, Theory, and Writing by Black Women.* Ed. Cheryl A. Wall. New Brunswick, N.J.: Rutgers University Press, 1989. 173–95.

Wilson, John Oliver. *After Affluence: Economics to Meet Human Needs.* New York: Harper and Row, 1980.

Wilson, Matthew. "The Rabbit Tetralogy: From Solitude to Society to Solitude Again." *Modern Fiction Studies* 37.1 (1991): 5–24.

Winter, Douglas E. "Less Than Zombie." In *Book of the Dead.* Ed. John Skipp and Craig Spector. New York: Bantam, 1989. 201–15.

Witt, Grace. "The Bad Man as Hipster: Norman Mailer's Use of Frontier Metaphor." *Western American Literature* 4.3 (1969): 203–17.

Woidat, Caroline M. "Talking Back to Schoolteacher: Morrison's Confrontation with Hawthorne in *Beloved.*" *Modern Fiction Studies* 39.3–4 (1993): 527–46.

Wong, Hertha D. "Adoptive Mothers and Thrown-Away Children in the Novels of Louise Erdrich." In *Narrating Mothers: Theorizing Maternal Subjectivities.* Ed. Brenda O. Daly and Maureen T. Reddy. Knoxville: University of Tennessee Press, 1991. 174–92.

Woodcock, George. *Anarchism: A History of Libertarian Ideas and Movements.* New York: New American Library, 1962.

Wright, Austin M. *The Formal Principle in the Novel.* Ithaca, N.Y.: Cornell University Press, 1982.

Wright, Derek. "Mapless Motion: Form and Space in Updike's *Rabbit, Run.*" *Modern Fiction Studies* 37.1 (1991): 35–44.

Wright, John S. "The Conscious Hero and the Rites of Man: Ellison's War." In *New Essays on "Invisible Man."* Ed. Robert O'Meally. Cambridge: Cambridge University Press, 1988. 157–86.

Wright, Neil H. "Of Pomerleaus and Pumpkins: Christianity and Paganism in *The Beans of Egypt, Maine.*" *Kentucky Philological Review* 2 (1987): 13–20.

Wu, Qing-yun. "A Chinese Reader's Response to Maxine Hong Kingston's *China Men.*" *MELUS* 17.3 (1991–92): 85–94.

Xu, Ben. "Memory and the Ethnic Self: Reading Amy Tan's *The Joy Luck Club.*" In *Memory, Narrative, and Identity: New Essays in Ethnic American Literatures.* Ed. Amritjit Singh, Joseph T. Skerrett Jr., and Robert E. Hogan. Boston: Northeastern University Press, 1994. 261–77.

Yetman, Michael G. "*Ironweed:* The Perils and Purgatories of Male Romanticism." *Papers on Language and Literature* 27.1 (1991): 84–104.

Young, Elizabeth, and Graham Caveney. *Shopping in Space: Essays on America's Blank Generation Fiction.* 1992. New York: Grove Press, 1994.

Zubizarreta, John. "The Disparity of Point of View in *One Flew Over the Cuckoo's Nest.*" *Literature/Film Quarterly* 22.1 (1994): 62–69.

Index

KATHRYN HUME, a Distinguished Professor in the Pennsylvania State University Department of English, is the author of *The Owl and the Nightingale: The Poem and Its Critics* (1975), *Fantasy and Mimesis: Responses to Reality in Western Literature* (1984), *Pynchon's Mythography: An Approach to "Gravity's Rainbow"* (1987), *Calvino's Fictions: Cognito and Cosmos* (1992), and many articles. Her research interests reach into various branches of contemporary fiction, both serious and speculative.

Typeset in 9.5/12 Trump Mediaeval
with Chunder and Orbital display
Designed by Dennis Roberts
Composed by Jim Proefrock
at the University of Illinois Press
Manufactured by Thomson-Shore, Inc.

University of Illinois Press
1325 South Oak Street
Champaign, IL 61820-6903
www.press.uillinois.edu